Monique Roffey was born in Port of Spain, Trinidad, and educated in the UK. Since then she has worked as a Centre Director for the Arvon Foundation and has held the post of Royal Literary Fund Fellow at Sussex and Chichester universities. She is the author of the highly acclaimed novels *sun dog* and *The White Woman on the Green Bicycle*, which was shortlisted for the Orange Prize for Fiction in 2010.

Monique currently lives in London, where she spends most of the day in her pyjamas, writing. You can read more about her at: www.moniqueroffey.co.uk

WITH THE KISSES
OF HIS MOUTH

A Memoir

MONIQUE ROFFEY

**SIMON &
SCHUSTER**

London · New York · Sydney · Toronto

A CBS COMPANY

First published in Great Britain by Simon & Schuster UK Ltd, 2011
A CBS COMPANY

Copyright © Monique Roffey, 2011

1 3 5 7 9 10 8 6 4 2

Simon & Schuster UK Ltd
1st Floor
222 Gray's Inn Road
London WC1X 8HB

www.simonandschuster.co.uk

Simon & Schuster Australia
Sydney

A CIP catalogue record for this book
is available from the British Library

Hardback ISBN: 978-0-85720-429-5
Trade Paperback ISBN: 978-1-84737-722-7

"Andromeda Heights" words and music by Paddy Mcaloon © 1995,
reproduced by permission of EMI Songs Ltd, London W8 5SW

This is a work of non-fiction. The names of some people and some
details have been changed to protect the privacy of others. The author has
warranted that, except in such minor respects not affecting the substantial
detail of events, the contents of this book are accurate.

Typeset by M Rules
Printed in the UK by CPI Mackays, Chatham ME5 8TD

♥

for love is strong as death
The Song of Songs

♥

For Demara and Rosie,
women of the light

PROLOGUE

the letter bomb

The night before, for the first time, we'd talked seriously about splitting up. For months there'd been stalemate: rows followed by long silences, followed by rows. We'd even tried counselling together and then he'd started seeing a therapist alone, a bad sign. One by one, in sworn secrecy, I'd confided in my closest girlfriends about our problems. I'd even told my mother what was going on – a very bad sign. Even so, facing the reality of the loss had brought on an onslaught of gut-churning dread and anguish. It was, after all, *my fault*. I knew this. It was me who'd ruined it all, months back, by admitting, finally, that I was restless; our relationship had been mostly celibate for some time.

I wept all night. Ours was an affair of the heart. He was my twinned universe and our years together had been rich, event-ful, loving and romantic. Now, all this felt long gone, ruined. The split was upon us, it was happening. How? Waves of grief washed over me, tears of disbelief. He slept on the sofa downstairs.

The next morning, we sat at the breakfast table in a word-less state. My face was red and crumpled. It was dawning on me that he'd been assessing the situation with a clearer head, thinking it all through: he knew this was pre-split time, a grim

1

but necessary part of any relationship to be endured. This had happened to him before, with two ex-wives. He was conducting these hours with what seemed to be a newfound steeliness. He'd come to his own stopping point maybe even months before. Now he only had to negotiate this dreadful time, not look me in the eye. I suspected he'd made plans of where and what he'd do next.

He made us coffee and toast. There was unopened mail on the table, including a brown manilla envelope with my name and address typed on it. It had been lying on the table for over a week while I'd been away visiting my family in Trinidad. Bleary-eyed, over coffee, I picked up the envelope and began to tear at the flap. He sat opposite, expressionless, attempting to read the newspaper. We were in pyjamas and slippers, dressing gowns; neither of us was good in the mornings.

I had so many things to say to him but nothing came. My body was weak from the sleepless night; my nerves prickled, like sugar in my veins. The thought of actually parting from this man, from our way of life, brought a feeling of mortal threat. I would die; surely I'd die if this happened.

I pulled the papers out of the envelope. Three or four A4 sheets of blue handwritten scrawl and a thicker sheaf of printed-out emails. I took a sip of coffee and began to read the letter. At first it made no sense at all.

Dear Monique, Please sit down; I have something shocking to say.

The letter was from a woman I didn't know. She claimed she'd had a passionate affair with my partner. She had fallen in love with him and he had rejected her. She was writing to tell me all about it.

I sagged in the chair. A small atomic explosion went off in every cell. What on earth was this all about?

The letter went on to tell me how they'd first met, where and when. She'd left her husband over this affair, had become so distressed that she had even stopped eating. She had thought of coming to our home personally, to tell me what had been going on. She wanted me to know what kind of man I was living with.

I looked up at him, suddenly cold. His head was still buried in the newspaper. It was then my heart broke. My eyes filled. I couldn't say a word. I looked down at the letter in my hands. There were emails too: emails from him to her.

The emails were proof of her claims. I managed to read fragments of them, but the shock made them blur. He'd promised to be with her. He'd fallen in love with her – I saw that written too. He'd promised her that he'd leave me, to be with her: *wait for me, wait for me*. But he'd reneged on his promises. So she'd decided he wouldn't get away with hiding their love affair.

In her letter, she said as much. Briefly, I was able to take all this in. She wanted to make her presence known, wanted her status fully acknowledged. She was doing what we, so far, had been unable to do. She was parting us.

I stared at him, hands shaking. 'What the *fuck* is this?'

'What?' He hadn't seen what I'd pulled from the envelope.

'This woman . . . has written to me. About your *affair*.'

He looked up and stared. His face paled.

'What the *fuck* has been going on?' I rose from the table. I stood tall then, tall and on the verge of a wildness I'd never known.

His mouth fell open. 'I can explain . . .'

'*Look*!' I shouted. I began to read from the letter. Terrible words were emerging from my mouth, amazing sentences. To me these words were violent, awesome. Like being walloped by lightning, like being run over by a truck. Overturned and bulldozed into the ground. She knew I was asthmatic! Knew about my novel, *sun dog*; had read it, even. She knew the hours I worked, when she could call him freely. She loved him, she said. And he'd rejected her. He'd ended the affair months ago, but she was still miserable.

'*Look*!' I screamed again. I began to read from the emails too.

'No,' he begged. 'Don't read them. They're poison. They've been edited.'

'I don't fucking care!'

Through a maelstrom of tears, I read scraps of the emails aloud. *I'm only with Mon for career reasons.* He'd been planning to join her, to be with her. Then he'd got cold feet. There was a flow of lust and fantasy in those emails, how much he wanted her. *I stare at your photo, I want to make you pregnant.* In those moments, I saw a picture of the affair, a proper full-blown wild and ardent love affair that had been raging alongside my own relationship – for how long? I didn't know and I didn't care when it had ended. Right then, the details didn't matter. I hadn't understood why our relationship was limping quite so badly, what had caused things to be so irreparable – at that moment it all added up. He'd already left our relationship. He'd stepped outside of it, gone elsewhere some time ago.

I stared at my partner as if he might have shrugged from a suit of human skin to expose green scales, fish eyes and roving antennae, as if he'd just revealed himself to be another type of creature altogether. The man I knew had once *adored* me, gazed at me with eyes brimful with love. People had often commented on it. I knew things were bad between us, but had never thought that he would have the courage, the sheer audacity, to have an affair; it was beyond contemplation. Apart from the previous night, we had always slept in the same bed together. The logistics of it – *how* had he managed it? Even though our life together had been chaste for some time, even though I knew deep down that the sexual energy not released between us had to go somewhere, I hadn't even *suspected* he could do this. Who was this woman? I stood and screamed at him – God knows what I said.

'Please, please don't read those emails,' he sobbed. 'Whatever you do, don't read any more.'

The cats we'd adopted together as kittens flew in from outdoors, as if they'd sensed the supersonic boom of our drama. They frowned at us. Their tails quivered. Paintings on the walls gasped. The walls sweated.

In those first moments, I could have killed him. I could have killed her, too, stabbed them both into a bloody mess; now I understand how these crimes happen, like this, when a bombshell arrives in the post. With the letters and emails in my hand, I legged it upstairs. I pulled on some clothes and bolted back down and out the front door.

♥

I'm a shit driver at the best of times. Tears flowing and hands leaden, I don't know how I managed to escape in the van, driving the mile and a half to Totleigh Barton, the writing centre we looked after in Devon, where I thought I'd be safe. A place for me to sit and read through the letter and emails properly, gauge the situation, calm down, drink tea, gather myself.

It was a Saturday, so I thought the centre would be empty. But I found it swarming with guests who'd rented the house and grounds for the weekend, efficient and cheerful types, togged up in green wellies and cagoules. I'd forgotten they were there. I turned round in the car park and sped back out and up along a narrow country lane. I didn't notice that it'd been raining and the lane was very muddy. Soon, I found myself stuck, wheels spinning and throwing up clods of wet earth. I gave up trying to get out and sat and stared through the fogged-up window. I held the letter and emails in my hands and tried to read them again and again, but was blinded by tears.

It was late January: 30 January 2006, to be precise. It was cold. It was winter, the season of death, hibernation. The frisky bullocks in the fields surrounding Totleigh had been slaughtered months back; the army of daffodils were curled in their bulbs deep underground. Lone roe deer foraged for roots and shrubs.

A wild terror tore through me. The world shrank. *How, what, where, when ... how could he?* I got out of the van and trudged back to Totleigh with the letters in my hand.

There, on that hilltop lane which ran beside Totleigh Barton, I had a sense that more than just these letters was amiss. I was a frizzy-haired island girl, a Trinidadian, but a city person too, a Londoner by adoption. I was very far away from any kind of place I called home. I'd put myself in a relationship which, at its foundations, was flawed: the physical side, the sexual force had never flowed between us. Instead, it had been weak, complicated; then it had entirely died away. He'd desired me but I'd never desired him. Why not? I never knew.

But I'd loved him with another type of passion. It had always been a puzzle. What was I doing with this man? There'd been this terrible problem and now it was exposed. I was exposed. How had I got it all so wrong? I shouldn't be trudging through the January slush in Devon. I'd no business being anywhere near a roe deer or a badger. I had the grief-crazed, toxic letters of another woman in my hands. I stumbled along and the rain began to come at me in horizontal sheets, stinging my eyes, slapping my face. I wailed with fury and self-pity.

♥

In the centre's office, I made two phone calls: one to my neighbour, Deborah Dooley, to ask for rescue from the mud; the second to my boss, Stephanie Anderson, to tell her what had happened. By contract, he and I were yoked together as centre directors. Our job was very busy: there would be no faking it. We'd been there four years and we had been successful and yet it was time to move on. We had already handed in our notice and were three months from leaving our posts. It was a quiet time of year, only six courses left to run. I wanted to ask Stephanie if I could leave ahead of the due departure date, if I could arrange cover and vanish. I left a message on her voice mail. Soon Deborah and her husband Bob arrived, ashen-faced.

My neighbours pulled the van from the muddy lane, drove me to their home and I stayed with them for a couple of hours, drinking tea. They were as shocked as I was. In fits and starts, in their kitchen, I managed to spit out what had happened. They gawped with horror. Mostly, I heaved and sobbed. Eventually, half-insane with grief, I went home and found him cringing but wanting to talk, hoping that 'talk' might be possible.

'Are you *mad*!' I spat.

I threatened to kill him. I told him if we slept the night in the same house, I'd stab him in the chest as he slept; that I'd cut his balls off and feed them to the cats. He packed and left twenty minutes later.

Stephanie called and I told her what had happened. She advised me not to drive as I was in shock; she said I should wrap up warm and sit tight, do nothing. I told her that I had kept trying to read the emails but couldn't though my tears.

'*Burn them*,' she said.

I took the letters out the back door of the cottage. There was a wind so I stooped close to the ground and lit a match. The flame flickered indigo and orange. My heart was in two pieces; I could feel it broken in my chest. I put the flame to the papers and watched it spread and destroy the words and the paper they were printed on. The ashes blew away and the cats chased after them.

♥

I'd been felled by one woman. In the aftermath, a number of other women stepped forward to stand me upright again.

Deborah Dooley was the first. Stephanie Anderson was the second. What a wise woman she was. For the next few hours I lay on the sofa and stared into space. The TV was on, some black-and-white romantic comedy. Lady Violet, the snooty fluffy cat, came and sat on my chest and glared at me, suspicious, as if demanding an immediate woman-to-cat version of events. Deborah came round with vegetable broth. Lovely, flame-haired Deborah. She had cried too, with her husband; they loved us both.

Deborah told me she had a friend staying the weekend; this friend was a Relate counsellor.

'Maybe she can help. Shall I send her over?'

I nodded, mute.

This was the third woman to save me. She listened to what had happened and at the end of my story she asked one simple question, one I may never have asked myself.

'What do you want to do *now*?'

I stared at the front door. Next to it was my suitcase, still unpacked from my three-week holiday in Trinidad.

'I want to go back home,' I whispered. 'I want to go home and write a book. I want time for me.'

'*Do it*, then,' she said.

The Relate counsellor's name was Sarah McCloughry. If she hadn't been there and asked me that question, I might have sunk into a terrible, terrible state. But in that moment, I knew what to do next. I would go home, back to my mother, back to Trinidad.

I'm still so grateful to these women.

Burn them.

Do it.

They gave me such clear and sound advice. I was to do as they bid. Fire and flight.

♥

It took forty-eight hours to extricate myself from my life. I bought a plane ticket and found cover for the centre. I terminated joint bank accounts, snipped up shared credit cards. I began to pack. The cats paced the house. I couldn't eat. I lost several pounds over the following week.

Two nights later, the shock was so bad I got out of bed

and knelt on the hard wooden floor and prayed for help. The prayers came all mixed up, in fragments, parts of prayers learnt as a child. Then I gave up. *Help me, oh Lord, help me*, I begged. The following night, I was sitting in bed and the phone rang. It was his father, a man with one lung and four ex-wives and a prostate the size of a grapefruit. He spoke just like an East End gangster. He'd abandoned not just my ex but also his fostered brother and another adopted daughter. He was a man hated by and alienated from his entire family.

'Can I speak to my son?' he rasped.

I roared at him. The lightning-energy I'd been struck by left my body, doubly charged, and hit this man, this decrepit hate-filled man, a man who'd neglected his son and failed to give him a role model to live up to. I bellowed at him, hurling abuse. I had refused to meet him in all the years I'd lived with his son. His name was Alan; my father had been an Alan, too. My father had also been, to say the least, a difficult man. I'd never wanted to meet this other Alan. That moment, I told him why.

♥

Nine days later, my entire landscape had altered. I'd packed up my belongings and was driving to London in a Luton van. I'd lost my relationship, quit my job and was leaving the cottage I'd lived in for four years. I had deposited my cats at the writing centre for the short-term, hoping to rescue them on my return. I wept. I couldn't believe what had happened. Couldn't believe my life with this man, my heart's true love, my companion of six years, was finished.

I couldn't help thinking, over and over again, about the

words written in *The Song of Songs*, a copy of which he'd given me, etched in gold and bound in engraved leather, the most romantic gift I'd ever received.

Stay me with flagons, comfort me with apples: for I am sick of love.

That's how it was. I was faint, as overwhelmed as the woman who speaks in the song. I was exhausted. And yes, sick of love.

LOVE STORY

'The dream companion I had longed for since I was fifteen'

Simone de Beauvoir on Jean-Paul Sartre

♥

the first love note

This love story begins eleven years ago. At 10 a.m., on a Thursday. Thursday 16 December, 1999. Lancaster University Creative Writing department.

He stood with his back to me, studying something pinned on the wall, or pretending to. He wore a dogtooth check trench coat and wide-leg tweedy trousers. On his feet were battered walking boots, which somehow managed to appear fashionable. He was tall, well over six foot. Big and tall and bald. The back of his head was fuzzy, wrinkled around the neck. A boulder of a head.

I'd seen his face before he even turned around. A photo of him in a local newspaper cutting adorned the department notice board. He'd just published a novel and was an ex-student. I'd walked past his face twice a week for nine weeks of that first term. The face in the photo was winsome and open, cast in a warm half-light, a face which liked the camera and knew how to compose itself and take up the frame. I'd peered at this face many times while waiting for my class – I liked the look of this man.

So, cheerful, I bounced over to him, wanting to introduce myself. 'Hi,' I said, tapping him on the shoulder. He turned.

'Eh?' he replied.

'Hi,' I said again. 'We're the writers.'

'Eh?'

'Your class. That's us.' I pointed to two of the other students loitering near the door.

A grunt.

But I wasn't thrown off. 'You've come to *teach* us, remember?'

'Oh, er ... yes.'

I looked up at him and smiled. His face was huge. Oval and wide, somehow sad, clown-like. Small eyes, peering with a soft intelligence through thick lenses. Close up, he was very different from the photograph. Not so winsome: a thug, a ruffian, unkempt. But kind of cute, too.

The workshop went badly. While he'd read our work, his feedback was wishy-washy, to say the least; he had nothing specific to say. He generalised and made vague comments, umming and erring, not wanting to be impolite or hurt anyone's feelings. Clearly, he had little or no teaching experience.

He'd liked my work, though, the first chapter of a novel, *sun dog*. There was a line about a crisp packet blowing along the pavement like a squid shooting off on the seabed. On the top of the first page I'd written my name in blue pen – Monique Roffey – on the left-hand corner. On the right-hand corner I'd written 'For I. M.' – his initials. Later, much later, he said he took that as a sign:

M.R. 4 I.M.

It was our first love note. That's what he'd imagined.

He also said he'd fallen in love with me before we met, with that piece of writing. He meant it at the time; he was a very romantic man. He said he fell in love with me *on the page*, that he knew he'd like me from what he'd read, that he was looking forward to meeting me. That it would be a meeting.

Meanwhile, in the workshop, I began to get a little impatient with his waffle. He'd wandered off the point and was trying to fill the gaps in his critical approach with tales of how he got published, about his early short stories, the bleak days of writing while parenting a child single-handedly. All very interesting, but he was failing to deliver anything that resembled an MA workshop. I looked at our regular course tutor and could see she was becoming impatient too. She began to ad-lib. So did I. It's fair to say we hijacked the workshop from him entirely. He didn't seem to mind, though; in fact, he looked relieved.

I was mad-crazy about becoming a writer back then, obsessed with the language of storytelling, with the technical aspects of narrative. Bossy cow with it, too. I think I was talking, talking, talking, a bit on overdrive that day. Trying to impress? Maybe. I noticed him looking at me in a cock-eyed, dreamy sort of way. Was he staring at my tits? I glared. This didn't stop him. I glared some more. But he kept looking at me with open interest.

I blushed. Yes: very different from the photograph. One of the oddest-looking human beings I'd ever seen. His forehead had a noticeable dent. His teeth were big and square. One gold tooth flashed in the corner of his mouth; others were nicotine-stained. But then I began to recognise a glimmer, just a glimmer of that winsomeness from the photograph in the way he smiled, a little crooked and mischievous – a boyish grin. Behind the large black-framed specs, his eyes were inquisitive. His manner was gentle and his voice, for such a big man, was soft. He filled the room with the aroma of wood smoke and cannabis. He reminded me of a big friendly marine mammal. A manatee.

'An ogre,' one of my classmates said later.

It wasn't love at first sight.

the no

In the café, during the break, he was encircled by some of the other writers on the course. I got talking to another student, a handsome younger man, Justin Hill, who was writing a novel too, *The Drink and Dream Teahouse*. The manatee and I didn't speak, only glanced at each other with speculative interest.

When the workshop ended, he was taken off to lunch. I was disappointed. I ate a sandwich with classmates in the same café. On the way back, walking across the university quad, I noticed him standing outside the campus bookshop, chatting to someone else from the class. I shortened my route to stop and join in. He was holding his mud-spattered brief-case and a bag of newly purchased books. The trench coat and cuffed suit-trousers, his duffed-in walking boots; he looked tramp-like, writerly. His appearance, from the neck down, was also worthy of note: his hips were voluptuous, like a woman's. He had the posture and mannerisms of a showy transvestite. He cocked his head when he listened. When he walked along a bit, away from the bookshop, I noticed he was pigeon-toed, yet he turned this into something of a flamboyant feature, ambling with a curiously upright gait.

On the quad, next to the entrance to the bus stopping point, we stood face to face.

'Anyone getting the bus into town?' he asked, looking directly into my eyes, a hopeful note in his voice.

'No,' I said, quite matter-of-fact.

He shifted, uncomfortable. His eyes looked wistful.

I could have gone, if I'd liked him. I could have found a reason to catch the bus into town with him, chatted on the way, maybe even made an excuse to have a cup of tea together. But my instinct was to walk away.

'Thanks for the class,' I said, meeting his gaze.

He nodded.

I smiled, curt and dismissive. Down came the barrier. Best to say 'no' to this confusing character, this man who needed a dentist and smelt of cannabis and who, despite it all, was winning all the others round with his charm. I turned and flounced off in the opposite direction.

♥

A month later, after the Christmas break, our course tutor let slip that the manatee had talked enthusiastically about me all through their lunch together. My heart fluttered. *Really?* Curiosity got the better of me, and, after the class, I plucked up the courage to ask her for his address to write him a thank you note. She looked askance as she gave it to me.

'He's a well-known womaniser, you know,' she warned.

I didn't care to hear this. I sent him a postcard anyway. So it was me who asked him out.

We met a week later in the Ring O' Bells in Lancaster. I was nervous, so nervous I uttered a brief prayer as I opened the door and entered the pub. He was sitting by the open fire, reading. When I approached, his forehead broke into beads of sweat. I noticed the book he'd put down on the table was some pulp fiction and made a remark to break the ice. He said it was about fascism; I was intrigued. Nearby, a woman sang ballads and played an acoustic guitar. I sat down, making sure I placed both feet square on the floor, earthing myself. I didn't want to drink, but I ordered a glass of wine anyway and over the course of the evening, drank myself into an intense soberness. The conversation didn't flow: we made the usual mutual polite enquiries about life and work. He stared at my tits. Again, I decided 'no'.

the yes

Even so, when he rang a few days later, I agreed to a second date. I'd talked myself out of meeting him again – he was too fat and funny-looking, we didn't get on – but I never made the call to cancel. I'm not sure why. Maybe I just needed to check my instincts were correct. So, a few days later, he picked me up from my student flat on the outskirts of Lancaster to go out for Sunday lunch. When he arrived I was playing the Neville Brothers – this seemed to liven him up.

That day, we drove up a mountainside in sheets of brown rain. On the way, without too much probing, he talked about himself; he said he'd recovered from a nervous breakdown. He'd spent two years in bed, unable to function, had once called the Samaritans for support. The person on the line had turned out to be someone he knew socially; it had been embarrassing. Prozac and therapy had saved him. I thought a breakdown sounded glamorous. He said he'd spent his youth singing in pop bands, had wanted to be a pop star. He sang a few lines from an Elvis song. I turned and stared at the side of his enormous head and the hairs on the back of my neck stood upright. A nervous breakdown? A voice like Elvis?

He hopped out in the downpour to open a cattle gate. Perhaps that's when I started to love him, when I heard him sing and when I knew he'd broken down, and when I saw him walking back to the car through the rain with his friendly-monster face. When he got back in the car he said: 'I'm a new man, I'm in a good place.' Yes, I began to love him then: this man who'd almost ruined his life. He'd broken, and healed. Failed, and resurrected himself. He was forty-one, alive again, back from the edge.

We drank beer in a pub in a village called Dent. This time the conversation flowed. I was loosening up, responding, in spite of myself, to his irrepressible charm. He chain-smoked, waving his fag about like a drag queen. He talked in civilised and sometimes theatrical tones, spoke of books (*Walden* was his favourite, by the American writer Henry D. Thoreau, a memoir of a year spent in a woodland cabin, experimenting with a simple life). He talked of religion: he described himself as an Agnostic High Church of England Buddhist. He knew much of the history and geography of Lancashire and talked a great deal about the Lancashire witches. He knew a lot about the whole of England, in fact. He joked and laughed, the sound rising from deep in his chest. Others glanced at him; it was half donkey bray, half

21

operatic boom. But he didn't seem to care or notice: laughter was something he owned and spread around him.

He wore the cuffed tweed trousers again, with crepe-soled shoes and a roomy ginger-coloured fleece, which he referred to as his 'bear costume'. We talked more about books. I mentioned some of my favourite authors: Camus, Steinbeck, Plath, Jean Rhys. He liked the kind of male English writers I instinctively avoided: Anthony Powell and Evelyn Waugh. A man of the working class, he insisted he was a 'gentleman.' And I could see he'd modelled his persona on this certain type of so-called gentleman writer. Those soft eyes rested on me with careful intent. He asked if I'd like to go back for tea in his caravan. I imagined a rather comfortable affair, a park home with proper rooms and a loo, something homely. So I said yes.

andromeda heights

In a farmyard on the outskirts of Lancaster, behind the farm-house, on a desolate muddy spot surrounded by brambles and clucking chickens, there was a small white hump, a two-wheeler caravan of the kind you might see pulled behind a family hatchback.

'You live in *there*!' I gasped. But he seemed proud, delighted.

'Welcome to Andromeda Heights.'

'What?'

'My home.'

I laughed out loud. I knew the Prefab Sprout song he was referring to. Paddy MacAloon – what a songwriter.

We're building a home on the side of a mountain
Above the clouds, next to the sky
And after our labours the stars will be neighbours
We'll take our place with them in space
We're not using concrete or plaster or wood
They'd lower the tone of our new neighbourhood
And mortar will crumble with age and neglect
We're building our home upon love and respect
And when we've built it we'll call it Andromeda Heights
And when we've built it we'll call it Andromeda Heights
And when we've built it we'll call it Andromeda Heights.

Sellotaped to the right-hand side of the caravan's minute door was a crude handmade Valentine's card.

'From my eldest daughter,' he explained. I suppressed a smile of incredulity and followed him into the gloomy, cramped space.

The caravan consisted of a damp and lumpy multi-duveted bed at one end and a desk with an ancient computer, half-destroyed by smoke at the other. In between there was a wood-burning stove, a Formica cupboard bulging with clothes and a tiny sink crammed with unwashed dishes. The air was musty and heavy with carbon from the stove. A thin layer of soot smothered every object. The interior of the van was grim, ashtray-esque. He put the camping kettle on to boil and sat cross-legged on the bed. I perched on a stool at the desk opposite. I didn't know what to think or say. I dared to look around. It felt inconceivable that anyone could live in such a place and be happy. But he seemed to be. It was where he'd written his first novel; it was the refuge he'd escaped to after years of lone parenthood to a teenage girl. It was his cave of peace and rest and work. If he needed a bath, he went to a friend's house. If he needed a meal, he went to a café, Penny's of Penny Street.

I marvelled. So, this was Bohemia. I'd found it here, at last. A person living for a noble cause – the life of the pen. A man who had rejected materialistic bourgeois society for the sake of exploring a higher way of living, that's what I thought. I was impressed. Impressed! By his poverty and dignity with it. Here was a *real* writer. Many of my literary heroes had lived rough. Jean Rhys had spent her last years in a galvanised tin hut in a bleak wet village called Cheriton Fitzpaine. F. Scott Fitzgerald had died of a tubercular haemorrhage in a friend's flat. Hemingway had lived in a shack in the Bahamas with tons of cats with six toes. I was also living in a pokey garret – which I loved – a half hour's walk from the campus. This was the type of writer I imagined I'd be; brilliant and self-destructive and living life on the edge. This was the kind of *person* I wanted to be. All of a sudden I was very pleased to meet this writer-gypsy.

A black cat wandered in from the yard and purred up to him, its tail erect.

'Hello, Cheeky,' he said to the cat as it arranged itself in his lap. He looked at me and smiled, then turned to the cat and bombed its head with a kiss.

That was when I fell in love with him. When he kissed Cheeky the cat. That was when I didn't go backwards or forwards any more. I was in it.

the things I didn't care to heed

That I didn't think him brainy the first time we met.

That he'd had a breakdown – that I'd thought this glamorous and didn't question him about it too closely.

That I didn't look up anything about breakdowns, that I didn't even stop to ponder what a breakdown was.

That he had been married twice; that he had left both wives.

That he was the marrying type.

That he liked books I didn't.

That he lived in a tiny filthy caravan. A caravan!

That my tutor had referred to him as a womaniser.

That I was thrown by (rather than attracted to) his strange physicality.

Having made this list, most sane right-minded women would run a mile.

But I was not the sanest or wisest of people. And I didn't make a list, not until now. I overlooked all the above. I was already writing our creation myth. I was entranced by what I perceived as the romance of this man, of who he was: poor, failed, broken-down and funny as hell. Also published, highly educated. Great company. I wanted what he had. To be a working writer at whatever cost, and the greater the human cost, the more exciting.

On paper, everything was bad. He wasn't the kind of man to introduce to my mother.

'Mum, I've met someone! He's broke and twice divorced,

a single parent, he lives in a caravan with a cat called
Cheeky and a chicken called Ginger. He has bad teeth, two
daughters and is newly recovered from a nervous breakdown.
But he's very funny. I love him, Mum.'

I was thirty-four. The youngest child and the only daughter. My family still hoped I'd marry well: a lawyer, a doctor,
someone who'd take care of me for the rest of my life. My
mother had all the hopes a mother is entitled to: she'd been
happily married herself. While she knew I was 'headstrong',
she thought this 'being a writer' thing was just a phase; that
I'd come round to a careful woman's life of devoted child-
rearing and allegiance to one man.

But even then, the word 'marriage' brought me out in a
rash. Like the spirited orphan Jane Eyre, I didn't like the
sound of the arrangement at all. It signified a contract which
had been thought up before the Victorian era, an unrealistic
goal, a prison for someone like me who planned to write and
travel and meet the world. I didn't want a surgeon who
worked round the clock, who was committed to a mortgage
for life. I respected this man's choice, the sacrifices he'd made
for his art.

st valentine's day

We courted for about two weeks, up until Valentine's Day.
Dinner dates, tea and cake, long walks, and not so much as
a kiss. I was beginning to worry it would never happen. The
night before V-day, I invited him and two friends round for
dinner and we played card games up in my garret room

until midnight. When my friends departed, we were left alone.

When are we going to kiss? I'd recently written on a postcard and posted it to Andromeda Heights. It felt like a romantic thing to do.

Now we were sitting on my narrow single bed.

'I got your card,' he said.

'I'm glad.'

He leant forward and kissed me on the lips. He was wearing a tweedy suit and as we began to undress each other, I wondered if he was the tidy type; would he want to fold his suit over the back of a chair?

Soon we were kissing and struggling with each other's clothes. He stopped and stood up and ripped off his jacket and flung it on the floor matador-style. Then he ripped off his trousers and flung them on the floor too.

I gasped. His body was vast. Like a Beluga whale. White as milk and ungainly. Folds of skin on his chest, soft tender breasts, a robust stomach which hid his genitals. His hips! Great swells of flesh which were soft and somehow mesmerising. It was the body of a man who'd expanded and contracted and expanded again. Carefully, he removed my jeans and laid me down on the bed. And then he kissed me from my toes upwards, kissed my insteps, my ankles, shins, knees, thighs, reaching my cunt where he sighed and gasped:

'You're so *pretty* there, so, so pretty!'

At thirty-four, no man had ever stopped to declare his love of my cunt. My previous lovers had, until then, been an unimaginative bunch. These were the most precious words anyone has ever said to me – then and still. To have a man declare his love and admiration for the softest, quietest place on my body, a place so hidden and mysterious that even *I* had no real idea of how it looked, close up. For the first time ever, I felt fully adored. Like a treasure, a fabulous and exotic work of art.

He threw himself into lovemaking in a most unself-conscious manner, kissing me, kissing every part of me. He was only seven years older than I was, but way ahead of the other men I'd been with. Sex, that first time, was an event, so different, so theatrical and intense, that it wasn't the right time to judge: *is this good, do we have it? Am I turned on?* Too much else was happening. In bed, as in all things, this man was showy, a romantic and oh, so strange with his big bald head and ogre's face. I didn't know what to make of him.

We woke on Valentine's morning smooshed up in my single bed. In the post, I received a card from him and a cassette tape of love songs he'd made. He blushed as I opened the gift in front of him. We devoured a cooked breakfast in a local caff and agreed to see each other the following evening before going our separate ways. I was fine with that; I went home and listened to the tape he'd made: 'Gypsy Woman', by the Temptations, 'Didn't I Blow Your Mind', by the Delfonics, 'Into My Arms', by Nick Cave. I stared out the window wondering what I'd got myself into. I listened to 'My Funny Valentine' – it seemed to sum him up. That Valentine's night I spent alone, thinking of him. He spent it at the local pub's quiz night.

♥

The next evening, we went to see the film *American Beauty*. As we walked there his suit trousers came loose around his waist. He jumped and danced along the pavement until they fell to his ankles and he danced a jig, flashing his bum. It made me love him even more.

After the film, we walked back to his caravan in the moonlight. Ahead of us a plastic bag was caught up in a thermal of wind, dancing an eerie lonesome dance, just like the plastic bag we'd seen in the film. The caravan was parked near a patch of allotments and I saw broccoli growing for the first time, sprouting in hard green nubs from stalks like goose necks. In the caravan, he threw me on the lumpen bed. He wanted to make love to me with the passion of all men. But when he was upon me there was something in his eyes, a wild glint which terrified me. His face was drained of blood. A vein stood out on his forehead.

'Stop!' I begged.

Had I made some terrible mistake? In an instant, the maniac's face dissolved; again he was the mild-mannered man I knew. Or rather, I was *getting* to know. For years afterwards, he'd bring this cry of 'Stop!' to my attention; I'd asked him to stop his passion. But he didn't know the murderous face I'd seen when he was above me.

I forgot this face. It fell away. I forgot this explicit glimpse of his dark side. He never showed it again.

♥

We spent many happy times at Andromeda Heights. On Shrove Tuesday, on his Bunsen burner of a stove, he managed to cook us lemon pancakes. Ginger, the chicken, proved to be female competition. She clucked fiercely at the door to be let in whenever I visited. From the caravan, he'd accompany me to the outdoor lav in the freezing cold dead of night and whistle as I peed, balancing on the broken seat. His bed was hideous: stiff with frost on the top layers, slimy and fungal on the inside. You had to break frost on the duvet and then unpeel the gluey covers and slide into the bed as you might slide into the gullet of a large dead fish. Once we were inside it, steam rose off the covers. We would lie there not moving for several minutes, our bodies acting as two huge radiators till the sheets warmed. Above us, squirrels skittered. They had bitten through two sets of electricity wires. When it rained it was like being *in* the rainstorm; when leaves fell it was like being in a sandstorm.

This was his second winter in the caravan. I soon realised it wasn't so much living, as surviving. The Bohemian ideal vanished. Life in the caravan wasn't the least bit romantic; it was arduous, filthy, damp and bone-chilling. Whatever food he bought went off; but he ate it anyway and often got food poisoning. Field mice, free-ranging chickens and grey squirrels were always trying to get in to nest. He began to spend more time with me in my garret where we made a raft on the floor out of bits of bedding. I would rehearse *Riverdance* in my bra and knickers to entertain him. He would impersonate the Queen in the nude. Once, he flung himself on his knees and put his arms around me saying:

'Could you ever love a dwarf?'

He always made me laugh.

When I had an argument over the washing-up with my sport-obsessed Danish flatmate he penned me the following poem:

Denmark

Of all the nations I loathe and despise,

The Frances, the Scotlands, the Spains,
There is one above all which makes my blood pressure
   rise
The land of those tossers the Danes.

Their watery bacon and horrid blue cheese
Are insipid and processed and boring.
Hans Christian Anderson and Kierkegaard
Just make me start dozing and snoring.

Oh jutting peninsula! Shaped like a cock
I guess that you think you are cute
But all that you are is an anagram of
Your greatest of kings, King Cnut.

He did more than cheer me up. He gazed at me when we were together, alone or in public. He took great interest when I talked about myself. He bought me gifts. Books. Flowers. Songs. He wanted to know who I was. Other men had loved me too, others had been admiring. But not like this. He called me his Helen of Troy. He called me pixie pants and honeybee and puddle duck. He told his best friend Paul he'd met the love of his life. I was star-struck by all this attention. I loved being loved like this. I loved being loved by *him*. He had a talent for love. His love melted me, dissolved my reserve, softened me up. I basked in his loving gaze. It felt healthy and good for me. I blossomed. It all happened so easily. Within a month, and without much question, we'd fallen into each other's lives.

donkeys

His car was a heap of shit, bought for fifty pounds from an uncle who was a part-time second-hand dealer. He believed in buying near-dead cars for environmental reasons and so our entire time together was plagued by shit cars. Dolly, Collette. Shit cars with women's names. Even so, we had many adventures in them. Neither of us believed in walking. Him, because he was a lazy bastard; me because, coming from the Caribbean, I have no notion of the habit of walking for *pleasure*. So we drove about a lot. We visited many beaches. On the way to one, we visited Sellafield nuclear power station and this started a tradition – we visited quite a few nuclear power stations over the years. We visited churches too – Whitby Abbey, Jervaulx Abbey. We fell in love with Blackpool, both in and out of season.

Once, in winter, in Blackpool, we parked the car opposite a shoe shop called Vernon Humpage. We hooted about the name for months, thinking it the best name for the hero of his next novel. We walked along the beach in the dark and the cold; we ate mushy peas and chips in the only fish shop open. In the summer, we rode the tram into Blackpool, the best way to arrive. This time, we walked the beach barefoot. We loved the pretty but patient donkeys all lined up in their fancy tack, waiting to give snot-nosed kids rides up and down the sand. I wore strange flip-flops we nicknamed 'toe-breros'. I once had a photograph of that day, of those donkeys; of him, the famous tower in the background, his trousers rolled to the shins, smiling and toothsome, holding my toe-breros.

your dad

His pop star career never happened. Instead, it mutated, via a string of other bands and some stand-up comedy, into a bizarre light entertainment musical comedy double act called Your Dad. This double act comprised my ex and his piano player, Chaz. Chaz secured the gigs and they travelled the country in his clapped-out car. Just them, some props and a keyboard. I'm not sure how or why the act got started: my ex said that when his pop career waned, he needed to keep singing, needed to dance and perform, to let off steam. It 'let out his dark side', he said more than once, but I never paid this enough attention.

My ex had a touch of the Eric Morecambe about him. Chaz, his 'Ernie Wise', however, was a shambolic man who looked like a horse-thief and ate with his mouth open. They irritated each other and yet couldn't live without each other. Their act was based on the premise that they were two embarrassing old men, just like someone's dad, pissed up in the pub, and taken to the mike. It was musical cabaret meets concrete poetry, so edgy and dark in places it was blue.

The first time I saw Your Dad was in Lancaster, in a room above the Yorkshire House. The room was packed with local friends and stalwart fans, a captive audience. He wore a pink ruffled dress shirt. He was thinner then, bald and lean and powerful behind the mike. He crooned love songs, stopping to make a show of singing 'Mona Lisa' to me. My heart swelled.

He sang other songs too, camping them up and twisting the words. He skipped about and wiggled his curvy hips and rolled his eyes like a naughty child; he stomped and swore and yes, revealed the darkness in him, flashing those black gold teeth and roaring at the vulgarity of his own jokes. He played a kazoo, waved a football rattle, threatened to French kiss men in the audience. That first night I saw him perform, I encountered a mixture of feelings: pride, awe, and a tinge of reserve in my belly because the act was so unashamedly hackneyed and recycled. But, he left the stage to great applause. I went to see him in the tiny dressing room and found myself in his arms, kissing him like a groupie. There was a knock on the door. When he opened it, a young woman, just out of her teens, stood there, glowing with phosphorescent lust.

'She fancies you,' I said to him when she left.

'Don't be ridiculous, she's one of my daughter's friends.'

But she did. Just another thing I let pass: women fancied him. Women of all ages.

Despite the act's poor taste, people loved Your Dad. They got lots of work, especially in festival season; he loved gadding about, the tents, the muddy fields, meeting other ne'er-do-wells of the road. At small festivals he was a big act, at big festivals he was on the outer fringes, a micro-star. Yet he brought with him the spirit and anarchy of what all festivals are about: he loved being last on the Glastonbury playlist. He was a travelling showman, representing olde England and upholding its ancient lore. Sometimes, Your Dad was so ramshackle that their keyboard collapsed mid-act. Often, they forgot the words, or the music. One or twice they punched each other on stage. They often ad-libbed, surviving off their wits just like the old fuckers they were sending up.

Your Dad? Yes, quite. It was some time before it hit me straight between the eyes. How very much this bookish charismatic man was just like my father. He even wore the same thick black horn-rimmed spectacles.

i'll look after you

Six months had passed. In July 2000, when my MA in Creative Writing had finished, I knew I wanted to leave Lancaster and return to London. By then, he and I were an item, a double act of our own. There was no question of leaving him behind. I invited him to come south with me, see how things worked out. He said 'yes'.

We stuffed all his belongings into a white Transit van. It didn't take long. Much went to Oxfam in black bin liners; some things, like the wood-burning stove, were left in the caravan. We both had very little – he the contents of a small hump, I the contents of a garret – so it all happened quickly. Before moving to Lancaster, I'd spread my few possessions, some books, clothes, and a couple of armchairs amongst my friends in London. We packed the Transit in a morning and headed south. It was exciting.

We held hands and listened to pop music all the way down. There was no master plan, no 'let's set up house'. I was leaving and he was coming with me. Simple as that. He'd been a father half his life and this was his big escape. His eldest daughter was twenty and settled in Lancaster. His youngest daughter was eleven and in Brighton with her mum, (ex-wife No. 2), so we'd be closer to her. This was a new life for him. He was embracing a metropolis, and well-earnt freedom. I was returning to a familiar life, a city I knew well and loved, a place with long-established friendships associated with my youth and its multifarious adventures and misadventures. But I was bringing back a new man, a grand love. I was sure everyone would like him, that London would be good for him, that we'd be happy.

We had very little to go on by way of accommodation or income. I'd found a room in a low-rent short-life housing co-op, bang in central London, a prize for a writer. I was intent on squeezing him in. In the meantime, he'd secured a small flat on a housing estate in north London, rent-free for a couple of months. The flat, which belonged to a friend of mine, had been sold, and while the deal was going through, it was fine for my ex to stay there. So we each had a landing pad. He had a little cash from the deal of his second novel; I planned to extend my loan and buy time to finish my first. We were coming to London with just our wits and talent and love to rely on. It was rather late in life for both of us to be living so hand to mouth, but, like many writers, we were also *choosing* rather than falling into this kind of existence.

♥

The minute we hit the outskirts of London we got lost. I knew the city well, but only on foot, by tube and by bus. I knew the parks and cafés and shops and pubs and clubs – but not the roads. He assumed I could direct him to my friend's flat. I assumed he could map-read.

'I thought you knew the way!' he snapped.

'I thought you had a frigging map!'

'Jesus. Where are we?'

'I don't know.'

'Fuck.'

'Shit.'

'*Fuck.*'

We argued and panicked, finding our way there in the small hours, arriving tired and lost and hungry. We made tea in the empty flat and went to bed in the empty bedroom. I wrapped my arms around him. I assured him all would be well from now on: he was with me. *I'll look after you*, I promised.

In the morning my friend rang to say the deal had sailed through and the new owners wanted to move in the following week. I rang everyone I knew and asked around for a flat, a room, anything, but came up with nothing. He rang his ex-brother-in-law's wife who lived in Hackney, a posh, jolly woman who loved him. She said yes, that he could come over immediately. She had a spare room, nothing big, but he was very welcome. Because of my place at the co-op, and because we were so poor, we hadn't thought of finding a flat together. The co-op was worth waiting for, would make living in London possible while we wrote books. And this was no ordinary housing co-op. The Black Sheep Co-op was infamous.

summer of love

103 Grosvenor Avenue was a grand Victorian townhouse on a leafy Islington street a ten-minute walk from Upper Street.

It had five floors, many large rooms with high ceilings, and a thirty-foot garden out back. In the early 1980s it had fallen derelict and was squatted in by punk anarchists who set up camp and painted the interior black. They brought their pets and musical instruments with them. It was a time of do-it-yourself social housing, when many of the city's artists and anarchist communities lived or squatted in the rundown and unfashionable areas of Hoxton and Hackney.

So, for the next six months, my ex and I lived apart, me at the Black Sheep Co-op and him a number 38 bus ride away in Hackney, with his ex-brother-in-law's wife. Within weeks, he landed a job as a bookseller at Quinto, a sprawling second-hand bookshop on the Charing Cross Road. We saw each other every day. I occupied the co-op's 'garden suite', a large room in the basement of the house with a window looking out onto the rose beds, and set to work finishing *sun dog*. At 6 p.m., after work, he'd knock on the door, often brandishing a bouquet of flowers.

One afternoon, the doorbell rang. I skipped up the stairs and threw open the door. My beloved stood there in his old suit, the suit he'd worn under his dog-tooth check coat the day we'd met, the suit he'd ripped off that first night in my garret. He was holding a bunch of red roses, and he was beaming with love. Then, inexplicably, he roared with laughter.

'What?'

'You wagged,' he replied.

'What do you mean, wagged?'

'You wagged your tail, just like a dog.'

'No, I didn't.'

'Yes you did.'

'Did I?'

He came forward with the roses and kissed me on the lips. 'Yes, you did.'

He was right. This man made me wag my butt like a dog wags its tail. I often hid behind the large lime trees when I saw him advancing down Grosvenor Avenue. I'd leap out and shout 'boo' to him, or bound up in greeting, leaping to kiss his face. Yes, I remember that: how I jumped and wagged and kissed his nose, his ears, his face, not quite licking him.

♥

That summer of 2000, he, a stranger to the city, introduced me to London. He showed me many sights I'd never seen and we did things I'd never done before. We walked the length of the canal from King's Cross to Camden; he told me all about locks and we emerged to crowds of people sitting with their pints, soaking up the sun. We walked the dead-straight Kingsland Road in Dalston, originally a Roman road. We browsed the shops of Stoke Newington and saw the spotted fallow deer in Clissold Park. Through him, and his job at Quinto, the intricacies of the second-hand book-dealing world of Charing Cross and Cecil Court were revealed; the runners and the dealers, all of whom he came to know on first-name terms, and the celebs who stopped by, the bad and mad book deals made there.

Together, we shopped for new clothes for him – he had very few items of normal clothing. Much of what he owned was stage wear, ancient braided comedy coats and jackets, the top halves of military suits of all persuasions (God, how happy was I, when, years later, moths attacked and ate the lot). His one pair of crepe-soled shoes was full of holes. But it wasn't easy going shopping with a curmudgeonly manatee. Once, in a shop on Upper Street, I forced him to stop and consider just *trying on* a pair of shoes, some suede moccasins. They were a bit of a departure for him, but they weren't uncool, just different. He was unhappy and huffed and made a fuss; the shop assistant had to jam the shoe on.

'Look,' he complained. 'They won't do.'

I'd averted my attention, trying to ignore the fuss. But I turned in time to see him kick his foot high, in a burlesque manner. The flick of his ankle sent the moccasin whizzing off his foot and out, out, out of the shop door, out into the air, at head height, above the pavement.

honk

In January 2001, when another person moved out of the co-op, my ex moved in. These were the co-op's last days. A central ceiling beam in the kitchen was so rotten that scaffolding had been erected *inside* the kitchen to keep the room from collapsing. The scaffolding was decorated with fairy lights and an enormous cheese plant. The kitchen was the only warm room in the house because the gas oven door was kept open as a makeshift heater. There were holes in other ceilings and holes in the floors. An old taxi klaxon had been fitted to the outside door and the word 'honk' scribbled in chalk. The co-op was well known locally, especially by the residents on the estate opposite: the only house on the street that burglars wouldn't even consider robbing – perhaps out of respect for the co-op's ethos, but more likely because they understood it was a scrappy hippie house. Old fridges and pieces of furniture were often put outside the front door to be recycled back into the community.

My ex and I were allocated two whole floors, the basement and the rooms above the kitchen. We arranged ourselves accordingly, with our bedroom downstairs and a shared study and living room on the higher floor. He brought his library out of storage, the one thing he did own. Books. Tons of them. He loved books so much he'd rather spend money on them than food. He ate books. Along with fags and sweet tea, they were his soul food.

We built a little nest on those two floors, a writerly den with heavy marmalade-coloured silk curtains and a 1920s sofa and a glass coffee table we found in a vintage store on the Holloway Road. The other co-op members were Ben, a peaceable chef who'd opened a designer soup kitchen in Old Street station, and Richard, a hippie and an inventor-designer, a house elder who'd lived there since the punk days. For some reason, perhaps because of his ancestral status, he became Uncle Richard to us. We lived happily with our new housemates; the four of us were an industrious team. There were no house pets, no cats or dogs back then. Just rats and mice, quite a few of both.

rats

Every night we huddled together in my old iron-framed French bed. Really, it was a large single bed, one made for a shorter (French) person. His feet stuck out the bars at the end.

With no heating, in the dead of winter, they often turned blue overnight, but, perhaps because he'd endured even colder conditions at Andromeda Heights, he never complained. Most nights we listened to the sound of rodents squeaking in the walls, inches from our heads.

We spent weeks falling asleep to the sound of squeaking walls, maybe months. Then, one spring morning, a Sunday, the sun pouring in through the curtains, filling the room with soft lemony light, I sat up in bed and yawned. My beloved was snoring lightly next to me: it seemed to me that my life was blessed. I was in love. I was writing my first novel. I was even signed to a literary agent. I was still young, thirty-five. I had my health, good friends, everything I'd ever wanted. I threw my arms up in a wide self-congratulatory yawn, almost hugging myself.

Just then, a rat the size of a rugby ball popped out of a hole in the wall. It sat on the carpet, two feet from our bed. Its whiskers were silken and long. It twitched and stared at me, as if it was cool to share the room, as if it had been going about its business.

'Oops, sorry, wrong exit,' the big rat seemed to be saying as the bleakest and most horrifying dread spread through my veins. I screamed until my throat was hoarse, screamed my beloved into a sudden wild and fitful consciousness. The rat fled. Vanished – poof – into thin air.

'Darling, what on *earth* is the matter?' he spluttered, seeing the room empty.

The next day, under my orders, the whole house was dismantled. Holes in the doorframes were patched. Rat traps were bought and bolted to the floorboards. Rentokil came and laid poison. We caught nine large rats the following week in the traps alone. Other rats were found dozy and stoned on poison, frothing at the mouth and lolling around the rooms.

Once, we found a dying rat on the stairs. It was blocking our path down to the washing machine. No one was brave enough to touch it or go near it in case, with a final surge of strength, it might sink its fangs into us. Me, Ben and Richard gathered at the foot of the stairs, nervous and scared. For some reason, we began pelting the hideous creature with pieces of broken chalk from the blackboard in the hall.

'Die, die,' we chanted.

But the creature didn't stir. It was scared too, dying a horrible death and unable to move.

Just then, my ex arrived home from work. He was appalled at what he saw; his housemates, a group of middle-class hippies, hurling stubs of chalk at a dying rat.

'Stand back,' he commanded. From the kitchen toolbox, he found a hammer. We made room for him and watched, aghast, as he clambered down the stairs and hammered the rat to death.

maria grubziňska

He was a romantic man. He found it easy to declare his love. Once, when ambling along Church Street, browsing in bookshops, he stopped in the street.

'I wish,' he said.

'What?'

'I hadn't been married before.'

'What do you mean?'

'I wish I'd waited ...'

I was dumbstruck. I didn't know if I felt the same way. His previous two marriages did mar things. Was I to be a *third* wife? Would that be wise? But his heart was open and his eyes brimmed with love. I believed his love to be genuine. He often spoke of his love for me and showed it every day.

Often, he brought me books from Quinto. One day, he came home and presented me with a slim black hardback. The board covers were exquisitely etched, the pages illustrated with couples embracing in fields of flowers, sheep, deer. There were ornate capital letters etched with pure gold. The pages were hand-stitched together. It was a handmade book, a limited edition made by a small press. There was a bookplate in the front flap, foxed and aged, with the image of a knight bowing to the statue of a woman cradling an infant. The name Maria Grubziňska was written on the plate. Once, this slim book had been a gift to this woman. Now it was mine. It was a copy of *The Song of Songs*, the erotic Hebrew love poem of the Old Testament. Maria Grubziňska and I had the ancient poem in common: had we both been loved, cherished, admired, just like the woman in the song?

I didn't know what to make of this gift at first. I thanked him, but it somehow made me pensive. He adored me so openly. But I didn't understand my own feelings, quite *how* I loved him back. I'd never been so engulfed in a relationship, part of something so much bigger than myself. It made me groggy and unfocused. I was aware I was taking a risk, that I was in the midst of an enormous life shift. But also, I felt distant and guilty. There was an unspoken problem between us: my body didn't respond to him. In fact, my sexual desire, my usual hunger and playfulness, had mysteriously vanished since meeting my ex. Where and why it had gone, I didn't know; but I was always aware and often troubled by this, as I'm sure he was. And so I recognised that the love spoken of in the Hebrew song was the same and yet entirely different to my love for him.

When I read *The Song of Songs* I found it enigmatic and endlessly fascinating. In traditional theological terms, the poem is seen by the Jews as a grand allegorical representation of God's love for the children of Israel. Christians also regard it as a poem about man's love of God, or of the Church. However, from the mid-nineteenth century, post-Enlightenment scholarship understood it differently, as a natural love poem. In fact *The Song of Songs* is not one long poem but a number of small poems strung together, where two voices, one male, the other female, call to each other and speak of human love.

The song opens with an expression of female desire for a man: *let him kiss me with the kisses of his mouth*. The woman in the poem says how much she loves the way her man tastes, like wine; how she loves the scent of him; how she yearns for sexual union. She is exuberant and impatient for intimacy. She wants him to be with her. She invites him to a tryst. Throughout the poem the woman is ardent; she often takes the initiative herself. It is a poem which celebrates and also warns of the potency of erotic love: *for love is strong as death*.

I wasn't sure what to say about this gift. It was an expression of *his* ardent love and intent; clearly he saw himself as the male voice in the poem. I put the book in my bookshelf and didn't want to look at it.

My agent put *sun dog* out on submission to editors. Because of the ongoing rat plague, we moved our mattress and bedding to the floor of our study. Again, it was my romantic idea of Bohemia. I loved our ramshackle adventurous life. One night, we gazed at each other.

'I love you,' he said.

'I love you back,' I replied.

'I'm sorry I don't have *more* ...'

'More what?'

'To offer you.'

But he'd given me the most famous love poem ever written.

'I don't care,' I whispered back. 'I love you.'

And I did. I stared at him as he slept, basked in his smile when he was awake. I couldn't wait to see him, talk to him, be with him every day. It was a strong brash love: *he is the one my soul loves*. I wanted his argument, his opinions, his take on everything. I'd hurt anyone who ever hurt him. And so, why? Why didn't I feel desire for this man I loved so much? I fell asleep most nights asking myself this question.

♥

That year, 2001, we decided to have a big Christmas celebration at the co-op, inviting some friends and his daughters to come and stay. We bought a tree and a huge turkey and some Fortnum's mince pies. On Christmas Eve it was like Santa's Grotto in the co-op kitchen, with everyone chopping vegetables and helping to prepare for the next day. Glasses of sherry, carols sung off-key – until we noticed spirals of wispy smoke snaking through the air.

'A heater on upstairs?' someone wondered.

'Must be.'

And then the sounds of urgent banging on the front door.

We opened it to see our neighbour, bug-eyed, clutching her cat.

'Fire!' she shouted.

Next door's bathroom heater had exploded into flames. Two flashing fire engines were already parked outside. His daughters and I stood on the pavement with our glasses of sherry and watched as the fire was extinguished. My ex arrived, through the crowds on the pavement, his arms laden with booze.

'Ho, ho, ho,' he sang.

'Thank *God* you're here!' *Thank you, God.*

That night we made it to midnight mass and I prayed for us, that we should be safe and happy. The next day, during Christmas lunch, which he cooked, we all told stories of the day we were born. I was riveted by his story.

'I was pulled by forceps from my mother's womb,' he said, exhibiting his forehead. 'See?'

This explained the strange dent in his brow. It was easy to see two marks, where the forceps had grasped.

'It caused me fits as a child. So my mother was very over-protective.' The story made me wonder. As an adult, my ex hated being mothered. And I didn't have mothering instincts. In the past, he'd chosen a string of aloof, queenly wives and girlfriends. Women like me.

New Year came. Soon it would be 2002. To celebrate, we went to a dinner party in Hackney at his ex-brother-in-law's wife's flat. The night evolved haphazardly and yet harmoniously as they sometimes do if you stick to a small patch of London on foot. We ended up at a house party nearby where we met lots of interesting people including Jake Prescott, an old anarchist who'd served ten years for bombing a Tory minister's home, a member of the Angry Brigade who'd known the punks at 103 Grosvenor Avenue.

It was the first time we'd seen in a year together. We walked home to the co-op around one o'clock, talking about anarchists and punks. We went back to the garden suite, to my iron-framed French bed. The rats had been exterminated.

We didn't stir until some time in the afternoon on the first day of 2002. It was dark down there in the basement; cold, too. The curtains were drawn and we were snuggled together, sharing the dim heat of our bodies. There was love between us and we lay in this love. He began to kiss me all over, moving down under the covers, down where he kissed and whispered love-clotted words, prayers to my cunt. Then he was on top of me and we were fucking until he collapsed full of the sweethappy sadness of orgasm.

'God, I love you so much, Mon. Love you, love you, love you,' he murmured, spent, his head on my stomach.

I put my hand on his head, unfathomably moved. I loved him, but it was as if my heart was struggling inside my chest. It was hard for me to register his love, to absorb these tender loving words. I basked in this love, needed it like a flower needs water. But I couldn't return it fully. I didn't know how. I *couldn't* love him sexually; something was blocking this. It was like a curse, to adore a man in every other way, but not in bed. Your Dad. That was key. I didn't mother him, but he fathered me. I know that for sure now, but I only half-guessed it at the time. I craved the adoring attention of a man just like my father.

♥

I was younger then, ten years younger. I was used to being disappointed by sex. Sex had never lived up to all my hopes and expectations. It was one of life's great unsolved mysteries. Vaginal and whole body orgasms were ideas I'd received from Hollywood films and books; they were well out of the realm of my experience with men.

So, I didn't care *enough* that sex between us was just 'okay'. Well, often more than okay. My ex was an ardent and selfless lover at first. I was the one who was tricky and complicated. My ex had breasts, ever so small, but nonetheless there, small, pale, hairy breasts. I didn't fancy them at all. While I knew I *loved* him, I had no physical appetite for him. Yet I ignored this conundrum. This was why I was so unsettled at receiving his gift of *The Song of Songs*; deep down I knew our love didn't match up to it. Desire? Mine had evaporated into thin air. I wanted to be with this man, but I didn't yearn for the taste or smell of him.

interview with a cat

In February 2002, we'd been together two years. Just around that time, we were shortlisted for a joint position: centre directors for the Arvon Foundation. The Arvon Foundation, a unique organisation, owns three large houses in the countryside and offers residential weeks for those who wish to learn more about writing. I'd had a tip-off from Andy Brown, the current centre director at Totleigh Barton, that his post would be advertised and so we knew when to look for the job in the *Guardian*.

We left the co-op for the interview in Devon on a chill and blustery winter's day. A tree in the garden had blown down overnight, as though a sign that our time at the co-op was ending. We stayed at a bed-and-breakfast near Totleigh Barton, run by the Neales, a friend's parents, and did mock presentations for them together that night. Being a performer, my ex was good at anything to do with show and tell. He charmed them.

The real interview was held at the centre, a majestic cob-walled and thatch-roofed manor house listed in the Domesday Book. It had been a working farm set within acres of green rolling Devonian land. You drive along a narrow country lane and then a thin concrete track to get to the house, passing through fields of frisky bullocks. Totleigh Barton nestles beneath. There's a hillock on the way down where the sight of the house below makes the heart falter. It is a thousand-year-old view and there is a sense of this antiquity as you gaze down. Your skin rises in bumps. You see a gentle picture of rural England, a house that possesses something of the earth's natural magic. We baulked at the same time on seeing this old house, even though we'd both seen it before.

'Jesus *Christ*,' my ex whispered. He squeezed my hand. The job of caring for Totleigh Barton would be an immense privilege.

We were forced to sit through lunch with the other shortlisted couples. We looked around and saw that we were in for a good run: one couple looked too dour and politically militant, another too quiet, a third was, well, just not quite something. Another couple were younger than us and attractive: our main competition. But we were the only couple chatting away to James Long, the Chairman of Totleigh's Committee.

I was contemplating how best to impress him when Cello, one of the proprietorial Totleigh tabby cats, sauntered into the flagstone dining hall. Cello was a famous Arvon cat. She had a habit of sitting up on her haunches, like a squirrel, and waggling her paws about while meowing for attention. For years, she'd delighted Arvon students with this circus trick, and, after Totleigh's administrator, Julia Wheadon, Cello was second-in-command at Totleigh Barton. Tail up, Cello mewed and trotted snootily past the other couples frozen with pre-interview fear, all perched on long wooden benches. Decisively, she leapt onto my lap and curled up. Her noisy purr seemed to say, 'You're in.' I smiled at James. He winked.

My ex had squeezed himself into a thin cheap suit and we'd shaved and polished his head so it glowed like a baby's bum. He looked like a big fat gangster at a wedding, what with his black teeth and wheezy smoker's cough. I wore an olive green knitted top with flared sleeves, very 1960s, and flared cuffed twill slacks. Red leather clogs. Suede coat. We had rehearsed who would answer what kind of question and took turns in being professional versions of ourselves. He gushed and fluttered his eyelashes and made literary jokes and asides. I was cool and succinct. Both of us 'oohed' and 'aahed' and 'dahling-ed' and camped it up just a notch. When they asked me how I'd handle a student who'd had some kind of mental health breakdown on the course, I was very close to saying that my ex had suffered a full nervous breakdown. Instead, I made the point that depression, anxiety, an array of mental health issues went hand in hand with the creative personality.

'Show me a poet who's never been depressed,' I said. I looked at my ex. He nodded in sympathy. I'm pretty sure they saw what kind of people we were; bona fide literary types. She's nice and bossy, will get things done. He's unique, a one-off.

As we left Totleigh after the interview, my ex was confident we'd won the job.

'They loved us,' he said. 'We've got it.'

I wasn't so sure. I thought the younger, better-looking couple would be hard to beat. But the next morning, Helen Chaloner, the then Director of Arvon, called to offer us the posts.

That night we huddled in the freezing cold in my old French bed, unable to believe our luck as we clung to each other for warmth. The temperature in our room was the same as in the garden. The job came with a free home, a cottage in Sheepwash, the village nearby, which meant we would soon be leaving.

The next morning we were woken by the sound of a tremendous bang.

'What's *that*?' I gasped from under the duvet. My ex got out of bed and opened the door.

Part of the plaster from the ceiling outside had crashed to the floor. Boy, was the timing right.

♥

A 'handover week' was organised and we spent a week shadowing our predecessors whilst they ran a typical Arvon course. We stayed at the Neale's B-and-B and got tipsy with them most evenings. On 1 April 2002, my ex woke me with a pinch and a punch and we went for a walk along the lanes. I was almost thirty-seven; *sun dog*, my first novel, had been sold to a publisher. It would be out in the summer. *Feels like we are on the brink of a new time together* ... I wrote in my diary. *We are at a place of peace.* We came across a lonely war memorial. At the foot of it were tiny yellow faces, clusters of pretty primroses smiling at us.

'My favourite flower,' he said and stopped to pick one for me. It was two inches long, fragile in his giant's hand. He presented it to me as a gift and I knew with this tiny prize there was something of him in it, his past, his family, his unspoken self. A small common springtime flower. That day he passed on to me a love for primroses too. I still have that primrose pressed in my diary.

We'd bought a decrepit 2CV from Uncle Richard's father. It was green and white and called Dolly. We needed a car for our new job and this one was all we could afford. When Uncle Richard went to get her for us, Dolly broke down on the way back. But my ex loved her on sight. Even though he could only just fold himself into the pram-shaped contraption, he cooed Dolly's name as if the car had a human life. He loved the minuscule windscreen and the wipers the size of his index finger. He liked being part of the 2CV club and waved at other 2CV drivers whenever they waved at us.

6 May 2002: Dolly was bulging. Two Luton vans were parked outside the co-op's front door, one stuffed just with books. Our friends at the co-op gathered on the crumbling, mortarless doorstep to send us off. We waved and blew kisses

goodbye to Uncle Richard and his mad inventions, to Ben and Wendy Jones, our co-op writer-in-residence replacements. We set off in convoy to Sheepwash, Devon, a place with no more than two hundred residents, our second big move together.

Sheepwash was a thatch-roofed village, situated on a hill. Unenclosed fields surrounded it, a chain wide and a furlong long. A tinkly river ran past it, full of brown trout. It had won England's Best Kept Village in the not too distant past. The village was arranged around a square and in the square there was the Half Moon, a famous old fishing pub, then run by newcomers. This was my first experience of living in such a rural place. I didn't know what I'd make of it; but my ex had lived in the country before, he was something of a country-loving boy.

We arrived on a balmy Friday evening. The cottage we had been given to live in was a bucolic idyll: an oak lintel above the door, cob walls and a slate roof. Two up, two down, a garden out back with views over the surrounding fields, a barn there too. I almost cried when we opened the door and walked inside. A proper home. With plumbing and heating – and rat-free. We unpacked for two days solid. We ate crackers and drank beer and slept on the old double bed, two floppy mattresses sandwiched together with a piece of hardwood. The following Monday was the May Bank Holiday morning and we were due to run our first full Arvon course together: a fiction-writing week, with Richard Beard and Elspeth Barker as tutors. We were nervous and a little tired from the move and the unpacking, but we couldn't wait to get cracking.

holding pattern

4 p.m., Bank Holiday Monday, 2002, Totleigh Barton. The house was all prepared for sixteen students to arrive: flagstone floors buffed, beds crisp with newly laundered sheets. The statutory Arvon Monday meal (salads, quiche, baked potatoes, cold ham) was in the fridge. We sat on the window ledge outside the kitchen waiting. Cello sat on her haunches and waggled her paws. When our very first student arrived we pounced on her, a small Malaysian woman who looked clever and bright.

Together, we led her to the bedroom she'd already been allocated for the week, the tiny thin-floored room right above the kitchen. We didn't know it then, but it was the worst room in the whole house: the noisiest and least private. We chatted gaily all the while, helping her with her bags.

We glowed.

She sniffed and glanced around the room.

'It's an Anglo-Saxon building,' my ex began, wanting to tell her about the ghost, the moat, the methods of making cob.

'Where's the nearest *bathroom*?'

'Well, um, not too far away . . . er,' he stammered.

'Actually, it's over on the other side of the house.' I stepped in. 'There are two baths there. Just through the main hall.'

She stared at us as if we were stupid.

'*Baths*?'

I nodded.

'But I'm *menstruating*,' she said.

'Oh,' I breezed. The handover notes hadn't prepared us for menstruation and baths. I felt myself stiffen with rising panic. I could see my ex quailing, visibly.

'Do you expect me to *sit* in my own menstrual *blood*?'

'Nooooo,' assured my ex.

My stomach rolled.

'I'm not sleeping *here*,' she spat.

'No, of course not,' my ex agreed.

'I want a room near a shower.'

'Of course, you do, Madam.'

I raised an eyebrow at him. *Madam*? Where had that come from? He peered at me; his little piggy eyes were innocent behind his specs. The luvvie stuff was his default manner: it always worked. He batted his eyelashes. I pursed my lips. Some kind of holding pattern was set up between us in those moments, a pattern that held for the next four years.

'Come this way,' I said.

We led her to another room, outside, to one of the converted pigsties, although we didn't mention that. I know he wanted to inform her of their history, but I jabbed him in the ribs to make sure he didn't. We settled her in the corner corridor, giving her one of the biggest and warmest rooms next to the shower.

Our first week as Arvon centre directors, it's fair to say, was a total disaster. Because it was a Bank Holiday, there were few trains. The minibus waited for hours at the station to collect the students. When it arrived, late, we threw open the sliding door to see the novelist Elspeth Barker sitting there, bleak-faced, filled with morbid incredulity at being made to wait so long in the minibus with the students and without so much as a bag of crisps. The students were all women, all unamused. The luvvie stuff didn't work on them. No one liked their rooms and many immediately wanted to change. I forgot to put the baked potatoes in at the designated time, so dinner was late and a little *al dente*.

We went to London the next day for the annual programming meeting and left the course in the hands of a relief director. On our return, we found the group had splintered into rival cliques and were bitching about the tutors, us, and each other. On the Wednesday evening, the guest speaker went missing, on his way to Totleigh. Everyone complained about the poor quality of the vegetarian option; half the group were vegetarian. One was a vegan. Two didn't eat wheat. One didn't eat anything red: peppers, tomatoes, anything. The food thing foxed us completely. On the Friday night, when I brought up the subject of contributions for the minibus on the Monday, one woman snorted and swore under her breath. We waved people off on the Saturday morning and I promptly burst into tears.

'Let's hold a staff meeting,' my ex suggested. And so, on that first Saturday, after our first course, we sat together in the office at Totleigh Barton and had a staff meeting of two. We *were* the staff. Over flagons of coffee, we dissected the week and what had gone wrong. Together, we came up with a few ideas about running an Arvon week. These were good ideas, ones which we built on and added to over the next four years. From then on, our relationship changed: my ex wasn't just my romantic partner, a fellow writer too, but now we were colleagues. Workmates. A new relationship began to develop between us.

the second love affair

The Arvon Foundation became a love affair within our own. I can say that now, eight years since we moved to Sheepwash and over four years since we left. I was surprised by my reaction to the job; at how much I cared about the grand old house, the founders, John and Antoinette Moat, the long-term Totleigh administrator, Julia Wheadon, and about what Arvon does. Apart from my own writing career, I don't think I've cared about a place of work as much before or since. Both my ex and I had in the past benefitted from the 'Arvon experience'. He'd won a place on a course about writing for radio, with Simon Armitage. I had come as a student on a fiction course taught by Andrew Miller.

After that first difficult week, we threw ourselves into the job. It was mad, on every level: challenging and crazy. But we both loved mad. The tutors were often colourful, to say the least. In our time, we met over four hundred professional writers of some sort. This was one of the great privileges of the job: to meet our peers, to listen to their work, often read out in the barn while still in progress. We had a chance to enjoy their ideas and enter into their post-dinner discussions and debate. It was a never-ending master class, especially for me, with just one novel to my name, still an apprentice to the pen.

Sociable people in different ways, we each got a chance to show off our hosting skills, our literary tastes, and, yes, our love for each other. I had the model of my parents to live up to: they were a flamboyant party-throwing couple, tempestuous too, like Burton and Taylor. I had this prototype of a couple imprinted on my hard drive. I knew how to be one half of a great dynamic. And so did he. God, we were camp, and, at times, purposefully dramatic. We found, to our delight, that many of the tutors had similar tendencies. That first summer we met Philip Hensher and his giant greyhound dog with its diamanté collar; the poet Paul Farley and his flammable Hawaiian shirts; Paul Hyland and his magic tricks; the singer Tom Robinson, who arrived with his shaman; pop megastar Ray Davies, who arrived, shades glued to his face (even during dinner), with his personal assistant; Charles Palliser, ever the quintessential writer, who arrived with a box of Bendicks mints for us and whose chin was dotted with shaving cuts blotted with loo paper. My ex, a huge fan of Palliser's novel *The Quincunx*, still uses that mint box as his pencil case.

mad fuckers

I fell in love during my time as a centre director for Arvon. In our four years at Totleigh, we also met over two thousand aspiring writers; student and apprentice writers aged eleven to ninety. The house we looked after with pride, but it was with the students that the heart of our second love affair resided. Arvon took up so much of our writing time that I think we would have quit in less than six months if we hadn't witnessed, week after week, the transformative process of an Arvon week. It happened without fail, to almost every member of each course, something known as 'Arvon magic', a phrase so twee that I always hated it, hated even saying it.

In reality, it wasn't magic at all, but lots of the *right kind* of hard work thrown at them in idyllic surroundings.

I fell in love with many of the students I met. The myth that 'there's always one' is true; yes, there were sometimes difficult students. But in general, they were not the least bit difficult; sometimes maybe just awkward or eccentric. Mostly the students were charming and polite, mostly they wanted to write. They made me love them; they helped me to be a nicer person. I wasn't as friendly as my ex. I found being nice and charming to lots of people week in, week out tiring. For the first time ever I was being stretched; I was being forced from my aloof tendencies. It was good for me. For my ex, being affable and available was the easy bit; he oozed loving hippie niceness.

But yes, for us both, it was the students who did it: Hom Paribag, a Nepalese writer who came with English PEN and said I looked like his sister; Aziz, the freedom fighter from Sudan, who came with the Medical Foundation; the young boy who kicked a football through the dining room window, leaving a neat hole in the glass; the woman who wore her cycling helmet when she read out tales of her disastrous love life, the woman who sat writing on a chair in the car park, the man who stood on the table and sang love songs, the couple who came together even though they'd split up, the Israeli woman who did Reiki on my headache, the kids from an inner-city school who thought sheep were cows. They are the reason why Arvon stole my heart: these mad fuckers who came to stay week after week. They came and they wrote poems and stories and caught a glimpse of how writing is crafted, a glimpse of their own potential. For those few days at Totleigh Barton most of them blossomed. They went home altered and we helped this happen. *Fuck*, it got to me.

sex and arvon

The students were, on average, mostly female. Arvon and Arvon-like writing centres have a reputation, amongst other things, for being nodes of sexual energy. Maybe there's some truth in this: it was one of our earliest female poets, Anne Finch, who said that literary creativity in women is the result of sexual frustration. She was talking about our foremothers, of course, those writers in the early eighteenth century, for whom even picking up a pen was considered monstrous.

But I wonder if some accuracy still lurks in this idea. As a female author myself, do I write because I am undernourished sexually? God – now that's a real possibility. The very fact that Arvon, like all writing courses, attracts significantly more female students than male students draws a link to the notion that women are traditionally less free, less used to being in positions of authority, let alone authorship, than men.

Enter, into this group of women, the established poet or author, an icon of romantic manhood. A blend of the feminine principle, demonstrated by his creativity, his ability to write sentences which make the heart soar, and yet a man in most other respects.

Just say this poet or author is handsome; or, just say this poet or author is scruffy, fat, or even piggy-eyed.

Just say this poet or author is bored with his own sex life, stressed by his familial constraints, off the marital leash for the week; or so he feels.

This poet or author, fat or thin, handsome or ugly, can do

something most other men can't. He can touch the feminine in himself and in doing so communicate uniquely with women.

Imagine the effect this poet or author has when he smiles and looks deep into the eyes of a woman who also wants to be a writer.

Get the picture?

A male poet or writer could come into the environs of Totleigh Barton and kill a woman dead just by fluttering his eyelashes. Many (and I'm not mentioning any names) did just that.

My ex, a fat, ugly, hilariously funny author was a big hit with the students, male and female alike. Even so, I never saw it coming. I always thought he only had eyes for me. In those earlier years together, people often commented on his love-drunk gaze. So I never imagined he'd roam, not even when things began to deteriorate between us, when we were rowing and our bed had gone stone cold. I was unwise about this; I took an awful lot for granted, mostly his love for me; that his love hadn't faltered, not fundamentally. I assumed that somewhere, he still adored me.

I was also wilfully *blind*. Arvon made me compartmentalise my time: X amount for the centre, the rest for my next novel. I kept my head down and my eyes shut. I retreated more and more. My ex would be at Totleigh late on the nights he was on duty, always there on a Friday night, creating a 'party-like atmosphere'. I was writing a doomed-to-fail novel, my second, and had become obsessed with saving it. He spent more and more time at the centre, at first to help me out, but, in the end, because he preferred being there to being with me. And so I didn't know or care to know if any of the students fancied him. I saw it as distasteful and unethical to chat up or have sex with a student, and assumed that he did, too. But he was very popular with the students. He told me once, much later, that several women *had* made passes at him, that he'd deflected them. I never knew about these incidents, or cared to know. I admit to a foolish pride on this front: no female student was my equal. Truth is, I underestimated the 'student factor' entirely.

fantasies, fantasies

I never fancied any of the students. Okay, maybe one or two. But there were a handful of the tutors who came through whom I fancied the pants off. So I was guilty, too, and yes, in some respects, I wasn't so different from the female students, in that I find men who write attractive.

Over those four years, a banquet of poets and writers passed through Totleigh. I basked in the company of these men who were excellent, even if only in one particular way. I'd always found it hard to find an intellectual and emotional equal. I'd endured years of singledom prior to meeting my ex. I had survived off writing, and reading good books, had thrown myself into numerous adventures to stave off the monotony of being in the world without a worthy companion. Before my ex, I used to think men were boring, easy, and less complex humans.

And then this stream of male intellect passed through my life, week after week.

I sinned. In my imagination, I committed adultery again and again, with some of these men. I conjured numerous fantasy encounters with them; I wanted to sleep with *other* men. I became not just sexually restless but tormented.

Months would go by without sex between us. And when it did happen, it was a crippled, sometimes bungled, half-loving encounter. He gave up on me, and I didn't care to show him where or how I wanted to be touched. I didn't even know myself. I began to wither from lack of sexual love. My desire for sex returned to me, after years of lying dormant all those years with him. It came back with renewed strength and I became the woman in *The Song of Songs*, lustful and looking for a tryst. I even started writing a novel called *The Tryst*. I was horny as hell but we weren't having sex. We didn't know how to love or please each other. He said that most of the other women he'd slept with orgasmed through penetration. I questioned this. Looking back I'm appalled at my lack of knowledge about my own body. It was a mystery to me, let alone to him. I was thirty-eight, and still a virgin to myself.

This was our most difficult time. Once we'd loved each other enough to accommodate this mismatch of desire. Now we were tense and overworked and resentful. We both needed sexual loving and release, but I didn't want him and he knew it and this made things fraught between us.

We began to argue in that cheap sordid way you see in Australian soaps. That all-loving look in his eye disappeared. He became patronising to me, said things to undermine me in front of other people. I withdrew. Night after night we shared a bed. I lay there sweating with lust for other men, barely touching him. I became repulsed by him, coming to bed in a tea-stained T-shirt and nothing else, just the flash of his cock. I pretended I was asleep. Awful, awful to end up like this. Once I'd wagged my butt at the sight of him. Jumped out from behind trees to boo him. He'd painted my toenails in Andromeda Heights, we had shared a rat-infested house, driven to nuclear power stations, played on beaches, travelled all over the country. We'd loved each other and yet it had been a hellish fickle love. To find a person to love so much but whom you don't want to fuck? I still curse the gods as I write. I still miss his laugh, ten years later.

But in those last months I was miserable. I'd no idea that he was making passionate love to another woman, the woman who eventually sent me the letter bomb.

My ex, in some respects, had *my* affair. He had the courage to do what I dreamt of doing. Those emails that I was sent. Without sex in our own bed, his fantasy life, like mine, was running rife. We were doomed. If my ex hadn't had an affair, maybe I would have.

'It's only a matter of time before one of us has *an affair*,' I once hurled at him during a row towards the end of things. His face was curiously placid: he was in the midst of one.

How stupid I was. And how textbook it all seems now. But I didn't stray. It takes guts. Maybe it also takes some past experience. In the end, fantasy got the better of him.

the curse of the eggs

Over those six years together, I gave him eggs. The first was made of turned beech wood. I presented it to him for his forty-second birthday weeks after we met. I left for Trinidad soon after and he said he kept the egg safe in the pocket of his ginger fleece, clutching it for comfort while he awaited my return.

After that, the egg-giving became a thing. Each time his birthday came round I'd delight in finding him a suitable egg. The second was an ostrich egg, all snubby and creamy and fat; the third was a glittery egg-shaped box. Another was made of polished rock, opals set into it. I began to get superstitious about the eggs. If I didn't give him one, something bad would happen; if I gave him one when it wasn't his birthday, then something bad would happen. He loved the eggs and displayed them on his bookshelf on little egg stands.

What were those eggs? Was I counting out our time together? Was I giving him eggs unfertilised? At the time, I wasn't too interested in getting pregnant. I don't know what they were, only that I gave him eggs and they were of me and they were of love.

The Christmas before the letter bomb, against my instincts, I gave him another egg. It was spotted, made of red glass. It was a mistake; or was it? A month later we were split apart.

the start of the affair

And yet, and yet, during those years in Sheepwash we'd been happy too. A double act. Popular and successful. I am plagued, still, by my memories of our happiness while we lived there together. Mostly, I remember his ginger fleece and the side of his large shaved head, a rollie clamped between his lips while he sang in the car as we drove all over Devon together, to the nearby beaches and the moors, to Welcombe, Dartington, the Scilly Isles, Lundy Island, to Cornwall. Holidays on the Greek islands of Symi and Patmos, a wedding in Spain, a carnival in Trinidad. We had many adventures together in those years.

Most of all I remember the effect of the Devon landscape on me, its gentle soothing effect on my spirits. A city girl, I'd never seen badgers in the wild, let alone red deer; I didn't know the names of wild flowers, had never seen a house being thatched before, never seen house martins return to the same spot, year after year, never witnessed a river bursting its banks, or lambs appearing, bullocks appearing at the same time, only to disappear. I had never encountered nature's active and insistent purpose on the world.

One afternoon, I left Totleigh on foot. It was July, and the harvest had begun. I walked back along the track. The farmers in the top field were making bales. The land everywhere was golden. I walked along and watched the men work; I gazed out at so much land which had been tended for centuries by man, and I felt a strange and humbling sadness ripple through me. I was alone, no one saw me come or go; and yet I felt both part of things and insignificant, the lonely shape of a woman, maybe the shape of many women who'd passed that way. I wept. Nature had ganged up on me. I wept as I walked home that midsummer's day. And something of that landscape and the time I spent there lives with me today.

♥

In the end, it all got too much for us. The lack of sex was causing an almighty chasm. My novel was dying and my nascent career was falling away whilst his was taking off. We were still arguing. Once, I lost my sense of humour and stalked out of dinner while a well-known writer was visiting. He caught up with me on the track and I turned and slapped him hard and ran back home in tears. Everyone still loved him. But I hated him. I was doing the lion's share of the admin at work. I was doing all the admin in our house too; I ran two homes. I was managing the students and managing my ex. I had no headspace to create. I was tired.

Then, after a trip to Bath, I cracked. We were chatting in our bedroom. Finally, at last, I summoned the courage to bring things up.

'Sex,' I said.

'What about it.'

'We don't seem to have much, do we?'

'No.'

'I wonder if we should have a trial ... separation. For six months or so.' I hadn't planned to say this; it popped out.

He was dumbfounded. I saw his face fall, his eyes film over.

'I mean, there's nothing ... you know ... between us ...'

He nodded. But as I ventured forth into this terrible subject I was unconsciously ending things, digging myself deeper into a well of sadness for us both, one we'd never clamber out of.

'I want to try sleeping with other people.'

He didn't know what to say. Then he looked me in the eye. 'Have you *ever*, you know ... fancied me?'

I didn't know how to reply.

That conversation had the effect of napalm on a field. November 2003 was the beginning of the end of things between us; we'd been together four years. We never had that trial separation, I never slept with other men, and we were never happy again. Somewhere, we still loved each other deeply, were profoundly attached to each other. We soldiered on. Now, I see we should have sought counselling *then*, but we didn't until it was too late. Six months later, in May 2004, he cracked and found solace in a female Arvon student, one whom I don't remember meeting because by then I was half present at the centre.

They met again at Glastonbury that summer, where my ex performed with Chaz and Your Dad. When he left for the site he remembered to take his brand-new sleeping bag but forgot to send his daughter hers. I rang him and screamed at him for being such a selfish pig. He sobbed and sent me a bouquet of flowers. When he returned, days later, dirty and dishevelled, having made love to her, he got into bed and held me close.

'I love you, Mon,' he whispered into my ear.

I was sick at heart. I still loved him, somehow, despite everything else. He was the one my soul loved. He cried into my hair. He cried because he was guilty, because she had met him at Glastonbury and they had started their affair.

GIRLBUTTERFLY

'The desire of the lover is the desire of one who delights
in learning and who loves knowledge'

Socrates

♥

the purple suede book

After the letter bomb, and the grim week that followed, I first fled back to the Black Sheep Co-op. It had been four years since I'd lived there. I stored my life's belongings in the basement and repainted the moth-infested vacant attic rooms. My ex, left behind in Sheepwash, was distraught. On Valentine's Day, two weeks later, he sent me a large bouquet and I agreed to meet him in Hyde Park. But it was a pathetic meeting; we stumbled around the gloomy February rain-soaked lawns in tears. There was nothing to say; what we had was blown apart. A few days later, I left the country, heading home again for Trinidad.

Back home, I worked on a new novel and played Scrabble with my mum a lot. It was a dire time: I could barely speak about what had happened. I took three months off. I was due some down time after Arvon – it was a much-needed break. From March to May of 2006, I wrote the first draft of my next novel, *The White Woman on the Green Bicycle*. My ex called me a few times. We cried on the phone, both of us miserable and suffering, both incredulous that we were now apart, an ocean between us. When he asked, I refused to go back to him. I was still too shocked. Writing a novel was the sanest thing I could do, under the circumstances, a new world to invent, a whole other story to investigate. It was something important to occupy my thoughts.

I flew back to London on 1 June, 2006. Temporarily, I

moved back into the Black Sheep Co-op, maybe an unwise thing to have done: to return to a place where we were once so happy. And yes, I was haunted by all the memories of the time we'd shared there. But I was a writer, still living hand to mouth, and I knew it was a temporary arrangement.

In another way, this was the right place to regroup. In London, at the co-op again, over that long blue post-break up summer of 2006, I began to write in a purple suede-bound book. The book had been a gift from Arvon, sent in haste, just before I departed for Trinidad. Our Arvon colleagues had been as dismayed as we were at our split; no one knew what to do with us, how to handle a goodbye party. And so, I was taken out to a posh French restaurant by my boss, Stephanie Anderson, and received this purple suede book in the post.

On 23 June, 2006, I made my first entry:

Being in a bad relationship is not the same as being in a relationship with someone you love which has turned bad.

That was what I'd come to. Our relationship had *turned* bad. I blamed the pressure of the job; in other circumstances, perhaps our sexual life could have improved, even flourished.

On 26 June, 2006, I wrote:

Have fantasies, fantastical dreams. Be a dreamer. Be dreamy. Tread the fine line between fantasy and real life. Fantasy enriches life – fantasy is the wick of love. Beware fantasy though. It is strong. Eros.

Those emails between my ex and that woman were still alive, dancing in my head. This is what had killed him first, then us, getting into a fantasy-based scenario. Projecting his hopes and desires, finding another woman into whom to pour himself, physically and emotionally. Proclaiming his lust via email.

I'd lost my life-companion. For the next year or so, this purple suede book became a substitute. It was a handmade book with silver gilt-edged pages. It became my confidante, my intimate.

Those first writings in the purple suede book were meditations. Ponderings on what had happened between us, how things had gone so wrong. Like Joan Didion in her memoir on loss, *The Year of Magical Thinking*, when disaster hit, I wrote a lot. I also went to the substantial body of literature on love and loss. I liked Stendhal's *Love*: 'You are unconsciously bored by living without loving . . .' Yes, without my ex, I was bored. No one to talk to, check in with, care about. No one to care for me. My ex had been a robust conversationalist; I was too. I missed the daily conversation between us.

John Armstrong's *Conditions of Love, the Philosophy of Intimacy*, was also interesting: 'The structure of our minds is set for love.' I knew this too. I was still 'set for love', I couldn't unset myself.

A Grief Observed, by the Christian scholar C.S. Lewis is a *tour de force* on loss. 'No one ever told me that grief felt so like fear. I am not afraid, but the sensation is like being afraid. The same fluttering in the stomach, the same restlessness, the yawning. I keep on swallowing.' Grief takes you physically, it affects the body; it yearns for the lost other. I could feel my heart murmuring, talking to me, *where is he*?

Others had loved and lost and written about it. It helped to know I wasn't alone. I was part of a community. Some in this community were dead, others were alive. I was part of an unseen group of the grief-stricken, those who had suffered the loss of love.

And, all the while, it was so, so hard to explain to others then – as it still is now – how I loved a man so much whom I didn't desire. 'Surely you're best out of it,' others said. 'Why are you so heartbroken? You didn't love him. It wasn't fair on him. This woman did you a favour.'

A favour? To be so ruthlessly bombed?

It was as if *proof* of the ideal love affair was lust. At the heart of all proper relationships had to be Eros, desire. But my love affair *was* proper. Time and time again others said, 'But you never really fancied him'. I realised that around me existed a very high ideal of what constituted a proper relationship: it had to be a combination of erotic love and friendship-love. Both must exist for a relationship to count. I wondered: did everyone else have this perfect mix? Had I been stupid? I had a sense that the grand love I had for him had somehow cancelled out desire. 'I am certain of nothing but the holiness of the heart's affections ...' said the romantic poet John Keats and I understood what he meant. My love for my ex had this quality, holiness. I refused to let others tell me what was what, what a relationship should or shouldn't be.

♥

That August, at WH Smith in Paddington train station, something happened. I picked up a new kind of book, a sex-blog-diary called *Girl with a One Track Mind* by Abby Lee.

I stared at the book. It was pink. I strongly object to the

pinkification of all products aimed at women. This book was pink and cartoon-esque, not the kind of book I'd ever buy. Yet I picked it up anyway. I took it off the shelf, almost sniffed it. It was about sex, a sex diary. Sex had become a subject I was interested in: the lack of sex in my relationship had fucked up my life.

I stood in the bookshop, read a few pages, and was instantly absorbed. Like the woman in *The Song of Songs*, the author was lustful and Jewish, a woman ten years younger than me. She'd been writing an anonymous online sex blog which had attracted millions of readers.

I took the book home and read it in one sitting. I was awed by this woman's voracious sex-drive, admiring of her candid approach to how she felt about sex, had always felt, since adolescence.

Abby Lee, I know now, is the writer and blogger Zoë Margolis. Reading her sex diary did something to me – and hopefully to lots of other single women of all ages. It opened up a world of possibilities. Sex shops, sex blogs, online casual sex dating, sex clubs, swinging clubs, BSDM. A Girl's Guide to Fuck Buddies, A Girl's Guide to Why Men Should Shave their Genitals. All of a sudden the world of regular internet dating appeared tame. What on earth was anyone doing looking for romance on the internet? The internet is surely the least romantic place to find love. But sex – wow. Yes, this seemed far more likely and appropriate.

Girl with a One Track Mind is written in frank, self-deprecating prose. The sex is often funny and titillating. But in the end, the heroine proves that she does have a heart, that she is looking for Mr Right after all. It was my story in reverse, almost. All sex, no love.

I finished the book and put it aside. But something about its adventurous spirit stayed with me. The heroine was part nymphomaniac, part buccaneer. I liked the idea that there was a 'world', a hidden population to be explored – a place for sexual seekers. And so I took note. I was already so lonely and yes, *bored* without my ex, so numb with grief that I was primed: I'd do anything for relief. I didn't know it then, but I was months away from following in the footsteps of Ms Margolis.

♥

The cats I'd shared with my ex were called Daphne (du Maurier) and Lady Violet (after Anthony Powell's wife). We'd left them behind at Totleigh Barton. While I had settled in London, he had moved to a town on the Welsh border. We'd kept in touch those summer months after our split, talking, emailing, crying, and arguing. Nothing could be resolved. We wanted to see each other, stay in touch; there was an old habit of knowing each other that didn't die quickly.

To make things worse, I heard reports that our cats were unhappy without us. My ex had visited Totleigh and Lady Violet, the fluffy queenly one, had tried to follow him on a walk away from the house across the fields. He'd had to carry her back. There were too many people coming and going. The new centre directors owned a big galumphing Labrador; they weren't too keen on cats. Violet spent most of the day hiding in the dilapidated barns. I was wretched with guilt. So my ex and I agreed on a rescue plan, to take them back to his cottage where they'd be safe. We also agreed, just this once, due to the long drive, that I'd stay overnight in his spare room.

The cat-rescue was swift. It was a Saturday and the centre was quiet; the current directors were relieved we'd come to collect them. Both cats were asleep in a bedroom upstairs. A dozy pair, I was able to lift each cat as it slept, and drop them in the cat boxes I'd brought. Once trapped, they were both silent.

We had a moment together, my ex and I, some kind of leave-taking, as we drove through the last cattle grid on the top field with our cats. It was September, 2006, seven months after our split. We were leaving Totleigh Barton again, together but separated.

That night, at my ex's cottage, while he was out rehearsing with his new band, I logged on to his computer to check my emails and noticed he'd been making playlists on iTunes for a 'Ruth'. A play list of love songs, including one particular song he bought me for Christmas once, cheesy as hell: 'If You're Not the One', by Daniel Beddingfield.

Now he was wooing another woman with *the same song*? Several of the other songs on the playlist I recognised, too. The tape he'd made me six years before: I'd listened to it dreamily – 'My Funny Valentine' had become one of our theme tunes. While he was at the quiz night I'd dreamt of him, all those years ago. Suddenly, it became clear: he'd made many tapes like this for many women. This was how he did it. I hadn't been any different. He had a collection of love themes and he strung them together for each new woman. How had I taken this man so seriously? Given him six years of my life? Ruth was a new woman, not the woman who'd split us up. I was amazed at the speed at which he seemed able to move on.

When he returned home I went ballistic.

'Who the *fuck* is Ruth?'

'Someone I like.'

'Yeah – so much you gave her that song you bought *me* for Christmas! You shit! You just *recycle* your love.'

Again, he was speechless at being found out.

I was incredulous he was so keen to replace me. *Me?* I'm fantastic. My mother has told me so – many times. He fell in love with me *on the page*, before we'd even met. M.R. 4 I.M. Surely he remembered that? Mon who'd soothed his bald head during his night terrors, who'd painted his toenails green in summer, who'd encouraged him into Birkenstocks, liberating his punk feet, who'd forced him to hitchhike in Greece, who'd led him into the job at Arvon, who'd drugged him on Kalms and flown him to Trinidad, who'd been a bloody great laugh. Mon of the Nuclear Power Stations. Mon of the Shit Driving. Was he mad? I was irreplaceable.

This happened just as I was beginning to *like* him again, maybe even come to understand the tragedy between us, if not forgive him. The next morning, we drove to the train station in silence and I swore to cut all contact with him thereafter. Not only did he have a 'Ruth' in his life, but he had my beloved cats, too. That's when I went into another time, a more demented state of grief. I knew nothing and understood nothing and cared for no one, especially myself. I'm a Taurean, a bull. I raged, intent on self-destruction. I had to *know*, to find out what had happened between us. I'd do anything to find out.

bookish ex-stripper

17 November, 2006. Ten months after the letter bomb. Late autumn. I happened to bump into my old friend Jason on Clerkenwell Road. I was en route to meeting another writer friend at a wine bar further down. I persuaded Jason to come along for a drink. But the wine bar, Vino Teca, was rammed and we ended up opposite, in the bar of St John's, laughing and chatting about one of Jason's friend's recent escapades on the *Guardian*'s Soulmates site. A man had shown Jason's friend a picture of his cock on his mobile phone.

It was funny and weird. Everyone was internet dating. There was no longer any stigma attached to it. The *Guardian* site was by far the most popular. This whole new era of internet dating had boomed in the years when I was more or less married. I'd emerged, single again, in my early forties, to find there was this new way of meeting people. But I had mixed feelings about it. I could see it was a positive thing, but also found it daunting. In a fit of optimism I'd once logged on to the *Guardian* site and lasted three days; I found the experience alienating. It was like shopping in a super-market, except not for apples or Ryvita. For a man. I didn't like it. It was distracting and overwhelming, and not at all romantic.

'I don't think internet dating is for me,' I moped. 'I don't want another boyfriend, not so soon anyway. I just want a lover.'

'You should try Craig's List then,' Jason quipped.

'Craig's List?' I replied, 'What's that?'
'A sex dating site. You'll find a lover there.'

♥

A week after that conversation in St John's, I was in alone on a Friday night – Friday 24 November, to be precise. I was in a strange autumnal mood: vengeful and furious that my ex had moved on, pensive and wistfully making notes in the purple suede book. I was reading books on the complexities of having a broken heart and still feeling inspired and titillated by the marvellous Ms Margolis. This was my mindset that Friday evening, the evening I placed my first advert on Craig's List. Vengeful. Wistful. And yes, horny. Or that's my excuse.

Well, for whatever reason, I did what my friend Jason suggested. I logged on to Craig's List – to their infamous 'Casual Encounters' section – looking for a lover.

Readers, go do this too, *now*, and then come back to this spot on the page. Only then will you be able to venture forward with me, to know what I saw – and just how shocked I was by what I found. If internet dating is like shopping for a mate, then the Casual Encounters section of Craig's List is like the bargain basement of all internet dating sites, a wretched place. Yes, please, go there right now.

Shocked? At first glance, it's a harsh world. Full of whores and perverts and sex freaks and sadists and people with the most one-dimensional (and badly spelled) sexual fantasies, fantasies of being sucked and fucked and whipped and humiliated. It is, on first glance, the land of the zip-less fuck, the territory of the oversexed, those who will do anything with anyone because they are *that* up for it. Wow. What a world to stumble on. Yes, I was astounded, at first. But then, on further perusal, not *that* astounded. Intrigued, fascinated, more like.

And then, and I think this is the real truth, the writer in me clicked into action – the person who believes, like the Irish short story writer Frank O'Connor, that stories come from 'submerged worlds'; that they are about outlaw figures trying to escape from these small, socially claustrophobic societies. And here, right in front of me, on the screen, was such a world.

Was I a common hack? An author in search of a subject? Or was I a furious horny bitch bent on doing something reckless? Maybe both; I'm sure the truth is somewhere between the two. But whatever the reason, I found myself writing the following advert.

Bookish Ex-Stripper

Mature, vivacious, rapacious woman still in possession of fine legs, great arse and a cracking pair of knockers seeks Lover, not Fucker, on casual but regular basis, for clandestine sex and sparkling conversation.

New to CL, I read a lot and so would like to meet a man who reads too. Novels, poetry. A man with an erotic imagination and a poetic ability with his hands and mouth. Is there anyone out there who'd like to read to me in bed?

Get in touch. Send a pic and your tel no.

Placing an advert on CL is free. But to do so you are advised to set up a Hotmail account in order to ensure privacy. I followed these instructions and made up a name for myself without much thought: 'girlbutterfly', butterfly being a symbol of metamorphosis, the Greek symbol of the psyche. It seemed appropriate at the time.

So, advert placed, I went to call my good mate Emma Daly in New York. We chatted on the phone for an hour at least. When I returned to my screen, a little tired and ready for bed, I found that eighty replies had sailed into the inbox of girl-butterfly.

♥

I didn't know where to start – or what I'd done, or what I was doing at all. I flicked open some of the emails and flicked them closed. They were alarming. Cocks. Faces. Lewd propositions. I instantly deleted some. What *on earth* was I playing at? In cyberspace it's so easy to fall down a black hole, find yourself in a darker world. What had I done?

Slowly, slowly, one by one, I started to read this outpouring of male sexuality, their offerings, their words, their ideas. I couldn't help myself. There were things I knew men wanted, but had never been asked for. There were things I could never have imagined *anyone* wanting. This was men laid bare. Men stripped of the niceties of courtship, of having to tone things down. *Suck me, fuck me*. Wanton maleness, undiluted male sexuality, right there, on my screen. I could fuck all eighty of these men if I wanted. None seemed to care who I was. The tone of the emails was cocky, audacious, funny, lewd, juvenile, dark, lascivious. Rude. Craig's List is for sexual adventurers, for those with high sex drives and high sexual self-confidence. All fancied their chances.

Did I? Was I their female counterpart? Could I be another Abby Lee? A worthy or likely match? I didn't know. Right then, I didn't know myself, not in this area, had never explored this aspect of myself, my sexual potential. I began to plough through those emails. Below is a short, but by no means comprehensive, list of some of the men who emailed me that first night.

Younger men – in their 20s
Married men – all ages
Attached men – all ages
'Professional' men
Writers
Journalists
A foreign correspondent
A 'wealthy businessman'
Doctors
An Oxbridge graduate
An ex-athlete
A teacher
Americans in town on business
Photographers
Academics
A policeman
A man describing himself as Othello
A vaudeville theatre director

And here is a list of what they sent in their emails:

Decent pictures of their faces and their telephone
    number (these all got serious attention)
Pictures of their cocks (flaccid, semi-erect, erect)
Pictures of 'Conan the Barbarian'-style torsos
Pictures of themselves with wife and kids (some had
    altered the faces of their wives and children with
    weird bubbles)
Pictures of their own artwork (one man was trying to
    sell me his)
Erotic art. One man sent a picture of himself wrestling
    with another man in a gimp mask
Self-penned poems, some sent reams of their bad
    poetry
Erotic fantasies
Short stories
Lists of books they had read; one man sent a picture of
    his bookshelf!
Some good poetry (Byron, Sappho, James Joyce)

I found myself making a shortlist. A shortlist! From heartbroken celibate to wanton player in just one hour. I thought of
the emails I'd burned earlier that year, the email-fantasy life
of my ex and his lover. *Waitformewaitformewaitforme.* Beware
fantasy – and the power of email. Cowards, braggarts, the
weak and the sick, even the desperate can sound attractive via
email. I was conscious of this strange twist of fate as I sat there
that Friday night, my screen aglow with hot florid erotica. The
same erotica which got my ex going, which replaced the lust
in our cold and unfucked bed, which ended in utter devasta-
tion, the end of our love.

I was aware of the lure of fantasy. And I couldn't resist.

The men who got onto some kind of shortlist were:

R – 34, a television journalist
W – 30s, who ran a family sign company
P – 35, a photographer
S – 45, a businessman
J – the vaudeville theatre director
D – 30s, an American professor in town for the week
N – who sent good poetry

All of the above were shortlisted on the grounds of some kind of appeal. Looks, yes, for I could afford to be choosy. A significant number of the emails were from men whom I felt I might come across in my personal life. Some looked handsome, many were young, many were professional and didn't seem too crazy. Some could have stepped out of my life, or near to it. Some had a direct and appealing approach – no cock, just a face pic and a nice message, polite, not freaky. Not weird. Easy.

It was late. A Friday night.

I thought 'what the fuck' and picked up the phone and called the television journalist. When I introduced myself I could sense his panic and disbelief. He gabbled, but was funny with it; he said he was 'high up' in the business, said he'd written a few non-fiction books. Clearly, he hadn't bargained on hearing from a real woman, not so soon, just a few hours after his reply to my advert. I was amazed at how calm I felt. I didn't care that he sounded nervous; he had every right to be.

We arranged to meet a few nights later in a pub he suggested, the Old Mitre in Ely Court, a tiny pub in the back streets of Holborn.

'I'm going to chat you up,' I said, breezily, as this new me, girlbutterfly. And I meant it.

mr wolf

'Looking for someone?' the barman asked. I nodded and blushed, scanning the room. The bar was empty. I faltered. The barman must have known what I was doing; it must've been written all over my face. What with this new era of inter-net dating, this must be a new phenomenon for landlords. Strangers, not friends, meeting over a drink.

My heart beat faster, just like when I went to meet my ex for our first date in the Ring O' Bells. Tension, the possibility of sex, romance, maybe even love. I felt deranged. No other friend of mine would actually *do* this: step out into the night for a random sexual adventure.

Richard, the TV journalist, was sitting in the tiny back bar. Stripy shirt, small round specs. Mid-thirties, much more handsome than his photograph. Greying reddish hair, freckles, a wolf-like glint in his eyes. He stood as I approached. I'd travelled up from my new part-time job in Brighton, a fellowship at Sussex University, and was a little train-worn. So it was the real me, not girlbutterfly, who sat down next to him, smiled, pecked him on the cheek and said:

'I'm not going to sleep with you tonight.'

He laughed. This broke the ice. Northern. He was northern. This made me fancy him outright. I have a general dislike of men of my own class and social background. I like big men, rough men, men with eye patches and cork legs and tattoos, northerners, working-class men.

We got drunk and chatted easily. We talked of money, love, and cricket. A Trinidadian, by default I'm always happy to talk about cricket. There was a couple sitting next to us who didn't say a word to each other all evening and we giggled at them. The hours seemed to pass, conversation flowed. It was almost a normal date, a chance meeting. We disarmed each other and got drunk.

Outside, we kissed in the alley: my first taste of another man's lips in years. I felt about fifteen. Happy. People watched us. We walked to the main road and without much discussion, flagged down a cab and sped back to his flat in Hammersmith, snogging all the way.

In his tiny flat, we fell into bed. He sank his mouth between my legs and I groaned. *Ahhhhh.* Thank you, God. It was that post-pub-rolling-round-the-bed-tugging-to-get-clothes-off kind of sex, him whispering 'Hold me', 'Ride me' into my ear. I did my best to comply. I hadn't had sex for over a year. I hadn't even *realised* this, I was that used to my celibate life. I'd been living without *this*! Glorious, it was glorious and fun to fuck around like this. This is what my ex had been missing too. This is what couples did. I'd had this kind of sex with my ex once: in a hotel room during the Abergavenny Food Festival, at which he'd performed. I could *count* the times. Once.

Richard was slow to come. At one point, we were shagging furiously, only half on his bed, me holding onto a wooden clotheshorse near the window as I bounced up and down. We laughed at ourselves. We shouted and broke into sweats. Afterwards, we fell asleep wrapped round each other in a thick duvet, caressing each other's skin, our fingers entwined.

His body was smooth and creamy; he had a pretty cock. He was a boyishly handsome man, a great kisser. The window was open and I drifted off listening to rain, my favourite sound.

In the morning, he brought me tea and toast in bed. We walked to the tube arm-in-arm and snogged at the station. We swapped our real life e-addresses and emailed each other later to say how funny and fun the evening had been. Boy, was I pleased. *Go girl*, I said to myself. Well done. Hello girlbutterfly. I saw quite a bit of him over the next six months. It turned into a largely sex-driven affair: dinners, the theatre, meals in his bed, always sex afterwards. Sex, sex and more sex, exactly what I'd been looking for.

thrown down a well

By midday after the date with Richard, sixty more emails had arrived for girlbutterfly. I had lunch with my good friend, the writer, Julia Bell. Julia, a sassy, straight-talking woman, was just the right person to 'out' myself to. When I told her what I'd done she didn't bat an eyelid. Rollie clamped between her teeth, she shrugged, as if what I'd done was my birthright, a natural and acceptable mode of behaviour.

'Get with the programme, baby,' she purred and blew me a kiss.

Programme? I wasn't with any kind of programme at all. Modern trends and fads weren't my thing. It was late 2006. I'd had a private email account for less than a year. I'd never even owned a mobile phone, never sent a text. Now I was using an exotic alias and plotting to meet men for cyber-sex via the net. I saw her point. There was a lot going on out there; get with it.

'You know something, Julia,' I said. 'Either I'm going to find the lover I'm looking for, or at the very least, I'll have done something interesting.'

Julia rolled her eyes and puffed shrewdly on her ciggie.

I knew that outing myself was important. Poor Zoë Margolis, the girl with the one track mind; she had tried to keep her real identity anonymous – and it had almost worked. But, in August 2006, days after her book was published, she was brutally exposed by the *Sunday Times*. All she'd done was indulge her desires, allow herself to be fully sexually active. But she'd been publicly burnt at the stake, as good as thrown down a well, which is what used to happen to libidinous women in the middle ages. Once, in the 1980s and 90s, it was gay men who were outed. They were 'other', different. Now, in the noughties, sexually 'too active' straight women were being targeted in the same way.

Society, I feared, still believed the sexually forward woman to be harmful to the fabric of civilisation. Zoë was still a Jezebel, a Magdalene. Or that sinner, Eve. Burn her. I felt unhappy that Zoë had even thought she needed to be anonymous.

At that time, Belle du Jour (Brooke Magnanti), and other female sex-bloggers were also hiding their real identity. This felt wrong to me. On the one hand, I thought it bought into the shame and social stigma of being openly sexual and female. On the other hand, I knew these women were right to conceal themselves. They were transgressing so many basic rules for women. Be nice, stay home, don't show off. Never hunt men. These sex-bloggers were revolutionaries. Outlaws, masked highwaywomen of the net.

In the end, I decided I wanted to make sure I *didn't* hide what I'd done – and intended to keep on doing. So I told all my close friends about using Craig's List. That was my first rule. Be out.

I continued to write in my purple suede book. I wanted to puzzle over and process what had happened between me and my ex. This seemed to be getting harder, not easier. Despite my vow to break contact, we'd seen each other once again and were in touch; it seemed to help. We were both still stunned and downcast. The initial drama had settled, but the real consequences of those emails were only just making themselves clear. We had lost each other. We still missed each other. My love for him seemed to swell, get fiercer. In another old notebook, I found a scrap of paper. On it was a poem he'd once written for me after a holiday on a Greek island, Symi:

0+0+0+0

I counted your hair when you were asleep,
A mop of particles colliding in a bubble chamber,
A hullabaloo of strange quarks,
A non-countable infinite nest.

I dreamt of water while you lay beside me,
Bubbling under the boat, running away from the wind.
Blue uncharmable sea dancing
Beyond figuring into the west.

How could the man who wrote this poem betray me? This

man had written me countless love notes, had, on numerous occasions, sprinkled my pillow with rose petals; had bought me flowers, books, *The Song of Songs*, and enriched my life immeasurably. How had this happened, and what was my part in this tragedy? I didn't know. I was in a new era, some kind of belated aftershock. I loved him. My grief raged. I was wretched and dumbfounded to be without him. I wanted to make amends for being such a cold unloving bitch. I saw Craig's List as means of investigating the conundrum of my lack of desire for him.

the company i was keeping

Out of curiosity, I began to peruse the Women4Men section of the Craig's List site. I wanted to see what kind of company I was keeping. Who were the other women out there using this site as well as me – and why? This is what I found:

Sexy Body in a Christmas Sale, 48, Greenwich
High as a Kite, 30, Surrey
Let's Heat Up These Cold Nights, 27
Warm, Classy, Sexy Lady, 23, Soho *(surely a hooker)*
Santa Claus Required. Apply Within.
Looking for a Young Stud, 30
Bored Superstar, 32
Looking for a Policeman, 25
I Want to be Your Muse, 25

No wonder my advert had done so well – a pretty unimaginative lot. Some of these women had posted pictures, showing their breasts; others modelled various types of lingerie, legs splayed, their buttocks proffered. Some were touching themselves. Some posted pictures of their open mouths performing fellatio on humungous cocks.

I wanted to meet these women. I wanted to ask them all sorts of questions – who they were and what did they do for a living? What were they looking for? Were there any other writers among them? Had any of them read *The Song of Songs*? I often contemplated posting an ad. 'Fellow CL women – Let's Meet'. Some were older women, some American, perhaps more comfortable with using this site since CL's Casual Encounters section is so much more commonly used in the US. These American women's ads seemed well worded and discreet. Other ads were weird, even funny. 'Anyone Watching *Newsnight*? Isn't it boring – come over and fuck me.'

Often I noted that women wanted to get laid because they were newly single (like me), or tired of their boyfriend, or unable to ask their partner to indulge in their fantasies of being spanked, whipped, urinated on, fucked while menstruating. I didn't think this was strange, to not be able to ask for the sex you want in a relationship. I hadn't known how to talk about my sexual needs either – to my ex or anyone else.

Every now and then, I saw a man advertising that he wanted either to sleep with a pregnant woman or to make a woman pregnant. God, I'd love to know what kind of women responded to those ads, if any.

Craig's List was a world to marvel at: ask for what you want. Simple as that. As a woman, just what *did* I want? Had I *ever* asked myself that question? What were my fantasies? What did I like?

I made a list. It wasn't long.

1. Sex in public places
2. Stripping for men
3. Filth whispered in my ear

Was that it? No whipping or spanking or being tied up in knots? As a woman who uses her imagination every day, for a living, I was surprised to find that I was woefully under-supplied with sexual fantasies.

When pressed, all of us can reel off favourite songs, bands, books, poems, films, food, fragrances. We all have a well-known and well-loved store of these aesthetic and sensual pleasures. In most arenas of the senses we've explored our taste in pleasure and know what we like. But sex? Did I have a single favourite fantasy, let alone a collection? Did I know what I liked?

If there was a Sexual Fantasy Store, just like HMV, what fantasies would I buy? Which section of the store would I spend most time browsing? Vanilla sex? BDSM? Sex with animals? Anal sex? Oral sex? Self-loving? Group sex? Tantra? Forty-one years old and I had no developed 'taste' in sex, no sexual self-identification other than: female, heterosexual. I despaired.

What did I think I wanted if I was to go ahead and use this site? I made another list:

1. To learn
2. To let myself get hurt (again)
3. To find other lovers

So, I made up a few Basic Rules:

1. Condoms. They were a must.
2. I would be nice, even charming to every man I met, chat them all up.
3. I would never send a picture of my naked body or even part of my naked body to any potential date.

I was very selective about whom I sent pictures of my face. However, being a writer, once or twice I got carried away. I also found myself sending some very dodgy erotic porn out into cyberspace, porn I wrote myself. With one man I got into a fantasy exchange involving sex in a farm kitchen – and then he melted away. With another, whom I later met, I wrote about wanting to be stripped and kissed along the back of the neck and fucked. He later complied.

God knows what's out there. At the time, I *did* worry it would all come back to haunt me and ruin my reputation, my career. Maybe one day it will. But at the time I was finding it was all far too interesting to let that stop me. I didn't know it then, but I was at the beginning of a very long and eventful journey.

Above all, my main rule was this:
4. Make notes.

I wrote about my experiences in the purple suede book. If I were to go out there on another date, it would be in the spirit of a quest, a pilgrimage towards selfhood. Surely going so boldly out into the unknown would bring rewards? I might get hurt or fall in love or, at the very least, I'd find stuff out. I knew this would be a good thing to do. I wanted to put myself way out of my depth.

I was forty-one. I'd had a great body in my twenties. Now I had the forty-one-year-old version of that body. The breasts and arse were still holding up, just, as was the face. I've always had to try harder than conventionally beautiful women at attracting men, so I was used to working at it. I have a well-developed 'personality', a good sense of humour, and, contrary to popular myth, men are drawn to female cleverness.

Over the next ten days, my Bookish Ex-Stripper ad received almost two hundred replies. I corresponded with a dozen or so of these men and in the end only met a handful. Date Two deserves special mention.

the rocket scientist

Professor Jack was from New York. A physicist, he was in town for a few days lecturing at a London University college. We talked on the phone. In his picture, he was shaven-headed, mid-thirties, cute enough. I also have a penchant for shaven-headed men. My ex was a skinhead. This man was an academic too; bald and clever, just my type. We arranged a time and place to meet and I waited for him outside Momo's, a restaurant on Heddon Street which had a separate bar.

Was I as nervous on that second date? Yes and no. I don't

think I cared. What was the alternative? Stay at home and organise my sock drawer? Write more long self-questioning notes in the purple suede book? Remain celibate, untouched, for months, even years? I knew this was part revenge for the Ruth playlist. But, in the end I didn't care *enough* how wanton my behaviour was. To this day, I still don't fear or care what others think about the times I went out into the night looking for sex.

He was late, arrived with a woolly beanie hat pulled low, leather jacket buttoned up, a long scarf wrapped up to his nose. It was cold, so cold it was about to snow. As he walked towards me, looking for the bar, a not-so-innocent abroad, I liked him already.

'Hello,' I said as he approached, and was pleased when he smiled and kissed me on the lips.

He was a sexy man. Friendly. Already, it was an easy date. We descended to Momo's subterranean Kemia bar, all caves and nooks and rich glamorous French people smoking hookahs, Middle Eastern funk playing in the background. It was much too noisy down there and the mojitos were almost a tenner each. Jack and I tried to be polite and open towards each other, but it was too loud and crowded. After one drink he said, 'Let's get out of here.'

Outside, we walked down the narrow cobbled street. It was very easy to be with this man; he had a natural way with me, with women, I suspected. We didn't walk far and neither of us spoke; we started kissing against the wall. Christmas lights twinkled high above us; a crowd of happy Friday night drinkers milled about. Heddon Street is where the cover of David Bowie's *Ziggy Stardust* album was shot; it felt sexycool kissing there. There was a charge between us. I was a total CL beginner but had a keen sense that this Professor Jack was the opposite. He had the air of a player, a man so at ease with our meeting that surely he'd done this many times before.

Soon we were in a black cab heading back to his South Kensington hotel, legs entwined, chatting.

'Are you bi-sexual?' he asked out of the blue.

Bi-sexual, was he nuts? I was just out of celibacy school, a newby to these nights. I was a heterosexual lunatic.

'No,' I replied. I wondered if he was hoping to pick up another woman for us to play with later.

'Are *you*?'

He shook his head.

What kind of sexual creature are you? I wanted to ask. *How do I meet other people like you?*

He was pleased to hear of my beginner status on the CL site, honoured to be one of my first dates. I was pretty pleased too, with this second date. Beginner's luck, no doubt. How the heck had I landed this sexual expert and what on earth was I going to do with him back at the hotel?

His hotel room was small, a single. I was a bit disappointed. He poured me a glass of merlot and disappeared to the bathroom.

With Richard, my first date, we'd talked for hours before getting to this point. There'd been the pub, drinks, conversation. Things had progressed as they would if I'd met him any other way. This time was different: Jack and I hadn't talked that much, not in the same way. Yet we'd clicked on the most basic level – the kissing was great. Now we were in a hotel room.

Shit. Be careful what you wish for.

This was what CL was all about, after all: coming together

for *sex*, not conversation. I stared out the open window into the night and thought: 'Forfuckssakes, Mon, whatonearth-haveyoudone*again*, how on earth are you ever going to tell anyone about this and what the fuck do you think you're doing? Go, run away – now.'

And then his hands were cupping my breasts and his lips were on my neck and, yes, he was whispering filth into my ear. My knees went weak as he peeled off my clothes. And then I was naked at the window and he was whispering sex-soaked words into my neck and then we were on the single bed kissing and fucking and wow – it was great.

Jack had manners. Bedroom manners. First we had slow, comfortable sex. Talking and smooching and fucking. When he came on my stomach, he excused himself to get a towel and wipe it away, just like a French waiter attending to a table. Then, we chatted some more, all wrapped up round each other. At one point, he ordered room service: smoked salmon sandwiches and fruit salad. While we ate, we discussed American politics and Seattle Grunge. He loved the Smashing Pumpkins and Hole and had nursed a crush on Courtney Love in his youth. I asked him all about Craig's List and for tips on how to use it.

Naked, we surfed the site on his laptop together and he showed me the other adverts he'd answered and the ads he knew, just by the language they used, were placed by whores. He never answered these ads. We stopped at the one advert placed by a woman. She'd posted four shots of her pert, naked creamy body. She seemed outrageously comely, yet somehow modest too.

'Is *she* a whore?' I asked. She looked like a very nice young woman. Surely not.

'Probably.'

I was shocked.

Jack was happy to talk about his use of CL and his sexual adventures on it. He'd been using the site for three years, both at home in New York and whenever he travelled abroad to other cities which had CL too. He'd met a woman the night before me, and his chest and biceps were covered in lilac-coloured bite marks. No doubt he'd meet another woman after me, the next night. He was single, a sometime swinger, had slept with hundreds of women using this site and sex clubs. Jack was thirty-five and firmly committed to a non-monogamous lifestyle but he swore he'd never slept with a prostitute. I was fascinated by his louche sexuality, the way he was so open, easy, and loving towards me, a complete stranger. I admired him for it. Perhaps his openness represented the first glimmer of the man I was looking for.

'I love to fuck,' he said. 'Fucking is my thing.' He was a lover of women, an enthusiast.

Jack wasn't looking for more than just this sensual connection; he wanted to taste, watch, touch, feel and fuck as many women as possible. Unlike me, he had spent time exploring his sexual tastes. He wasn't sleazy or creepy, or grabby – quite the opposite. He offered himself in the most comfortable, even humble manner, a sexual operator *par excellence*. I wasn't intimidated; instead I was intrigued and wanted to learn from him.

In fact, I wanted to be like Jack. I saw a flash of my own potential in him. I'd had a similar experience once, years back, in Jerusalem, when I'd met a well-known Irish writer; in fact the first writer I'd ever met. I'd seen myself as a writer too, then. I'd had a moment of self-identification. Now Jack showed me another part of myself that could emerge, if I paid it enough attention.

Even though we'd had regular vanilla sex, I'd held my own. How? Fuck knows. Sheer bravado. I love being naked; that helps. Not everyone will find using a casual dating site easy. I now know that being an actively sexual being is some kind of calling. Was I being called, finally? It felt like it. Like I was finding a part of myself which had been lying inert – for men like Jack and for nights like this.

The only time I sensed a slight unease in Jack was when I stared at him while he ate his smoked salmon sandwich. I'd been trying to understand his emotional ease.

'Don't look at me like that,' he said. He smiled as he chewed.

'Like what?'

'With those eyes. Like how you're looking.'

I shifted my gaze. *So*, he wasn't cool, after all. He was fine with sex, but not so fine with the human quality of my curiosity.

'Have you ever had any disasters using Craig's List?' I probed.

'Sure,' he said. Once, one of his female students had answered one of his ads and he'd replied, blowing his cover. Another woman had become a stalker.

Jack gave me advice: always meet in a public place and never take a man home. Always go back to *his* house. It was much safer that way. This became another of my new rules: never lead a strange man to your door. I hadn't yet considered the dangers of this kind of dating. So far I'd met two rather excellent men. I had assumed neither of them would hurt me. But there'd been many unpleasant types I'd deleted from my inbox.

'Men lie,' Jack warned. 'They lie about who they are and what they do.' I took serious note of this. Good thing too. In the USA there's been a Craig's List Killer. In April 2009, only a year after I last used CL, a man called Philip Markoff, a Boston University medical student, was charged with the murder of a masseur he met on Craig's List, JuLissa Brisman. In April 2010, Markoff committed suicide in his prison cell, and in September 2010 Craig's List USA removed its adult services section from the site.

Jack and I fucked again. This time we were more active, new playmates just starting to get the hang of each other. His cock was smooth and slender, somehow ladylike. His jock's body was slightly running to fat. He was a Lover not a Fucker, again exactly what I'd asked for. Was this beginner's luck? Yes.

When the concierge rang up to ask if his 'guest' was staying the night, he became short-tempered at being cornered (for extra tariff, presumably).

'Yes,' he snapped and slammed down the phone. I was a little embarrassed. He asked me to stay the night then and so we slept curled around each other, while outside it began to snow.

In the morning, he walked me to the hotel lift, kissed me on the lips and whispered 'Thank you.'

Earlier he'd said he fell a little in love with every woman he slept with. It was a line, I knew, as was this 'thank you'. I didn't mind. There were fresh bite marks on his chest, rosy red – mine.

I skipped home. I didn't quite punch the air. Over the next couple of weeks, Jack and I swapped a few emails and then he melted away into the black hole of cyberspace. Last time I heard from him he was chasing European snow bunnies in

Colorado. I never saw him again. I was a little hurt because he said he'd wanted to see me the next time he was in town. Hurt. Good. I wanted to hurt myself.

the man on the phone

In January 2007, a few months after I first started using CL, something very unexpected happened. I had sex on the phone for the first time.

The man in question had contacted me via my Bookish Ex-Stripper ad the previous November. Like Professor Jack, he was also American, a teacher based in Brighton. He was mid-thirties and dark-haired; handsome, very handsome indeed in his photograph. He'd come to the UK to be with his long-distance English girlfriend and she'd promptly dumped him. He was heartbroken, lonely and not sure why he'd contacted me. We talked on the phone for over an hour that cold November night. He was an English teacher and we discussed the novels we admired. His voice was soft, well-modulated. He was charming and erudite, no sex freak, no pervert. He made me laugh. We flirted on the phone but didn't arrange to meet. This was a queer conversation to have with a total stranger, yet we communicated very naturally. This man was bookish and sophisticated in his tastes and outlook; it was like talking to someone I already knew. We talked about the human heart, about our experiences of love. He was in a similar place to me, sombre from lost love, newly single; we'd found each other on a *sex* site. He'd liked my ad; I'd liked his photo and response. Simple as that.

During that phone call we counselled each other, made friends, if you like. He was flying back to the States soon but there was a slim chance he'd secure a teaching job at a private school and if he did, he might return. When we said our goodbyes I assumed I'd never hear from him again, this man on the phone. Steve, let's call him.

So, when Steve rang a couple of months later, I was delighted to hear he was back in the country; he'd decided to work in the UK for the coming academic year. We talked, made each other laugh. Again, we discussed our broken hearts. Again, the connection was effortless. We talked for at least an hour. Then, there was a long pause.

'What are you wearing?' he asked.

His voice was tentative at first, but he got my attention.

I described my thin vest, my jeans, the black lace underwear beneath.

'And what would I see if I stood at the foot of your bed?'

I described my French iron-framed bed, the detritus of going to sleep which lay around it: what books lay open on the floor, what body crèmes and lotions and lubricants lay on the small table beside my bed – and what I liked to do with them. I described the curled-up position I lay in, the colour and texture of my skin.

And then he was whispering words of sex down the phone, and I returned them. Words. Language – my favourite thing. This man knew how to use words: Lick. *Frisk*. Grind. He shared some of his fantasies, said how much he'd like to watch as another man made love to me. His voice was tender and sincere.

I caressed myself as he spoke. I slipped my hand to where I was wet. We spoke words of lust to each other, and then ...

come here, where are you? Very quickly, we worked each other into a mutual ecstasy.

'Don't come, don't come *yet*,' he pleaded. I waited and we came together, for my part in a back-arching body-shuddering torrent. We lay there, spent, whispering more words to each other while cradling the phone. I lay breathless and dazed, stroking myself as he said to me: 'I feel dizzy now.' Wow.

Less than a week later we spoke again. It was mad. There was chemistry! Chemistry between us – just from the language we spoke to each other down the phone. All we had to go on were photos and the tone of our voices.

This conversation was different:

'I want you here,' I said. 'Beside me.'

'I want to be there too.'

A long silence.

'*Fuck*, why aren't you here?' I whispered.

Another long silence.

'What are you doing?' he said.

I told him I was touching myself.

'*Fuck*.'

Silence.

There was palpable tension between us. Eventually we stirred each other up again, into hoarse whispers, into sad-sweet groans. It was shockingly sexy. Ridiculous, given how we could so easily meet.

We made love on the phone again, whispering filth and sex and breaking into sweat. After that he became 'the man on the phone'. Once, we did decide to meet, but he got cold feet and cancelled: he 'wasn't ready', or something like that. Disappointing, but okay. But we continued to talk on the phone. It was so other, so different. I went along with this new type of affair – why not?

Sometimes Steve rang and we'd talk for hours without sex. Books, love, art, family, we'd chat for an hour or two and then say 'goodbye my friend, goodbye'. Other times he rang and from nowhere the sexual energy sprang forth, and we'd end in a storm of gasps.

This continued for over a year. Sometimes, he'd call late at night and I'd have to be very quiet on the phone as I squirmed and thrashed, for fear of what my flatmates might think. No man was with me, yet my cries and moans were loud and luscious, as if I had a lover in my bed.

Steve and I became friends on Facebook. We sent each other private messages. It was another link we made with each other – again, in the dark vault of cyberspace. I could see who his friends were and he could see mine. Over the phone I often recounted my adventures on Craig's List. He seemed to like to hear about them; they titillated him and I knew they did.

Did my escapades scare him off? Possibly. After a while, his communication got a little fraught and dramatic; in one email he called himself a 'liar and a coward'. And then he didn't reply at all to one of my messages. A year had passed, longer. Enough was enough. I'd never meet this man. I tore up his phone number, deleted his email and de-Facebooked him. Best to stop it all in one go. It was a mad affair, going nowhere. We'd met in cyberspace and vanishing back there felt the most apt way to end it. I wanted to disappear. For a couple of months all communication ceased between us.

Then, one night, tipsy from a party, I traced an old email from him and sent him a long message saying I was sorry he never replied to my last message. A day later, I received a lengthy missive. He said he'd enjoyed my honesty, had found it refreshing, that I'd gained his trust and coaxed him from his shell. He apologised for the time he had taken to reply to my last message, he didn't want to play games with me; he'd been annoyed to see me disappear from Facebook, implying it was me who'd played games. He wondered if I might be willing to 'put up with a friendship with someone you might never meet'; if so, he'd be willing to keep in touch. I said no; this was just too weird. I said goodbye. As I write, years later, I find I'm still curious about this man. Though we never met, ironically, he's the only man of this era I'd like to meet again.

♥

In early 2007, in the weeks and months after meeting Professor Jack, I went out and met more men. I found, to my great surprise, that I was a natural at this form of social engagement. There was a long line of dates; I noted them all down in the purple suede book. And – forgive me, dear reader – I gave my dates marks out of ten. Professor Jack was a nine. I'd judged him to be a near perfect casual encounter: a robust individual, a sexual adventurer, easy to be with, good company and *safe*.

Over time, I came to form a few more ground rules and a plan of attack.

5. My personal safety. I always let a friend know, via email, where I was going, when and with whom. In those days, I still didn't own a mobile phone; this was the only way for others to keep track of me.

6. On the date itself, I made sure to be consciously positive

and disarming with the men that I met. I composed a few good questions as ice-breakers.

What's more important? Love or Work?

Who has been the love of your life?

Have you ever had a supernatural experience?

And so, none of my dates were boring. I made good chat.

7. I kissed those I wanted to kiss. This was crucial to the date going any further. Quite a few of the men I met kissed badly. One, an Irishman who'd studied at Oxford and Yale, a witty polymath and excellent company, suckered himself to me like a vacuum cleaner. When I complained, he begged good-naturedly for kissing lessons. He was a funny, clever man, but no way was I going to teach a man in his thirties how to kiss.

I was also aware, in some uncanny way, that I was in the process of acting out something which I'd already manifested in prose. I'd been working on a novella called *The Tryst* for some years. It was about a woman who could not fuck her man; who adored him but didn't desire him. She begins to lose herself in fantasy lovers. The couple go to a bar and meet a woman who turns out to be an imp from the underworld; she invites the imp-woman home and this creature destroys their lives. So here, years later, were the flesh-and-blood manifestations of those fantasy dream-lovers, the dreams I'd converted into fiction. It was life turned to art emerging back into life again.

I was deeply flattered to be forty-one and admired and fancied by younger men.

'You're so screwable,' Richard had said. He'd sent admiring emails, complimented me on my body. It was welcome and reassuring to be so appreciated as a physical and sexual human being at an age where this had come into question. From using Craig's List, I found out that this part of me, my sexual life, was very much still open. Young men fancied me, older men too; this idea of ageing and becoming invisible, no longer sexually attractive to men was a myth. I'd been expecting it to happen once I'd turned forty, but it didn't. Out there, somewhere, a lie has been circulating in magazines, in the media: older women lose their sex appeal. Rubbish. It's not true.

♥

Meanwhile, my ex and I had been sending each other long and heavy-hearted emails. Incredible that me and him, our team, had ended in a slum, that we were no longer together, being us, having fun, sharing our life. Images of 'us' plagued me as they do to this day, our unique combination of yin and yang, his benevolent chaos, my ridiculous bossiness. His bald head, my curliness. His bold anarchy, his charm, his beguiling manner, my strong-headedness, my nose in the air. We'd suited each other, we were a match. My friend Philip Cowell, who'd been a colleague at Arvon, said he'd cried when he heard we'd split. Karen May, our colleague at the Ted Hughes Arvon Centre at Lumb Bank, had also rung me in tears. We'd caused others to love us. I was struggling to live as one part of this rogue act.

Twelve months on from our split, we were living in separate parts of the country. I was still unable to see past his betrayal. I was still shocked, still miserable at the loss of him. We met at Trevi's once, a local café just off Upper Street. He looked older and unkempt, like a homeless person. I used to shave his big bald head. One birthday I'd bought him a badger-hair shaving brush with which to swab his face and skull. I'd often sat on the rim of the bath and lathered him up. Without me, he'd let his patchy skull grow. It sprouted hair unevenly so that his head appeared ravaged by moths. His teeth had grown blacker from his rabid increase in smoking. I feared he was teetering on the verge of a major depression. He'd secured another book deal from his publishers for *The Electric Pilgrim*, an investigation into atonement for his sins. Back then, he'd wanted to write about us, too. He'd bought an electric bike on which he hoped to tour the country. But he couldn't write a word.

'You look pathetic,' I said to him.

'I *am* pathetic,' he replied. 'Pathetically happy to see you.'

I loved him then, but felt a pang of revulsion for the state he'd sunk into. He had a new girlfriend too, this Ruth – I doubted he loved her. He looked like the tramp I'd first met, except now he didn't seem so romantic.

I loved him. But I also despised him. Looking back, it was the very last meeting where we could have realistically discussed getting back together again. A year had passed. I missed him, but my casual sex dating encounters were giving me new ideas about myself.

♥

After this meeting, I launched myself on a renewed dating campaign: I wanted to fuck myself into oblivion. I wanted to find a Lover – okay, maybe even two. But I found that I was often more chatty than horny or sexually predatory. Many of my dates were more like bizarre social curios; they made me think of the grotesque southern gothic stories of Carson McCullers.

One date was with Howard, a dashingly handsome forty-five-year-old lawyer who had Bond-esque qualities and a bad limp. During our date we got talking to a sozzled barfly who joined our table. For an hour – at least – I was chatting to two complete strangers, both of whom I found interesting. The other man was a writer too; he'd recently placed a book with an editor which was about a famous Russian spy. He'd just visited Lenin's old home in Islington.

At the end of our date I kissed Howard at the tube station. The kiss was odd, tongue-less. I said goodbye politely and moved on spiritually. The writer emailed me the next day, asking me out on a date. I said no. I took notes. Meeting for sex via the internet provided me with a wealth of human experience. So many men wanted sex; instead they met me.

More emails came in reply to the Bookish Ex-Stripper ad, including this:

Well-read 45-year-old seeks novel lover with poetic legs for thriller in the bedroom.

I laughed at this and got in touch but the sender never replied to my show of interest.

The novelty factor of using the site was starting to wear thin. I became reckless. I indulged myself in all kinds of e-porn and e-fantasies which went amiss in cyberspace. One man, Charles, who seemed shy and polite by the tone of his emails and the photo he sent, asked me out. I said yes. Then, he accidentally forwarded me a picture of himself bound up in ropes. I came to know that while CL had so far offered some excellent men, as well as some strange and freakish encounters, there were many pitfalls too. I made a list:

Craig's List – some hazards I encountered

1. One man sent me a fake, more attractive, picture of himself. Then a real picture of himself (oddly, he was still attractive) – then bombarded me with freaky images of BDSM sex.
2. One man sent me 13 emails, his photo, his telephone number and a poem by Byron, 'My Soul is Dark'. We swapped heated fantasies. We planned to meet behind the Bs in the poetry section of Waterstone's – and then he disappeared into cyberspace.
3. Several men seemed very enthusiastic to meet, then changed their minds, saying they'd got cold feet.
4. Many men, after some questioning online, turned out to be married (my one big No).
5. The problem of Englishness. For English men this was a new game. They were awkward and uncomfortable and secretive. Americans were much freer and easier to deal with.
6. No Strings Attached. The motto of the site. Was this possible? None of my dates had been string-free. Quite a few of the men expressed an interest in following up our date.
7. I discovered there *were* other writers were out there. I was approached, disconcertingly, by two other male novelists, both well known and with one of whom I shared an agent. I started to fear I might encounter an undercover journalist.
8. The roving few. A small bunch of men were regulars on the site and answered almost every advert I ever

placed, including a black man who sent a pic of himself naked, except for a pair of shades. His cock reached to his knees.

9. A much younger man I'd been corresponding with sent an email, mortified, to say he'd just found a genital wart. Luckily, this was before we were due to meet.

10. Lots of the men who answered my ads were physically unappealing and either too broken or too needy or sounded freaky. Trailing for the few 'possibles' became demeaning.

Even so, using Craig's List seemed like an antidote to my situation. In my purple suede book I wrote:

My adventures on CL are the perfect solution. X was such a significant relationship that this is the only logical and sensible way to fill the gap. By having many men. Maybe I will learn something about men. To look for another relationship now would be silly. I may not have another important relationship for many years.

This didn't disturb me in the least: I was preoccupied with grief, and with these outlandish and unpredictable meetings.

the gay cowboy

Only one of my dates felt bad, like a one-night-stand from my youth. A one-night stand gone very wrong indeed. This was the Gay Cowboy. In response to my Bookish Ex-Stripper advert a man sent me a very confident, if not cocky email – and a picture of himself in a cowboy hat. He was handsome and tanned, with an open face. It was the one time I ever pinged off an outright 'yes' to anyone. We met two nights later at the Jorene Celeste on Upper Street; within minutes we were drinking wine and kissing on the sofa. He was skinnier and older than his photo suggested. He told me, rather too quickly, that he was loaded. He worked in the music business. Let's call him Fred.

'So,' he said, staring hard at me. 'How are we going to conduct this affair?'

'Affair?' I replied.

'You and I. This. How does it work?'

'Let's get through tonight first,' I suggested. An Alpha male, already trying to control things? Yes.

It was a rash decision to go home with him, but I did. We jumped into a black cab and sped back to his designer home in Camden. In the kitchen we kissed and soon I was naked, sitting on the kitchen countertop. Then we were upstairs in his white designer bedroom, on his bed.

'I don't know what to do with you,' he said. 'I'm cock shy.'

I think I'd gone mad by then. I was capable of being wildly forward and fuck-happy.

'Do nothing,' I said. 'Sit back and watch.'

I lay on the chaise longue in one corner of the room. I spread my legs and began to pleasure myself. He came closer and gasped. His eyes glittered as he gazed down at me.

'You're so beautiful like that.'

It was a moment of sheer exhibitionism on my part. I loved it and so did he. I love men watching me pleasure myself. It's an awesome sight, to see a woman laid out so open and in touch with herself. He reached for his camera.

'Please stop,' I said. There were to be no pictures of me, ever.

We moved to the bed.

He had an agile body and a thick, meaty cock. We fooled around, but something had happened. I'd taken the wind out of his sails. We lay down on the bed and talked about the very moments we were sharing, why he couldn't get hard.

'All this is too much. All this is wrong,' I said. 'This no strings attached sex.'

'Yeah,' he agreed. 'It's all too quick.'

'There's been no build-up, no fantasy between us. We're strangers.'

'Yeah.'

'We don't care about each other at all.'

'I know.'

'I think fantasy is *needed*.'

It was a moment of epiphany, lying in that man's bed. Fantasy is a necessary ingredient for the build-up of desire: without it, we aren't stirred.

We abandoned the idea of sex. Instead we went downstairs in kimonos and ate a meal he prepared in his kitchen: duck pâté on mini-pitta breads, with cranberry jam and a squeeze of lime. We drank designer floral tea from a Japanese teapot; he had many jars of exotic tea leaves. We talked about life and death. We were both sleepy.

All was okay until then. It was after this that things began to get edgy.

When we returned to his bed instead of wanting to sleep, he suddenly wanted to fuck. He produced a bottle of lubricant and put on a Supertramp record. 'You're right, right, bloody well right.'

Shit, I thought. I'd now entirely lost the spirit of things. I hated Supertramp. But I let him fuck me. I think he was trying to catch up, to get what he'd wanted out of the date. And so we fucked and it was rough and empty.

'Get on your knees,' he said at one point. His voice was cruel. I didn't say 'No'. I didn't say 'Fuck off'. I'd put myself in this place. I wasn't in actual danger, but I allowed him to fuck me and I did something I didn't want to do. I hadn't done that in years. I don't think I'll ever have a moment like this in my life ever again. It was an act from my distant past, from a time when I was less conscious, a lesser individual, from my early twenties, from those years when I wasn't in possession of myself.

In the end, I stopped him. But not soon enough.

We lay next to each other all night without a word. He kept putting my hand on his cock which was huge and hard. I kept moving it away. We lay for hours in a mute, warped silence.

At dawn I got up and found my clothes. I looked down at him.

'You can let yourself out,' he smirked.

I went down the stairs and out into the cold dawn air; I almost ran to the train station.

This was the worst of all my dates: *get on your knees*. But I'd got what I wanted, too, in a way: I'd got hurt again.

the ethical slut

I went on more dates. Was I deranged? Yes, maybe. Would I recommend other women, readers, to use Craig's List now? No. Not unless you are as demented and as miserable as I was. This was most unusual behaviour. This is the sex of the lonely, the sex that satisfied base needs and instincts. It is primitive and heartless and only suits a particular type of woman, a confident predator who can honestly revel in moments of free sexual love. I did it because I was restless, because I wanted to fill my life with stuff, with drama, with human experience. I missed the company of my ex. I pined for him. I yearned for him. I often cried myself to sleep. I loved him. But I couldn't be with him. He was seeing another woman. This Ruth. I was beside myself with despair.

When I was with him all those years I never knew or understood how much I loved him. But now that he'd gone, I knew. My love for him poured forth in volumes. I craved him. He was mine and I was his.

Bollocks to this Ruth, I thought. I would *find* my desire for him.

I continued to go on these dates. They were a way to survive being single. I told myself I was educating myself, that I was in the midst of trying to classify my love for my ex. I was investigating sex just like some kind of Dawn Porter or roving 'in the field' reporter.

After Fred, the cowboy, right the next day, I met Spike, a professional clown who came from Texas. He'd sent me a picture of himself cycling down a street full pelt, a cantaloupe exploding from a gunshot over his head. It was stunt. He was a clown in the *Archaos* tradition, into pyrotechnics and escapology. One of his acts involved struggling from a flaming straightjacket while keeping a goldfish alive in his mouth.

We met for coffee and talked. He had punk hair and was covered in tattoos, but he had a soft voice and doleful eyes. He talked about his dog, his Triumph motorbike. But I was just hours from the clutches of the Gay Cowboy and this man didn't move my spirit. I mentioned my previous night's encounter and he nodded sagely.

Coffee over, we hugged next to his bike. His front spokes were covered in red and yellow butterflies.

'I'll be in touch soon,' I said, knowing I'd made some quiet decision to the contrary: this man, for sure, would be kinky as fuck. He bent close to me, lips on my neck, and whispered: *don't throw yourself to the masses.*

Next, I met Martin. He'd sent me poems and a picture of himself at a piano with a candelabra on the lid, a moody, romantic shot. His emails had been articulate, honest and open, maybe the best I received in all that CL era. We met in the Snooty Fox opposite Canonbury Station. Martin said he was a gardener; he was studying horticulture. He was young. Quiet and shy. He was a decent, if a little sexually frustrated, young man (in truth, everyone using CL is a little sexually frustrated).

It was all getting so easy for me. With each date, I was amassing experience. But I came to understand that for most of the men I met, I was their first Casual Encounter. Usually, my dates were awkward and unsure of themselves and the protocol of such a date. With the exception of the Gay Cowboy, I was in control. I set the tone, made the men feel safe. I disarmed them with good chat. I was determined to destigmatise the 'meeting for sex' reason for our date.

Martin and I talked easily. At one point, when we discussed novels, he said his favourite piece of literature was the last page of *The Grapes of Wrath*. I almost fell off my chair. This is my favourite page of fiction too, my literary G-spot. So I kissed him then and there, with tenderness and love.

'Would you like to see me again?' he asked.

I said yes.

It was a Sunday night. After a second pint, we walked back to the station and kissed again, up against the station wall. He said he liked chatting to me. He said that all through our date he'd been trying to decide if he liked me.

We kissed some more. His cock was hard against my stomach.

He left to catch his train and when I looked the other way I saw that the men from the Turkish shop on the corner had been watching us. I felt ashamed. I went into their shop every day. We bantered and they liked me. Now they'd witnessed me in the act of being a man-eater. *Shit*.

But I knew using CL was somehow good for me; it was giving me a lasting skill. Years later, I still find the idea of asking men out on a date quite unproblematic. I'm not frightened of being rejected. I've created many good dates. I know I can more than adequately negotiate a wide range of conversations and mishaps during them. Besides, some men love being asked out. Suicide rates are higher in men than women. Many men I've dated have one thing in common: a photo, somewhere in their flat, of their younger more exuberant self, the *them with more hair*. Just like women, many men lose confidence as they grow older.

More than anything, using CL gave me a unique insight into male loneliness. So many men out there are on their own. Some are even committed to the idea of being single, and, just like women, waiting for a soulmate. But so many of these happily single men have also, contrarily and endearingly, wanted to share of themselves. I have been shown photo albums by single Alpha males, copies of treasured books, copies of self-published books and magazines. I have shared toothbrushes, dressing gowns, seen men to be equally in need of a good mate as women. Using CL, I listened to enough tales of loved dogs, motorbikes and martial arts to know that most men crave intelligent like-minded female company. Probably more than a good shag.

All sorts of men were emailing me during this time. I'd placed other ads: *Let's Sin. Spoon Buddy Wanted*. It was funny, thinking them up.

I never saw Martin the gardener again: he disappeared.

But I continued to see my first date, Mr Wolf, the northerner. He was easy going and we got on well enough. We went out together and then we fucked like bunnies back at his flat. I posted another ad, *Puss in Boots*, something about wanting to dance naked around a bedroom wearing just knee-high boots. It drew lots of attention. Even Mr Wolf replied, not knowing it was me. When I revealed myself we both laughed it off. He knew I was still using CL and I could hardly complain if he was too; we had never discussed if our affair was open or closed.

I began a long email correspondence with another erudite man, a sexual seeker, 'William', who got too much information out of me, who was intrigued that I was a writer. He recommended I read a book called *The Ethical Slut*.

♥

Reading *The Ethical Slut* by Dossie Easton and Catherine A. Liszt was the second turning point in what had been, until then, a witless and unconscious quest. This was an actual *handbook* on how to go about having more than one lover; it had instructions on the ethics of getting it right. These two American women laid out ideas and a pragmatic code of conduct for those who want to live outside the box of conventional monogamy. Like gay people who had reclaimed the word 'queer' and black rappers who reclaimed the word 'nigger', they wanted to reclaim the word 'slut' for the sexual nonconformist and turn it into a term of approval. They believed that being openly sexual and intimate with many people is possible and rewarding:

> 'To us, a slut is a person of any gender who has the courage to lead life according to the radical proposition that sex is nice and pleasure is good for you. A slut may choose to have sex with herself only, or with the Fifth Fleet. He may be heterosexual, homosexual or bisexual, a radical activist or a peaceful suburbanite.'

The book explains that sluts want different things. They want different forms of sexual expression, sometimes different people, men or women; sluts are adventurous and curious. Easton and Liszt are keen to stress that sexually adventurous people can also have children, a mortgage and a career. Sluts believe that sexual love is a force for good; they believe that pursuing a wide spectrum of sexual pathways, if consciously chosen and mindfully followed, is both positive and creative. They point out that whilst the word 'slut' is full of negative connotations for women, the word 'stud' can sound like a compliment to a man.

I saw some connections. Like the authors of this book, I saw myself taking risks, some of them reckless, in the name of sexual exploration. Like them, I also wanted to be thoughtful about the process. I wanted to bring choice and a degree of consciousness to what I was doing. I wanted, in short, to be more ethical. I had already decided to 'be out' about being so sexually active. Now I was reading the words of other women who felt the same, women who were taking a stand for the right to be as fresh and ready for the blowing as a field full of dandelions. I was with them.

Sluts are people who like sex and the company of diverse people; they are not necessarily bold sexual athletes. Sluts are wary of a 'monogamy-centred culture', of a lifetime of pair bonding, one sexual partner forever. The authors believe that longevity is not the best criterion for judging the success of a relationship. They argue that one-night stands can be equally intense and fulfilling – as was my experience with Professor Jack. I understood then that Professor Jack was an ethical slut, too. I'd tried to work out why he was so different to other men I'd known. That was it. He had manners. He was conscious.

The ethical sluts had a code of practice:

1. Avoid hurting others.
2. Avoid taking sexual risks such as HIV and other STDs.
3. Sex must be consensual and respectful.
4. Sluts are committed to emotional honesty.
5. Sluts are committed to supporting themselves and their partners in dealing with conflict thrown up by their sexual practices.

The Ethical Slut is a well-known practical guide, not just for sexual seekers but for those who wish to practise polyamory – loving more than one person. It offers practical skills along with rules and ideas for making this possible. Published in the late 1990s by a small press, it is Californian in feel and outlook, so it's not surprising it is little known here.

First Abby Lee, the girl with the one track mind, had inspired me. Now these two women, Easton and Liszt, had grounded and educated me. Combined with my adventurous spirit and my quest for knowledge, my dating took on another spurt of energy. I was now active and more informed. I found I had my first words of self-identification beyond heterosexual and female. I was an ethical slut in the making.

I went on yet more dates. I no longer thought of CL as a pool of seedy riff-raff; this site was a great toy-box. I was on a learning curve; and I was learning one big thing: that the human heart is prone to romantic fidelity, to idolising, to lovemaking, to linking sex with love. This was something the ethical sluts skipped around. The authors saw it as a problem of social conditioning; they wrote that by breaking the rules you could change them. They believed it was possible to avoid or change this so-called heterosexual ideal.

But I wasn't so sure. I wasn't becoming polyamorous: quite the opposite; I was learning that very few of the men I met and was communicating with could deal with the 'sex alone' concept of the site. Most wanted to develop things. A drink, a date, then sex. Or, sex and then more of an ongoing and friendly connection. Almost none of the men I met, apart from Jack, knew how to be sexual and boundaried on the first date. Being like Jack, being a conscious ethical slut, took some practice.

I met more men. There was Peter, whom I snogged in Charterhouse Square, a spectacular surrounding, an assembly of medieval cloisters which today houses forty male pensioners. It is private, secluded, a portrait of ancient London, a fine place to kiss anyone. But he kissed like a baby.

We went our separate ways. I met another man, Paul, in a very expensive cocktail bar in Soho. He was humourless and money-obsessed and bore a faint whiff of misogyny.

Then I met a barrister; let's call him Lucien. He appeared raffishly handsome in his photograph; he'd called to chat a few times and sounded funny and confident – and posh. He had answered a new advert I'd placed in which I'd called myself an 'ethical slut'. He said he was an ethical slut, too. He sent me a picture of his erect and dancing cock. I went against my rules (always meet at night, night-time carries more sexual charge) and agreed to meet him during the day, at the Queen Boadicea on St John Street.

Lucien was the only man to reject me. He turned up on his bike and immediately I sensed I wasn't what he was expecting. I didn't look like my rather glamorous photograph. I could sense him adjusting his expectations, maybe even preparing himself for just one drink. I was a little thrown. I'm like a ventriloquist when it comes to making men fancy me. I can 'throw my voice', if you like, project, create an illusion; I can exude the confidence of a woman who is far more beautiful than I am. But sometimes I can lose my nerve.

Until then, I hadn't encountered any disappointment from my dates. Quite the reverse, in fact. Now I was going to have to work at this date, and I wanted to because I found this Lucien attractive. We talked, both quite cagily at first. He'd two ex-wives, (like my ex); he even said something – 'we're all going to hell in a handcart' – which my ex often used to say. His name was very similar to my ex's real name. I started to feel unnerved. Lucien was yet another clever polymath, an A-grade man. Here I was, yet again, with a man whom I felt I would have been pleased to meet naturally, to have been introduced to by a friend. I wasn't meeting A-grade men socially. Good and clever men, I was coming to realise, were using the site like I was; because they were bored with the constraints of their ordinary monogamy-centred lives. They wanted to meet a slut like me.

Lucien and I talked about English law and its general tolerance, about the tragedy of Iraq. It was a tense conversation, neither of us relaxed. After two drinks he said 'goodbye' politely, as I expected he might. We kissed briefly outside the pub. He got on his bike and rode off.

I walked home, back along Upper Street. I was put out. I rested my hand on my heart. It felt bruised. Yes. A small dull pain. I was glad. It meant I *could feel*. I thought of my ex, how he'd gazed so lovingly at me. I thought about how I'd never given him half the sexual loving I'd given so freely to these men, these total strangers. I was somehow balancing out the loss of him. I missed him and this mad sex thing was filling the gap of life experience I had had on tap every day with him. I walked back to the co-op. The feeling of rejection wore off along the way: by the time I got home it felt like a small arrow ping.

my lifestyle

In March 2007, I left the Black Sheep Co-op for a spacious flat in Harlesden. I moved in with a couple, my friend Emma and her partner Matthew. They knew nothing of my quest.

Initially, when I told my girlfriends, they'd greeted the news of my sexploits with a mixture of amazement and feminist support. They thought it was a wild thing to do but they were open to it; they were curious and maybe even a tiny bit envious. But mostly they thought it would be a short phase, perhaps just a few weeks. Well, it was and it wasn't a phase. This period of my life lasted eighteen months. The first six were the most active. But I noticed, as time went on, that a certain sense of distaste for what I was doing descended over one or two of my friends, the very ones who had been open-minded at first. These female friends were mothers. They began to withdraw from wanting to hear any more about this kind of dating. I can see why: mothering and wanton casual sex are worlds apart.

Mothers, understandably, are often too tired for sex, the very opposite of libidinous. They are attendant on a suckling infant, maybe even having to negotiate a jealous or needy partner. New mothers are also recovering, physically, from pregnancy – swollen breasts, stitches in the nether regions. They have given birth, they're producing milk, they're on call twenty-four hours a day. This is no time for stockings and sex toys, for discussing clandestine dates made in cyberspace.

And so it became impossible to talk about my adventures with a few of my female friends. Our lives were too dissimilar. There was also the stigma of this kind of date. In their eyes, there was no comparison to meeting a man 'properly', that is, socially. Meeting men the way I had been wasn't regarded as equal to meeting a man in the course of real life. Even though all of these men were human, some excellent, some just the kind of men they themselves would have been interested in, these men I met on CL didn't count.

Some friends thought I'd developed an unseemly habit; it had become 'a lifestyle'. I suppose it *was* a lifestyle and yes, it had an aspect which could be seen as seedy. I'd never want to paint this part of my sexual quest as particularly admirable. Yes, I met some very interesting men. Yes, I learnt a thing or two. But some of it was edgy and loveless and awful. My friends who were mothering were right; it was no way for them to behave, nothing to aspire to.

When I moved in with Emma and Matthew I was careful at first not to mention my sexploits. When they announced that Emma was pregnant I was super-careful. I didn't always tell them where I was going of an evening.

It was months before I spilled the beans to Emma. I'd written ten sonnets about my CL encounters. I let her read them. The poems were very graphic and to her credit she reacted graciously to them, saying 'wow, Mon', but that's all. Over the months of her pregnancy, Emma and Matthew and I had become exceptionally close. As her bump grew, we all relaxed. We cooked together, threw parties, met each other's friends. We became obsessed with reality TV: *Big Brother*, *Strictly Come Dancing*. We lived through the dramas of a shared domestic life: we were invaded by bed bugs, putting our bed-legs in little pots of water. They endured my shit poetry. They knew of some of my plainer forays into the real world of dating in my forties. I often came home and recounted tales of dates gone wrong and much drunkenness.

In my purple suede book I wrote: SAVE THE CATS. I'd grown obsessed with my cats. I wanted them to be with me. But I was living with a pregnant woman; it wasn't an ideal household for cats. I missed them so much.

I'd developed a weird type of love: cat love. I'd never before loved an animal. But I loved those cats. C.S. Lewis in his book *The Four Loves* talks of man's love for the sub-human: by this he means man's deep love of his country, of nature – and our natural affection for animals. 'Man with dog closes a gap in the universe,' he says. I agree. I asked my ex about the cats a lot, I wanted regular reports on how they were doing. I wasn't pleased to hear they were doing fine. Violet, the fluffy one, the one who'd always been indifferent, even snooty towards him, was actually settling down. I felt wretched about it. I'd lost a man, his children, my cats, a home and a village, Sheepwash. A year on, I was still thick with all this loss.

One day, when Emma was heavily pregnant, she found me in tears at my desk. I'd heard from Deborah, my neighbour in Sheepwash, how happy my ex was with this new Ruth. She'd moved, with her children, to live in the same village, virtually next door to him. It signified the defining 'end of things'. I could no longer be in contact with him; it would be demeaning. Emma found me sobbing to myself. With her huge bump, she came and sat down on the floor outside my office and listened. She told me of a similar lost love. *Ah*, women. How we tend to each other, nurture each other so. I grew to love Emma dearly. We'd been friends for ten years, but this was a new kind of sister-love between us, born of our separate situations. I was coming to terms with a death of sorts; she was about to give birth.

♥

April 2007, I turned forty-two. I was having phone sex with the man on the phone. I was still dating Mr Wolf and I was still meeting other men. An ex-Arvon colleague and chum got married in Shropshire. My ex was at the wedding. I wore an expensive Kenzo dress, tried to look as ravishing as possible. Apart from cat updates, we hadn't seen or spoken to each other in six months. During the party, we slipped away and walked in a nearby apple orchard and talked about how much he'd fucked up and how miserable we both were. I asked him to come back to me but he said because of 'the sex thing' it was impossible. Besides, he was committed to this new relationship with Ruth.

Later, he asked me to dance. I said, 'No, absolutely not. You don't get to dance with me again.' This was a terrible moment. We'd never dance together again? Had it come to that? He then danced with lots of other women and I watched as a tall glamorous woman with long legs and long blonde hair flirted with him. I wept and left the wedding early.

I stayed the night at The Hurst, Arvon's centre in Clun. The centre directors there, Kerry Watson and Peter Salmon, had a little girl, Pearl; the day after the wedding, it was her third birthday. My ex and I were both invited to the party. There were balloons and cake and fizzy pop and little children gadding about. I arrived to see my ex and another man with a banjo, sitting on chairs under an oak tree, singing to a captivated group of three-year-olds. My ex had his head buried in a songbook, an enormous gentle man perched atop a rickety chair on the croquet lawn.

It wasn't fair. Even three-year-olds loved him.

I'd *never* get over him.

The next day, we drove out into the countryside and stopped at a roadside bench and talked while staring out at a rolling green field, studded with sheep. I asked him again to come back to me. Again he said no. I was stuck. I loved him with my heart and head. From the waist up, I was dying of loneliness. My sexcapades weren't the least bit important compared to my love for him. I never told him about them because they were so hard to explain. But mostly they were not, in the long run, cancelling out my love of him, or replacing my love for him with the kind of divine and all-engulfing sexual loving that the woman yearns for in *The Song of Songs*.

A few months later, I happened to visit another friend in the same village where my ex lived and decided to pop over and see him. I found him in a bad way. His small cottage was in chaos, thick dust on every surface, enough to trigger my asthma and make me wheezy. Dirty plates crammed the sink, books and magazines were all over the floor. He seemed to have given up on keeping himself and his surroundings clean. It was a tell-tale sign, another hint of the major depression that had begun to descend on him. I was worried. I told him the place looked terrible, that he looked terrible. He didn't care. For months afterwards I heard reports that his living conditions had deteriorated. He was living in a hovel. It was so bad that the violet cat began to shit inside the house.

As I write of my own heartbreak and madness, I can see I never knew or cared to know or take on board *his* anguish. This is a story about two people. He'd also been trying, and failing, to write about what had happened, about the love-sex conundrum between us. He was just as dejected and tired as I was.

Recently, on a tube ride, I made a list of all that I *didn't* know about my ex during the period after our split.

I didn't know:

1. What the pain of our separation was like for him.

2. What the pain of my sexual rejection was like for him.
3. The depth of his post-split depression.
4. The acuteness of his shame regarding his affair.
5. How bad his sense of failure was.
6. The nature of his love for me.
7. The nature of his loss of me.
8. If he, too, was as heartbroken as I was.
9. If he was ever plagued, as I was, by memories.
10. If he had actually *missed* me, missed my company as I missed his company.

From The Hurst I went back to London, where I saw Mr Wolf. Mr Wolf was mad on sports and, a month later, he took me to Paris for the French Open.

Paris is for lovers. But not for fake lovers like we were. It rained. We went to see the Eiffel Tower. I took one look at it and thought of my ex and burst into tears. Mr Wolf was also out of sorts; he missed another woman. The tennis was rained off. We went to the Louvre and had a long conversation about politics. We went out for expensive meals. I started to go off him. I even started to be mean to him. The hotel was pokey and the breakfasts were inedible. We argued. On the Sunday night we walked around and found ourselves in the Sacre Coeur with midnight mass in full swing. Both Catholics, we walked in and sat there and cried a little. We were both tearful about being there, in Paris, with the wrong person. We left and walked back through Montmartre to our hotel. It was a dismal trip. On the journey there, on Eurostar, he'd had an erection all the way. I'd cradled it in my hands. On the way back we barely spoke.

WITH THE KISSES OF HIS MOUTH

the wisewoman

In late May 2007, my great friend Curly drove me back from a party and parked on my road for a post-party chat. We started talking about my ex and soon I was in floods of tears.

'I can't seem to stop this,' I sobbed. 'Every time I talk about him, I cry.'

Curly nodded. She had also loved and lost.

'I'm *bored* of being like this. I'm boring my friends. I'm boring myself. I don't know what to do with this grief. It won't go away.'

'I know someone who might be able to help.'

'Who?'

'My friend Michele.'

Until then I hadn't thought of 'going professional' with my grief. I'd seen a bereavement counsellor when my dad had died fifteen years earlier. That had helped. There had been Sarah, the Relate counsellor, who'd said the right thing in the hours after our split. *Do it.*

Maybe Curly was right. Maybe now was the time to call in some help.

From May to August 2007 I went to see a good, kind counsellor, Michele Bosc, about what had happened to me. Seeing her, over four months, proved not only timely but little short of miraculous. Our first session was a long one: three hours. She liked to start her sessions this way, to 'get the cards on the table', she said. It was the first time I had ever recounted, in any detail, what had happened to someone who didn't know me. The whole thing with the sexless relationship and the letters from my ex's lover and the split and me running away and bellowing at his father and how I'd had to leave my cats, one of which was now missing. And, above all, how much I'd loved him. When I finished my story she had tears in her eyes.

Here are the notes I made from that first meeting with Michele on 15 May 2007:

1. I had been slowly, in my own time, preparing to split with my ex, but my preparations for grief were interrupted by the trauma of receiving the letters. My natural grieving process was broken. There'd been the catastrophic drama of the letters. Now my grieving process was resuming. This was why my grieving process had taken so long.
2. Was it just the sex that was missing in the relationship – or something else? Is this 'something else' to do with me? Is this 'something' still going on? If so, what is it?
3. What I said to my ex about not being attracted to him, sexually, is the worst thing a man can hear.

Below are my notes from our second meeting on 22 May.

1. Were we the victims of stereotyped ideas of romance?
2. Love has no archetype.
3. Was it possible I had outgrown my ex even before we met?
4. He was swept up with me, not the other way around. Something I had not previously imagined.

5. I was in the midst of a grand metamorphosis, he was part of it.
6. Loving attachment needs to be fed or else fades into affectionate regard.

These notes continued until the end of that summer. My CL dating died down a little. I went to see Michele, and I continued to read a lot.

Limerence – I stumbled on this new word in my reading. It was coined by the experimental psychologist Dorothy Tennov, author of *Love and Limerence*, in the mid 1960s. Tennov interviewed five hundred men and women of all ages and walks of life about falling in love and found that their experiences were similar. Limerence is the obsessive and intrusive early phase of falling in love. The French call this a *coup de foudre*, the English call it a thunderbolt. Whether it hits you on the head or sneaks up on you, it is the word for the precise moment that you come to know that you have selected someone for your love. To make this choice, sexual attraction is not enough. It is more than just finding another person sexually attractive; limerence is a state of grace, it is the tender feeling of admiration for another human being, the recognition of another as a worthy companion.

This was how I felt about my ex. I had felt limerence. I began to broaden my reading. The sex adventures, talking to Michele. It was all very good for me. Michele introduced me to the Seven Cycles of Change, which apply to all things, not just love: New beginnings, self-organisation, complexity, turmoil, chaos, letting go, rest/rejuvenation. I was oscillating between two stages, between 'chaos' and 'letting go'. I pinned her Cycle of Change diagram above my bed. I'd look at the 'letting go' bubble and wish desperately to be there. *Fake it till you make it*, some would say. But it wasn't a case of acting things out. I just couldn't get there. When I first met Michele I'd told her that I didn't want to move on. Moving on felt like leaving him, the part of my life I'd loved so much, where I'd flourished to maturity, where I'd been so happy, even when I was miserable. I still wanted to be in this phase of my life. I wasn't ready to leave it behind. I was consciously wallowing, maybe, messing around in the aftermath of the disaster that had ended so much happiness.

Eighteen months had passed since the split. I did lots of relief centre directing for Arvon and the Welsh writing centre, Ty Newydd. I worked on my novel. I kept myself busy. Socially, I met some nice men whom I liked and who seemed to like me. But nothing 'happened' between us and I began to find meeting men in the normal way a bit tame. Using CL, meetings were always illicit, edgy. Meeting men in real life felt much too ordinary. I was starting to notice how muted sex can be in the real world, how little people flirt openly and show appreciation for each other as sexual beings. When I met men for dates on CL, the atmosphere between my date and me was charged. Around men in general, in real life, this wasn't the case. I began to wonder if my peers, those in their forties, had lost their confidence around sex; that, or they'd lost their sex drive entirely.

♥

With Michele, I was working on the love problem. Through my wild dates, I was addressing the problem of unfulfilled sexual potential. But I was still a long, long away from finding it. These dates were some kind of an education around sex, but they taught me nothing about bliss, about the pleasure which lay locked in my body.

One afternoon, restless for sex, I logged on to CL and found myself answering a nice-looking man's advert (answering men's ads was something I rarely did). By 7 p.m. we were having a drink in a pub in Soho. Henry was young, sweet, shy, clever, an ex-Cambridge graduate. He was my sixteenth date. By then I'd developed a calm and relaxed approach to these meetings. He was nervous. I didn't fancy him: it was something about his bowling shoes, and he was shorter than he'd claimed, which is very common. We had two drinks and then I said, 'I think I'm going to go home now, alone.'

He nodded. We left the pub. But, as we were about to part ways, he said, 'I don't care if we don't have sex. I like your company. I'd happily talk to you anyway. With or without the sex.'

Just when I thought I'd seen and done it all. I should have known better. This is why I was dabbling, still doing this kind of thing: for the surprise factor. Because these meetings were still unpredictable.

My sad little heart surged. I looked at Henry and my eyes went a bit flimsy.

'Okay,' I said. I smiled at him. Because of all my sessions with Michele, I was soft as pulp.

We went to another pub, The Cock (yes) near Portland Place. We chatted some more and then we kissed outside on the pavement and he said he'd like to see me again. I thought: *Really, come on now, young man.* Carpe diem. *We may be blown up by a terrorist cell tomorrow. We may all be decimated by a dirty bomb. Now is the only time we have. Let's fuck.*

I dragged him to a spot behind the big church on Portland Place. There I wedged myself into a crack, bracing my legs against the facing wall. At last it had happened. I *was* Kim Basinger, having sex up against a wall. Except there was no waterfall cascading down over us. I was having sex in a public place: we could get arrested. Finally, one of my fantasies was coming true. This poor young Henry, he'd come out for a quiet Sunday evening drink with some woman he found he liked to talk to. And he got *me*, a grief-obsessed nutbag, randy as a hippo. He came home with me in the end. But things weren't quite so sexy in the morning.

Henry is the one date I feel bad about. The only man I really used.

Men and women use each other and sex happens to be a very common way for us to do that. Sex is exciting, dramatic; it distracts us from everything, from rejection of another, loss, grief. My grief was ever-present in those first two years after our split, like a cloud, a weather front. I now see it was a form of exterior depression, clinging to me like mist.

broken heart

In September 2007, there were two big events in my life.

The first was when my ex rang one afternoon in a state of alarm. He said his heart was beating rapidly. He often had panic attacks, but this was different. I hadn't seen him since the April wedding, though we'd been in touch via email throughout the summer.

'It's *not* a panic attack,' he said. I could hear the genuine fear in his voice. In the aftermath of the death of his first wife, he'd suffered a nervous breakdown; he'd had panic attacks, off and on, ever since. I'd lived through many with him. They'd worsened in our last year together, the year he'd had the affair and suffered so much guilt. He was having cognitive behavioural therapy to learn how to deal with them. But I could hear he thought this was *different*. Not a panic. This was real.

'Listen to me,' I soothed. 'The CBT is to handle a panic attack. Fine. But now listen to *yourself*. You just said this is *not* a panic attack. Trust yourself. Go to A and E. Go immediately.'

He did.

They hooked him up to a monitor, did some tests. They discovered that he had developed atrial fibrillation. He was put on beta-blockers. More tests were done over the next six months which confirmed that he will have to stay on beta-blockers for the rest of his life. His heart was out of whack. Stress, anxiety, God knows what else. His heart was broken; properly broken.

On 30 September 2007, my flatmate Emma gave birth to a baby girl, Lois. We all loved her immediately. She was tiny, perfect, and unique. Emma was over forty and the birth was textbook even though doctors had told her she'd never be able to conceive. The day Emma and Matthew brought Lois home from the Chelsea and Westminster Hospital and laid her down on the special nappy-changing table, we all stared at her in wonder.

She cried.

We stared.

'What do you think's the matter?' Matthew said.

We didn't know.

'Maybe she's hungry,' I said.

'She just ate,' Emma replied.

'Maybe she's tired.'

'She's just woken up.'

We stared at her some more.

She cried.

'I know!' I stammered, as if struck on the head. 'Maybe she needs her *nappy changed*!'

I was right.

But it was hard to get a clean eco-nappy back on. We all tried. Eventually, I think Emma managed; only it was on back to front. My life became a romantic comedy: *Three Forty-somethings and a Baby*.

the men with wives

Against my own rules, and for very specific reasons, I met two married men on CL. In each case we agreed to meet for drinks, dinner and not sex.

I met James for dinner in Chinatown. He and I had been corresponding for a few weeks. He said he was on also a journey of sexual self-discovery; he claimed he was 'developing a mature outlook to non-monogamous sexual relationships'. Although he was married, he was making this journey alone. His wife, whom he loved dearly and described as his soulmate, had a progressive wasting disease and was physically unable to go out into the world of sex clubs and join him; if she had been able to join him then she would. I explained that

I didn't like to meet with married men, but I was intrigued by him. Our emails had been fluid and gracious. We'd even talked on the phone. I suggested that maybe we could just meet for dinner, to swap stories. He agreed.

James was handsome and slender and courteous. I told him about my ex, about my dates. He told me about his disabled wife, about his ventures into all types of sex clubs. Looking back, I didn't challenge him enough about why he hadn't gone out to sex clubs with his wife. In those days, I hadn't come across events such as Night of the Senses, that were disability friendly. At certain clubs and parties there are numerous sexy and sexually active people in wheelchairs. The TLC Trust website, run by Tuppy Owens, which uniquely addresses the issue of sex and disability, was also unknown to me. Sex workers and sexual surrogates who work with disabled people were not yet on my radar. All that was to come.

I'm not sure if James and I swapped any information which helped each other. I'm not even sure why we met. It was an odd evening. I went on a hunch, because of my quest. I went because of some kind of half-baked humanitarian cause. Here was another soul trying to get out of the box of lifelong monogamy. He loved his wife. She'd sanctioned his quest. She even knew he'd come to meet me. I began to see that my idea of marriage was limited. My parents' marriage lasted forty years; fidelity, monogamy were its basic rules. But what about illness, disability? What do couples do for sex then, and what of a number of other setbacks?

Now, as I write, I hope this man's adventures have led him to places where he and his wife can enjoy being together. I respected James and reviewed my ideas of the married men who contacted me: not all of them were cheating or lying, betraying their wives. James was the first married men I actually *met*; he was conscious, ethical, and he was exploring a more flexible and open type of relationship.

The second married man I met described himself as a cross between Sean Penn and Viggo Mortenson. I was amazed he could say something so cocksure about himself. Sam was a writer too, a fairly well-known writer, it turned out. I coaxed him out with the lure of a drink in broad daylight; no sex, just a chat. He said yes. I told him I looked like Barbra Streisand, circa *Yentl*. He didn't laugh.

We met in Soho, at a bar on Beak Street. To my surprise, he did look like a cross between those two very attractive Hollywood stars. He was mid-fifties, comfortable in himself. I liked him immediately. He must have been dazzlingly handsome once. He still was, only worn. His was a simple and common tale. He loved his wife, but the sex had dried up between them years ago. They'd been together over twenty years; they had kids. He had no intention of leaving her.

'I just miss sex.'

He'd had a couple of encounters on CL, both charged, sexually, but meaningless.

I listened with great interest. It was becoming clear to me that just like me and my ex, many people live in a stable monogamous relationship – without sex. It occurred to me that human beings crave this 'social monogamy', this social safety, the companionship of a human pair bond. A home, a life together, a garden, pets. This was why so many of the men I met had wanted more from our dates. They craved the intimacy of friendship and social contact. This, indeed, was what I'd been missing too; I found it so hard to live without the companionship of my ex.

Agape. This is the strongest type of love, the superior love; it's a selfless giving love, what keeps people together. You can love someone so much you can live with little or no sex in your relationship. But how long can this type of arrangement last? For me, it was four years. Even early on, the sex was once a month, then once every two months and then weeks and weeks of no sex. We enjoyed every other aspect of being together, but not sex. Now I wonder if this is common, that couples can get by because there is another strong love that feeds two bodies, heart love.

Eventually, however, there will be fantasies, one of you will crack. One will wander or desire others. Perhaps humans are socially monogamous, but sexually polyamorous. Even if the sex in a relationship is good, for all sorts of reasons, some people, maybe even most people, still want others.

Jesus. Where do we go from here?

Michel Foucault, in his seminal work *The History of Sexuality*, says that in the seventeenth century the state and church ganged up to outlaw any kind of sexual conduct outside heterosexual monogamy. Ideally, I think church and state would have liked to ban sex outright. They realised, however, that sex was necessary for economic reasons: so that the masses could give birth to future generations of workers. So they decided that sex was 'okay', but in the narrowest of terms and under certain circumstances, only within the confines of an outwardly stable marriage. Marriage is a sacred sacrament, a Holy Union.

Three hundred years later, this exterior bullying still holds sway. We are still rule-bound, guilt-bound, harassed and tortured sexual citizens. We stay in our sexually desiccated marriages and relationships because we have been told for centuries that it is illegal and immoral to step outside the heterosexual model. Men and woman can and do stay in sexless unions for years, even decades, rather than open things out or think up new rules.

I told this handsome older married man about my novella, *The Tryst*. He said it sounded interesting.

'Wanna read it?' I knew this was cheeky. But we were getting on well.

'Sure,' he replied.

'It has plot problems. I'd love your advice.'

We parted company. Later, I sent him the manuscript. He sent me some sound feedback. Now, years after this meeting, I remember one thing he said: *sexually lascivious women were once treated like witches. Either burnt alive or thrown down a well*. It made me angry to hear this. It also made me determined to write this book and to put my name on the cover.

larvae, pupa, butterfly

I loved my alter-ego, *girlbutterfly*. I found I couldn't dismantle her. She had been courageous; through her, I'd learnt a lot. I'd learnt that I was like the woman in *The Song of Songs*, that I was sexually exuberant and ardent and felt free to take the initiative. But, over the next six months, my adventures dwindled: their novelty factor wore off. After a while, I lost all interest in CL. There was a fabulous man whom I met in the Park Lane Hilton, a well-educated German who spoke a number of languages and loved art. We talked for ages over a bottle of champagne in the rooftop bar and then had sex in his enormous suite overlooking Hyde Park, the city's lights glittering beneath us. There was another man, a financial lawyer in a big City bank who was dealing with the first days of the credit crunch, who came over to spoon with me in bed but we ended up having sex. There were two or three men I met for drinks and left at that, including a handsome American man whom I met in Soho, who'd paid for a taxi to deliver me to a pub where he sat.

Over eighteen months, I'd placed nine separate adverts, met twenty-four men, written ten sex sonnets and several poems. I had only slept with six of these men, seven if you include the man on the phone.

In October 2007, I de-Facebooked my ex and told him there could be no communication between us. Since the wedding and seeing him sing to the party of toddlers on the croquet lawn at The Hurst, we had remained in touch; again, it wasn't right. We didn't communicate again for another six months, not until Valentine's Day came round again. On Valentine's Day, 2008, I cracked. I'd been single for two years. I emailed my ex a sonnet I'd written about him hurling his moccasin out of the shoe shop on Upper Street. The letter bomb had split us up, but hadn't managed to split this image from my memory.

Valentine's Day was our anniversary, the anniversary of the time he'd laid me down on my garret bunk in Lancaster and kissed me from my toes up to my cunt, murmuring: 'You're so pretty there.'

I was coming to the last few pages in my purple suede book. A good sign. But I was still troubled. I'd stare at the Seven Cycles of Change pinned to my wall. Try as I might, I was still not out of the 'letting go' part of the cycle. Maybe I still wasn't even in that part of the cycle.

One of the very last things I wrote in that book was this:

I know an era has passed. But I still miss X so much. I think of him every day. He still feels irreplaceable, like we had a time never to be replaced or bettered.

It was around then that I opened a file on my computer called MEMOIR. My adventures had been wild, random and inter-esting – but so far inconclusive; so I decided they were not all over. I decided that 'I' was my next project. I'd investigate my sexual life, my sexual desires; maybe I'd develop a whole *range* of them. I'd go shopping in the sexual HMV store, cul-tivate a part of me that the state and church hoped I would bury in lifetime of chaste monogamy. I hadn't used my sexu-ality to have children. I wanted to break out of the box I'd been put into. As it turned out, my adventures, my proper conscious quest for the development of my sexual self, was just about to begin.

THE TANTRA DIARIES

'Life shrinks or expands according to one's courage'

Anaïs Nin

♥

conscious touch

November 2008. Six months later.

The young man lay naked on the massage table. His body was pale and sleek. He was slim, his torso sculpted and taut, no scars or blemishes, the body of a young god. Beautiful lithe arms, beautiful lithe lingam which rested inert between his legs. Demara washed her hands in the oil she'd warmed earlier. She slicked it over her hands and arms up to the elbows, encouraging me to do the same. Then she cupped her hands and filled them with oil, letting the liquid run freely through her hands, along her forearms, dripping in a stream, anointing the young man's stomach.

He sighed deeply.

'First, we'll do a ritual called "imprinting",' she explained. 'Where the man is "called into his body".'

I nodded, knowing nothing and willing to learn everything. Demara's hands were small and pretty, almost like a little girl's. She used what she called 'conscious touch' as she began to run her slickly oiled hands along the young man's chest. She bent close, her mouth an inch away from him, blowing cool air onto his skin. Her long red silky hair danced along his belly. She bent even closer and her bosom brushed his thigh. She focused her consciousness into her fingers, touching him with the lightness of a butterfly's wing. I watched. The young man's skin rose in bumps. His lingam grew stiff. His eyes were closed and he looked peaceful. I watched as his body came to life.

I followed her lead. We worked together in a spacious attic room with a slanted ceiling and skylights, the blinds pulled shut. The walls were adorned with masks: half-cut Venetian ballroom masks, masks of Shakti, Kali, other goddesses. One was a whole-face mask, scarlet and gold, framed with feathers and coarse hair. Tribal, a female warrior mask. On the walls there were framed photographs of men, ordinary men, faces we might see every day, icons of modern day Shiva in the various ages of his life. There were fat towers of candles in iron holders and standing candelabras. Long peacock feathers, curlicued ostrich feathers, fans of inky green plumes in jars and vases along the wall. There were whips too, made of finely splayed leather and pink and purple suede, and a line of shiny black patent stilettos: Vivienne Westwood, Louboutin, Manolo Blahnik, a pair of silver sling-back dancing sandals. There was a low seating area in one corner and pillows on the floor. The air was heady with scents extracted from trees and flowers. Frankincense; neroli; juniper. A lamp in the corner glowed phosphorescent, like a jellyfish, faintly pink and then lavender.

This was Demara's 'sacred space', part-temple, part-harlot's boudoir. We wore lace basques and sarongs, our feet were bare. Here, Demara performed similar rituals to those once bestowed on men in bygone times by the priestesses and sacred prostitutes of the Egyptian temples. In his book, *Women of the Light, the New Sacred Prostitute*, respected masseur Kenneth Ray Stubbs draws a link between these ancient sacred whores and some women who exchange sex for money today. 'What makes women of the light unique is that they exchange consciously. Even more important, they provide a context of compassion and wisdom in the exchange. They are teachers of the heart.'

The young man shifted. Demara and I took two long peacock feathers and caressed his body from head to toe in long
delicate strokes. When we touched him with our hands, we
touched him with tenderness and care, as though poring over
an ancient papyrus-leaf book. We touched him with reverence, running the tips of our fingers along his body,
whispering tender words. We touched his hair, kissed him
lightly on his forehead, temples, lips, stroked his shoulders
and neck. We brushed our breasts along his chest, gazed into
his face; *'You're a handsome young man,'* we whispered. *'Thank
you for the gift of your manhood.'* We kissed his fingertips, his
arms, let our hair, our breasts, fall about his face.

Demara signalled that it was time for the massage proper
to begin. That day, I was to watch most of the rest: I was her
student. The young man wasn't a real client. He was an eager
friend of hers, keen to offer himself as a 'model' for my tute-
lage. He was open to my presence, my questions, to almost
anything. Over the next thirty minutes, Demara demonstrated
a number of massage strokes around and on the young man's
lingam with deft ease – maybe twenty different strokes in all.
Some she called 'healing strokes'; others were purely stimu-
lating – these can produce an instantaneous erection. Long,
languorous strokes were used to spread the man's sexual
energy when the stimulation led to twitching, or what she
might see as premature ejaculation. All the strokes were
devised by Joseph Kramer, a US body worker and pioneer in
the field of erotic massage, and had names: 'Opening the
Gates of Consciousness' (massaging behind the tip of the
head); 'Cock Shiatsu' (a two-handed pulsing movement);
'Cock Cradling' (cradling the cock in both hands). I watched,
awestruck, as she pulled and tugged at the scrotal sac (this

looked quite rough), as she gathered his testicles up and scratched his balls, then ran her nails along his cock. The young man sighed and groaned. She ran her hands along his pubic bone, again, spreading out energy. I watched as she skied her fingers along the shaft, as she cuddled and coaxed and rubbed the head in circular motions in the centre of her palm. All the while, as she caressed this man she whispered words of love. A stroke called 'juicing' produced a deep groan. He opened his eyes and whispered 'Yeah.'

I was amazed. I'd never even tried *half* these tricks. I never knew a man's lingam was so dexterous and flexible that it could be swivelled around 180 degrees.

'How does all this *feel*?' I asked him.

'Incredible. I've never been so relaxed and so horny.'

I ran my hands from his stomach up to his collarbone. The young man opened his eyes and looked at me.

'Usually the man does all the work, you know. You try *not* to come or you try to come. You have to try so hard,' he whispered.

I nodded as if I knew. 'Wow. Er . . . would you bring a girl-friend to come and learn from Demara?'

'Definitely.'

God, how I wish I'd been taken to see Demara aged twenty-six. I wish I'd had some instruction in this fine art, and watching her, pleasuring a man really *is* an art. I loved watching what she was doing, seeing how much this young man was enjoying her gift. And then, having observed, I tried my hand too, and found, to my delight, that I took to the skill. We are good at things we like, I think. 'How am I doing?' I said at one point, keen for feedback.

'Yes,' was all he said.

'Will I do?'

He nodded and seemed far away.

I was proud. Could I do this for a living, like Demara? I always needed an extra income to support my writing. I tucked the idea away in the back of my mind. No, no of course I couldn't ... and then, well ... er. Yes. Then, maybe. Demara made very good money from 'touching cock', as she puts it. And doing it this way, within ritualised space, with so much reverence, made it all seem good, natural.

Demara has one stroke, the Hand Jive, which is the final stimulation, a two-handed up-down motion designed to be the masterstroke, the endgame. She clasped her hands together, as if praying, lacing her fingers, making a tightly meshed hold. She slotted this around the young man's cock and began to move her hands smoothly and steadily up and down the shaft. By then she was controlling not if but *when* he would climax. I was fascinated at how slow and undramatic this was. One, two, three, and he ejaculated in a hot stream over her hands.

She looked up at me through her long red hair and winked

'Never wank a man off,' she advised. 'All that furious jerk-ing. It's not sexy.'

Demara was a new friend, the first woman to ever give me a sex lesson. I'd met her in March 2008 on a tantra workshop in Somerset. She was an erotic masseur, yes, a woman of the light, and a generous one too, happy to teach me some of her skills.

That night I slept on the futon in the corner of Demara's temple. Or rather, I tried to. But I couldn't sleep. Instead I wept. I wept because I was ashamed of myself, at how closed

I'd been, not just with my ex, but all my life. I wept because I'd never touched a man like that before, never kissed or cherished any lover like that. I'd never expressed such clear adoration for any man, given of myself in such a free and open way. In the past, I hadn't thought to explore the vast ground of intimacy between sex and friendship, all the hundreds of ways to give of myself, to demonstrate love, erotic or otherwise. There had been sex, often quite a hurried affair, and then the time spent together which wasn't sexual. There had been no hours of pleasure in between, nothing like this. It all made sense: why things had gone so wrong. I'd never loved my ex like this. I didn't know how.

All through 2008, I still thought of my ex every day. I still missed his face next to mine every morning, on the pillow. I used to start each day peering into his face. It was a kind of meditation. It made me happy to gaze at him. *He is the one my soul loves*. But, as I came to see it, this 'high' spiritual love had doused the flames of the baser sexual love. He wanted none of this weird sexless love. *Of course* he'd wanted none of it. What man would? What man, made of flesh, with a beating heart, what hot-blooded still-alive man would stick around with some kind of crackpot nun? What man would *want* a nun, a woman who worshipped him for his mind only?

There are different types of love; we all know that. The Greeks had named them: *Eros, Agape, Philia, Caritas*. This love I named myself: *Castrato*. This nameless sexless love was a strong love, too; it hadn't died or gone away, not even after two years. In fact, the love I felt for him seemed to get grander, more heroic, after our split. I missed him desperately. I *endured* my days. I was lonely and constantly cheerless without him. I was dead without him: one half of a double act. I was Ernie

Wise after Eric Morecambe had gone. I missed his donkey bray at *The Simpsons*, a laugh that shook the house. I missed his ridiculous waddle-walk. His tapered hands, I missed them too. His flat-as-a-spade arse. I missed him sitting in the bath with fags and tea; I missed kissing the stems of his glasses, sitting on his knee. I missed walking hand in hand. I missed his presence in all its forms.

enter, madam rose

When I'd moved to Harlesden in March 2007 with Emma and Matthew, by complete chance, I found myself round the corner from my old friend Rose Rouse. The night I moved in to the flat, Rose came round with a bottle of wine to celebrate. I'd been using CL and regaled her with my most recent adventures. She listened politely. She brought up something called The Art of Being and waved a leaflet at me. I read it sceptically. It looked fluffy. Pastel pinks. A couple were embracing on the cover, laughing. Inside, there was a great deal of blurb offering 'a profound affirmation of your natural sexuality' and other stuff about 'reclaiming your sex as a gift of whole being'. Rose said the leaflet was for a tantra workshop, that there was some nudity involved; she said I might like it, might even get a lot out of it. I was dismissive.

'I don't like all that stuff, Rose. I like sex quick and mad and hot.'

She wasn't convinced.

'I do.'

'But you're missing so much.'

'Trust me, Rose. I don't want any of that hippie shit.'

Rose managed to talk a close male friend, Matthew Bowes, into doing this Art of Being course. *Good luck*, I thought. *Rather you than me*. But to my dismay, Matthew returned buzzing, raving about the course. Rose went to meet him for lunch in a café nearby to debrief. Clearly, something interesting had happened but I didn't care or want to know what: I wasn't about to get naked with lots of people in a big hall. I didn't want to do any group psychotherapy or work on my 'feelings'. Bollocks to that. Rose and Matthew were mad. Matthew had already done too much therapy; Rose was a bohemian who'd done everything. They could both jump in a lake.

I don't know when my resistance slackened. I was still miserable; I'd been having therapy sessions with Michele Bosc. Despite his depression, my ex seemed to be settling down with this woman, Ruth. He was moving on. But I couldn't get over him so easily. I'd been split *from* him. I hadn't split up *with* him. There was a big difference.

I'd been replaced. Almost immediately replaced. It hurt like crazy. How could he live without me? I couldn't live without *him*.

I wrote to him, he wrote back. There was a flurry of letters between us.

I called him. We talked for over an hour. I begged him to think again. I had no idea on what grounds I wanted him back: all I knew was that this love for him was worthy of still taking seriously; that, with some support from someone like Michele, we could venture into a new era. Those were my vague ideas. He said, 'But you don't fancy me. I want to be *fancied*. You rejected me. I felt so hurt. You'll never know how.'

'But you and I are *supposed* to be together,' I said. 'You don't love this Ruth. You love me. I love you.'

Was I deluded? Partially, yes. I wasn't able to see the full picture, not then. I clung to one truth. We'd shared an extraordinary time together. For a few years, we were wed. We blossomed with each other. We'd grown each other, been good for each other. It had been a creative partnership, there was a spark between us; he had activated a part of me. There'd been a hook. I believe now that ours was the archetypal attraction of two creative spirits. I'd loved him, even admired him. We'd been productive together, active, happy; this was what I was alluding to: so much *had* worked. But he was more realistic.

Rose and I went out a lot. We became even closer as friends. Rose was like a vitamin pill. Bedecked in feathers and flowers and furs, her life an array of launches, art openings, travel and dancing. I nestled in her glamour and her sanguine female wisdom. Rose had a son, an ex of twelve years, a past life lived to the full in places like New Orleans and Jamaica. She'd done it all: long-term monogamy, motherhood, a career in journalism, and she was still *out there*, in her mid-fifties. I saw her as more fulfilled and more adventurous than many friends my own age. When Rose rang one day, full of the joys of yet another workshop with The Art of Being, something shifted.

'Humph,' I said.

'What does "humph" mean?'

'Bollocks,' I said.

'Get a life,' said Rose.

'Fine. I'll do that course then, in March. Okay, I'll do it.'

easter 2008, glastonbury

So, in March 2008, two years after our split, my CL adventures
dwindling, I found myself on my first workshop with Jan Day
in Glastonbury, Somerset. Until then, I hadn't been on any
kind of conscious quest; all I'd done was seek knowledge and
gain experience in a reactive way. I was out there but very
much on my own. No support or wisdom, no teaching.

I was allocated a caravan for a bedroom. Almost exactly the
same as Andromeda Heights, a white hump. Except prettier,
with clematis trained round the door. I was thrown. I was ill,
too, with a raging cold and arrived with bottles of pills. The
weather was grim for mid-March. There was a howling wind
and pelting rain when I arrived. I was kept awake by the
storm, remembering what it was like to sleep with my ex all
those years ago in Lancaster, the squirrels skittering on the
caravan roof. I dreamt of the time my ex saved Lady Violet
from a similar storm in Sheepwash, when she got lost in
the vicar's yard next door and we heard her mewing in the
downpour. He went to fetch her, climbing over the adjoining
wall. The image of him, lurching through the door, soaked to
the skin, clutching our bedraggled cat, haunted my dreams. I
shed tears in my sleep.

On my arrival at the centre, I'd found two men in the hot
tub. One bald and sexy, one old and whiskered. Both naked.
I froze and backed out the door. Rose had been careful to say
nothing about the course, for fear of scaring me off. But she
had mentioned the hot tub. I *hate* hot tubs; I hate their whole
association with Nordic casual group nudity. There was

nothing casual about sex as far as I was concerned. Nothing sexy about group nudity. Nudist beaches and naturist camps, the very idea left me cold – like graveyards for those with sagging buttocks and flattened breasts. Sex, to my mind, deserved more respect. Nudity was something to be done in private; fine one-on-one. Already, I knew I was on the wrong course.

There were primroses everywhere, sprinkling the country lanes with chaste yellow flower heads, like smiling faces. Primroses, his favourite flower. They made me feel gloomy. In the morning, the storm had passed and the sky had cleared. I wandered the lanes and picked a few primroses and put them in a jar in my caravan. No one and nothing could cure my prolonged melancholia. Not this Jan Day who was facilitating the course. No one. I was ill with flu and besieged with nostalgia as I made my way to the only part of the course which was compulsory, the dynamic meditation before breakfast.

dynamic meditation

Jan Day, the group leader, stood in the open space, a barn-type area, holding a microphone. I didn't want to like her, but I did. She was tall and leggy, with flame-red hair pulled back in a ponytail. Pale-skinned, blue-eyed and dressed in loose-fitting clothes. She stood with her feet apart, braced. She was very feminine and also kind of kind of dazzling. Energetic. And English. An English eccentric, just like my ex? Yes. Rose hadn't mentioned that this woman would be so strong and charismatic. I liked resting my eyes on her; immediately I felt safe. I liked her. *Phew*.

There were twenty of us in the group, aged twenty-five to seventy-five. Gender-balanced. Fat, thin, old, young, glamorous, less so. I knew nothing about these people. We hadn't yet had the chance to talk. There'd been a meal the night before, but most of us had been too unnerved to chat freely. There were a few others who weren't part of the group, Jan's assistants. I was glad of them, that our numbers were enhanced with others who knew what was to come. Demara was one of them.

Jan had talked us through the meditations and its four stages:

1. shaking
2. wildness
3. chakra opening
4. stillness

She demonstrated each one. I watched, baffled, as she shook her entire body and then rolled around on the floor in a bestial manner, as she growled and clenched her jaws and her hands, expressing a primal fury. Then she stood in a still state. I had no idea what all this would do, but I decided I would sure as heck give it a try.

Cue music. New Age music. Music very reminiscent of Your Dad's 'Whale Song'. I bit my lip. I heard my ex on the mic. *'Breathe,'* he whispered, full of malevolent intent. I closed my eyes and tried to forget him and his ridiculous waddle, his manatee face. But images of him came to me, skipping across a stage, yodelling and doing knee drops and chasing after audience members trying to escape. I was like a junkie trying anything to get off the real thing. Methadone, alcohol, doing a 'Geographic', the Twelve Steps. Now, this shaking.

We had all been given blindfolds, airline masks, for our eyes. *Good*, I thought. I didn't want to see anyone.

Jan guided us.

The music picked up. It became more frenetic.

'Shake like you're sitting on a donkey on a bumpy road,' she coaxed.

The idea was to try and shake up and then upwards the sexual energy lying dormant in the first chakra.

Many spiritual schools of thought believe the body has hidden portals of energy which are called chakras: the Hindus think there are seven; North American shamanic traditions say ten or more. The Tibetans and Chinese believe in chakras too. 'Chakra' is the Sanskrit word for wheel and it's believed that there are 'wheels' or vortices in the body through which the body's *prana*, chi or life-force flows. They run in a straight line through the centre of the body, starting in the perineum, then just above the pubis, the sternum, the heart, throat, forehead and finally, the crown. The idea behind the shaking was to awaken the energy in the first chakra, or root chakra; this is 'serpent energy', the energy of the mystical Kundalini.

The air became worried with cries and the sounds made by people's bodies shaking. It was weird and exciting. *Shake, shake, shake.* I couldn't quite get it. My hands flailed. Everyone around was shaking. Twenty or thirty people shaking themselves like crazy. I shook too. My legs, backside, arms. I shook and shook till I thought I'd shake my head off. But nothing like a serpent seemed to be awakened in my groin.

No snake-energy coiling up there. People around me were making odd noises, grunts, groans; some were shouting. I kept shaking. Nothing. I liked doing it, though. I fought the urge to hurl myself into a massive shaking fit, throw myself on the ground.

The music changed. Jan guided us so we were kneeling on our mats. There was a palpable rage all around me. This was the 'wildness' stage. I peeked from under my blindfold. People were tearing pillows to shreds, tearing off their clothes, rolling around naked, howling and growling and screaming. It was mayhem, but somehow beautiful, too. Harrowing. Deranged. I loved it. I couldn't muster a whimper, though. I curled into a ball. Not a peep. Not even a whisper of rage. Nothing came out, nothing of the little girl neglected by her impatient father, nothing of the woman damned by another woman, her life blown apart by a sheaf of letters and emails. No anger for my ex, his betrayal, his moving on so swiftly. I wasn't used to this licence to express whatever lay dormant, impacted. This was *too free*, too much. I shrank. I listened as the room bellowed. Bedlam, or worse. People were roaring like the storm the night before.

And then the room was still. We were to let this energy move upwards, guide it up and out of the crown chakra. I imitated what the others were doing. The music continued. Some people had keeled over. Others were blissed out. I lay on my side and thought *forfuckssakes, Mon. What on earth have you done now?*

That was Day One, Hour One. This was before we had even had breakfast. This was warm-up. The course hadn't even begun. I vowed to strangle Rose Rouse when I next saw her.

the tantra diaries

My purple suede book ran out of silver gilt-edged pages. I began writing in A5 Moleskines instead. On 23 March 2008, while on the course, I wrote:

Primroses everywhere. Tears and primroses for X. I still think of him every day. I do not believe for one moment he loves this other woman.

Much was bothering me on the course, just on Day One:

1. One of the men looked just like Captain Mainwaring from *Dad's Army*. I didn't think I could let him touch me. Even though I didn't know what to expect, I assumed touching would be the least of it.
2. I couldn't stop myself from thinking of John Fowles' *The Magus*. That we had been somehow tricked there to be toyed with; we were the playthings of some sinister sexual magician or billionaire.
3. No alcohol. Would I make it through the week without a glass of Pinot Grigio?
4. Early on, someone commented that I was a person with a big 'no'. Actually it was much worse. I had 'fuck off' written on my forehead.

♥

On Day Two, 24 March 2008, I wrote:

Fuck, now it starts to get tough. Today we all took our clothes off. I have an agonising fear of being touched by someone I don't like. Having to endure rather than enjoy another's touch.

Yes, at one point we were asked to disrobe, but even this was optional. This was done in stages, first with blindfolds on, just to feel our way into the experience, then with blindfolds off. And yes, this was odd. I stood in a hall and took off my clothes quite slowly, garment by garment and so did everyone else.

Afterwards, we stood in a circle and were encouraged to walk around and have a good look at each other. It was funny and strange. All shapes of body, and yes, I had a good look. One woman with wounds under her arms, these wounds still dressed. Another with a Brazilian shaped pubic haircut. Spot, moles, creases of skin. My breasts have grown larger over the years, no longer the pert missiles they were; was I less confident of their new shape? Yes. I was self-conscious of them but generally okay. One man, an ex-actor, decided to moonwalk backwards across the circle, butt-naked.

g-spot

On Easter Sunday 2008, at 7.30 a.m. I wrote in my diary:

Slept quite well. But woke up at 5 a.m. Shit. I'm here. Like being in hell. I'm exhausted. Today is make or break. I'm close to leaving. Perhaps I really am on the wrong course.

Soon after I wrote this, the men and women on the course were separated. I was relieved. This timely act meant that I didn't run away.

That day, in groups of three, in a room exclusively female, I touched women for the first time. Women! Tenderly, lovingly, sexily. They touched me. And I got into the hot tub – with the women. We all sat huddled in a circle and talked about our sex lives, our desires and fantasies, and these ranged from the most basic heterosexual fantasies and frustrations to thinking about sex with animals.

We talked and then later, in a structured exercise, we stripped for one another. In small groups we served and honoured and pleasured each other. When it was my turn, I lay naked on my back while two women ran their hands all over my arms and legs and stomach and breasts. It felt safe, and also sensual, erotic. I enjoyed it. I found delight in this kind of touch from my own sex. *Jesus*, God, a whole world of possibilities was opened up. I'd never have dared, *ever*, to ask a woman to touch me, touch me consciously and lovingly. This felt shocking and was way beyond my experience; I was moved in a way that's difficult to speak about.

My G-spot. It had been hidden from me all my life. It was the Holy Grail, a legend. But, during my turn to be served and honoured, Demara came over to me and, with her expertise, slipped her fingers inside me, massaging my yoni, feeling her way, until she pressed and – *oh*.

'Yes!' I exclaimed.

It was there all right.

'Do you feel like you need to pee?'

'Yup.'

'That's your G-spot, honey.'

It was a strange, awkward feeling, deep inside me. In that moment, a dull, dim groan stirred in me; I had a sense that *I* was stored there, some unknowable self. If she kept massaging this spot lightly, I felt I'd die of some kind of inner explosion of peace.

She didn't persist. But she'd found it. Quite easily. She'd *searched*. No man had ever tried to find my G-spot. Not even my ex. A woman! After all my years as a sexually active heterosexual adult, a woman, not a man, was the first to find my G-spot. A professional erotic masseur, admittedly, but, nevertheless, yes – I have a G-spot. I know many women reading this may think otherwise. But you're wrong, it does exist. Get a woman to find yours too!

After that, there was little stopping me.

I was out of the box.

I spent the rest of the session being explored and exploring the other women who chose me to be with them. Glorious.

Reclining backwards with her legs open, Demara showed us many forms of self-pleasuring, using her own yoni (Sanskrit for vagina, it means the source of all life). She showed us a technique called Round the Park, circling her fingers around the clitoris, and another which involved plucking the pubic hair upwards. Wow. Jan then showed us her bag of sex toys, a crystal wand, some geisha balls, giving instructions on how to use them. The wand was an exquisite object, swan-necked, Perspex-plastic, bulbous at the end for pressing on the G-spot. When she slipped it from its red velvet pouch, I gasped and knew I'd buy one as soon as I got home. The geisha balls, also known as 'love eggs', are small oval balls which women can keep inside them; they give an immense and comforting private pleasure. I imagined myself in Tesco's, shopping, my eggs swaying inside me.

Female ejaculation was another Grail, a mystical fable in the field of female orgasm. It had the status of the grandest of all states of female bliss. Some women ejaculate easily, others never. But, here too, Jan gave advice on how to achieve this miracle: give yourself a couple of hours off to self-pleasure. Drawn the curtains, switch off the phone, light candles, burn incense, create a sensuous space and then explore yourself. Use a mirror.

I was happy to be alone with the women. It was easy and comfortable being with my own sex. Between lesbian women, there can be similar tension and edginess as between straight women and men, but that day, amongst a group of heterosexual women, a kind of '*agape lesbia*' descended. It was a quiet blissful self-love, a milk-bath of sisterhood, an encounter with my own sex that I'd never found the opportunity to experience, let alone savour. I sank into a sublime comfort.

I crossed a line that day: I became 'ambi-sexual', a word I came across years later which denotes a sexual orientation close to bi-sexual but bi-sexual lite. It happened very naturally, in a very safe environment. When women get sexing with women, it's a type of loving men cannot recreate or compete with. Woman-on-woman sex is honey-velvet-drunkenness, a generous and nurturing form of same-sex-love. This was all new: that I could feel so sexy and happily so, without men. All of sudden I could see what men saw in the sexual nature of women: breasts, nipples, skin, hair, the hidden folds between women's legs; all of a sudden I understood.

That day I wrote:

Thank you, Rose. I am in a different place. This has been life-shifting. Disorientating. I am not crying any more. Something bigger has happened to me. Easter Sunday today. Resurrection!

We met the men again, later, in a formal ceremony. I was ill, exhausted and overturned. I didn't care to greet them. I liked being with the women. I was tired of men and all I knew of what they could offer. One, my ex, had almost broken me. I used to be so spirited. But I had been so mournful for so long – too long. Men could fuck off. But that day, I was too weak to be bolshy or complain. It wasn't 'fuck off' to men or the whole of mankind, more like 'go easy with me'.

Later, when a touch structure was suggested by Jan, I was outvoted. We did an exercise where the men and women were brought back together in an intimate way. Each person was to be touched, loved and nurtured by a group of the opposite sex. I was resistant, and while most of the others disrobed, I kept my clothes on.

I lay on a mattress while three attractive men 'served' me, caressing me lovingly, consciously, my legs, arms, stomach and breasts. Tears ran down my face. Being caressed by three men? This had never happened before, either. But here it was safe, easy. They were the right men; around me there was an atmosphere of grace. Jan and her assistants were holding the space. And this was a new type of space, ritual space; soon my dress slipped off – *ha*. This re-acquaintance with men after the day languishing with women had been set up in a respectful manner. It was a way of re-integrating men. I writhed and moaned under their conscious loving touch,

I basked in the appreciation of their gaze. I felt okay about men again.

♥

That week in March 2008, in that barn in Glastonbury, I practiced tantra for the first time. I did this in a number of group 'structures' and games. So experiential is the practice of tantra that it's very hard to do justice in words to the power of these simple humane practices. Many were ingenious. All were challenging. I'll describe just one, a game called Yes, More, Goodbye.

I found some people in the group attractive, others not at all. The idea was to move around the room and experience each person through touch, to touch and let yourself be touched and to see if you or that person wanted more and if so how much. If not, you or that person would say 'goodbye' and move on. I found it utterly foxing. Men I found attractive came up to me and touched me and said 'more' and so did I. This was sexy – but then quickly, far too quickly, they said 'goodbye'. I didn't know how to play this game at all. When a man said 'yes' and then 'more' in the past, it had often led to sex. But here men were saying 'yes' and then 'more' and then *moving on*. For the first time I was experiencing what it meant to play with the sexual urge, to exercise choice, delay gratification, to explore the middle ground of 'maybe'.

Through the week we touched each other, in groups. We explored every inch of each other's bodies. We gave instructions on where we wanted to be touched and how and where we did *not* want to be touched. I was touched by several people all at once. We talked a lot, in large circles, on the floor. We danced around naked to music. We danced clothed. We talked some more. At no time was there any pressure or expectation to remove clothes. I could have gone the whole week with my clothes on.

At one point, yes, I got a little over-touched. It was all way beyond the boundaries of all my past experience. In my diary I wrote:

Managed to tell the group that all the touchy feely stuff is getting on my nerves, that all I want is to be hugged. I got lots of hugs. That was lovely. I feel better now. I need to lie down.

When I questioned her later on her approach, Jan said: 'Sexuality is a powerful tool. In my groups we use sexuality to take people to their edge, to their uncomfortable feelings. They are encouraged to make friends with these feelings and therefore dissolve some of those no-go areas.'

Indeed, I was being pushed way out of my comfort zone. I'd surprised myself at how far I could stretch, at how flexible I could be. I was rather pleased. I was also learning a new vocabulary. There was a tantric lexicon. It was exotic and poetic. I loved these new words and rolled them round my tongue. I made a list:

Kundalini
Yoni (sacred place)
Lingam (wand of light)
Crystal wand
Geisha balls
Loving touch
Conscious touch
Sky dancing

The primroses in the jar wilted. The break-up seemed less important. Finally, in that week, the drama of the split had been eclipsed. This tantric work was far more interesting than me and my broken heart. This was the beginning of a new time: a time of self-revelation. It was what I'd been yearning for, new things to know and think about. I'd been feeling sluggish. I wanted to learn more. Tantra was all about learning to be intimate. Jan was teaching the art of love, something mothers should teach their daughters; once, in ancient times, they probably did. Tantra provides this knowledge. It is some kind of elite school, Intimacy School for those who seek this knowledge.

I'd learnt a lot using Craig's List, mostly about men, their sexual needs, their loneliness. But meeting for casual sex is all about getting a base need met. This work was far more subtle. This was about the art of touch, of trust, the art of opening the heart: in many ways it was back to basics.

In my notebook, I wrote:

In the early days X had tantric energy, a purity of heart and spirit which I loved. I can recognise this now. He had broken down, repaired himself. He had a softness to him.

egolessness and timelessness

I went home and read all that I could. I found out that tantra is a Sanskrit word meaning 'web' or 'weave'. It comes from the verbal root *tan*, meaning 'to expand'. Georg Feuerstein is one of the most lucid contemporary Western writers on the subject. 'According to esoteric explanations, tantra is that which expands *jñāna*, which can mean either "knowledge" or "wisdom".' Tantra, he says, is a continuation of earlier ancient Hindu and Buddhist teachings. Buddhist tantra descends from the Buddha himself; Hindu tantra regards the *Vedas* (collections of prayers or rituals) as its starting point.

While tantra is a broad-based ancient esoteric teaching, it's most renowned, even sometimes reviled in the West, for its teachings on sexuality. This is often known as 'left hand' tantra or red tantra. It's been stigmatised in the West because *anything* regarding sexuality has been stigmatised in the West, especially something which sounds so exotic, so avant-garde and foreign. The God-awful Sting and Trudi Styler are linked to tantra. We've all seen those narcissistic naked torso-shots of Sting in his yoga pyjamas. Madonna is linked with the Kabbalah, Tom Cruise with Scientology, Sting with tantra. It would be easy to write tantra off as another spiritual celebrity fad.

Left hand tantra, as far as I've come to understand, aims to show practitioners of tantra (tantrikas) that sex is linked with the divine. Tantric sex is spiritual sex, sex where one's partner leads you to God. Think bliss-inducing whole body orgasms, non-ejaculation for men, think mindful, spirit-full, holistic non-goal-orientated sex. This kind of sex takes conscious practice. Tantrikas have, in my experience, a very practical attitude towards sexuality. They see it as something that can be worked on in a practical way. Through a number of structured practices, which include many types of meditations – work on the body and the body's seven chakras, work on intimacy, on one's own demons – one's sexual landscape can transform or expand.

The most recent and infamous 'master' of tantric teaching in the East was the late Osho, otherwise known as Baghwan Sri Rajneesh. His name comes up time and again in contemporary Western tantric circles – a stumbling block for those who are only aware of him from outside these circles. Osho and the ninety-three Rolls Royces and the pictures on YouTube of men with Uzi sub-machine guns guarding him. Bald-headed, orange-robed people banging drums and worshipping a man who sucked on nitrous oxide and loved magic tricks? No thanks.

The stories of Osho are wild and many are true. Osho was an Indian professor of philosophy who set himself up as a spiritual teacher in the early 1970s in Mumbai. First he spoke in small spaces, private rooms, gathering small crowds of (mostly Western) disciples, but by 1974 he had set himself up in an ashram near Pune, which still exists today as the Osho International Meditation Resort. In 1981 he moved his base from Pune, India, to Oregon, USA, to a vast plot of land called The Ranch. However, this newer and larger commune disastrously collapsed in 1985 after his main assistant, Ma Anand Sheela, planned and executed a number of bio-terror attacks on salad bars in The Dalles, Oregon. Soon after, Osho and Sheela were arrested on a number of serious charges. While Osho was heavily fined, given a ten-year suspended sentence and ejected from the US, Sheela, admitting to the crimes, was also heavily fined and given three 20-year sentences, although she was later released for good behaviour after serving only two years.

Osho died in 1990. Today, all the information on him is out there. He spoke copiously, for hours at a time; all his books are transcriptions of his speeches, and are still available. *Sex*

Matters: From Sex to Superconsciouness is his most famous, the one that earned him the label of 'sex guru'. Reading this book, I came upon something remarkable:

> 'First, in the moment of orgasm, the ego vanishes and ego-lessness emerges. For a moment there is no ego; for a moment no trace even of "I am" ... The second thing that happens is that for a while there is no time ... These two are the most important elements of religious experience: egolessness and timelessness. And these two elements are what account for the mad drive of humans towards sex. The craving is not for the body of a woman or a man ... not at all. The craving is for a taste of egolessness and timelessness ... no sooner than the ego disappears, there is a glimpse of the soul; no sooner than time disappears, there is a glimpse of godliness. There is a religious experience, a spiritual experience, underlying the craving for sex.'

I liked this a lot. It made perfect sense. Those moments we chase, moments of orgasm, they are, in fact, a chase after an encounter with the divine. Yes, *of course* this is what sex is all about. Using CL, I was chasing after men, after cock, after a base need – and also, a moment with God.

If I could explain tantra to anyone it would be this: if sex is a drive towards an encounter with the divine, then tantra is a conscious practice which helps to extend that encounter.

What Osho *did* do was translate the tantric teachings of Lord Shiva's 5000-year-old *Bhairav tantra* – which means 'techniques for going beyond consciousness' – a collection of 112 tantric meditations, calling them *The Book of Secrets*. Today, despite the enormous scandal surrounding him, many of his former pupils, or *sannyasins*, who have nothing to do with his criminal activities, are now continuing his early tantric teachings in the West. People like Diana Richardson, Margot Anand, Alan Lowen, Jan Day (an ex-student and co-teacher with Lowen) and Ma Anand Sarita all spent many years working with Osho or in Osho communities outside India.

ancestral widowhood

When I returned home I rang my ex immediately. 'I think I'm bi-sexual,' I blurted. 'And more. Can we be friends?'

'Friends?'

We hadn't spoken for six months. But he was relieved I'd called, that we were back in touch. Some real forgiveness and reconciliation now seemed possible. Through tantra, I'd been given a chance to see more fully into the sexual mechanics of our relationship. Maybe, with more of these workshops and experiences, I'd come to know why I'd chosen to be with him.

Two years. That's how long it took for the sorrow to start to leave me. Two years for something *else* to happen. My grief and mourning had become embarrassing and irksome, even to myself. I spoke of it only to Michele. *Get a life*, Mon – move on. But this had not been so easy for me. I come from a family of widows. I have inherited the tendency to grieve deeply over lost love. The women in my family are Keepers of Romantic Grief.

All kinds of tendencies and traits run in families: ginger hair, depression, alcoholism, beauty, maverick behaviour, asthma. One of the things that runs in my family is widow-hood. I come from a long line of women who married for love and stayed married and who lost their husbands through death.

My great grandmother Nona, Irma Mifsud, born in Pisa in 1874, was only married for two years before cholera car-ried off her handsome young husband. He was a doctor and they were living in Alexandria at the time. She was left a widow at twenty-three with a toddler and a newborn and vowed never to marry again. She wore black all her life and brought up her children with the help of French nuns. She made a living as a teacher and a seamstress. Family legend has it that she embroidered trousseaus for the daughters of Egypt's King Fuad. Nona was an indomitable matriarch, the strongest person I've heard of in our family of strong people. I never knew her, but the stories of Nona are many. She once bashed her son-in-law, my domineering grandfa-ther Clement, over the head with an umbrella so hard she broke the umbrella. She was much feared and loved. She lived to be eighty-seven – making her a widow of *sixty-four years*.

Maman, my grandmother, Laure Garrana, was born in Alexandria in 1900. Daughter of the formidable Nona, she had been cloistered in a convent as a child and was a very different type of woman: reserved, beautiful, exquisitely mannered. At nineteen she married an older man, Clement, a distant relative and wealthy businessman whom she adored. She had eight children but only four of them sur-vived. When Clement died of a combination of epilepsy and post war-depression, Maman was fifty-three and still rav-ishing. When she was ejected from Egypt in 1956, during the

Suez Crisis, she went to live in Trinidad, to be near my mother. There she taught French, and also sewed hand-embroidered clothes. At one point, she opened a maternity boutique. Like Nona, she was a staunch Catholic. She said her *chaplet* every day of her life. She couldn't cook but sang like a nightingale. She liked to dress up (I take after her in this respect). She had seven wigs, all beehives, one for every day of the week. She was always immaculately turned out; never without her girdle and stockings and patent court shoes and lipstick and rings; dandyish little kerchiefs of chiffon tied at her throat. Often she was seen walking around Port of Spain with her parasol held aloft. Many of my friends were taught French by Madame Garrand (she had changed the last letter of her name, so as to sound less 'foreign'). She died a few weeks before she turned one hundred. She died of old age, in her bed, in my mother's arms. There'd never been a question of another man, or a love affair, a second marriage. She had been a widow for *forty-seven years*.

My mother, Yvette Roffey, was born in Port Said in 1931. Blonde, green-eyed and extrovert, she had lots of male admirers. My mother was an archetypal blonde bombshell: rude health, a natural beauty and great sex appeal. French was her first language, Arabic her second. She spoke Italian, too, and learnt English at school. After the war, when my father was posted to Port Said with the Royal Engineers, Mum worked as his secretary. He tried his chances dating her, but had lots of competition. When his tour of duty was over he went back to England and wrote her wonderful letters for four years. He romanced her *on the page*. She wrote back, sending him miniature Hollywood-style glamour photos of herself. When his parents put pressure on him to marry a nice young woman he'd known all his life, he asked my mother if he could back come 'to visit'. Mum says when she saw him descend the aeroplane's flight steps she just knew. Her heart leapt.

They courted for two weeks in Port Said. When he proposed on a bus she said 'yes'. A week later, there was a civil marriage ceremony; a week after that, a big white wedding in a Catholic church. Her whole family waved her goodbye from the port. It all happened in under a month. They'd never so much as kissed. She loved my father and only my father all her married life. Their marriage was never boring. I witnessed much of it myself. They were my model: they matched and complemented each other. They entertained a lot, threw great parties, they danced and drank and yes, they fought. I once saw my mother throw a glass of rum in my father's face, still one of the most exciting things I've ever seen. When my father died, when my mother was sixty-three, she fell into a profound grief. They were married for forty years. When he died, shockingly, in our swimming pool, she jumped in after him, trying to haul his lifeless body to the surface. She screamed and screamed till the neighbours came running.

My mother has been a widow for seventeen years and counting. She still mourns my father; she's still lonely without him.

I know how she feels. It is in my particular DNA to grieve romantic loss. It's in my inheritance, my family map. I wasn't aware of this till it was my turn. In total, these women, Irma, Laure and Yvette, have mourned their lost husbands for *one hundred and twenty-six years*. For me it was two years, two years thick with loss. And then I saw what was happening and decided it couldn't go on. I got off lightly by comparison.

attending class

Practising tantra was the first actual 'sex teaching' I'd come across. It was a revelation in the area of sexuality, the one subject it's hard to gain experiential information about, outside our own relationships. It's absurd. We go to university to improve our minds, we go to the gym to improve our bodies, we go see psychotherapists to improve our mental health and self-understanding, we go travelling to improve our knowledge of the world. And yet, when it comes to sex, gaining knowledge of our sexual self, a fundamental part of human personal life, there seems to be nowhere to study.

Instead, most of us muddle through, pick things up from our hit-and-miss personal experience. Some of us are lucky, some not so lucky. Some of us give up, especially as we age, have children. We withdraw, contract. But at this point in my life, I saw a unique chance to learn and practise. It was the area of my relationship which I'd ignored and sacrificed. I'd also withdrawn. Failed? Yes. Suddenly, I was woken up. I wanted to attend class.

propinquity

In May 2008 I wrote:

I'm anxious and not quite myself today. My flatmates are leaving.

All through this time, I'd been living with Emma and Matthew and their baby, Lois. When people see a lot of each other, through work, life or living conditions, they tend to form close friendships or relationships. It's called the 'propinquity effect', a term coined by a group of American psychologists in the 1950s. And this effect had taken hold of me and my co-habitants of our Harlesden flat. We had all grown close; we'd grown to care for one another. I had grown reliant on them for a by-proxy world of family support. Emma had grown reliant on me for female companionship, a spot of hands-on co-mothering and a link to the outside world, one she'd had to relinquish short-term.

Emma counselled me on love; it was common for me to appear at the top of the stairs, dishevelled and railing about some date gone wrong, whilst she was nursing Lois. She'd roar at my antics. We'd sit and have a calming cup of mint tea. I'd stare at the baby on her breast and know that my life was a million miles from hers and hers from mine.

Over eighteen months, Emma, Matthew, 'Mrs' Lois and I had bonded into a functioning, if a little eccentric, family pod. I had been part of the baby's life since she was one day old. She had me in her line of vision; she saw me as part of her tribe. I was one of her 'people'. She was often in the baby bouncer on the kitchen table whenever I went to make another pot of coffee to fuel my morning's writing. Lois was the only baby I'd ever lived with or got to know at all. This little baby girl was part of my daily habitual life.

In my thirties I'd been too busy becoming an author to think too much about having babies. My ex already had two daughters and so the subject didn't come up at first. Once, early on, he did say he'd have been 'honoured to have a child' with me. But I was too busy developing my full potential. Then, years later, nearing forty, when I did begin to hum and hah and think about babies, it was too late. Our relationship was foundering. There was no way he would agree and we were not having any kind of sexual relations.

But, one night in July 2008, I went to the Groucho Club in Soho with my great friend of twenty years, Sean Thomas (aka the writer Tom Knox). We got talking about babies. Sean, the father of two little girls, said:

'*You'd* make a great mum.' We'd both drunk quite a bit.

I stared at him, a little disconcerted. 'Well, I need a man to help me with *that*.'

'What about me?'

'*You*?' I spluttered.

'Yes. I'd give you a baby.'

'Really?'

'Yes. I'd love to.'

'Bloody hell.'

I was stunned. But I cocked my head and squinted and saw, in a flash that yes, Sean, a friend of twenty years, might make the perfect sperm donor. But I'd come to quite fancy him since I was single.

'I wouldn't want to do a turkey baster thing,' I shot at him.

His face went dark.

'I couldn't tell my child I did it that way. We're friends. We fancy each other. Let's have some fun doing it.'

But he became more serious-looking and didn't reply.

When I got home I told Emma about Sean's proposition; she shrieked with laughter.

♥

Also in the summer of 2008, I was invited to a tea party to celebrate Arvon's fortieth birthday at The Hurst in Shropshire.
My ex and I were in email contact and his relationship with
Ruth had recently ended, so we arranged I would spend the
night at his home. We had dinner at a posh restaurant and
talked. He looked more tramp-like than ever. Those blackened
teeth, a hacking smoker's cough, a ticky heart which he constantly massaged with his hand, as if it might stop at any
moment. At his home, our snooty Violet cat didn't recognise
me at all; she was in another life.

But, over that dinner, a new peace began to settle between
us for the first time in years. This was our first meeting in
which I was able to surrender all defence. Only once in our
post break-up era had he ever shown frustration with me and
my moods, my ups and downs. Early on, in the months after
the split, he'd been sober and humbled. Like me, he couldn't
bear an outright ban on communication. Later, as time wore
on, as I was struggling more to accept the permanence of our
separation, he was patient and contrite. Always open and
compassionate, even when I grew mad and tearful. Somehow,
another affair had rumbled on between us; our post-love
affair.

'It's good to see you,' he said. 'If I go away again, you can
come and stay and look after Lady Violet, if you like.'

'No way. I'm not looking after that cat. She's forgotten me.
She can look after herself.'

I never told him of my cat nightmares. My guilt dreams.
How I'd given the cats away when push came to shove, had
run away, saved myself and put my writing career first.

But it was at that meeting in Presteigne when things began to shift. It was summer, a time of nature's abundance. I wanted to end the war between us. He was so physically war-torn.

The next day, at the Arvon tea party, an old shaman-type poet with long grey hair read a terrible poem about death and the underworld. We were all perched on benches on the croquet lawn. I sat at one end, my ex at the other. When the poet began to read, I felt my body begin to heave and then corpse. We'd listened to so many awful readings together in the barn at Totleigh. One little-known elderly poet had read out a memorable line: *the countryside around Scunthorpe is like a flat cunt.* Tears began to leak from my eyes.

I dared to lean backwards and peek at my ex. He was leaning backwards too, his face alive with mischief, his eyes also leaking tears.

♥

I was moving forward, *thank fuck.* I was still reading a lot. I was conscious of being in a state of evolution. I was in the process of sexual liberation. I'd already begun to question the 'monogamy for life' model laid down for us by church and state. Now I had a new working case study for relationships. Jan Day and her husband Frieder Fischer are married and committed, and they have room in their marriage for harmonious connections with others. Soon after the Arvon tea party, I watched the 2008 BAFTA awards on TV and read the next day about the actress Tilda Swinton, who has two partners, the artist John Byrne whom she lives with, and a younger man, also an artist, Sandro Kopp, with whom she travels the world. It was Kopp who escorted her to the BAFTA ceremony. 'The arrangement is just so sane,' she said.

I wondered if our relationship had needed this flexibility, if this was the non-monogamous model I was trying to describe when I spoke to my ex in November 2003, when I talked of having other lovers. Was it such a horrifying proposition? No. But these ideas, I now know, are complicated and sophisticated and only for those with clear mutual interest in another way of loving. They take contracts, agreements and only work if both partners are in a position of strength, if both can mutually say 'yes'. This was not the case for us.

sketched in the act

In May 2008, I used CL for the last time, advertising for a 'tantric lover'. I found one. We met for tea and cake at the Welcome Café in Euston. This man, Lawrence, let's call him, was one of the most handsome men I've ever laid eyes on: long sandy-reddish hair, iridescent blue eyes, tall and clad in a leather jacket and jeans. He turned heads as he walked in and I was conscious, throughout our conversation, that women were gazing at him. When he spoke his voice was educated and upper middle class. He'd stumbled across tantra through an old girlfriend and had been in more than one open relationship.

'What about sex parties?' I asked, keen to find an escort to these kinds of parties myself.

He nodded. 'Yeah, I've been to a few. Had a blast.'

'Who did you go with?'

'A friend.'

'A girlfriend?'

'No. She wanted to try them, but when we got to one, she chickened out.'

I nodded. In dimly lit mornings, mornings of fantasy, I'd often imagined this type of sexual group encounter. If confronted with the reality of such an encounter, would I also chicken out? Like Professor Jack, this man was a conscious sexual seeker and a liberated operator. We talked for hours. I explained some of my journey, that I was new to tantra.

Meeting for tea and cake in the afternoon is not conducive to sexiness. Our talk was almost a swapping of notes and adventures. I wasn't sure what to do with this handsome god. Chatting to him felt harmonious and soft. He was very tantric in his manner, with lots of eye gazing; his face was open and serene. He'd been comfortable with how we'd met and why, and had been honest, or so I felt, in describing his past relationships. With those great big blue eyes, it was hard to return his gaze. This meeting was almost chaste. When we went to pay for the bill, the pretty young waitress blushed and there was a sexual tension between them. I thought, for a moment, she was going to hand him her phone number; instead she pushed a piece of paper into my hand.

'What's this?' I asked.

'It's just something I do, you know, to pass the time.'

On the scrap was an intricate line drawing of Lawrence and me deep in conversation.

'Thanks,' I said. Lawrence smiled in appreciation and we left. I guessed he was used to having this effect on women. At the station we hugged and kissed each other on the lips. I felt sure I'd never see him again.

When I got home, the flat was mayhem. Matthew and Emma were packing up and moving out. They were going travelling to Europe for the summer months. I was sad they were departing; they were my family in London. They were taking Mrs Lois with them. I didn't tell them about Lawrence; it was still hard to explain the nature of these meetings to anyone, even them. I pinned the line drawing of myself and Lawrence to the wall next to my desk. I felt disconcerted that someone, a sweet young waitress, had taken the time to make a rather old-fashioned image of us, two strangers meeting via the internet to see if they might like to have a sexual connection. I was wrong about Lawrence. We did meet again.

the man with the mandolin

After the course in March with Jan Day, I signed up to do another tantra course soon after, called Energy and Consciousness, with a man named John Hawken. On the train to Cheltenham to spend the weekend working with him, I was hijacked by a well-known poet and Arvon tutor.

I was sitting in the quiet carriage and scoffing a sarnie when I looked up and saw the poet John Hegley coming towards me down the aisle, holding his mandolin.

'Hello,' said Hegley (Heggers to me and my ex).

'Er ... hello, Mr Hegley,' I stammered.

'Mind if I join you?' he said, dropping his mandolin case onto the seat opposite me.

'Course not.' I like Heggers. We're not friends as such, though I have a friendly disposition towards him. Heggers and my ex were friends. Hegley had heard what had happened to us.

'So, why are you going to Cheltenham?' he asked.

'To do a workshop. Why are you going?'

'To perform at a festival.'

'Oh.'

'What kind of workshop?'

'A yoga workshop.'

'Yoga?'

'Sort of.'

'Sort of?'

'It's complicated. I'm doing research for a book.'

'What kind of research?'

'Workshop research.'

Heggers, I could see, wouldn't be easily thrown off. He changed the subject. 'So, will you and X ever get back together again?'

'No.'

'Why not?'

'I don't know. It's complicated.'

'That's a shame.'

'I know.'

'What happened, then?'

'It's complicated. I dunno. I love him still, and he loves me. But he won't come back to me. He's been with someone else.'

'Really?'

'Yes.'

'I saw him recently. He had a toothache,' he said.

'He's always got bad teeth.'

'So what's this workshop you're going on?'

Long pause. Heggers looked happily expectant.

'It's a *tantric* workshop.'

'What?!'

I laughed. 'Yes. Research.'

'Jesus Christ.'

'Yes, I know. It's called "Energy and Consciousness". I'm hoping it might help. You know. Help me with a broken heart.'

Hegley nodded. I could see he both understood and yet wanted no further talk on this tantra business.

'Tell you what.'

'What?'

'Your ex needs a fucking tantric dentist.'

the tantric shaman

Saturday 31 May 2008, I wrote:

John Hawken is a wise man.

'He looks like an old Cornish pirate,' said Robert, his kind-voiced course administrator.

Attached to John Hawken's name were words like shaman, sky dancing, sexual magick. I was intrigued. When I found out he was running only one course which single people could attend that year, I jumped at the chance to sign up. Without doubt, there was some kind of mystique around him.

'John Hawken?'

'Oh, he's very dark.'

'He's funny-looking.'

There's this idea that tantra teachers should be somehow god-like and beatific in their appearance, handsome or

beautiful, sunny, open-faced, silken-haired, beaming, radi-
ant – and also pristine, beyond the casual, the scruffy or the
disorderly. In general, they live up to this ideal, especially
the women, who present themselves as sylph-like and über-
feminine. They often wear lots of pastel pink and discreet
layers of flowing skirts and flowers in their hair to emphasise
their goddess qualities. They dot their foreheads and have a
way of being bright-eyed and eerily composed.

John Hawken is a tubby dishevelled man. His hair is often
worse than bed-head, all tumbling this way and that or plastered to his head; his eyebrows resemble the wings of a bird
of prey. His teeth are like a mini-Stonehenge, broken, gappy
and spread (a tantric dentist, yes) and his beard is rough and
unkempt and spattered with grey. John's belly is almost caul-
dron-shaped, just like Obelix. Ancient Nike trainers and
tie-dye pyjama-type pants are his uniform. He wears specs.
Very obviously, he doesn't given a toss what others think of
his appearance.

His credentials are impressive and maverick. He studied
medieval literature at Cambridge. He then worked in the
experimental theatre world in Poland with Jerzy Grotowski's
Theatre Laboratory. He has sailed all over the world, and
lived in a bus which is now decaying outside his Cornish
home. He describes himself as a 'body-centred humanist
psychotherapist'. He has studied the work of Wilhelm Reich
and his particular field of energy work, bioenergetics, as well
as tantra for years with French arch-tantric diva Margot
Anand.

John Hawken is also a shaman, a person who can contact
spirits. Though he was trained by a North American shaman,
a woman who calls herself Arwen Dreamwalker, he is a

shaman in the old Anglo-Saxon tradition. He says he discovered the earth's magic and its places of natural power during his boyhood in Cornwall. Leylines, stone circles. Magic ponds. 'Piskies'. Strange, naturally-formed outcrops of rock. He came to know their energy and their healing properties as a young boy, and he made a point of learning more of this magic as a man.

I don't remember any formal introduction, any handshake or hello, any meeting of eyes. I just pitched up and joined John's space, a small workshop room at this centre in Cheltenham.

That first night, in an ice-breaker exercise, I found myself in a mad dance, touching fingers, hands, heads, 'third eyes', backs and arses with a group of strangers. John was sitting, watching, magus-like and barefoot, wearing his tie-dye pyjamas. His young Czech partner, Gabriella Rimska, was part of our group. Gabi is milk-skinned, with strong Slavic features, a ravishing beauty and, yes, one of those female tantrikas who radiate openness and inner light. That first night John demonstrated a 'touch structure' on Gabi, a type of massage called the 'cat paw' massage, kneading the skin a bit like a cat does when milk-treading. This ended with something called 'opening the jade gate', which sounds like it might be a place in the genital region, but in fact it's at the base of the skull.

I buddied up with a handsome young man, there with his girlfriend who was suffering from depression. Some tantric groups are a mixture of single people and couples. The couples, in these circumstances, can choose to work together or with others. I've now worked with many couples, both separately and together in a threesome; so far, it has been trouble-free. Tantric couples are usually open. They have often made some kind of prior agreement about working with other people. Tantra is not a sex club or a swinging club, a place to have sex or pick people up; so, from my point of view, the times I've worked with couples, there's never been any kind of jealousy. I'm not there to make a move on another person's partner. The 'structures' are a form of therapeutic 'work' on intimacy; they are often very effective and powerful. They're effective because they depend on the willingness and open-ness of people to participate in these games. Tantra, as I've heard said many times, is a *practice* not a theory.

So, we practised the cat paw massage. The young man was light with his hands and he'd done this before; he gave me a sensuous full body cat paw massage which ended with him opening a space I didn't even know existed, at the base of my skull. I lay there in a strange half-conscious but blissful state for several minutes. Something had opened: it felt like my face was open, or maybe my neck, or my nose. Tears welled in my eyes.

In my diary that night I wrote:

Tantric Mon – some new kind of archetype is emerging within me. Who is she? It's exciting to be on the move, to be inside, aware of the process of metamorphosis. I'm not only transforming internally, but outwardly, physically. I can see lines in my face, grey hairs, droops and sags on my once pert body. For the first time ever, I bear witness to this time shift. I've never witnessed myself growing before; not when changing from girl to adolescent, from adolescent to young woman, from young woman to mature woman. But I'm now wit-nessing, consciously, another of these grand changes.

tantra – types and archetypes

So many people who read, I find, read *too much* and depend on reading for their main source of access to knowledge. For some, the life of the mind is all. Books, films, music, art, all these aesthetics satisfy the unconscious human drive for wisdom. I find these people lazy and boring. Often they can be writers and poets: all that conjuring and venturing *inwards*. Little real outward journey, few risks taken. Writers sit on their arses and write all day: what the fuck can they know about anything?

Tantrikas are *not* clever know-it-all writer types; they are not clever know-it-all types full stop. In general, they are people who are not prepared to put up with the inertia or despondency of any of the Western social or psychological malaises which come from working too hard and living for too long without love. Tantrikas learn through doing.

In my experience, tantrikas are an open-minded bunch, most of them highly educated and adventurous. Often they have an edge, a secret type of nature, which makes them intriguing. They describe themselves as spiritual seekers. They are often well travelled and have come from varied and interesting fields of work; tantrikas I've met include academics, farmers, filmmakers, vets, therapists, journalists and masseurs. On that first 'Energy and Consciousness' weekend there was the usual eclectic tantric mix: a young tall wildman hippie with long hair and a beard who did body work and a lot of dance therapy, a middle-aged woman who also liked to dance and who suffered from man-disappointment, an aloof passive-aggressive black chick, an older man, a cat from the ashram in Pune who described himself as a 'messy sannyasin'. There was also an angry-looking man in orange clown pants, a handsome Indian god-like young man who was still suffering from events in his childhood, the attractive younger couple (she, depressed), a curly-haired black woman who talked a lot about the esoteric teachings of Alice Bailey and the 7 Rays, and me, a grumpy writer nursing a broken heart.

On Day Two, after some dancing in the morning, we all sat round on the floor in a circle to discuss why we were there. The stories were wild and vivid and heartbreaking. I can say, now, that I lied about myself. I told of a colourful background in the Caribbean, of coming from a culture where people were bold and fun-loving, natural exhibitionists and storytellers. I told of my parents who were 'sexually alive to each other', how I was torn from this more vibrant society only to be thrust into a cold flagstone-floored convent boarding school run by nuns in Surrey; how I had to learn to tone down my act for the English. Though all of this was true, I spun the romantic story of myself. I mentioned nothing of my aloof father, how he never spoke to me, or showed any interest in me as a child.

my flawed and crooked self

That morning, John Hawken talked a little about Wilhelm Reich. Tantra, body work, body-centred psychotherapy – in all these circles the name Reich comes up again and again.

Reich is the guru of the body. He formulated all manner of theories around the body's energy, the orgasm and what he calls the process of the body's armouring.

Reich, an ex-student of Freud and a respected psychoanalyst, experimented on the cutting edge of energy work in the 1930s and 40s. Reich was a radical; some would say he was the archetypal mad scientist. He built 'orgone accumulator' machines which collected energy and also conceived of a 'cloud busting' device (since iconised by Kate Bush) which would harness thunderstorms. Reich understood that some kind of universal energy pulsed through every living creature on earth. He saw the heartbeat as the basic energy movement; he identified the self as merely a flow of energy and point of consciousness. If energy stops flowing and becomes blocked, he reasoned, it can become deadly.

John demonstrated to us how to 'energise' a part of the body by using the three 'keys' of movement, breath and voice. He shook, blew on and made a loud *ahh*ing-sound close to one of his hands. Exposing his hand to these forms of energy, he explained, would 'charge' it up.

So we tried it. I shook my right hand for several minutes, then blew on it and used my voice without inhibition, making a loud guttural sound. Yes. My right hand felt more electric and alive. We then experimented with trying to bring the 'charged' hand closer to the non-charged hand. There seemed to be some kind of resistance, a magnetic field around the charged hand, making it hard to press the two hands together.

John then talked of the 'energy body', a kind of second invisible body which interpenetrates the visible body, and at the same time expands beyond it, a type of forcefield if you like, a micro-field of energy which pulsates around the visible body. Each of us stood upright while two others 'swept' the energy around us up from our feet to our head. Those doing the sweeping made gigantic fanning motions using their hands like wings, fluttering the energy surrounding the body up in great circular movements. The effect was convincing: I could feel a stir of energy around me. My body tingled, yet I hadn't moved a muscle. John then explained that energy is formless. Energy can enter the body and 'take form' in an emotion, such as anger. We can *give* energy a form. We can take an action with no single particular charge, and give it a charge.

'The self is independent from form, from energy,' he said. Practising tantra is to practise using energy differently, to be conscious of energy and to know how to use it, to *choose*, if you like.

'Tantra is a bid for freedom beyond attachment,' John further explained. By this, he meant freedom from past patterns of behaviour. I thought of my ex. I couldn't get unattached. There was a way to change this, thank God. But it took some practice.

We next played a game where we were invited to 'jump' in and out of various forms of emotion. Anger, joy, fear. We ran around the room in a formless state and when he named an emotion, we jumped into it, as if trying on a suit. We howled and screamed and cried and laughed as we tried out our different 'forms' of expression, consciously choosing to turn our energy into these forms of emotion.

I wanted to know more. I'd never considered that by bringing greater awareness to how I used my energy I could change the way I behaved; I could, in fact, *choose* how to behave. All of a sudden I was on edge. I liked my flawed and crooked self. It suited me to be unconsciously motivated. I was wounded, and, as a writer, I had an excuse to remain ignorant. I was blind, intentionally, because I wanted to turn the darkness in me into prose. I wanted to remain a working writer, not banish my ghosts; I wanted to be an alchemist of sorts, to turn the shadow into art, into something which might be worth passing on to others. But this new information about energy was explained in such a rational way, it didn't scare me off.

the poster boys

Tantra has its small but quite well-defined canon of Western literature. Along with George Feuerstein, men like Daniel Odier, Ken Wilber and David Deida are its academic poster boys. These men, mostly American, have all studied various types of yoga, tantra and Eastern meditation techniques. In the mid-1980s, Ken Wilber was linked to the now deceased and some would say criminal (others would say evil) Adi Da Samraj, a self-styled guru living in a Jonestown-type community in Fiji: Wilber has, since 1996, publicly distanced himself from Da. Wilber and Deida are Western men of ideas and together they have investigated and merged Eastern and Western scholarship and teachings in order to address, amongst other things, the age-old conundrum of modern Western male-female relationships. These men take the subject of the human heart seriously. Not only are they friends, but both men are prolific writers and thinkers. Deida is a co-founding member of Ken Wilber's progressive think tank, the Integral Institute. As far as I can see, the Integral Institute (based mostly in cyberspace), is a super-modern and well-organised version of the ancient model of philanthropic school of thought. It is an attempt to collectivise and spread an integrated working ideology as a working map or key to figuring out life's big questions.

Wilber, a brilliant scholar, was married for five years and lost his wife to cancer. In the grief of the aftermath, he locked himself away for three years and did nothing except figure out his Theory of Everything. Wilber gets my vote because he knows about the loss of love. In his autobiographical *Grace and Grit*, which he co-wrote with his dying wife, he says: 'Real love hurts; real love makes you totally vulnerable and open; real love will take you far beyond yourself; and therefore real love will devastate you.'

Wilber, like the scholar C.S. Lewis, who also lost his wife to cancer, is a man who loved and lost and his great cleverness was no defence. He was taken down and, like all of us, had to face his own self-resurrection.

David Deida, on the other hand, is best known for his workshops on sexuality and his work with men and male sexuality. Also an ex-devotee of Adi Da, his most famous book is the irksome (to any feminist) and portentously titled *The Way of the Superior Man*.

Deida, it seems to me, has had a single good idea about the present sex war. Deida feels that men and women have become too similar, too homogenous, and thus the sexual polarity between them has disappeared. In the 1960s and 70s men never did any 'work' of their own to catch up with the feminists. Two generations on, he says masculinity is in need of a rethink. Men, especially sensitive middle class men, get pussy-whipped and hen-pecked and have become an army of broken men. Men who work with David Deida do so because they want to do this 'work'; they want to re-identify themselves; they want to re-establish a new archetypal status on this earth. They go, in a way, to try and find a new path for themselves, so they can move forward with their modern female counterparts. This, he says, is going forward into a Third Stage. Deida, it could be said, is leading the way in trying to make men better for women and women better for men. In doing so, he wants to re-establish some of that old chemistry between men and women. He is *not* trying to get men to go backwards; but he is trying to encourage men (and women) to retrieve a core dynamic that was lost when women rose up and fought for equal rights. This core dynamic is our sexual attraction for one another.

the ugly man

Summer, 2008. By then I'd attended just two tantra workshops. I went to parties. I met men. They were uninteresting to me. They were either too vocal or too stale and set in their singledom, or too promiscuous. Most worked on the assumption that women *always* wanted 'more'; some assumed relationships were a trap. Was this what happened to people in their forties? Were we all jaded from love? Time and again, out there in the dating game, I met with dispirited men, and dispirited women, too. I knew people who'd been single for *years*, maybe even a decade. I knew people who'd been celibate for years, too, and not by choice. I knew people (mostly men) who didn't want to get involved, who said they 'weren't ready', that they couldn't commit – *to what*, I often screamed inside, *you egomaniacal prick*. Who, in God's name, decided that men are strong on matters of the heart and women are weak? I kept meeting people who'd somehow ground to a halt in their own love and sexual life. People who were dried up and half-dead. They were pre-occupied with 'not getting hurt' again.

At one party that summer, I met such a man, a man who'd been around forever on the West London scene. This was how the conversation went:

'How are you?' I asked.

'Okay.'

'How's things, love, sex, seeing anyone?'

'No, I keep myself to myself these days. I'd rather be alone than seeing someone.'

'Why?'

'Women want too much. They all want kids. I already have kids.'

'Really? I don't. So, how do you survive? What do you do for sex?'

'I'm celibate at the moment.'

Moment? I could tell this was a fib, that he'd been celibate for years, that his sexuality was stuck. He'd be lucky if *any* women fancied him at all, he emitted as much glow as a 20-watt pearl bulb. He was making his celibacy seem like his own choice.

'I've been going to workshops,' I tried.

A blank stare.

'Men and women can take each other to God, you know, a higher realm, during sex.'

He began to look shifty, like he wanted to escape.

'Tantra workshops.'

He paled.

I didn't continue. He moved off quickly. I stared into the bottom of my plastic cup of cheap merlot. *Great*. The word 'tantra' tends to dry up a conversation instantly; even a boring one.

I'd been frustrated with my London life before. So much so, that in 1997, when I'd recovered from a horrible auto-immune illness called Churg-Strauss Syndrome, I packed up my belongings and left town. I went to the Middle East and taught English for a year in East Jerusalem. I couldn't stand the feeling of waiting around for my life to begin; the type of people I had found myself mixing with suppressed my spirits and de-activated my creativity. So I departed, looking for other pastures. That summer of 2008, I was in a similar funk: gripped with self-righteous indignation, bordering on depression.

In June 2008, I was invited to teach a school group, some talented sixth-formers, at The Hurst for Arvon. My co-tutor was the poet and writer Tobias Hill. I'd never met Tobias during my time at Arvon. But I had heard lots about him from the other (female) centre directors, especially how dishy he was. Tobias, from his press pics, resembles Mr Rochester. Pale-skinned and dark and tall and handsome. But I was determined not to like him too much; I was sure he'd be posh and aloof and maybe even jaded, just like the other men I was meeting.

I was wrong. Tobias was really nice. Shy and nice and clever – and married.

I didn't think I fancied him at all, not at first. But then, after a couple of days, I began to think, *okay – so he's cute*. Yes, okay, I can see what the other female centre directors meant. Yes, okay – Tobias Hill is handsome and – okay – I was just about to start *fancying* Tobias Hill, when my ex rocked up as the guest reader for the week.

In our new era of peace, I'd suggested him for the spot. A performer, he'd be perfect for the kids: he'd entertain them and give us the night off. And he did read a very funny story about a posh dinner party hosted by a couple called Mungo and Katinka Needam – and mimicked all the snooty accents all the way through. While the children had sat politely through the readings Tobias and I had given the evening before, they sat rapt as my ex minced around and bellowed and ranted, giving a performance that would have blown away a packed auditorium. He mashed the place up and stirred up the kids.

'Children can't tell jokes,' he teased during the Q and A after his reading.

'Oh yes we can,' they raged.

'Rubbish, no they can't.'

Yeah, he got them all in a tizzy over that. He even managed to *sell* them his books, a rare feat to a group of disaffected yout'.

'See what my life was like?' I whispered to Tobias.

I found myself sitting behind him, on the sofa, with Tobias. Again, against my will, I was downcast. Also happy and dizzy – because my heart was still with the ugly man. No matter how handsome Tobias Hill was, my heart belonged to the uglier man.

I had loved a monster.

I loved a monstrous man with all my heart.

I had tried everything to shake off this feeling.

♥

In July 2008, there was another setback. I was deranged with boredom. Restless for sex, for adventure of any kind. A voracious longing for my old life took hold. Yes, I was moving forward and yet there was a new wave of being drawn back. I was still pestered by memories of this old way of being. I wanted to be loved again, like I had been. *Oh,* how I'd been loved and fuck, was I furious with being so unloved and having to mix and try to flirt with the dead-eyed men of West London.

In the years of my singledom I had formed a trio with two men, both friends of twenty years, Chris Neale and Sean Thomas. Our trio had formed by accident, after one summer barbeque in 2007 at Chris's house in Shepherd's Bush. After everyone else had left, we went out and got drunk. First there was Soho House, where we drank margaritas and almost ripped the pool table to shreds. We were so addled by cocktails we stumbled out without paying the bill. Then there was a lap-dancing club. We drank buckets of gin. I came home and fell into bed fully clothed, still in my shoes, and woke up in the same clothes clutching a plastic lemon squeezer.

That July summer night in 2008, the three of us went out drinking and it happened again. We got messy, inebriated. Chris got talking to some young blonde women, leaving Sean and me at the bar.

Sean and I were both single; we'd known each other for over twenty years. I got it into my head that it was time for us to kiss. The last time we'd met at the Groucho Club, he'd come over all amorous and kissed me on the stomach while we were sitting on a sofa. I figured he might like to try it on the lips.

'*Kiss* me,' I dared.

His face froze.

Casual sex dating sites, tantric sex, I think I thought I could do anything with anyone. I could take on all comers, even Sean, who I knew had a very . . . well, let's say rich and varied sex life.

'No,' he said flatly.

'Just here, on the lips,' I pointed to my lips.

'No.'

'Why on earth not?'

'Because I love you.' He whispered this in a drunken slur.

'Oh, piss off.'

We kissed. Sort of. Well, Sean was pretty, er, hesitant. He kissed me like he would kiss a hirsute midget.

Then, yes, dear reader – I did it. I went for the flies on his jeans. I was sure he'd be hard after kissing me, a hot vixen. And I was hot. Hot and mad. A tiny bit drunker and I'd have thrown myself on my knees and buried my head in his crotch there at the bar. Oh, *God*. I unzipped him and pressed my hand to his groin.

But he wasn't hard.

He raised his eyebrows.

I stared up into his face.

It only just dawned on me that he *wasn't* overwhelmed with lust. I got cross and hissy. I left the bar in an almighty huff. I weaved across the busy main road and fell into a taxi and when I got home I staggered through my flat, tearing off my clothes, leaving them in small piles behind me.

I woke to find the little castles of clothes all over my flat. I woke to the feeling that I might actually be unable to be happy again in this life.

I'd gone mad.

I knew Sean would phone or make contact at some point over the weekend. But he didn't.

By Sunday night I was deranged with mortification. I emailed Sean, who pretended that he couldn't remember a thing.

That July night was a turning point. I rang Jan Day and asked for help. She offered to give me twelve counselling sessions to help 'integrate into my life' what I'd been learning with her in the tantra workshops. I readily accepted. Help. At last. I needed help *again*.

end of act one

In August 2008, I went to teach for the first time at the Writer's Lab in Skyros. I had a blast. A fun and talented group of aspiring writers to teach, some of whom became friends. Free room and board, excellent powder sand beaches. I was graced with the company of a vivacious and accomplished colleague in the form of Dina Glouberman, the founder of Skyros. A litter of kittens was born in Dina's cupboard: it was a sign. Then I had a very powerful dream: our black cat Daphne, the one who'd disappeared, was alive and well. She appeared in my bedroom, her coat glossy. She jumped onto my bed and purred up to me; she had come to visit me to reassure me she was safe. I felt comfortable in this kind of set-up, and I felt loved again. It was Arvon-by-the-beach – with souvlaki thrown in. I came home refreshed. I was okay again.

There was a younger man in Skyros; everyone fancied him. At a barbeque on the beach we flirted and briefly kissed on the lips. But I had a sudden and weird hunch about him. He reminded me of someone.

'What's your birthday?' I asked out of the blue.

'Fourteenth of March,' he replied.

'Oh, shit!'

'What?'

I stared. I was right; I could even guess the date of birth of the type of man I was attracted to. My ex was born on 14 March. What hope was there for me? At the time I'd also made friends with another man, a writing student; I was aware I found him attractive, too. He was also born on 14 March. Creepy.

In my diary I wrote:

I feel like a widow, the family curse. I will always miss X. The Song of Solomon. I am sick from loving him. I am alone on this earth without him. I am like the woman in the song. Wanting to go out and find him in the city, asking 'where is he', panic-stricken.

I thought about the woman who'd sent me those emails, two and a half years earlier. I decided to write her a letter:

To the woman who sent me those emails,
Never approach me. Never make the mistake of coming near me. If you do, I will unleash a fury upon you. You did a villainous thing. You ruined my life. I hope you are living a sorry and miserable life.

I never sent this letter. Two days later, on 12 August 2008, something terrible happened.

The phone rang.

It was Mike, the removals man who'd driven me and my belongings to the flat a year earlier. Mike, who'd said he'd keep safe half my worldly possessions. When I'd moved in with Emma and Matthew, the flat was just too small to fit everything in. I didn't know how long I'd stay, so I hit on the idea of storing what I couldn't bring with me. When I asked Mike if he had storage space, he said yes. I had to choose there and then what to leave behind with him. It was this:

Furniture, including a Chesterfield sofa covered in crimson poppies

A library of books

Boxes of old manuscripts

Papers and boxes of precious letters

A hatbox full of handmade linen and lace made by my great grandmother

Family heirlooms

Treasure collected over the last ten years of living and travelling

Svend Bayer stoneware pottery collected during my time in Sheepwash

Ten years worth of photo albums, many stuffed full of pictures of me and my ex.

'I'm afraid I have bad news, the worst,' Mike said.

'What's that?'

'There's been a fire.'

'Oh.' My heart went cold.

'I'm afraid everything has gone.'

'What do you mean, *everything*?'

'It's all gone. Nothing is left. Two trailers have been destroyed. One of them was yours.'

'Everything?'

'Yes.'

I hung up the phone. I sat down on a chair. I didn't sob straight away. I just sat and stared. It wasn't possible immediately to comprehend what had happened. That all those precious and valuable things had vanished. Torched, destroyed by fire and made into nothing. They'd disappeared back into the cosmos. Everything I'd collected all my life, parts of me, all gone. I'd been an avid amateur photographer. I'd never wanted a digital camera. I liked the old way of film and photography. I had, over the last decade, meticulously put together, with almost a documentary approach, the pictoral story of my life. My photo albums were substantial, fat and leather-bound. Four alone contained the photo-story of my life with my ex.

I rang my ex.

It was then I sobbed. He was upset, too. On many evenings he'd watched me pasting photos of our adventures into those big albums. He didn't cry. I wailed. Then I put the phone down.

I was pestered with images of those photos for months afterwards. I still am today. Unlike many people who never look at their photo albums, I used to take great pleasure in gazing at them. I have many of those photos in my head because I used to look at them so often. I still get flashes of these pictures from time to time. I wasn't able to use a camera or take a photograph for a couple of years, not until I went back to Skyros in 2010.

The fire signified the end of an era. The end of a time, not just the end of the affair with my ex, but the end of Act One of my life. I no longer own photographic evidence to prove that I have had a life before the age of forty. It's all gone.

Fire destroys. But it also purifies. Fire had transformed all I had treasured back into pure energy. All of my past had turned to ash and fluttered away. I had set fire to those emails from that woman.

I was low-spirited for days, weeks, after the fire. But, in the end, I came to see that all we are is energy anyway. One day, I will vanish too; my ashes will flutter away. That fire was the first step to understanding all that I was learning with Jan Day and John Hawken: what it means to be truly free, to live without attachment.

THE STONES

'Love is a matter of inner nature, not relationship . . .
love is a state of being. It is an inner component
of one's individuality'

Osho

♥

the festival in spain

On the August Bank Holiday, 2008, Rose and I flew out to Reus, a small town in Southern Spain. Our destination was an International Tantra Festival, which was to be held in the pine-forested hills above and behind the city of Barcelona. I'd almost cancelled the trip. The deadline for my PhD in creative writing was at the end of September. My life's possessions had burnt down. I was in no mood for a festival and I didn't think I could spare the time. But it was a past tutor and mentor who talked me round, saying I deserved the break, that it would be impossible to settle to work straight after the fire. She was right.

As the taxi drove us up into the hills we caught glimpses of the house where the festival-goers would be living for the week. Gaudi-esque multi-coloured onion domes flashed at us from the pine trees.

'Jesus,' I whispered.

The house was an eccentric millionaire's bauble, one of his many homes, no doubt, dotted over the world. The estate consisted of three buildings: the turreted main house, a rustic *finca*-style residence higher up in the forest and, near the finca, set back a little into the forest, a round and spacious 'temple' with a vaulted ceiling.

'*Wow,*' gasped Rose, when we were dropped off.

Yes. Wow. The main house was imposing and outlandish: colourful harlequin-style domes and Disney spires, curlicued

Moorish windows. One turret was choked with climbing ivy; tall sculpted pines nestled behind it.

We met Edwyn, the co-director of the festival, at the door. He was posh and roguishly handsome and covered in tattoos. Originally from Willesden, he was an acrobat and tantrika, boyfriend of Astiko, a willowy, fit, forty-something blonde woman, one of the festival's main tantra teachers. John Hawken was the star attraction. It was through John that we'd heard of the festival at all.

In my diary I wrote: *Coming here – possibly a mistake. The place is very weird. Those into self-development always talk about their 'stuff', which is a generic term for having unresolved personal problems. They always talk about needing to do 'the work' (a frame of reference the mystic Gurdjieff invented). They talk about their 'needs' a lot too, which feels unrealistic and selfish – considering half the world needs running water. They need a good thump in the head, that's what they 'need'. They could do with reading Moby Dick, David Copperfield, or Emily Dickinson. That would cheer them up. Lots of people are still reverent and loyal to Osho. As usual, I'm the only quizzical soul here. Amazing how no one questions him: quite likely these people never read a newspaper, as if they don't care to find out what the whole world knows about him.*

It was at the festival that I saw my first person wearing a *mala*. A mala is a large wooden beaded necklace that followers of Osho were given, along with their new sannyasin name. My friend, the author Tim Guest, who died in August 2009, got sent his in the post, along with his new name, Yogesh, at the age of four. The pendant of the mala was an oval-shaped locket; inside the locket, a black and white picture of the smiling Osho. Orange clothes (orange being the colour worn by ascetic Hindu holy men) and a mala were the sannyasin's uniform. The mala-wearer in question was a big burly Spanish man, not too friendly looking; he had some bongo drums and seemed to be part of the Spanish contingent. Could someone really be wearing a mala with a picture of Osho, eighteen years after his death? Could anyone be that ignorant of all Osho's wrongdoings? I glared. Yes, this big burly Spanish man was wearing a mala. Good grief. I couldn't tear my eyes from him.

devotion to one master

The Spanish festival was full of Osho-ites. Astiko, the teacher, had also spent time with Osho in Pune. Devoting yourself to a master? Submitting yourself to the ideas of one man? Every cell of my body screams that this is wrong. Over half the world is run by unelected governments; violence of the most extreme kind is perpetrated by all these states on their citizens with impunity. Half the world's population lives in appalling poverty, ground down by dictators who give them no freedom to think for themselves.

In Europe, where we have a healthy disregard for extremists and fanatics, men like Osho struggle to exist. But in the East and in the USA these men, be they TV evangelists, 'plastic' native American shamans, or similar self-styled gurus, can and do survive and teach all manner of crossbred ideas. They live in the desert, they set up think tanks online, they re-name themselves and they sell their supposedly new ideas in the form of workshops and courses to anyone seeking knowledge and understanding. Wilhelm Reich and the orgasm, Osho and sexual love, David Deida and men and women, Harley SwiftDeer and his Deer Tribe; I was beginning to put together a lineage of twentieth-century all-*male* mavericks who teach sex. Of course the subject of sex would attract mavericks, but it is more than a little spooky that all these teachers are men.

Western tantra, wherever it is taught – be it in the UK, California or Europe, is almost exclusively taught by ex-students of Osho or students of his students. My main conflict with it? I don't wish to align myself with the thinking of any one man, ever, no matter who he is. And yet, clearly, I'd been having some of the most stretching and thought-provoking times of my life while working with these teachers, these followers of Osho. I was benefiting from the work passed down from this self-appointed guru.

the man with the crotchety leg

There were fifty or sixty people at this festival. The group expanded and shrunk according to the rag-tag caravan of performers who joined each night, mostly circus friends of Edwyn's. There were young and not-so-young hippie women, some loving couples, lots of Beta males, ex-Pune sannyasins, mad Germans. The Spanish pot-smoking tantrikas were also bananas; sexy, too. There were a few obligatory Czech beauties, tantra being big in the Czech Republic. Everyone made an effort to make themselves understood and many of the workshops were interpreted from English into Spanish or vice versa.

Early on, we were thrown into the usual games and structures. In one particular structure, all the men (the Shivas) made a large circle on the outer edge of the temple. They sat cross-legged on the floor. The women (the Shaktis) sat in a circle opposite them. John gave us a number of breathing techniques and exercises to do together, using the chakras. At every new exercise, the Shivas moved around three or four places to the right.

Then John announced we'd do an exercise about 'being held'. All the men, he explained, would each hold a woman in his arms, hold her as he would his lover, wife, daughter or friend, hold her with the love and faith and goodness in his open heart, hold her on behalf of *all men*. This didn't sound too alarming at first. The men shifted around three places. I found myself facing a rather odd-looking Spanish man called Paco. He was very square in the body, podgy in the belly. One leg was stiff and he didn't seem to be able to bend it, so when he sat down his leg stuck out to one side. He had a strange way of looking at me too; he peered, rather fiercely, as if he wasn't quite sure what to make of me. He didn't speak a word of English. When John gave the signal that we Shaktis should moved forward and allow ourselves to be held, this strange awkward-looking man held open his arms.

Tears welled before I even moved. Tears abseiled down my cheeks, just seeing this man opening his arms to hold me. I inched forward. Paco peered at me. We locked eyes. I was surprised to find my body softening. I curled my back towards him, like a cat, in order to nestle into his embrace. He wrapped his arms around me. They were warm and strong. I sighed. It was soft and sad there. His embrace tightened. He rocked me in his arms and whispered tender Spanish words

215

into my ears, words I couldn't understand. He held me and rocked me and even sang a little song, and I felt tiny and found myself weeping. I'd never, until then, been held like this. Not by a man.

I didn't even realise that I'd never been held like that. I didn't know. My father? Never. Boyfriends? No. Not even my ex, not that I can remember.

Once, maybe once, aged twenty-eight, when I answered the telephone to my hysterical mother, shouting down the line that my father had died and that I should fly home. Only then was I held like that by a man. His name was Tom Ingoldby and he was my flatmate at the time; in the mid-90s we shared a tiny but homely flat in Kensal Rise. Tom was awake when I answered the phone, past midnight. One minute I was sobbing at the news, the next I was being enveloped in Tom's arms. Tom was a big man, over six foot; he had arms like oak limbs. Yes, I think Tom Ingoldby is the only man I can ever remember holding me in that way, and it was at a time of dire emergency. Which, of course, begs the question: had I ever *let myself* be held? And if not, why not?

massage

The next day we practised breath work using the pelvic floor. Synchronised breathing in and out through the first and second chakras while rocking the pelvis is, apparently, very good for stirring up your sexual energy. This, indeed, enlivened the lower half of me, and I found myself in a heated embrace with Adam, a young man with blue eyes and strawberry-blond curls. That day we did some '5Rhythms' dancing too, a spiritual dance practice. After lunch, while Rose had a tantric tango lesson, I took myself off to visit Karsten, the resident masseur.

Karsten was tall and blond, German and dreamy-eyed; he floated around in his vest and sarong looking suitably tantric. He offered two types of massage: 'holistic' massage and 'tantric' massage. He'd described the difference between the two: holistic massage was a regular full-bodied massage; tantric massage was the same except attention was paid to every part of the body, including the genitals. I nodded breezily, while my stomach knotted. *Did he say genitals?* At that point, no man had ever searched for my G-spot, let alone massaged my genitals. Both were new ideas I liked the sound of – a lot.

Karsten's massage parlour was in fact a small cubicle in what must have once been the servants' block on the estate. Despite my curiosity, I'd firmly decided on a non-tantric massage. Instinct? Yes. I wanted to work up to the Full Monty, what is also called (for women) a yoni massage.

When I turned up, Karsten had prepared the space.

'We will both be naked,' Karsten explained in the matter of fact way the Germans are famous for. Germans and nudity. Here I was again, allowing myself to be relaxed, pretending to be casual about sex in the Nordic hot tubs and saunas sort of way. I couldn't decide if I was being an utter twat, ridiculously *not* myself, somehow not the least bit Mon, or whether I was being the reallest and deepest most natural me. If, in fact, somewhere underneath, I was a born nudist.

Either way, Karsten and I did Namastes. I was a Western anti-hippie. In the past, I had even hated festivals. Again, I wondered, what on *earth* was I doing? Namaste? Me?

We Namaste-ed and then I lay down on my stomach, naked, and shut my eyes. Karsten was a tall, well-built man. Soon, his hands were on me. Through glimpses, I was aware of his smooth lingam close to my ears, neck, face. He rubbed oils into my skin. Incense was burning. Soft music played in the background. Soon I was loosed from all connected thoughts. I hovered on the brink of sheer relaxation and erotic dream. His hands kneaded my hands, my fingers, neck, back, legs, then turned me over. His hands were on my thighs, breasts, face. In the East they get this so right and use it in the every day. Ceremony. Ritual. In a situation like this, so intimate and yet so boundaried, something happens between two people. Trust happens.

I'm glad that I chickened out of having a full tantric massage experience first time round. Because something hard to define happened between me and Karsten that first time together. Small and unusual communications between us. Moans, sighs. He was tending to me. He was demonstrating his ability, his agility with his hands, his loving touch, his method, his expertise. He knew what he was doing; I was in good hands. Yes. By the end of the hour and a half session I knew I would come back for more.

el lobo

John Hawken is a man with many tricks up his sleeve. He gave us lots of games to play, usually in the evenings. The most spectacular, which he called The Garden of Delights, was spread over two days. This was to be tantric sex meets the Olde English country fayre, a chance for the Shaktis and Shivas to offer a fair of stalls, each stall offering a sexual pleasure. It was an ingenious idea. Immediately, everyone got into a tizzy over trying to decide what to do, especially the women, as the Shaktis went first.

Rose and I decided to do a stall called Feathers and Ferns which involved caressing men with peacock feathers and, well, long ferns. Fairly tame, I know. Next to us was the delectable tantra-orientated dominatrix, Jasmine: stilettos, fishnets, corset, fretted suede whip in hand. The Spanish male tantrikas queued for a whipping, or what they called 'an English type of sex'. There were 'the beach girls': one svelte beauty teased and paraded about in a bikini and beach umbrella while the other lavished caresses and kisses on their male customer. There were all kinds of massages. All kinds of teasing and touching and sucking and caressing, even foot-washing; everything except full-blown intercourse.

Night fell. We were entertained by a man with holy orange robes who'd spent many years living in a remote cave in India with only monkeys for company. An Indian-style circus performer. He entered the temple with a crystal ball balancing on his bald head. He enthralled us for at least an hour with that ball, gliding it over every part of his body with grace and ease, so much so he roused the onlookers to a standing ovation.

The next day it was the men's turn to offer their sexual pleasures. We Shaktis were kept away from the temple as the men prepared themselves for us. The buzz and laughter coming from the temple made us all nervous and excited. There was a whiff of competition in the air. It was charming and mysteriously unnerving to witness men almost giddily preparing to entice a group of women.

When we entered the spacious dome-shaped hall there they were: thirty or so men waiting to pleasure us. They wore sarongs and feathers and flowers and each had carefully staked out his stall, his patch of the fairground. Ivan, our surfer roommate, had paired up with a doe-eyed man to offer 'chest-ecstasy' – a stall where women would have only their breasts caressed by two handsome men. There was a man named Jesus, naked, offering his speciality – arousal by his breath. There was Appi, a colossal Spanish man with long hair who offered shamanic 'healing'. There were two English men, Jon and Andrew, with whom Rose and I had become friends, offering every type of touch going; they were garlanded and crowned with flowers and grinned mischievously. There were two men with turbans who had a whip, both resembling panto 'Orientals', the idea being that you confessed your sins to the bigger, fatter one, the holier one, and the other carried out the punishment.

My first stop was El Lobo. El Lobo was a Spanish man called Tony. He was squatting, completely naked, grinning like a wolf. In front of him was a simple sign which had caught my imagination. It read:

I WILL DEVOUR YOU SLOWLY

I laughed. Tony growled in response. I was wearing a sarong. I laid myself down on my stomach, not knowing what to expect. Tony pounced. He began at my feet, growling and biting and kissing and snarling and slavering. My reaction surprised me. It surprises me even now, as I write. I *squealed* with delight. I writhed and laughed and shuddered and laughed and squealed even more – and *adored* every minute of it. Tony, as promised, devoured me slowly, eating his way up my legs, nibbling and chomping his way to my buttocks, my back, eating my waist, my breasts, my arms, my legs, every part of me. And I was apoplectic with pleasure. I howled and chortled and laughed and wailed and fake-protested and mock-thrashed with terror which was in fact pure rapture. I visited other stalls, of course, but none as surprising and joyful as El Lobo.

eating the cook

That night, the last night, an 'aphrodisiac's feast' was held in the temple. We were blindfolded and fed tidbits by the young Spanish kitchen staff, sushi and tiny parcels of food on cocktail sticks. Food was passed from mouth to mouth, kisses stolen here and there. By then, the small group of English people had given up trying to speak any kind of comprehensible Spanish and stuck together. We weren't supposed to talk through the meal, but we chatted and giggled anyway. I was glad I'd made it through the week. I was bruised and sore and dirty and had enjoyed myself enormously. I hadn't thought about my ex much: he was a festival man, but would have hated this one. Thinking about the fire which burnt my belongings didn't bring an immediate stab of pain; even the fire which had burnt those letters, years before, seemed distant. Now I was a 'conscious seeker' in the field of love and sex and relationships. It felt like a new job.

There was a commotion in the centre of the hall.

Was I seeing right?

A man was being carried in, on the shoulders of some of the cooks from the kitchen. He was brown and glistening. I stared, trying to train my eyes to see correctly. Yes. He *was* glistening – with *chocolate*. His body was prone, arms held outwards as if preparing for a crucifixion. His torso was laden with fruit. Mangoes and peaches, pears and strawberries. Blueberries. A majestic Himalaya of whipped cream rose up along the centre of his body, from neck to navel. His cock was decorated with baubles of passion fruit, cherries, meringue puffs, purple pansies. The second course was announced. Him. The young cook was dessert.

The chocolate man was placed on a plinth on the floor of the temple. Within moments the diners, almost all female, fell on him. We English women were too flabbergasted to move at first. The cook had been both on the outskirts of and some-times part of the week's events; he was lovely looking and had a spiky hairdo. He had seemed sweet and shy; we'd all noticed him. We watched as the Spanish tantrikas gobbled at him, their heads down like a pack of hounds. Abegan, a Jack Nicholson look-alike and ex-sannyasin, laughed.

'My girlfriend is eating the cook's *prick*!' he exclaimed.

I watched, a little baffled and curiously immobile. It hadn't quite dawned on me yet to join in. It was too much of a spec-tacle: this young man being devoured by a pack of females. It was funny, too. Women's faces were smudged and smeared with chocolate. They fought over pieces of fruit, over who would eat what. And then it happened: then I was *in* the hungry cook-eating gang. On hands and knees. Bum in the air. I don't know how I got there. All I know is that one minute I was gazing at the sight, enthralled; the next, I was part of it, my head buried in his chocolatey loins. Rose and our other new English friends were with me. They laughed as I came up for air. I'd been licking chocolate off the cook's firm stomach.

'What?' I gasped.

'Your face!' they hooted.

'What about it?'

'You look drunk,' said Jasmine.

'Evil,' said Jon.

I don't know what I looked like. I guessed that my face, chest and hands were slick with brown muddy chocolate.

life is sex

On the last day of the festival, I made my way to Karsten's makeshift massage parlour. It was set back from the temple, somewhat derelict, surrounded by a bed of fallen pine needles. He occupied the end cubicle and something which resembled a sacred space had been prepared: figurines of the Buddha, flowers in a vase, incense burning. A mat and a towel were laid on the floor. This time, when Karsten and I did Namastes, I was in a very different mood. I was calm and ready for the full tantric massage.

I lay down on the towel and he went to work on my back and shoulders and legs. Weeks of my life fell away. The fire, what was lost. My ex, what had gone wrong. I closed my eyes. Karsten's hands were on me. Insistent, careful. They massaged these worries out of my consciousness. The body holds memory, holds trauma in its cells, or that's the theory held by many. And it feels more than just a tenuous idea.

Reading those emails and letters over two years earlier. The outing of an affair in such a toxic way. *I have something to tell you.* The horror of those words ... *I'm just with Mon for career reasons.* The months of numbness which followed. I hadn't really cried. I'd been struck numb, had ploughed all my energies into writing a novel. Where else was the shock and dismay of these events stored than somewhere deep in my body?

Tears fell as Karsten massaged me. By the time he turned me over, my face was damp. It was the first time since the letter bomb that anyone had touched me so thoroughly. His hands delved the tissues of me. A deep sympathy and generosity shone in his eyes, in his whole demeanour. He was naked. So was I. Then I was on my back. We gazed into each other's eyes. He massaged my stomach, breasts, arms and more tears came. He pulled me closer and wrapped my legs around his waist. He began the final part of the massage, the yoni massage, on my hips and inner thighs, massaging the muscles in slow circular movements, massaging away what was stored there, stroking and caressing the entire area. His thumbs and hands moved rhythmically. We watched each others' faces. He inched closer. It was tense and sexy.

In such intimate moments, the heart opens: I wanted to love this man. But I didn't. He was almost a stranger. He inched closer. His fingers massaged my pubic bone, my entire vulva. I smiled. It was easy. My legs wanted to open wide. I shifted, parting my thighs. He shifted. I was open. Open wide. He smiled. I smiled. His fingers explored me. Bliss as his fingers began to massage my clitoris. I opened wider still. His fingers moved in slow circular movements. Groans escaped me. Sadness, the sweet melancholia of sexual release. The melancholia held within me for over two years. Tears and ecstasy. My hips lifted up off the floor. It was almost unbearable not to be penetrated there and then. This was *the time*, the moment every woman arrives at when the foreplay is good. The 'fuck me right now' moment. The moment when she will die if she isn't penetrated.

The massage had turned into a sexual act. This was expert foreplay. But Karsten didn't even come close to fucking me; I don't think it even crossed his mind, even though my body was tender and open, and thrust before him in a way that begged for a physical coupling, the most natural conclusion to what we'd been doing – the massage had been going on for hours now. Hours of this tenderness, hours of this nakedness. I was beyond myself.

He changed his method to long strokes up and down. I opened even wider. My back arched. I'd never been pleasured by a man so seamlessly. Until then, only *I* had ever been able to do this for myself. I fought the urge to join him, guide him, as I had so many other men, to do it with him. But I trusted him. And he needed no guidance. He continued with his slow deft strokes. I squirmed and opened even wider, if that was possible. I got stuck in, as did he. If he wasn't going to fuck me, he could have me anyway. It was loving and open and crazy.

His fingers entered me. Long fingers delving up into the ridged place past the entrance to my yoni. He slid his fingers in and out and then his fingers touched the place in me where heaven resides, where heaven is guarded safely. He massaged this spot and our eyes locked and within moments my body gave of itself, a slow, dazed melting feeling and an orgasm washed through me unlike any other. I gasped and maybe even lost consciousness for a few moments. I lay there, out of myself, lost. Not tearful. Like I sometimes feel after a day spent by the sea. All the water leached from me. Like a tide had been drawn out of me, drawn out from the waters in me. Karsten got up and left the cubicle. He was well-endowed and I noticed he was semi-erect. When he came back, with two glasses of water, he lay down next to me. We gazed into each others' eyes.

'Fucking *hell*,' I whispered.

He caressed me.

'You're fucking incredible.'

He smiled. He knew.

'You have a gift for being open,' he said.

I nodded. I think, deep down, I knew this too.

'That was sex,' I said.

He nodded. 'All life is sex.'

'I wanted you to fuck me.'

'We can have sex now, if you like.'

'I don't think so. The moment has passed.'

He smiled.

We lay together on the floor of the cubicle for some time.

♥

On the last morning we said our goodbyes. Rose and I had made good friends in Jasmine and Jon. They were Londoners too, we knew we'd see them again. We spent the morning hugging and kissing our new Spanish friends. I avoided hugging John Hawken; his energetic tantric embrace could be hazardous. He'd hugged me once before, and left me charged up and volatile. I was due to do the second part of Energy and Consciousness with him in November 2008. I'd see him again. The young Spanish cook was group hugged.

Then I did something I've never done before, or since. Uninvited, I gave a man my phone number. I didn't wait till he asked, didn't even try to bring the conversation round, or vaguely offer it. Nothing coy. I went up to a man and thrust a piece of paper with my number and email address into his hand.

'Come and see me sometime in London,' I said. 'You'd be more than welcome to stay.'

Of course, that was Karsten.

How on earth would I return to my flat in Harlesden? I thought of my lunge at my friend Sean Thomas, the social torpor of my life in West London, how I was so restless without a companion. I thought of Paco, with his crotchety leg, holding me; Tony, El Lobo, devouring me; our roommate Ivan bringing us plums every morning. Karsten and his hands which could deliver me to heaven. How could I piece this into the story of my daily life, of the humdrum that awaited me? I wanted to digest it all, make sense of everything.

I needed help. And I was a lucky woman. Help was at hand back in London – waiting for me, in the form of Jan Day.

the second wisewoman

Before the fire and before the festival, I'd already rung Jan. I was expanding and learning so much in tantric workshops; but integrating these new ideas into my real life, into the modern Western world with its modern Western habits of being closed and defended, was proving difficult.

How was I to stay open to all these new experiences and

not lose my balance, or worse, get depressed, frustrated? For the next twelve weeks Jan and I spoke once a week via Skype. Her advice was solid. Here are some notes from the first five sessions:

1. I can have everything. My old life and the new life emerging. Don't devalue my old way of living. If I start to think that some of the things and people in my old life are now boring, look at this feeling of boredom in myself.

2. Intimacy is non-sexual. Make space in my being to take it *all* in, every person I meet, every leaf on every tree. Every encounter creates more space. Be in a world which includes everything, not just what I want.

3. The romantic love dynamic between adults should be adult-to-adult. She pointed out that my relationship with X was child-to-father. To change this dynamic is a long process. Notice which men trigger 'father feelings'. Personal growth means to change the places where I got stuck. Perhaps X served a good purpose.

4. Note to self: Purpose? Is that all we were to each other? I can see he was a father substitute – but more than that, too. He exists in his own power. He attracts many people to him. I mourn him for his own uniqueness.

5. Gently ask myself – would I do it again? What *wasn't* okay with X. How did X manage to deceive me? What clues in his past behaviour did he give me about who he really was?

6. With other men – look for the same clues. Look for

things you don't like – embrace them – so they don't have to hide them.

7. The goal of meditation is to be in the world fully. In deep meditation connection can made with both the material and spiritual world. We need one foot in each world.

There was more, a lot more. But this was the gist of things. Jan was guiding me through a process which I believe happens to us all, the thing Jung wrote a lot about: individuation. This is the process we all go through by dint of being alive in the world. We love, then love dies. We lose love. We grow older. We go on, in one way or another. We love again. But – with Jan – I felt I was interrupting the cycle right at this point. Next time round, I wanted to love differently.

♥

In October 2008, two men appeared in my life in the same week. The first was a writer, Luke, whom I met on an informal day of tantra between friends at Jasmine's house in Islington. The second was Pete, who worked in the film industry; I met Pete on a brief foray into the world of regular internet dating on Guardian Soulmates, on which I lasted all of three weeks.

Luke and Pete couldn't have been more different: Luke was dark, medium height, intellectual, mercurial, big into all the same kind of work as I was. He'd met Ken Wilber, had worked with David Deida, had done lots of 'men's work'. He had an interesting sexuality as a result. Luke was very much himself, very male and yet very open, soft; somehow there was a feminine quality to him. He was bloody brainy too, brainier than me.

Pete was shaven-headed, six foot, an amateur athlete, sat-urnalian in his demeanour. He was a skinhead from Coventry, metro-sexual, working class, a strange mix: big into cycling, astrology and bongos. Pete was effortlessly 'street'. While Luke was also edgy, with him it came from his intellect, his brain power; Luke was middle class. I don't think these two men would ever choose each other as friends.

'It would be a pity if you met another man right away,' said Jan. 'You've only just started this process.'

'But I *feel* different.'

'So enjoy this time. Experiment.'

She was right. A new growth spurt, gathering some new self-awareness, doesn't add up to an instant and fundamen-tal change in one's behaviour. It does, however, bring with it a sense of optimism. I remembered my first night in Demara's temple. *Things will be different.* That young man laid bare on the table, speechless with all the tender love he'd received. Jan, Demara, they had secrets. Becoming better at love was a new and worthy mission.

two dudes and a foolish old king

At the tantra day at Jasmine and Jon's, there'd been a number of intimate structures which included nudity. During one particular type of massage, I'd got naked with Luke, and so we'd got to know each other in a way we wouldn't if we'd spent the day at a barbeque or picnic. Over the course of the day, I came to think he was a bit out of the ordinary, a bit of a dude. We swapped numbers and a week after the workshop I invited him to a book launch in Brixton.

Luke turned up on crutches, a curious look. It was a spacious room and the book launch dissolved as we talked. We found a booth and quickly sank into a meaty conversation: books, love, tantra, working on the self. His injured leg rested on my knee. I rested one hand on it as we talked. Comfortable and easy, we were wrapped in each other's company and that thing happened when men and women engage in eye contact and descend into intimate conversation. Atoms started to whirr.

'We're having a moment,' he said at one point.

I stared. We kept talking. My stomach churned. I fancied the pants off Luke, but this took me by surprise. I baulked. *Notice which men trigger father feelings.* Answer: very clever men trigger father feelings. Here, a very clever man was doing just that. We kept talking – but I couldn't hear him properly. I was in some kind of space bubble.

Then, from out of the blue, he said something odd.

'No.'

'What?'

'Just no.'

'What do you mean, no?'

'You're making eyes at me.'

I must have been. That, or worse. Was the neglected child inside me leaping up and down? Was she proffering herself, her own heart, up to him? Could he already guess what effect his attentions were having on me? Did I look like a love-struck moron?

Jan was right. Things don't change overnight.

The conversation dried up. I didn't say much in reply; I only knew I needed to go, and quickly.

Even though he was injured, Luke drove me to the nearest tube and it was awkward for a few minutes as we exchanged pleasantries. It was a weird meeting. Good and then very bad. I thought he'd been a spectacular prat saying 'no' out of the blue; I thought he'd been the one making eyes at *me*, 'we're having a moment', not the other way round. I wanted to deliver an elbow to the thorax, club him around the face and chest, then run off. But instead I got out of his car and mumbled goodbye. I had Jan to report back to. But I *had* learnt something. It's the clever ones: really clever men bring out the child in me.

My father was a clever man. Always reading. For days he'd disappear, his head buried deep in a novel or biography. Funny how I've turned myself into a person who *writes* books, the very thing which so absorbed him, the thing that distracted him from noticing me. He died before he ever had a chance to read a book I wrote. It's not rocket science: in an attempt to get my father's attention, I make the very thing which blocked his view of me.

Stranger things happened between Luke and me after that. Over the next six months we forged a very modern sort of friendship – via email. We swapped notes. Poems. Chit chat. We recommended books. Luke had said 'no', I'd heard that clearly. But he was a very unusual man. In the new spirit of openness, I let my pride go; I allowed this *other* relationship to develop with him. We went from a bad date to cyber-friends, to proper friends. We have lunch these days at raw food restaurants; we go to poetry readings and films, share fruit in darkened cinemas. Luke talks with mesmerising honesty. He can still hypnotise me. But we are consciously practising a male-female friendship. This is a good thing: all my other male friendships have emerged without any conscious practice.

Pete was a very different story. We met in the Cock and Bottle on Artesian Road in W11, chatted easily, eyed each other up, drawing closer to each other as the evening progressed. Our fingers touched. He walked me to the bus stop and we sat on a bench, waiting for the bus. He looked at me and said.

'I won't kiss you right now, though I'd like to.'

I looked at him. I wanted him to kiss me, yeah. Right there on the bench.

'Best we wait,' I replied, knowing this was true; kisses are best when waited for.

I hopped on the 52 and sailed up Ladbroke Grove.

'What kind of men do you like?' one of my female writing students asked me recently.

'Clever as fuck and working class,' I replied, without a pause. Pete was very much my type, then and now.

Soon after, Pete came over for tea and stayed for dinner and then sex. He came for tea, dinner and sex quite a few times after that. Mostly, he came round on his bike. Once, when I had flu, he arrived with ginger cake and we sat on my bed, me in my silk kimono, him in strange split-toe socks – and we talked. We talked about astrology first and later I told him of my adventures, CL and tantra and Demara. He was the first (and only) man I told it all to. I knew he was titillated, but also conscious of being part of my investigations. He was also the first man to receive the benefits of my new tantric 'skills'.

'You're learning how to touch,' he said, by way of feedback after my first efforts. 'I had this lover once, Pauline, she touched me like I touch myself.'

'*How* did she touch you?'

'She just had perfect touch, hands like velvet.'

I was a bit envious, but it was a moment of realisation, that men also keep quiet about who does and doesn't touch them right.

Pete was lithe and fit. He had a very robust cock and was athletic in bed. I'd been a little fronty with him at first, explaining I wasn't monogamous. He took this in his stride, saying he didn't mind.

'You've got capacity,' he said more than once. By this I think he meant capacity to be open.

Truth was, I was still inventing this non-monogamous self. At the time, I wasn't sleeping with anyone else: but I wanted to keep the door open to this possibility. I'd never been non-monogamous before. Even though I'd read *The Ethical Slut*, I didn't know what I was doing. Despite my interest in keeping other lovers, Pete came round once a week for three long autumnal months. I went round to his flat on Portobello Road once or twice. We ate dinner at the Moroccan on Goldhawk Road. He was a big fan of Henry Miller and I re-read *The Tropic of Cancer* and decided firmly that I wasn't. We were skirting round the possibility of a full-blown love affair. He'd never stayed the night; he liked to cycle home.

Then, one night in November, something happened. We'd been watching Obama's presidential inauguration on TV, laid out on the sofa, legs entwined. Afterwards, or maybe even during, we had sex and this time it was different – I felt his cock reach *right* up. Some women will know what this is like. When the physicality of penetration is so precise and exacting; it overreaches the target. The cock can touch the heart inside a woman – or that's how it feels. A man can caress a woman's heart with the tip of his cock. In the sweat of an embrace, legs and arms all over the place, bodies met, when a man enters, and when his cock is rock hard and feels two feet long, it is the proverbial death by sex. Death and deliverance. A woman is cracked open. Her brain is hurled from her. Mine was thrown out the window on to the street. The heart is reached, the heart engages.

'Hello heart,' I whispered to myself. *You're back*.

♥

The next day, as luck would have it, I met up with my ex, who by then had ended things with Ruth and moved on to another woman. By this point, I no longer cared whom he was seeing. One affair, a humungous break-up, then two new girlfriends in two years, a ticky heart. In some ways he'd gone far madder than I had in the aftermath of our split. We were friendly enough, on email. He had even stayed the night once in my flat in Harlesden. During that stay he'd said: 'I feel a little better these days.' He stroked his heart as he said this.

'I do too,' I replied. I felt better, much better. Two and a half years later and we were both only just feeling a little like our old selves.

During that visit we took the tube from Willesden Junction together, the train shuddering to a halt in Queen's Park. An innocent and child-like expression spread across his face. He beamed at me and my heart surged at the sight of him so happy. And then he said something unexpected.

'Shed.'

I looked up. Indeed, we'd come to rest in a long glass Victorian train shed, one I'd never noticed before, even though this trip was an everyday event. Shed. A whole universe of knowledge and love for him came packed in this one word. Shed. I knew, in that moment, how he felt. I still cared about his love of sheds. His love of trains. It hit me then: just how would I ever come to love another man so thoroughly again?

♥

A month later, we met again. It was November 2008. We went to the bonfire night in Lewes with the poet Catherine Smith. In Lewes they are potty about bonfires. Once, seventeen protestants were burnt at the stake in front of the town hall for treason and the townsfolk, in the spirit of resistance, have been burning effigies of the Pope ever since. My ex wanted to go for research for his next book; I'd been the year before and had found myself dazzled. Here was dark old pagan England. I'd missed him then, missed his appreciation for the habits and customs of England; he was born in Newhaven, not too far from Lewes and I knew he'd find the pageant enthralling – strangely, he'd never been before. Last time I'd watched lovers kissing and children brandishing torches of fire. I'd written a poem for him about the town's mayor being thrown into the Ouse. This time, I was glad to go with him.

He was a wearing a corduroy suit and a ten-foot multi-coloured hand-knitted scarf. He was fatter and his teeth were shot. He didn't drink much because of his heart medication: he constantly massaged his heart. My heart was newly opened up.

I loved him. I didn't love Pete. I loved this tooth-decayed bastard. I adored being with him. His piggy eyes, his woman-hipped waddle. I delighted in being in his company. And I could tell he delighted in mine. *The clever ones bring out the child in me.* My ex was very clever too: and yes, he fathered me.

We muddled through the crowds on the streets. We even held hands. We were holding hands and muddling through the ancient, densely-packed streets of Lewes together. Had we always been like this? He and I and the grand and fascinating world around us? I couldn't shake him off, couldn't shake off this feeling of ease and comfort around him. He was my partner in this world or the last. He was my other half, my best friend, the only other person I gave a damn about. Father? Husband? With him I was whole; I was calm and settled and not alone. We were a strange king and queen, the two of us: a foolish old king and a bossy good queen.

We went up to a friend of Catherine's flat and watched much of the parade from on high. Fizzing sulphurous pink lights. Processions of people brandishing burning crosses. Papier-mâché effigies on rolling carts. George Bush with a rocket up his arse. Barrels of burning tar. Smoke and gunpowder in the air, massive ear-splitting cracks as bangers hit the ground. Fifty Morris men in two lines, dancing down the high street. We knelt by a window together and oohed and aahed at the sights. Our hands touched. We ate prawn *vol au vents* and drank warm punch.

'*Burn* the Pope,' he shouted from the window. '*Burn* him!'

Being a lapsed Roman Catholic, I kept very quiet all night. It was Wednesday, 5 November 2008. I was forty-three. He was fifty. We'd spent almost a decade either together or *trying* to be apart.

'*Burn* the Pope,' he shouted louder, waving to the crowd, as bald and medieval-looking as the Pope himself.

'Calm down, dear.' Again, for one night, we were a double act. It was so easy to slip back into how we'd been.

Later, with Catherine, we went back down into the crowd to watch one of the three-storey bonfires. The field was cold and muddy and there were throngs of people. The fire billowed to the heavens. We watched the beautiful, wretched pyre. But we didn't stay long. We threaded our way back and soon found ourselves walking along a wall above the crowds going the opposite way. The wall was maybe three feet high and three feet wide, wide enough to use as a walkway. At the end of the wall Catherine and I jumped down. But he didn't. Instead, he made a fuss, like the foolish old king he was, and in the end four younger men came forward from the crowd and carried him, in a chair-like position, off the wall. They put him down and he laughed loudly and we walked back through the crowds, arm in arm, till we got back to Catherine's house.

It was long walk and on the way he came down with 'the aura', the crown of lights signalling a migraine. Water is the only cure for his migraines and as soon as we entered Catherine's kitchen we gave him a pint of water and put him to bed in a dark room. Next door, I lay on the sofa and rested my hand on my heart. I thought of the way Pete had penetrated me. I couldn't fathom what was going on in my life. I'd lost the map. Pete's cock touching my heart. But my ex, whom I loved, my ex touched my heart, too. Touched my very soul. *The one my soul loves.*

I didn't sleep a wink all night. I tossed and turned and then, in the small hours, Gino, Catherine's overweight ginger tomcat came and sat on me. He stared disparagingly down into my face, as if to say *get off my sofa.*

Cats and men. They could both get lost.

In the morning, I went in to see my ex. He was inert and

lumpen, huddled under the duvet in a heap. He groaned, still thick in the head. He'd come down with numerous migraines in the last six months of our life together. I didn't know it then, but they were a symptom of his guilt over his affair. I went and made him sweet tea. I brought it to him and stood over him.

'Thank you, Mon,' he said.

'S'okay.' I wanted to get into bed with him and wrap my body around him. I thought this would be a good time. Just go to him, like I used to. Comfort him. Love him again. But I turned and left him quietly in that dark room.

In London, on my return, I sent an email to Pete saying 'something has happened.'

'What?'

'My heart has engaged.' He knew what I meant; my heart had engaged with him.

'So soon?'

He went weird on me after that, evasive. Jan advised that I try to stay open; but I couldn't. Before Christmas, I said 'Goodbye, no hard feelings.'

where's the drama?

Days later, in November 2008, I went to stay at Field of Dreams, John Hawken's home in Sancreed, near Penzance in Cornwall. It was dark and wintry and John had a blizzard of a cold which I immediately caught from him. There were ten of us who'd done the introductory weekend in May and decided to attend the second part of this particular 'training'.

The group comprised six strong and attractive women, all between thirty-five and sixty-five, and four men with a similar age span. Two of the men seemed broken in spirit; another told me, quite early on, that he suffered from impotence. The fourth was a handsome and flamboyant young Indian dressed head-to-toe in designer Adidas sportswear. If any kind of generalisation can be made about the 'types' of people who come to tantra, it might be this: there are the 'broken people' and the sexually flamboyant. I would categorise myself as a flamboyant with a broken heart, somewhat midway between the two.

The ten of us plus John Hawken and his partner Gabi were to spend nine days in deep immersion in the practices of tantra. John's home is nestled in the bosom of the wild Cornish countryside, a spot close to sacred ponds and wells. These days John's part of Cornwall is inhabited by incomers and second homers who regard him, a native of the country, with some suspicion; the local tittle tattle is that he runs some kind of brothel.

During our first morning, we introduced ourselves and then John talked a little about tantra. Generally speaking, John explained, when we experience pleasure we expand and when we experience pain we contract. Excitement can cause pleasure and therefore expansion. We can relax into excitement and a sense of well-being is experienced. Excitement plus expansion gives us pleasure. Excitement plus contraction gives us fear. When we are aroused we generally feel excited. However, there is often an element of uncertainty too, hence contraction. Therefore, our sexual encounters often have this mixture of excitement and expansion, and uncertainty, or contraction. There is often this ambiguity, or even fear, around sex. We all want to feel sexual arousal, pleasure – and yet we choose to get rid of this pleasure quickly in the sex act. All the fuss of romance and courtship often ends in an act which lasts eight to twelve seconds. Hence, he explained, it is ironic that the greatest pleasure of sexual energy is getting rid of it.

Most of us, he said, never allow ourselves to *be in* the excitement, be in the energy. Most of us load sexual energy with expectation and attachment to result, i.e. orgasm, and get caught up in the yes/no thrill of ambiguity. We are used to this drama, like we are used to having too much salt to flavour food. We *like* the 'maybe' aspect of our sexual liaisons. Tantra, he said, gives us the choice of how and when to dispel sexual energy; it teaches us to relax and savour the feeling of expansion.

'Tantra is hard to sell,' he said. 'Where's the drama in it?'

Tantra, he continued, is all about the freedom to choose, to be self-aware about sexual tension; it is about keeping sexual tension conscious. Conscious tension has the qualities of a wave: it keeps its form and its flow of energy is fluid.

'Relaxing into pleasure is a technique. We can say yes to pleasure and let go of impulsiveness. Tantra looks for bliss, which is a passive quality of pleasure. If we let go of suffering, we enter a natural state of bliss. Simply being alive is an ecstatic state. Indian masters teach the same ideas via meditation. The key to finding bliss is to unravel habits which invoke suffering. Addictive behaviour, for example, brings suffering; it also brings ambivalence into sexuality. Bliss is a birthright. Trust the pleasure principal, it is a guide to what is true.'

Energy. It's a word I've used in the past with little thought or understanding, a generalisation I've used without meaning. On Day Three of the course, as if to provide proof of all this expansion and contraction theory, John decided to put us through a cocktail of 'bio-energetic' techniques. He called this process 'streaming', the idea being that these techniques, all thrown together, bring about a 'streaming of energy' in the body. John wanted to demonstrate to us what our body's energy could do, what it could feel like once it was all shaken up.

We did this exercise in pairs. I paired with an attractive woman called Annie.

First, we shook, shook up the Kundalini from the base chakras. This gets the body hot and fired up, as it were. Done right, Kundalini shaking alone is enough to send the body into a super-alive state.

Second, we did something called 'the bow'. I stood with my arms open in front of me, bent at the elbow, pelvis tilted forward, head up, a curved posture which opens the body.

'Now use your voices,' said John. 'Don't be inhibited. Invite the universe to embrace you.'

People began to call out. I did too.

'For fuckkksssakes come and get me,' I bellowed to the skies. 'Come and get me, I'm here. Waiting. Come and get me.' I was furious. I stood in the bow and howled my head off. Reader, I recommend you try this at home: it's exhilarating.

Next came a 'bio-release massage'. I was bent over double by my partner, head over legs, while she slapped her hands hard on my scalp, neck, shoulders, arms and back. This was a most peculiar type of massage, designed to cause shock impulses. The one giving the massage snatches or grabs energy from the muscle tissue and drags it away, across the skin.

This is followed by a brushing technique, where energy is brushed down the legs and up the spine.

Annie then brought me up into a 'soft standing' position, my body tingling and vibrating with this onslaught of twenty minutes. It was at this point that John Hawken came around to each person and laid his hands on us. With me, he put his hands on my kidneys. Floods of tears emerged. Snot poured from my nose. I babbled.

'I'm *sick* of being strong,' I sobbed.

'Good,' he said.

'I'm sick of being the strongest person I know.'

'Good.'

'I've had enough. I've had enough of this.'

He raised his eyebrows and there was a Puckish glint of mischief in his eyes. He moved on. I was dimly aware of another person in the room bellowing, someone John was touching.

Next, in this melted state, Annie did some Kundalini drumming on my sacrum, up my spine to the skull. The energy was then brushed up to the eyes. She stood in front of me, and we gazed into each other's eyes for several minutes. I could barely recognise her. Then she laid me down on the floor; she delved her fingers into the base of my skull, opening the jade gate. I was shivering, exhausted. She worked on my legs, opening and closing my knees in a kind of butterfly movement. I was to breathe in time with her. By then I wasn't sure what I was doing. Was there a feeling of energy streaming all through my body? I don't know what I can possibly say about the experience. I was a mess; my body's flow of energy stirred, but no, it was not exactly streaming through me. Again, somehow, I'd been thrown from myself. As with

Karsten, I was elsewhere, out of myself. I was sick of being strong. This was a good place for me to be; open and way, way out of my depth.

When it was my turn to be conscious, Annie went into a storm, her eyes bleary with being so shaken up. John laid his hands on her and she wept. I saw another woman in our group erupt into the whole body 'streaming' process, her body convulsing with energy which looked like an almighty orgasm. John made a V with his hands and cupped it to the woman's heart to channel the energy upwards. Can I say she was faking it? No. Her body was trembling and the energy moving upwards through her was visible and moving in a flowing stream; her eyes had rolled back into her skull. Another man, one of the 'broken men', the man who was bellowing during my turn, developed a red raw patch on his chest where John had laid his hands. Through the next nine days this raw patch didn't heal; in fact it got worse. It oozed clear fluid and bled, like stigmata.

That night I retreated to my tiny damp fuchsia-pink bedroom. In my diary I wrote: *The bar has been raised, we have been stretched. John put his hands on my kidneys and I bawled like a baby.*

fantasy turned to mantra

Workshops went on from morning till night. It was relentless. Breakfast, workshop, lunch, workshop. Some theory, then practice, then dinner. Then more workshops. One evening we were asked to write down a sexual fantasy. I wrote the following, a fantasy I'd had about Luke:

Luke is practicing celibacy. I am menstruating and don't feel the least bit like sex. He picks me up from the tube station and we go back to his house. We are on his bed: low lights, background music. Clothes come off. We don't speak much. With his finger as a pen, he dips it into the well between my legs and paints a red line from my yoni to my navel and then up to the point between my breasts. He dips again and paints a line under the moons of my breasts. 'Words', I whisper. On my stomach he writes GOOD. Underneath, he writes HONEY. He smiles. We laugh. 'More', I whisper. FLOWER, he writes on my thigh. He dips again and draws a sunflower on my knee. I begin to paint too. My finger draws black-red blood from the well. I smear the blood-paint across his white chest, swirl the paint up to his neck. I write the word PRINCE at the base of his neck. I mark his collar bone with dots. We kiss.

We each wrote a fantasy. I'd had a lot of practice, those ads I wrote for CL. I imagined we'd have to read the fantasies out to the group, that this would be a time for me to show off. But no, John asked half of the group to spread out, sit separately in the big wooden-floored room. To make a shrine around us, a place for another to sit. We did this. Lights were dimmed, incense lit. We were asked to read our fantasy aloud, as though reading a prayer or a poem, reading it privately, to ourselves. The others would come and 'visit', kneel and listen with utter reverence to our words. I liked this idea a lot. This honouring of *lust*, the filthy and profane cousin of *love*.

I began to read my fantasy out loud. One by one, others in the room came and knelt at my feet; they listened to what I'd written. I read my words slowly. I thought of my unrequited lust for Luke. Spoken aloud, the fantasy was released; it was born into the world. It was spoken about; it was passed to another. Like a genie, a jinn, some ne'er-do-well spirit, the fantasy was let out of the bottle.

Then John asked us to circle ten or twelve words on the page. I circled celibacy, menstruate, clothes, well, breasts, words, good, honey, more, flower, black-red, blood, prince, kiss. He asked us to invoke these words, as incantation, as a love-prayer, a lust-mantra, an honouring of the sexual desire. We did this. I whispered the words all run together; it sounded like a song, or something a temple priest might say, sexy mantra-speak: *celibacymenstruateclotheswellbreastswords-goodhoneymoreflowerblack-redbloodprincekiss.*

It reminded me of those emails I received in the post, *wait-formewaitforme.* And also of *The Tryst*, the fantasies I'd had for other men, those I wrote about and turned into prose. Fantasy emerges from the shadow part of the self – that's a no-brainer. We keep most of our fantasies to ourselves. Sometimes, we out them, we laugh them off, but mostly they visit us in the quiet and enigmatic hours of the morning, or when we are in a daydream, a semi-detached state, floating beyond the realities of our limited lives. Fantasy, like poetry, is an elevated form of human communication, our life lifted *up*. Fantasy is better than life, fantasy is the poetics of the soul, what we *could* or might be if anything was allowed. Fantasy, while often dark, is good for us. It is an essential form of self-expression. In fantasy we are our super-self; our deepest and most unformed self, which is allowed off the leash, allowed to be itself. If my ex hadn't retreated to fantasy, where or how else would this darkness have expressed itself?

my shadow cv

Early on, John had asked us to notice and be alert to our personal demons. 'A demon thinks 'I'm right' – that is the symptom of a demon,' he explained. 'Righteousness, a sense of being in the right, a zealous crusading energy, that's demon energy. A demon is unable to question the self; a demon has no respect for anyone else's reality'. He asked us to notice, collect and name our demons, to watch our blames and feelings of guilt within the group, especially with any figure of authority – i.e. him.

Over the next few days, this was my list of personal demons:

Broken men – I hate weakness in others, especially men.

Moral superiority – a major demon – I'm often sure of myself, that I'm right and can make others feel in the wrong.

I'm ugly – I've been pestered by this since adolescence, since my big nose was pointed out to me in the dormitory at my convent boarding school.

Pride – I can be queenly, grand, say friends and also my ex.

Fuck off – I tend to attack anyone who attacks me. I come out fighting and bash up anyone who fucks with me.

Yes, nice and thorny. It's alarming to look at your 'shadow CV', your shortlist of dark and difficult tendencies. Imagine putting that forward during any job application or interview: Monique Roffey, writer, Orange Prize shortlistee, PhD – also proud, morally superior, hates weak people, thinks she's ugly and will thump anyone who's mean to her.

'If you can play with your demons, then you are free,' said

John. 'If you *can't* play with them, then they control you. If you are in denial about these demons and can't let go, then they have you in their power. The words "I'm not" are dangerous, they suggest a strong demon.'

The idea around 'erotic punishment' is simple. We have demons and we judge each other around them. If we don't like a person or a person hurts us due to their demons, we tend to withdraw and then punish them morally, or we let them know, verbally, why we don't like them. We punish each other every day, either with words, or by withdrawing our energy. Sound familiar?

With erotic punishment, acted out in games between consenting adults, people are allowed to 'play' with punishment. There's no real motivation behind the punishment, no reason for it; once the demon is taken out of the scenario, then the person with the whip can experiment with power. The theory is this: a person who carries a lot of anger can use BDSM (Bondage and Discipline/Dominance and Submission/Sado-masochism) as a way of playing with this demon. They can express a kind of 'staged anger', they can vent pent-up energy in a formal scenario which has 'safe words' and rules. The person's anger can be released – but no one gets hurt. This is the 'energetics' of BDSM. Demons are played with – and released. Moral judgement doesn't come into it. Darkness can be transformed. Most people who are attracted to BDSM find it liberating, they find that wielding power in these scenarios keeps them from being demonic in real life.

'BDSM is transformative,' said John. 'To heal blame we learn to drop being right, being moral, and do it for fun. To heal guilt, the punishment stops being a way to hurt ourselves for being bad. It becomes a way to affirm naughtiness.'

erotic punishment

BDSM and tantra may sound like opposites, one hard and dark, one soft and light. But both share the conscious use of energy and the crossover is well known in both sexual communities. During those ten days, John was keen to introduce us to the energetics behind conflict, behind the demonic, and how we could choose, if we so wished, to play with our demons through erotic punishment.

In BDSM, a person can spank, cane or flog another person just for the release of it, just to see what arises in the power dynamic. It's a *game*. Whips, paddles, canes are all used in BDSM sex. All these can be seen as instruments of torture or weapons. We instantly recognise them as being connected with existential 'life or death' situations. This is the reason why BDSM sex has such a strong taboo, such an edge to it and why so many people feel a strong hostility towards it. We associate pain with fatality, with our own death. Being tied up, being whipped, is what can happen when life and limb are threatened. I'd always seen BSDM as a little creepy, a little too goth for me. And pain? Oh, I'm a total baby. My pain threshold is zero; I like being tickled, not whipped. But having it explained to me like this made me rethink it all. I could see why it worked for some.

The group was set a game in which some people were masters and others slaves. John explained it: 'Masters and slaves both exhibit demonic, or undesirable behaviour. The aim of this game is to become conscious of when these energies arise more subtly in everyday life. Sometimes we can be very bossy or domineering, other times we can be subservient. This game reveals these tendencies to us.'

While I was interested in witnessing my bossy/subservient sides, I found this game very difficult. Although I understood the theory, I didn't want to allow others to dominate me and I didn't feel comfortable with dominating others. So, I was allowed to sit out and watch. No matter how things were explained, I couldn't see myself obeying a master, as the others did. I watched, baffled and even a little shocked, as people allowed themselves to be tied up, used as footstools or dogs, allowed themselves to be ridden around the room and shouted at, beaten and caned. So what if it was all a game? This wasn't my type of game. Maybe I couldn't *play* with my demon of 'pride'. Maybe. I accepted that. But also, I couldn't let another person treat me like their slave: I come from the Caribbean. Not that long ago, slavery was an existential 'life or death' way of being.

Nor could I treat another like a slave. I didn't want to reverse the power deal. I didn't feel happy, even in a formal game, to ask another to bend and scrape and jump to my attention, wash my feet, lick my toes; I had no appetite or desire to ask another person to be at my beck and call. Maybe I have my demons locked up. Maybe. But this wasn't for me.

John seemed disappointed. I did try using the whip and found it very odd indeed. I wasn't sure how to use it: the concept of playing with it seemed radical. I didn't get any real pleasure out of flogging my fellow students. I even tried the whip on John – with disastrous results. He instantly felt real judgement coming from me, or thought he did – and called the whole game off.

But, late that night, during a more ad-hoc evening

workshop, I had a couple of fun, even erotic, BDSM experiences. We were encouraged to do most of this workshop in our rooms if we wished. The handsome young Indian god came to visit me in my fuchsia-walled boudoir. He brought a suede whip and asked me to lie down on the bed, my arse exposed.

'What a lovely arse,' he said, stroking it. 'We haven't seen enough of it in the workshops.' I laughed and he brought the whip down on my buttocks. *Whack*. The whip was soft suede, it didn't hurt.

'Be quiet. Now. I want you to tell me the story of Little Red Riding Hood.'

'Okay,' I said. I began the story. 'One day ...'

'No, that's wrong. The story begins at night.' *Whack*.

And so on. It was funny. I was punished for every sentence I uttered. I couldn't get anything right, no matter what I said. For every part of the story I repeated, I was lightly flogged. My arse was stroked. I giggled. I got lost and disorientated. I didn't know what to say to please my master. Eventually, I relinquished all power. Everything I said evoked a loving flog. There was one rule: *his* rule and it was unclear. He was the master. I stopped trying to figure out his method and relaxed, enjoying his domination over me. This was kinky, soft BDSM. I liked it.

Next, with my prior consent, I was visited by Sexy Sandra. Sandra was forty, but looked thirty; she was lithe and blonde and foxy. She was learning Kinbaku, the art of Japanese bondage, and made me an intricate but pretty knotted bra-harness. In the harness, I knelt on all fours on the bed as she flogged my buttocks.

'Ooooh,' I squealed. It was weird; again, things could be just as sexy woman-on-woman. Sandra was only mildly dominant; she was silent, almost studious, as she trailed the whip across my back, shivered the suede strings across my buttocks. The harness was a work of art and felt kinky to wear; I looked neat and tight and feminine in it. It was a light constraint, the smooth ropes were bound across my breasts and it was pleasurable to press against them. The knotted harness seemed far removed from its dark history of torture. I liked being trussed up so artistically by a woman; the energy between us was casual and yet sexual. Yes. That was good. Maybe I could get into BDSM lite.

the merry maidens

The next day we all got in John's minibus and drove out to the Merry Maidens, a Bronze Age stone circle which stands in a field not far from a main road near St Buryan in Cornwall. The circle comprises nineteen stones, the so-called maidens who, legend has it, were out dancing on the Sabbath and for this sin were turned to stone. Two bigger stones lie to the north of the circle; these are called the Pipers, men also turned to stone while running away from the dancing women.

It was a grim November morning. We trudged from the minibus to the centre of the stone circle in cagoules and hats and gloves. We sat on the ground in a disaffected half-asleep huddle as John explained that the circle was built on the St Michael Line, an ancient path or ley line which ran from St Michael's Mount off the Cornish coast right through to Hopton in Norfolk. True, many ancient churches and sacred sites, including Avebury and Glastonbury, are built on this line, many of which are dedicated to St Michael. Neolithic man could detect lines of the earth's energy, or that's the idea, and so many ancient trackways were built along them. This is the theory put forward by Alfred Watkins in 1925, at any rate. His book *The Old Straight Track* is a bible for ley enthusiasts.

Bollocks to all this, I thought. Ley lines. Pah. All hokum. Archaeologists don't accept ley lines and there's a good reason why not: no scientific proof.

John explained that because the circle was built over this ancient ley line, the energy within the circle was also ancient – and powerful. It could be accessed quite simply, though, by spinning in the centre of the circle, and keeping one's eyes on the stones. Then, the stones would dance. They'd dance for you with such force they could hurl you to the ground. The mystery of the circle would unlock itself; you would experience its sacred and cunningly hidden energy source.

Yeah, yeah. Right. Petrification legends are common with stone circles, the idea that people, usually young women, were caught dancing on the Sabbath and punished by being turned to stone. There are stone circles up and down the country called things like 'X and her daughters' or 'the X maidens', or 'the X/Y dancing stones'. There was a time when the Christian church encouraged these myths in an attempt to banish pagan rituals and keep Sundays holy.

One by one we circled the stones, touching each one in a ceremony of formal greeting. Each of us sat next to a stone, using it as a backrest, while one by one we had a turn at spinning in the centre. If you turned left into the spin, your back into it, the idea was you'd spin into a downwards spiral of energy, twisting into the earth. If you turned right, you'd twist upwards, into the sky. I sat and watched as each one of my fellow tantrikas went into the centre of the circle and span – or tried to. They were turning rather slowly, not really spinning, and yet they seemed to be quite unsteady on their feet. One or two wobbled and fell over. I thought they were being dramatic, making a bit of a show of things. I also noticed that each had a similar reaction: after a few minutes of backwards or forwards stumbling around in the centre, each person's face lit up in an ecstatic smile, a smile of recognition.

I was one of the last to go to the centre of the circle. I was a little nervous by then. In the centre I chose a piece of flat grass. I opened my arms wide, and fixed my eyes on the horizon line of stones. I decided to turn left, backing into my turn. I watched the stones. I turned and turned and yes, they moved. They moved as if by their own accord. They didn't move as I moved. They moved separately. And they moved fast. In fact, they seemed to take off, to spin very quickly around me. Yes, they *whirled*. I found myself spinning backwards in an attempt to keep up with them. They span faster than I did, as if they were leaping off the ground, as if they were indeed dancing in a mad whirling barn dance around me. The stones were linked in some outer wheel, some outer force. I laughed out loud. I felt powered. Charged. A huge rush of energy filled me, filled up my chest. It was hard to stay upright. The stones span around me and at the same time I was besieged by an exterior rush of force. My breathing changed, becoming slow and laboured. I felt total exhilaration. I laughed, as the others had. I span and span and threw my head back and laughed as the stones whirled around me at a different speed, much faster than me. Even though I felt I was spinning madly, rushing round and round in circles at the speed of knots, the stones span *faster*. I thought I was running around in the centre of that circle, as if I'd been taken from under my feet and spun. The stones rushed past, faster and faster, a giddy speed. The more I span, the faster they moved. And all the while I was being trammelled by a force. I was being somehow *energised*, filled with a natural power.

I stopped spinning and tried to stand still. I couldn't. I was swaying on my feet. The stones were still. They were just big stones. But I was utterly disorientated. I couldn't take a step. If I had, I'd have become unbalanced. My breathing was heavy and slow. In fact, I was out of breath. After a few seconds passed, I made unsteady steps back to the stone where I'd been sitting. I couldn't sit down; I was breathing like I'd just run for miles.

'Wow,' I muttered to the woman sitting at the next stone. 'Was I spinning very fast?' I knew I *had* been. I knew, of all the others, I was the one who'd done something different. I'd spun like a top. I'd gone for it; I'd hurled myself in a wild spin.

'You hardly moved at all,' she said.

'What? I was *spinning*. Running on the spot. That's what it felt like.'

'No. You were virtually rooted to the spot.'

pure math

John said some things during the course of the week which were revelatory. He talked about the possibilities which open to us if we use our energy *with intent*. For example, with our own personal energy there are choices to be made:

We can contract – or expand.

We can do this densely – or diffusely.

Our energy can be penetrating – or enfolding.

On a train, for instance, when we don't have a ticket and don't want to be seen, we can choose to contract in a diffuse manner, and so almost disappear. Conversely, if we want to get people's attention – we can expand our energy in a dense manner. Density works to feel safe, we often block others with density; a 'dense block' is a safe block and can be used to wall others off. 'We can do anything with our energy – if we do it with intent,' said John. 'We can play with it if we become more conscious.'

Yes. It all made sense. I could see that I'd over-used a dense block for most of my adult life. In the past, I had put this dense block on for almost everyone, dodgy men, good men too, an over-discerning filter – even when it wasn't necessary. When things began to go bad with my ex, I put a dense block on him *and left it on*. He did the same with me.

'Fifty per cent of what goes wrong in your life can be explained by an energy block. Our energy habits are picked up from someone who didn't know how to use their energy either,' said John.

It made me think of why some men gave me the creeps, men with a very penetrating gaze. Now I understood why they made me squirm: bad use of energy. Overuse of it. When we first met, and for a long time afterwards, my ex's energy was enfolding and diffuse. His gaze was soft, benevolent, his emotions were generous, he made grand romantic gestures. Once, early on, he picked me up in the dead of night from my garret flat and drove me to a tower in a field just to look at the moon and the stars. He was open, diaphanous in his love for me.

Conflict, John explained, arises between people on an energetic level. The best way to deal with conflict is to deal with the energy first – then the content. Forget using moral justification, the 'I'm right' mode of solving conflict. 'I'm right' signifies the demonic. Take responsibility for anger, deal with it rather than blame. Sort out the energetics of an argument first by letting things cool. Then come back to the reasons for it. Couples punish each other by withdrawing their energy from each other; often there is a heated battle full of moral justification, followed by a stand-off. When this happens again and again, bad energy is stored up. In many cases, as in mine, couples can withdraw their energy from each other so much that the relationship dies. A collection of problems which are not sorted energetically (through loving touch, sex and other forms of contact) can add up and kill off a partnership. Arguments are often 90 per cent energy and 10 per cent content.

It made perfect sense. I had a textbook relationship breakdown. No sex life. No loving touch. No physical energy between us whatsoever. All this energy withdrawn. All our arguments were solved through moral justification. I looked back in dismay. *I will love differently. I will be better at love.* I thought of Demara again and her temple, the love we bestowed on that young man. My father paid me no affectionate attention as a child or adolescent. I can't remember him holding my hand, let alone offering a hug. Cuddles from Daddy? Never. He was a most undemonstrative man, closed to everyone, even, at times, to my mother. How would I ever stop or reverse a lifetime's habit of grabbing and getting men's attention? I learnt to inhibit my desire for loving touch as a child, due to repeated rejection. As a result, I often try *to get* men's love and attention too quickly. I've been webbed up in this pattern of behaviour all my adult life.

♥

Those nine days with John Hawken signified a learning curve like no other in my recent adult life. Through working things out in energetic terms, I came to this:

> *My ex provided enfolding and diffuse energy, his gaze was loving for the most part of six years. He provided the energy and love I'd never received as a child. I melted into this love, this good man's appreciation. I was seen and loved by a bookish man, a man who even had a double act called* Your Dad. *But there was no sexual desire on my part, no sexual energy: that would have signified incest. I drank in his love and rejected his sexual energy, as I would have with my real father. I was so love-starved I denied myself sex, too. The grief and devastation of the loss of my ex is also the loss of the father I never had. It is father loss; I have been grieving the loss of a good father.*

And yet, and yet, it was also a great and singular love affair. I have no doubt about that. *He is the one my soul loves.* Is 'soul love' a base love, a love for all the archetypes of the opposite sex? In *The Song of Songs* the woman calls her beloved king, shepherd, lover and brother. She is passionate with this all-engulfing love for the man. I know something of this love. My love for my ex was father love and brother love and occasionally, or maybe at first only, the love of lovers.

Tantrika, a practitioner of tantra. Yes, I left the Field of Dreams a confirmed tantrika. Like the term 'ethical slut', which I was also happy to call myself, I felt I had another new term of self-definition. I was no longer only 'female, hetero-sexual'. I was expanding, escaping past confines; I was an ethical slut, a tantrika, mildly bi-sexual. And I was leaving old ways behind. Thank fuck.

the man with no name

I first heard Ma Anand Sarita talk at a tantra festival held in the Chelsea Town Hall on the King's Road. She was impres-sive. She spoke, Osho-style, without notes and uninterrupted, in a clear and un-preacher-type manner for well over an hour. Sarita is probably the best-known and most prolific tantra teacher in the UK. My new friends, Jasmine and Jon, had spent two years in a 'couples training' with her; they and everyone I'd met in the tantra world spoke highly of her. Sarita doesn't just have a following but her own tantra *school*. In March 2009, a few months after my time in Cornwall with John Hawken, I signed up for Sacred Sexuality, a course taught by Sarita in a big house in Somerset.

The house is a pale stone building, two floors, mostly given over to rather basic single and double rooms and dorms. It has a conservatory, lawns, a pool, a topiaried garden and a large hall where various teachers like Sarita can conduct work-shops. We were to spend 80 per cent of the week in that hall.

Again I found myself the lone geek. The only one with doubt, with awkwardness, with questions and scepticism and an open addiction to coffee. On those early tantra courses, I used to stick out like a sore thumb. I harboured such discomfort around what was to come that I was often always on the point of leaving rather than being there. Even now, I struggle and can get moody. Nothing is easy in these week-long workshops. Every time you pair up with someone, usually of the opposite sex, it's often for an intense, possibly naked, out of the body, super-conscious experience.

The first session on that first morning, I coupled up with a man who didn't want to be named. He called himself 'No Name'. I'd clocked him on the first introductory evening. We were all asked to take to the centre of a large circle (35-plus student tantrikas) and introduce ourselves in any way we saw fit. This man said he didn't want to tell us his name, he wanted to be nameless for the week, and then he did a little backwards walk around the room, waving one had in a mock-royal gesture. I distinctly recall looking up the moment he passed me. I gazed into his long-chinned handsome face and one word sprang to mind – TRICKSTER.

So 'No Name' and I buddied up first morning, first day. It was then that I noticed a leather thong around his neck, from which dangled a small red leather pouch. Again, I was suspicious; it seemed very 'on show' and portentous against his bare chest. What was in it? A shark's tooth? A piece of his frontal lobe? He'd just come from an 'initiation ceremony', he explained. Like Luke, and like a couple of other men on the course, he was part of a 'men's group'. This meant it was likely he was an aficionado of Deida and was working towards greater understanding of his masculinity. I was meeting a number of these 'men who did "men's" work': I was very on the fence about them; I nursed a mixture of envy and suspicion. 1. I wanted to be in a men's group myself, because I knew they would be fun, and because sometimes I want to be a man. But 2. also, with time, I began to know (first hand) that these men all displayed one rather alarming human trait, the very thing they were trying to correct: utter flakiness. But, overall, I decided, like everything else at that time, it would be best to 'stay open'.

Sarita demonstrated the morning's meditation practice of 'chakra breathing'. Watching her was spellbinding. She and her younger male co-tutor Suta sat opposite each other, in the lotus position, knees touching. They began to breathe in and out in a conscious manner, with a notable emphasis on pass-ing this breath between them, first through the root chakra, and then upwards through the other six chakras; the stomach, solar plexus, heart, throat, third eye and then out through the top of the head. While doing this, they both looked utterly possessed. The more the breath entered them, the more they were taken over, so much so that towards the end, Sarita was flailing her arms in the air and wobbling and probably 'streaming' with energy or alive with the serpent of the Kundalini, or something of that nature. Both she and Suta had obviously been switched on – or activated. We watched.

When the demonstration was over I turned to No Name and said: 'Come on, let's do it.'

And so we did.

I think we managed a good imitation of what they had-done, ending up rolling all over the floor, gasping for breath and out of ourselves. I know I'd inhaled a great deal of air very quickly, and had tried to do so in unison with my part-ner, No Name, through my seven chakras. Whatever happened, the process was wild and exhilarating.

No Name and I lay on the floor, wrapped up close, eyes dilated and glistening. Our hearts were pounding. He stretched out his hand and placed it on my heart and we lay like that for several minutes.

'I caught a glimpse of you somewhere there,' he said.

'What do you mean?'

'I caught a glimpse of your heart.'

'Hmm,' I replied. I didn't like anyone passing comment on my heart. Very sore subject.

'You have a very *homely* heart,' he said.

I wasn't quite sure what he meant. Homely? Did he mean motherly? Kind? A tear threatened to emerge. I dabbed it away. I wished he hadn't said that. But he had; it was a compliment. No Name was okay, after all.

We worked together in another 'big structure' the next day. It was late in the afternoon, Day Two, and again we'd ended up on the floor, exhausted, wrapped around each other. We said intimate things, talked of love, of who we were and how much we wanted to change.

'I think you're pretty,' he said at one point.

'Thank you. But I've always been the ugly duckling amongst my friends.'

'God, I'd like to see what *they* look like, then,' he laughed.

We talked so long we were late for dinner. I was touched. What woman wouldn't be? After that, No Name and I agreed to meet once a day to swap notes and exchange the events of our journey. Our mission was mutual: to stay open. A man tells you you're pretty and that you have a homely heart? It's difficult, under any circumstances, not to feel moved. But this is tantra world, an adult playpen on love and sex, a place where everything said or done needs to be filtered and much of what is said and done would never even be considered in the real world. It was an extra-real world. And so I forgot the image of his face, the hand-waving and the word TRICKSTER. I was succumbing to the extraordinary texture and challenges of the week: dynamic meditation before breakfast, followed by workshops, sexy people, nudity, twelve hours of being 'on', alert, encouraged to connect with the same and opposite sex in an intimate way, rising to and failing at the various structures. It's hard not to get swept up, overwhelmed. And so, yes, I forgot my initial impressions of this man.

heart penetration

As with John Hawken and Jan Day, working with Sarita proved revelatory. Sarita had her own approach, much of it taken from her decades in Pune. Her workshop passed on several different types of chakra work and meditation. Every morning there was a different type of meditation before breakfast. With Sarita I first practiced Osho's famous own-brand dynamic meditation. This consists of five stages: breathing rapidly through the nose, chaos and catharsis, ten minutes of jumping up and down shouting 'hoo-hoo', dance and then stillness. Osho devised this meditation specifically for Westerners who, he said, were too busy in their minds and couldn't achieve stillness without a jolly good clear out first, hence the hoo-ing.

There was more.

Chakras. I knew all about them, or so I thought, until Sarita said something quite astonishing.

'This is how they work,' she said, demonstrating by inter-lacing her fingers so they were lined up in a weave-pattern. 'Men penetrate women with first, third and fifth chakra, the sex, the solar plexus and the throat.'

I nodded, fascinated.

'Women penetrate men with the second, fourth and sixth chakra, the womb, heart and head.'

The heart? I was transfixed. Women penetrate men with their *heart*? Of course. This tantra stuff was so unexpectedly rational, so practical. Again, this sounded sensible, almost familiar: she was pointing out something I didn't know I already knew. Men penetrate women with their sex. Women penetrate men in a more emotional way – with the heart. An old feminine intuition rose up in me, an ancient wisdom. Now it was being fully revealed, even demonstrated for me to see. I knew this would be a good way to proceed. In future, I would wait until I felt I'd penetrated a man fully, with my heart, before I allowed him to penetrate me.

So much happens in these tantra weeks. Tons happens inside the workshops and then even more happens outside, during meal times amongst the group. People flirt, reject each other, buddy up, swap buddies, fall in love. This group was partic-ularly diverse and eccentric. A man called Ahan with long white hair woke most mornings and danced half-naked on the lawn, greeting the sun. I spotted him once from my bed-room window. There was a hulking man called Teejas (James, from Reading) whose wardrobe included a maroon towelling bathrobe and leather gauntlets. There was a small group of Irish tantrikas, gorgeous people, and, I have to say, easily the maddest people there.

No Name and I had managed to meet twice for debriefs. On the third day I wrote in my diary:

Will this connection soon fizzle out? Will one of us withdraw? Shut down? Can we both stay open? Can we make three more meetings at 7 p.m.? He is trying to be open – so am I. I want to stay open and trust him to stay open too. Each man here fulfils a part in my re-configuration. The other day a man called Pradip (Paul) said to me: 'The heart cannot break. Only the heart's armour can break.'

disco

There was an underlying objective to this week. The general idea was that we'd revisit the early stages of our lives in order to reset them. The seven to fourteen stage was mostly centred around one event – the teenage disco.

It was Friday night and we were encouraged to dress up. There would be no alcohol and we were asked to 'go for it', to indulge our most teenager-like sexual urges. Arlene, a slant-eyed Italian lesbian who resembled Gina Lollobrigida, was nervous and didn't have a dress to wear – so she came up to my room and borrowed one of mine. She hadn't been with a man for a long time. She was nervous about the disco and so was I. The idea was this: aged fourteen, some of us had been in the thick of the disco (as I had). Some of us had been in there snogging and getting off with the opposite sex. Others had sat around and watched, feeling awkward and left out. This staged disco was a chance to reset what had happened:

for us *all* to join in. The wallflowers could go mad, indulge themselves. The snoggers could bow out.

This made me very uneasy. The truth, for me, was that the teenage disco had been in every way horrible. No matter what part you played in it. If you were in the midst of it, snogging, it was one form of hell; if you were left out, it was another. That night, during this staged disco, many of the soft tantric men transformed: they went mad and ran charging around the room like fourteen-year-old boys on amphetamines. They groped and grabbed. One man, wearing nothing but a gold asp round his neck and a pair of designer underpants, came towards me, arms outstretched, like a mummy. I dodged and fled. Many of the women entered the spirit too; none seemed as phased as I was. Throughout all my era of casual sex dating, I'd never felt *depressed*. But I felt depressed as I watched Arlene flailing around and being groped on the dance floor. I felt depressed as I saw men and women descend on each other without thought or consciousness. It was messy and ugly watching adults act like fourteen-year-olds.

In the end, I sat this disco out, on the sidelines. I watched as No Name and a woman dressed in a cobweb-style goth dress pulled a mattress into the centre of the hall and got stuck into what looked like full-blown intercourse. Others had gathered in groups and were also 'going for it'.

The theory of this scenario left me cold. Surely there was another way forward, another way to tease out the scars and insecurities of teendom? A shy young man came over to me. He had long hair and a kind face; he'd been a virgin until he was twenty-seven. We kissed and fooled around a little. Around us, there was mayhem. Just before midnight, I made my excuses and left.

In the morning, I was even more depressed. I spoke to Sarita and Suta and explained I thought the whole thing was awful. They knew it was awful; it was supposed to be awful for some. They explained it was all 'part of the process'; I was where I was supposed to be.

'I think I want to leave.'

'Stay till lunch time,' Sarita urged. 'You might feel better later.'

I didn't like quitting. The only way to fail a tantra course is to leave it. That morning, in the big hall, I lay down on the floor and thought: *what on earth more do I have to do to cure myself of love for one man?* I'd done everything I could. I'd stick my head up an elephant's arse if I knew it would be the antidote for heartbreak. I'd do anything to feel better, to regain my spirits. Tears welled. No Name saw me and came over and put his arms around me. I was so low I couldn't speak.

The next exercise was a session in breathing the universal divine energy up the chakra system. Using something called 'the fire breath', raising the breath up the chakras, it could induce divine whole-body orgasms. I'd tried this before, in one of John Hawken's workshops and had breathed myself into delirium.

That morning I didn't bother to try. I lay there while all around me, the hall filled with groans and cries. Some were definitely faking it. One woman, though, wasn't. She was shrieking with preternatural ecstasy, thrashing and rolling around, beyond herself.

When it was over, I got up and walked out. I went to the bedroom I was sharing and opened my diary. In it lay a newly pressed primrose I'd picked only the day before. Primroses were out again. It was three years since we'd split, a year since my resurrection in Glastonbury on my first tantra course with Jan Day. Tiny angelic primrose faces smiled at me from flowerbeds, from beneath the manicured hedges of the hall. It was 14 March, 2009, my ex's birthday. I picked up the phone in the room and dialled his number.

'Hellooooo?' said his soft voice.

'Hello, dear. It's me.'

'Hello, dear.'

'Happy birthday.'

'Thank you.'

'Have you had lots of nice cards and presents?'

'Er ... no.'

'I'm in Somerset. On another tantra course.'

'Oh, God.'

'I've just been in a hall with lots of people having full body orgasms.'

'*God* ... I don't know how you do it.'

'Neither do I.'

'It's insane.'

'Are we meeting in two weeks, then?'

'Yes.'

'I'll be staying at the vicarage.'

I put the phone down. Two weeks later I was planning to go to a hen night in Madley, a small town in Hereford. Jasmine was getting married to Jon. We hens were staying with the vicar's wife. It was an hour's drive from my ex's home, so we'd agreed to meet, go for lunch and maybe a long walk. I'd stay the night in his spare room. I was looking forward to it. A month earlier we'd talked. I'd told him that I was still bored without him. He'd said he was bored too.

We'd discussed doing some kind of a long walk together, along the canal, from London to Birmingham; it was a project he was hoping to sell to his publisher. I'd thought, *maybe we've come to that time*. Time for a proper talk. Maybe it was the time to speak about either a clean break or a new time together. Maybe a few days' walk would be a good thing: banish the romance entirely. Bring us down to earth. Maybe we'd argue and hate each other and then I would have the closure I needed. I needed to hate him again, I needed to be with him again, so I could say – *yes, you're a pig, I hate you, it's better we're apart.*

have i ever hurt you?

I didn't leave Sarita's workshop; the feeling of desolation lifted. I stayed on. After lunch it was sunny and some of us women lolled on the loungers by the pool. No Name came bounding from the main house, across the lawn and hopped on my lounger, straddling it. 'Can we work together next?' he said.

'Okay,' I nodded.

'I'm not playing at being fourteen any longer. I'm working my way up in age ... to be with you.'

I laughed. I wasn't particularly disappointed that he'd gone mad with the woman in the goth dress at the disco. We'd danced early on and I had found him much less appealing, something to do with the strange horsey noises he was making. Next we were about to do a big structure around being twenty-one to twenty-eight. I felt it would be interesting to reconnect with him. We hadn't worked together since Day Two. Our 7 p.m. meetings had slipped.

Half an hour later, No Name came bouncing back out of the house and jumped back on my lounger.

'Now what?' I said.

'Err . . . I *can't* work with you next.'

'Oh, really.'

'I need to work with Sue, from the disco last night. I promised her I would. She's upset. We need to work things out.'

I looked at him. The word TRICKSTER flashed before my eyes. I thought, *you stupid, stupid man*.

'Do what you have to do,' I said.

'Can we work together later in the afternoon?'

'Um . . . okay.'

That afternoon, we went into the main hall. Sarita explained that we were going to do a ritual around forgiveness. As children, we are very needy for love and touch. When we don't get enough, a child thinks they don't deserve it. As a result, we can push love away as adults, thinking we aren't worthy of it. Intimacy is all about opening to receive this love. But in order to do this we need to forgive those who have wounded us. The ritual was a simple one. We were told to partner up with someone of the opposite sex. I partnered up with D, a slender grey-haired man in his mid-forties with blue twinkly eyes. The idea was this: I'd sit on a chair opposite him. He would kneel at my feet. He would ask me one simple question, a question spoken on behalf of all men. 'Have I ever hurt you?' I would then respond. Then he would say: 'Please forgive me.' I would say: 'Yes.' Then he would kiss and wash my feet. The ritual would then be reversed. Simple.

Couples lined up facing each other in the hall. Mostly the women sat in the chairs, men at their feet. There was silence, a few moments of composure, before the ritual began. Then Sarita gave the word. D leant forward and said:

'Have I ever hurt you?'

Before I could utter a word, the hall exploded. Violent tirades. Rants and screams and men and women shouting terrible things to whoever sat in front of them. I put my fingers in my ears. Screams and bellows disclosing all manner of abuse. My eyes filled. I couldn't speak. Until then, I'd wondered what I had in common with all these people in the hall. But then I knew, in that explosion of rage and fury around me. All these adults in a room, shouting that they had never been loved as children, they hadn't been loved or touched; they had been neglected, shut out, criticised. One woman was shouting about her dead brother; another about being left alone for years. I looked at D opposite me. I was too deafened and distracted to talk. I listened to the others, whose sadness and rage was at once so recognisable and similar to mine and yet also so much worse. Or perhaps, as I said to D, my anger was long cold. I'd often exploded at my father as a teenager. I couldn't shriek and scream. I told D of my father, the man I'd never liked or loved much, the man I'd been scared of as a child and whom I had grown to dislike from around the age of ten, whom I'd grown to judge and despise as a teen, who'd been nothing but a disappointment as I grew to know him as an adult. He had hurt me. I said nothing about my ex.

D nodded. 'Please forgive me,' he whispered. Then he kissed and washed my feet. I was happy to let him do this. I liked this man. He smiled at me. In tantra we are asked to look at a single man as all men. D's face was boyish, despite the salt-and-pepper hair. I was glad someone had said sorry. It felt like an honourable statement.

When D sat in the chair, I knelt before him.

'Have I ever hurt you?' I asked.

He looked at me long and hard. Then slowly, slowly ... tears came. 'Yes,' he said and buried his face in his hands. I saw his tears fall through his hands on to the floor. His shoulders heaved as he began to sob. His ex-wife of twenty years had hurt him. I listened to how his wife had withheld sex and hit him; how he'd failed her. I listened to his infidelities, how sorry he was, how much he loved her and how much she'd hurt him and I found, again, my eyes filling with tears for this man and for all of us, how much we hurt each other. When he was finished sobbing I begged him to forgive me and kissed his feet and thought of my ex, and how much I'd hurt him, how I'd also withheld sex, how I'd driven him mad. I was *so, so sorry*.

'Please forgive me,' I begged this man and kissed his feet and washed them and wept.

After this ritual, No Name came over to me.

'I can't work with you later,' he said. 'Sarah wants to work with me. I promised I'd work with her too.' I was so flabbergasted I almost laughed. He'd been putting himself about a bit. I looked at him.

'Listen, you *little shit*,' I hissed. 'You can't just cancel arrangements like this, not twice. I am NOT going to work with you again. Do you get me?' I glared. 'Why don't you *fuck* off?'

He nodded. He didn't seem to mind or care that I'd been so

WITH THE KISSES OF HIS MOUTH

blunt: he was having some kind of personal orgy of self-development. He hurried away.

bum sliding and sky dancing

Saturday night, the last night of the course. More massage. This time we were supposed to ask a member of the opposite sex for whatever pleasurable touch we wished for. I buddied up with D again, with whom I now felt very comfortable. We wore sarongs and nothing else. He was good with his hands and we talked as he massaged my shoulders, breasts and face.

'Did you do this for your wife?'

'Oh yes, many times.'

'My ex never massaged me. If he had, things might have been different.'

'I massaged my wife and she still hated me.'

'But this feels amazing. I'd love any man forever who could touch me like this.'

'Are you sure? You'd get used to it.'

'No, this is wonderful.'

I relaxed and wanted to fall asleep, to relax into this man's hands, to trust this man and all men; I wanted this trust of men back. I wanted to like men again. I thought of No Name, what a fool he was. I sighed and this nice middle-aged man put his hands all over me. It felt like we'd crossed many wide and thorny deserts of our lives together in a short time.

When it was my turn to massage him, he lay on his stomach and then made a strange request.

'I'd like you to slide down my bum.'

273

'What?' I laughed.

'Slide down my bum. Then down my legs.'

'You're silly!'

'Go on, have a go.'

'Okay.'

I squirted massage oil down his legs so they made a slick slide. I took off my sarong and rubbed oil into my bum. And then I slid – yippee – down the bump of his bum, just like a BMX biker, then down his legs.

'Again!' I squealed with delight.

I slid and squirmed and slid and wriggled till I choked myself sick with laughter. As with Tony, El Lobo, I delighted in this ridiculous play. God, it was funny. A relief to be giddy again, with a man.

After a while, I stopped.

'What now?' He turned over onto his back; he was naked, his torso, genitals and legs were exposed.

'Do what you like with me,' he said.

I grinned. He had a lovely cock. I wanted to put it in my mouth.

I began some kind of tantric heart-chakra pre-massage ritual which Demara had showed me. I vibrated my hands on his chest and his lower abdomen and then began a slow massage of his chest and groin and thighs till he was erect. I was naked. I let my breasts rub against him. I let my hair fall in fronds all over him and caressed him with gentle caring love. Despite Demara, this show of love was still new to me. Man worship. Phallus worship. I took his cock in my hands and began to massage it in slow deft circular movements. He groaned. He exhaled, then began to use the 'straw breath', sucking air up his chakras as I continued with my phallic massage. His eyes rolled backwards in his head. He seemed to go somewhere else as he breathed, as I stroked.

I didn't bring him to a climax, there wasn't enough time. We were given forty minutes to pleasure each other and the first half of this, at least, had been taken up with bum sliding. When the chimes rang, D was still breathing as through a straw, still elsewhere. I stopped and lay down next to him. I liked this man. We kissed and hugged, as though we'd just had sex.

'You went off somewhere there,' I said.

'Yes.'

'Where did you go?'

'Sky dancing.'

I'd heard the words before, but had never had it explained.

'What does that mean?'

'I was up in the sky, dancing up there. The breath helps to get up there. But once you're there, you can stay up there for ages. It's like flying.'

'Wow. Really?' I was impressed that with my own work I'd taken a man sky dancing.

'But I didn't give you an orgasm.'

'That's not important,' he said. 'You took me flying. Ejaculation is just like landing the plane.'

These were impressive words. They implied he felt there was no attachment to orgasm. This was the great theory behind tantra, that orgasm isn't the goal. At that point I hadn't slept with any tantric men, but I was very keen to see if the theory held sway in practice. Were tantric men very different lovers?

slap

In my diary I wrote:

It would be unwise to stay open to No Name, a foolish man. I must learn to choose who I should open my heart to. This course has been fruitful. Difficult and fruitful.

On the last morning, Sunday morning, I bumped into Sue of the cobweb goth dress on the landing of the ornate spiral staircase in the main house, two floors up. She looked teary and fragile. It felt like a long time since the disco, but in fact it had been just over twenty-four hours. No Name had moved on, she'd been part of an exercise.

'Are you okay?' I asked her.

'No.'

'What's wrong? Is it that twat?'

'Yes.'

'What happened?'

'He said he wanted to rent a room here, to spend last night together, that he wanted to be with me.'

'Really?'

'But he worked with Sarah all night, then he asked me to wait for him. I sat up waiting. But he talked to Sarah in the hall for hours. I waited in the living room and he didn't come.' Her face was puffy. 'I thought he liked *you*,' she said. 'He kept saying he wanted to work with you.'

'Oh *God*, he's a jerk.' I hugged her. 'I don't fancy him at all. I'd rather sleep with you than him.'

She nodded and a thin smile emerged. She'd had intercourse with him in the name of developing herself, in the spirit of the disco game. But it was my guess that she'd slept with men and been abandoned in the past, perhaps many times. This man had said things he hadn't meant. He was grabbing all and everything he could.

'He's a dick, don't worry about him,' I said. But I could see clouds of despondency gathered in her eyes. I peered down the curved oak banisters, down, down – and saw that there, two floors beneath us, the ratfink dick-brained No Name was standing. He hadn't seen us. He was deep in conversation with another man.

'*Look*,' I whispered. 'He's down there.'

We peered down.

'Come on, ' I said. 'Let's go and slap him.'

She shook her head, horrified. 'Nooooo, I can't.'

I felt a dim glow of pleasure grow and then spread in me. A hiss of tinder. A little wick lit itself. And then . . . I was aflame.

'I can,' I said. Then I was off, down the stairs, flying like frigging Scarlett O'Hara, racing to get to this cretinous man before he moved from the spot. And then I was there, feet away from him. By then, I knew his name. Sid. His name was Sid. I shouted it out. 'Sid!'

He turned.

My little hand was already drawn back, poised. As he turned, I brought it down on his face: *SLAP*. God, it felt good. It felt right and just. My hand landed square on his jaw. His eyes bulged. He couldn't believe what he saw. A raging woman standing before him, eyes fired with right-eous indignation. A woman who'd come to deliver a blow on behalf of all women. For that was at the heart of the tantric message. One man represents all men. One woman is everywoman. Poor Sue hadn't the energy to fight back. I had. I wanted to make this point for all women. We're human. Not toys.

'You're an arsehole,' I said. 'A total fucking *arsehole*.'

His mouth fell open.

We stood, rooted to the spot, and glared at each other. No other words came. None. I could have rained blows on him; I had the desire and passion to do so, to beat him to the ground. Instead, I turned and stalked out.

I saw my mother slap my father as a child and later, as a teenager. At first I was awed, and then I came to recognise the female face-slap was something to be admired. My mother's face-slap instilled respect in my adolescent Catholic heart. Once she even used it on me, aged fourteen, when I was unreasonable and mad and a total brat. She slapped me hard across both cheeks and it shut me up instantly.

My mother told me a story recently. She got cold feet on her wedding day, the day she married my father, with whom she stayed for forty years. All dressed in white and an hour before the ceremony, aged twenty-four, she went weak and limp and fearful. She wailed to her mother, my grandmother, that she'd changed her mind, she couldn't go through with it; she'd made a mistake; she didn't want to leave home, to marry this English man. My grandmother was the most composed and serene woman I've ever known. She never raised her voice, let alone her hand. But on that day, my mother's wedding day, she picked my mother up by the collar of her beaded Ottoman silk dress and slapped her hard across the face.

'*Fermez la bouche*,' she rasped. '*Il est un beau homme*. And you are going to marry him.'

And so I know, from family lore and from personal experience, how well it works. Along with widowhood, face-slapping is in my feminine family tradition. Both are dramatic and effective forms of either withdrawing or delivering energy. One, a form of self-punishment; the other a form of punishing others. I come from that punishing Catholic tradition.

In the last twenty or so years of my adult life I have used the face-slap judiciously. Only three times have I ever slapped a man. I slapped my ex-boyfriend Rupert once, at a university party, for being unchivalrous. It worked wonders, he came round instantly. I slapped a man with orange upright hair whose name I now forget, a younger man I dated years back. I slapped him for saying that members of the IRA should be rounded up and shot. This slap also worked. Eerily, both these two men were sons of Conservative MPs. And I slapped No Name, for treating this poor Sue like a plaything and for being an affront to womanhood. I'd be surprised if anyone has ever slapped anyone else at that big hall, a haven of self-development. Sarita and Suta, I'm sure, would be horrified. But John Hawken might not be horrified. I had gathered and guided my energetic forces to the right target.

I froze the twit out for the last day of the course. But, given that we had done so much work on forgiveness, I softened around tea time, only hours before the course ended.

'Do you wanna talk?' I asked.

'I'd like that very much.'

We toured the topiaried garden. I wasn't going to give him much time.

'Thank you for the slap,' he said.

'What?'

'Yeah, it was great.'

'Are you kidding? Sid, you've been a jerk. There are people here who've been abused.'

'I know. But I'm here with my own stuff. I've never been slapped before.'

'I'm surprised.'

'Nah, mostly, all you ever get from women is the usual bleeding heart stuff.'

I was shocked: *bleeding heart stuff*. My heart had been bleeding for years. Had his ever bled at all? I didn't slap him again. But he deserved to be punched. I'd recently taken up boxing at the All Stars Gym on the Harrow Road and I reckon the next man who says something like this to me will get clobbered.

I walked away, again. I was lonely again. Tired. I went home to Harlesden. I didn't talk about this course much to anyone. I'd lost five pounds from all the Kundalini shaking, dynamic meditation and raw food. It took me about two weeks to recover my spirits.

divorce

A week later, Rose and I drove to Jasmine's hen night celebration in Madley, Herefordshire.

We hens had stayed up all night singing songs in rounds and dancing in the crypt of the big old church in Madley. In the morning we'd all naturally gathered around an ancient oak in a next-door field. We were chatting and hugging the tree – when I spotted my ex knocking on the door of the vicarage. We shouted and waved at him and he waved back and started to make his way across the field, walking slowly towards us. There were eight of us hens and I felt awkward as he approached. I wanted to be proud of him with my new tantra friends; this was the ex I'd talked a lot about. Rose was there. She knew him but hadn't seen him since we split. He was older and fatter than when we'd first met. Big and old and fat and yet still striking to look at. I wanted to tell them that he was once younger and slimmer and cuter, but I didn't. I walked out towards him.

'Hello,' I said.

He looked troubled. I went to hold his hand and he made a show of shaking me off.

'Oh,' I said. 'Not in a good mood this morning.'

'Humph,' he growled.

I introduced him to the hens. Jasmine was swinging from a low branch of the oak; she was four months pregnant and her bump was tidy and round under her tight sweater. She was still wearing her jaunty oak-leaf crown.

'This is Jasmine,' I said. 'She's getting married next month.'

'Congratulations,' he said.

Rose kissed him in greeting. I introduced the other hens and we made polite chit-chat. Then we all walked back towards the vicarage and he took pictures of us gathered at the front door. When we'd talked on the phone at the hall, we'd planned to go for a pub lunch. It was a sunny spring day. In the hallway of the vicarage, as I was about to say goodbye to Rose, I suddenly had an idea.

'Do you want to join us for lunch?'

It was a strained moment. Rose looked at my ex. He bristled. 'Er ... I'd like some intimate time alone with you,' my ex said. Rose, wise, wise Rose looked at me and nodded.

'Of course,' she said.

I blushed. 'Okay.'

We said our goodbyes and walked to his car.

His car.

His car was everything I needed to remind me of who he was: a man prone to excess and depression. The back seat was crammed with empty cartons of milk and chocolate wrappers. At Totleigh, I often found rudely violated chocolate bars in the storeroom cupboard or on the floor. Quite often he would attack a chocolate bar, taking one or two shark-bites from it and then toss it over his shoulder. Often, he did the same as he drove. Our cars always had half-ravaged chocolate bars littered all over the back. He also did this with milk cartons. He drank milk a lot, by the pint, because he said it was good for his voice. He would drink a pint in two or three gulps and toss the empty carton over his shoulder and it would land somewhere behind him.

The front seat of his new car, a silver Honda, was disgusting. He hadn't given up smoking since he'd developed his heart condition. I knew he was still fighting depression and could see his smoking had got *much* worse. The front seat of his car resembled the aftermath of volcanic eruption. A fine layer of soft grey ash covered everything. The dashboard was snowy. The ashtray was stuffed and numerous fag butts were scattered all over the front seat floor and the gear-stick area. The passenger seat was covered in ash and butts and chocolate wrappers.

'I'm not sitting in there,' I said.

He laughed, only half-embarrassed, and found a newspaper from somewhere in the back seat. He blew some of the ash from the passenger seat and put the newspaper down for me to sit on. It all came back to me. Andromeda Heights. The days in the white hump of a caravan. The half-tramp I met and fell in love with ten years earlier. In those days, I'd thought his sooty smoke-choked and filthy caravan a fine place for a writer to live; it was Bohemia. I'd thought his squalid home and lifestyle somehow noble, the squirrels skittering overhead, and gnawing through the power cables, the trips to the outside lav in the dead of a winter's night. Our love story had begun amidst our mutual first endeavours to be working writers at whatever cost. Ten years later, I'd moved on. I sat down awkwardly in that filthy car and tried not to touch anything.

'I am the only woman *in the world* who will like, let alone love you, with a car like this,' I blurted.

He laughed.

'Can we go see a stone circle?'

He nodded. 'Yeah, I know one not too far from here.'

I was relieved. I wanted to show him the magic of the stones. He'd be impressed. The car, a mobile rubbish dump, shook and coughed as we drove along.

He drove me to The Four Stones, near Kinnerton in the Radnor Valley. These are four stones, set very tight in a circle. The stones are broad and fat and resemble a nest of sumo wrestlers huddled together. They're very near the road; I was a bit disappointed. They were too close together, or so I thought, too close to show him. But there was enough space for one or two people to stand in the centre, only just. *This won't work*, I thought. Bugger. Even so, I went into the centre and threw my arms open. I rested my eyes on one of the big stones and began to turn ever so slowly to the left.

An almighty heaving feeling instantly emanated from the stones, a massive power, as though I was in the foot of a towering ocean wave. I turned a little more. The stone-energy surged. I turned and ... *whoa* ... I stopped. My ex was watching, puzzled.

'There's big energy here,' I said. I didn't care how mad I looked. The stones were very powerful. 'Come and have a try.'

True, the space in the centre of the stones was the size of a bus shelter. But maybe he would feel it too. He stepped inside the stones as I left. He threw open his arms and turned and then stumbled a little.

'What do you feel?' I asked.

'I feel a bit ... dizzy.'

'Dizzy?'

'Yeah.'

'You haven't even moved.'

'I feel dizzy and sick.'

'That's the stones.'

He stumbled around a bit more. I wanted to laugh. He is a funny person to look at, colossal and bald as one of those stones. I knew then I could still get him to do anything to please me, that he still loved me. We were still fun together.

'Can I go now?' he begged.

'Yes, okay.'

He stepped out of the circle.

'You didn't really get it, did you?'

'No, I don't think so. I was worried someone I know might drive past.'

'Like who?'

'Everyone around here knows me. What if they saw me?'

'Okay.'

We left and drove to Hay-on-Wye for lunch. I wished there'd been a larger circle to show him my new discovery. I just *knew* he'd love it.

At Hay-on-Wye, I bought a sheep's-milk ice cream and we walked the streets. In one bookshop window there were remainder copies of a book by a well-known Irish writer with whom I'd had a liaison, years before I met my ex. He spotted them and made a bitchy remark. He was still jealous of this Irish writer-rogue. I was pleased he was jealous. We ate an unremarkable Sunday roast in a pub. He wanted to know more about my tantric adventures, but, as always, I found them impossible to describe. I've always found it hard to explain what happens and what I was learning. Tantra is a *practice*.

'I'm learning to be more conscious around my sexuality,' I stammered. It was hard to tell him what I'd been doing all the lonely years without him. He'd had two relationships. There had been eighteen months with Ruth and then six months with a younger woman. That had ended too. I hadn't ventured into another relationship. He'd been replacing me with other women. His replacement technique hadn't worked. My adventures, while illuminating, hadn't cured me of my love of him either. I still felt so unhappy to be without him. He was a stupid arse. But there was a resounding human empathy, almost telepathy between us.

We finished lunch and walked back to the car.

I assumed we were about to drive back to his home. His elder daughter would be there, whom I hadn't seen in years. I was looking forward to seeing her. I'd get to see the cat too,

Lady Violet. I got into the filthy car. We sat in the car park for a few moments before he said: 'I want a divorce.'

'What?'

'I want a divorce from you.'

'What do you mean?'

'I want you to be okay, without me.'

'What?'

'I've met someone. I've fallen in love.'

'What? *When?*'

'A month ago.'

'What's her name.'

'Lesley.'

'You cannot be *serious*. Lesley?' I scoffed. Leslie was the name of a satirical character he'd made up years ago. Leslie Alaric MacFaddean Spume (FRLS) was a top of the second division twentieth-century post dada-ist concrete sound poet. He was the Poet-in-Residence at the Potato Marketing Board and he was working on a collection of nature poems called 'Mumbles'. A friend of Larkin, dear old Harry Pinter, and Ted Hughes, his wife Mimsy had died in a water-skiing accident off Gozo. Leslie was seventy-two; he had a brother, Sir Hilary Spume who lived with his companion Eric and their house-keeper Mrs Cutler. My ex pretended he was Leslie Spume's official biographer. He used to do stand-up routines as this alter ego, Leslie Spume, and blog as Leslie. At Totleigh, when poets came to stay, my ex would use Leslie's blog to out the gossip he'd heard.

'You cannot possibly make love to a woman called *Lesley*,' I spat.

'Er ... Yes, you're the second person to point that out.'

'Lesley? You're kidding.'

'Yes. Her name's Lesley. She's been on *University Challenge* and I'm in love.'

'Jesus Christ.'

He started the car. The news was dumbfounding. I couldn't believe it. As he drove, this new love story unfolded. They'd met on an internet dating site, 'Ivory Towers', for clever people, people with a university degree. She lived in Northern Ireland. She was a librarian. He'd gone to visit her. It had been love at first sight. They had met twice in the last month and they were *in love*. It had happened. Finally, three years later, it had happened to one of us. It sounded bizarre and a bit desperate. It sounded fishy as all fuck. He'd fallen in love with me, too, at first sight. Was this normal, or a tendency of those who are narcissistic? To project, to throw themselves, make everything happen quickly, dramatically. It sounded as if this Lesley was someone he'd projected himself onto. He loved *University Challenge*, he loved all quizzes. He was a quizzer who loved *University Challenge* and had invented a comic character called Lesley and it was as if he had spun this new woman called Lesley out from all the *prima materia* in his unconscious. In the same way that Cathy wailed 'I am Heathcliff' – was this new Lesley somehow *him*?

I felt sick. I felt dire repulsion. I wanted to stop and get out. Tears fell. They fell and fell and began to flood. I hiccuped and coughed tears.

'Let's go for a walk,' he said. He drove me to a nearby forest where we sat in the car. I collected myself a little bit. Then we got out and walked. There wasn't anything logical or sensible to say. By then, Karsten had been in touch and we'd planned a weekend for him to come and stay. I had exchanged numbers with D, the slender man with the twinkly blue eyes. I knew I'd see him again. But I felt I needed a big card up my sleeve. I felt I needed to say, 'Well ... here's my news. I've met someone too, now you mention it.' But I had no such big card to throw down. I felt pathetic and dumb and tired of it all. I knew he'd loved me once. I knew all this had hurt him too. But I suspected he hadn't loved me half as much as I had loved him. I suspected he loved easily. That he could just fall *in*. I knew he wanted to get on with his life. So did I. Tantra, all my new ideas, most were so very hard to explain. And, besides, I wasn't sure if the sexual dynamic between us would ever change.

We left the forest and went back to his house. His daughter, by then a young woman in her late twenties, was there and so was the cat, Lady Violet. The cat ignored me. His daughter and I gossiped and drank wine and cooked spaghetti bolognaise. It had taken me two years to win his eldest daughter's trust. But I had. I was good at Christmas and I reckon that swung it. My ex had a kip.

I just about managed to be alert and civil as we ate dinner. Then I asked to be excused. Upstairs, in his bed, I started to weep again. Lady Violet came in, her great French tickler of a tail up; she stared at me and then went out again. In a corner of his room he kept a display cupboard which he called 'his shrine'. In it, all lit up with fairy lights, he had displayed various mementos of our time together, including all the marble and stone eggs I'd given him over the years, all my unfertilised eggs. I was forty-three. Too late for babies. I'd never have babies. In his shrine were all my eggs, standing on little plastic plinths. I'd given him six years of my life and seven polished eggs. My best fertile years. Instead of babies, I'd written books.

My ex came in with two cups of tea. I was weeping.

'You shit,' I said.

He sat down on the bed which was on the floor. He watched me as I wept. Despite all the irregularities of how my ex had met this new woman and despite how unromantic it sounded, I had a feeling that somehow this really was the end of things. He *had* fallen in love this time, or had told himself he had – and it amounted to the same thing. He seemed calm and stable, he seemed to know himself. We had come to this – the death throes. The natural end.

We had spent six years together and three miserable years *not together*. Since our split, the emails and phone calls and meetings via Arvon and elsewhere had never stopped. We still spoke to each other with the casual affection, intimacy, and sometimes irritation of a couple. We'd never shut down all the lines of communication. It would have felt wrong and impossible to do so. Our time together on the planet as mismatched lovers was soon over. But now I was sobbing uncontrollably.

'You know,' he said, 'I *am* a big personality. I know that. But the cure for me . . . isn't me.'

I huffed. I drew deep breaths.

'I know that,' I said. 'Of course I fucking know that. I've been trying so hard to find a cure for you. For our love. But I haven't found one. I don't think I'll ever find another love like ours ever again. That's what I'm most scared of. That this is it. You and I. That's it for me. I'll never find another man to love again.'

'What can I do to help?'

I looked at him, choked.

'Hold me, please.'

He put down his cup of tea and came across the bed and put his arms around me. I put my head against his chest and sobbed myself blue in the face. It was all over. I'd done everything I could to get over him. To some extent all the things I'd done had helped. And I was older, too. I was in a different place. I was soon about to be published again. But I was still so lonely without him. No one to talk to. And no one to see me. I *got by* without his company. I would be okay to go on without him. But only okay. Never great. Never dazzling again.

I sobbed and sobbed and eventually I was so tired he left me to sleep in his bed. All night the fairy lights winked in the cupboard in the corner, illuminating those eggs.

LIBERTINES

'Sex is as important as eating or drinking and we ought to
allow the one appetite to be satisfied with as little restraint
or false modesty as the other'

Marquis de Sade

♥

april fool

When you have a date with a man you've met on a tantra course, chances are you've either had him sobbing in your arms or cradled his cock in your hands. Both were true with D, the slender twinkly-eyed man. We met at Victoria station a couple of weeks after Sarita's course and three days after my ex's request for a divorce.

I liked D of the salt-and-pepper hair and the good hands. We'd got on effortlessly. He seemed natural and relaxed during the course, not needy or on the pull, and we'd swapped numbers and emails. I knew we'd meet again; it hadn't felt loaded between us, just easy. And so, when I saw him leaning against the railings outside the station, with a wry grin on his face, I jumped into his arms with relief.

'Good to see you again,' I said and meant it.

He winked and kissed me on the lips. We headed for the nearest bar. There, we chatted. Both Taureans, we drank a lot, ate tons of designer nuts and chewed the cud like two old Friesians.

He was a man's man, originally from the East End of London, and he used his blokeish charm with confidence. Blokeish confidence is a sure bet with women and yes, with me. Soon I was eyeing him up and a small tension stirred between us. Sex? Isn't there almost always this possibility when men and women first agree to meet, however casually? Earlier, he'd mentioned that he lived on a boat and had suggested meeting near it or on board. I'd said no to this; best we meet in town, in a bar, a public place, somewhere neutral, which wouldn't be too familiar to either of us. I knew 'boat' meant 'sex'; it meant 'let's do some massage'. I'd turned down this suggestion in favour of some time to get to know him.

After three glasses of chardonnay and four bags of nuts he said: 'How about we go to a restaurant near my boat for dinner.'

Three glasses of chardonnay. This man was easy-peasy company, funny and nice. Was it happening much sooner than I'd guessed? Did I want 'boat?' Did I want sexy boat sex? I didn't know. I didn't take full responsibility for my actions there and then – I can say this now. What trouble could I get myself into this time? Just what could go wrong with this man, who, I'd forgotten, was big into BDSM sex? I was forty-three. Old enough. Nothing could surprise me.

'Okay,' I said. 'Where's your *boat*?'

'It's a yacht,' he said. He kept it moored in a marina on the Thames.

We black cabbed it there. I'd never been to any kind of marina or dock on the river before; this one is right next to the Tower of London, rather glam, a bit like a glittering American shopping mall crossed with a mainstay marina. It speaks of new money and Miami. An old 'Iron Bridge', a relic of the *olde world*, of Plague London is bizarrely displayed on a trolley type contraption. There are a few chain restaurants lined up in a row. Of course, there are lots of very expensive-looking yachts moored there, too. From the dock you can see Tower Bridge, you can see the Gherkin. You are very much in the heart of the city, except on the dark lapping water.

The only restaurant open looked like an up-market American rib-shack, all wooden floors and oak beams and checked tablecloths. We went there. The steak was excellent; the waiters were attentive and so was D. He asked me lots of questions about myself. This is Chat Up Technique 101. It makes a woman feel appreciated for all her charms and human qualities, not just for her good breasts or her nice bum. Attentive males, especially on a first date, will usually get laid sooner rather than later. Attentive heterosexual males are normally 1. pretty rare and 2. very experienced womanisers.

He was doing well and we both knew it. When he asked me about my ex, tears fell freely (he was a tantric man, this was cool) and I told him it wasn't a great subject to talk about. I dried my eyes. I said I'd loved my ex deeply, but our sex life was complicated. I told him that my ex wanted a divorce, and of course this sounded mad. D's wife also wanted a divorce – a legal one. The conversation moved on. By the time our pudding arrived our chit-chat had turned to foreplay; we'd begun asking each other sexually explicit questions over our crème brûlées. Very quickly we finished them and got the bill.

On the way to his boat, we looked up at two helicopters, circling high overhead. The newly elected President of the United States, Barack Obama, was in town and the choppers were part of Her Majesty's Government's efforts to make sure he wasn't murdered by terrorists while he was their guest. The choppers, Tower Bridge, the Gherkin, the glittering condo-style buildings; the date had gone well so far. I was well fed, sexed up and with a nice man, one by whom I was happy enough to be womanised. I was wearing a Portobello Market rabbit-fur jacket, faded and torn blue jeans and Hush

Puppy boots. *Roffey, you're still cookin'*, I told myself. *Roffey, you're such an arse*, I also told myself. *What the fuck are you doing here?*

When we got to the boat I 'Mmm-ed' in genuine appreciation. A Caribbean girl, I've been on many yachts, but I meant it. It was a sleek fifty-footer with a teak deck and fine lines. I've never been much of a nimble-footed gazelle and he had to haul my fat arse aboard. This got us laughing. It was a balmy night. While he rolled a spliff downstairs in the cabin I sat on the top deck and surveyed the situation. Okay, here I was. I was on the boat. *In for a penny, in for a pound.* I liked the helicopters chopping above us. It felt Bond-esque on board that swan-like yacht. I felt a little like a Bond-style heroine, despite the haul arse thing. I got to thinking that we were in some kind of theatre. There was good lighting, action overhead – I got to thinking I should say or do something dramatic.

He sat down opposite me on the deck and lit the spliff. The night was warm; I shrugged off the rabbit-fur jacket. As he talked, I lifted my shirt and flashed him my stomach. He paused and I thought *here we are. Two can play at this. If you're going to womanise, I'm going to be a woman.* I began to run my fingers along my stomach, caressing myself. He watched my fingers and kept talking for another minute before he came forward and kissed me slowly and languorously. *Thank you, God.* A great kisser. We hadn't kissed on the course. His tongue was thick, but he moved it around my mouth in a tender, exploratory manner and soon we were kissing and groaning, him on his knees, my legs wrapped round him. A full leg-lock, body-lock, hugging groaning moaning smooch of a kiss. We stopped. He stared into my eyes.

'I need to piss,' he said. I laughed. Nothing could throw me by then. He left me on the top deck, the choppers for Obama circling overhead. I turned to look at Tower Bridge. The gates were up, like arms. I couldn't believe my luck. I shrugged from my shirt and bra so that I was half-naked on the top deck, happy for all to see. He came back and knelt in front of me.

'It's bloody difficult trying to piss with a hard-on,' he said.

I laughed.

'Shall we go downstairs?'

'No. I like it here.'

'Here?'

'I told you I was an exhibitionist.'

'But these other boats, they're my *neighbours*.'

Chop, chop chop, came the sound from high above. I smiled.

'Do you know what turns me on?'

'What?'

'Helicopters.'

I pulled him closer with my legs and we began to kiss again. Just as I was about to relax completely and swoon into a flow of loving softness, he stopped. His body became rigid. He pinched both my nipples.

'Owww!'

'Right. We need some *safe words*.'

'What?'

'We need safe words. The playing ritual has begun. We need to make things safe. Red. That means you like it hard. Amber is medium. Green is soft. He held my nipples like he was arranging jumper cables under the bonnet of a car.

I stared, incredulous.

'What the *fuck* are you talking about?'

'I always use safe words when I have sex.'

'Always? Really? I thought safe words are for when you tie someone up. For when you might hurt someone. I never agreed to being tied up.'

'We still need safe words.'

'No, we don't.'

'Yes, we do.'

'You're *kidding*!' I snatched my shirt and put it back on. I thrust him away from me. Whatever the female equivalent is of losing an erection, it had happened to me. How could he have missed what was going on? The universe had conspired to give us everything a man and a woman need to get it on. Easy conversation, good food, a romantic setting. Lights. Choppers. The boat. We were moments from moving downstairs, moments from rolling around on his bed, from terrific sex, from the kind of sex that makes you realise that it's okay after all; it can be so harmonious between men and women.

But no. This was a man just loosed from a twenty-year marriage. He'd never before got a babe aboard his boat. He'd panicked. He was trying to control things. Jesus God, turning my nipples like knobs on a control panel. *The playing ritual has started*. What was with the David Attenborough-type voice over? I pushed him away and grabbed my rabbit-fur coat and looked at my watch. It was midnight – fuck. I was miles from home, on a madman's boat – well, no – a nice, fucked-up man who'd read me all wrong and who wouldn't hurt me, but it was time for some instant calculations to work out what was best to do. How on earth would I get home? Taxi? Thirty quid. Shit. Yes, that was what I'd do. I'd listen to him for a bit; I wouldn't leg it immediately. I would give him ten minutes or so, then leave.

He sat and stared at me. I hunkered under my jacket. He handed me the spliff. I smoked some of it and let him talk. Ten minutes. That's how long before I would hop off that boat and head for the taxi rank. He began to ramble. Something about how he'd recently been on a cruise, about how he'd been the only single man and how all the single women, all in their mid-forties, had come on to him. How they'd been *older* (though not older than he was) and desperate and therefore unappealing. I've never so instantly frozen and hardened at a man's words.

'Stop,' I said.

'Why?'

'Because I don't think I like the way you talk about women.'

'What way?'

'I *mean* the way you were describing those women. Do you know how old I am?'

'No.'

'I'm forty-four. In three weeks.'

He blinked.

'I'm the same age as those middle-aged women you're describing.'

'But you're different.'

'I'm middle-aged.'

'You don't look it.'

'I'm middle-aged and you're a fucking arsehole. You're a middle-aged man, too. And you look it. And you're an *oaf*. What gives you the right to talk this way about women?'

His face fell. I handed him back the spliff. This was a man committed to tantra; he'd even once described himself as a 'tantric master.' Like Sid of the Slap, he was no such thing.

Minutes seemed to tick past. He smoked and stared and I sat and stared back.

'No one's ever spoken to me like that,' he said. 'Normally it's women who get needy and clingy. It's women who queue up to try and get me. I should throw you off my boat.'

'Good. I'm leaving anyway.'

I'd become instantly stoned from the few pulls on the spliff. It had muddled me up. My legs were weak. I realised this meant that I couldn't hop off the boat: I'd barely been able to get on it. I looked at my watch. It was 12.40 a.m.

We began to argue. And I mean argue. Like two bulls. For the next two hours we rampaged all over his boat arguing, stoned as stoned can be. We argued on deck, we argued down in the cabin. We drank. We cried. We said deeply personal things to each other. He showed me photographs of his wife, his grown-up children. We sat in two big leatherette armchairs and agreed that all this talking was very tantric; that yes, we were being real. I could have left, could have sped away in a cab. But no, I stayed and maybe yes, we were really 'experiencing each other' in a difficult place. We talked and ran around the boat until I was exhausted and it was well past 2 a.m. When he said, 'Come on, come and sleep with me, in my bed,' I said 'Absolutely not'. Then he got cross and hurled pillows at me from a cupboard in the belly of the boat. I hurled them back. We had a pillow fight trying to arrange a bed for me in the bow of the boat. He was annoyed that after all the kissing, talking, arguing and spliff, I didn't want to fold myself into his arms that night.

He was so stoned and bullish that he erected a makeshift curtain from a towel in the corridor outside my cabin.

'You're being an arse,' I laughed.

'Just so your ladyship doesn't get the wrong idea. You can have your privacy.'

'Great.'

I smiled, but he turned and stumbled back to his cabin.

'Good *night*,' I called after him from my bunk.

That night I didn't sleep much. I stared through the port-hole and thought of my ex. He was a bit of an arsehole too. I was *definitely* an arsehole. We all were. Why was it so difficult to get things right? Or was it me? Yes, probably it was. I couldn't see where I was going wrong. I wasn't getting very far with the goal of how to love better. I was running into trouble with every man I met. I was a fool, an April Fool. I was born in April. Soon, I'd be forty-four. Tantra? So what? I felt like I'd learnt nothing at all, nothing in the last twenty years, nothing since the first time I had ever had sex.

In the morning, we drank strong black coffee and he walked me to Tower Bridge tube.

'I'll understand if you never want to see me again,' I said.

He smiled. We kissed briefly.

'At least it wasn't a boring evening,' I tried.

He looked exhausted; sheepish, too. He smiled.

But yes – to my surprise, I did see D again.

my first time

At this point I felt that despite my quest, I'd learnt nothing, or not enough. I was *in* it; my ideas were still sketchy, still forming. This was a time of exploration and I was taking notes but not nearing any conclusions. Where and when had my sex life begun and what had I learnt in the years before my quest? My 'first time'? It was there, in my past, a half-forgotten scene in my head. As for many, the first time I had sex was a rather dismal event: I was ashamed of it for years afterwards.

My first proper boyfriend was called Joe. He had long brown hair and wore (much ridiculed) clogs and cut-off jeans and he had nice legs and looked a little Pacino-esque. He was the funny man of my brother's 'lime' (group of friends) in Trinidad. He was older than I was, twenty-one – and cool.

I was seventeen. I went out with him one long summer in Trinidad and even though I was as randy as a goat, I didn't let him 'go the whole way', for fear of what the girls might think when I got back to the convent in England.

This is true. Convent schoolgirls are much maligned, but we were all virgins, at least up until the sixth form. If anything, I felt pressure to *keep* my virginity rather than lose it. Joe and I did everything we could BUT have sexual intercourse. My father once caught us making out on the family sofa. Well, more than making out. Joe's head was between my legs. My father didn't utter a word in the darkness of the room; he simply appeared at the other end. We froze as he calmly made himself an Alka-Seltzer at the bar. As soon as he had gone, Joe panicked and said he should leave. But I replied, '*He's hardly going to come back!*' Joe stayed. The story is a famous one in the annals of my adolescence. Joe and I fooled around in cars, on the golf course, at my parents' house, at his parents' house, on the beach, at parties; everywhere we could. But we never made love – and I regret that now, because I wish I could say that my first time had been with him, a man who loved me and whom I've known and liked the rest of my adult life.

I lost my virginity two years after the summer of Joe. It was the autumn of 1984 and I was nineteen.

I was sitting at the main student bar on the old Air Force barracks at Fifer's Lane, where the University of East Anglia housed its first year undergraduates. I was in a state of distress. It was my first night as an undergraduate and I'd been herded to this off-campus ex-RAF bar by a group of women on my corridor. The women I'd come with had big hair and pasty skin, and they were a different type from those I'd grown up with at the convent boarding school. One was clearly anorexic; another was blousy and Welsh and over made-up. Although I'd been fending for myself since the age of twelve, it had been within the confines of a rather rarefied world. I'd come from day trips and exeats and covert social gatherings with boys; that and the freedom of holidays in Trinidad. I was sitting on the edge of a big group of these new types of women when a tall handsome blond man spotted me and smiled.

'Will you hold my leather jacket, love, while I'm at the bar?' I nodded.

'Can I get you a drink?'

'No thanks.'

I was troubled and tired. But this older student seemed like he might make things a little more bearable.

He came back and we got talking as he nursed his pint. He was in the fourth year, he said, just out for a drink that night.

It didn't even occur to me this might be suspicious: a *fourth year* was in that particular bar on the *first* night of term? This was an older male student in a far-away part of the campus where the new academic year's intake of female students had gathered. It never occurred to me that he might have gone out to prey on first-year female students for sex, so that he could 'fuck a Fresher'. I didn't even know until later that week that this was a common term used. I wasn't aware that during this first week older male students went out to Fifer's Lane *specifically* to hit on younger women who'd just left home, who were ill at ease, out of their depth and vulnerable.

We talked easily and I thought this handsome slightly older man was rather nice and dashing. At closing time he said:

'Shit, I've missed the last bus home.'

I didn't know what to do.

'Can I bunk with you?'

'Uh, I'm not sure.'

'I can sleep on the floor.'

'Er . . . okay.'

When we got back to my room I made him a bed on the floor and he lay there while I lay next to him in my single bed. We talked from the bed-floor position but soon we were kissing and he was no longer on the floor but in my bed. All of a sudden it was happening, I was about to do it for the first time, there and then on the first night of term. I was very much caught by surprise, but okay with it nonetheless. He, I know now, had been planning this all along. I was a score.

'I've never done this before,' I said to him, as he was about to penetrate me. 'I want you to know that.'

But he showed little regard. If anything, I think he gasped. Maybe he couldn't believe his luck. Not only had he pulled, but a virgin.

The sex was a non-event. It all happened in moments, neither good nor bad, neither quick nor slow, nothing. No pain, either. He came and we fell asleep. Isn't that the way it so often happens first time round – and, horribly, many times after that? For me, this strange experience was made shameful by the later realisation of the how and why of my companion's intent. He preyed on me and I had been too naïve to see it coming. In the morning, he got up and caught the bus back to the main UEA campus and we never spoke again. For years I swore my closest chum, Emma Daly, to keep this secret because I was so ashamed of my slip-up. I was ashamed I'd been so easily undone.

Outwardly, it appeared that I had gone out and got laid and had sex; a shag, a quick fuck on the first night of my university career. Outwardly, it might have appeared that I was sexually confident, even voracious. But the opposite was true. It was a mistake. And it was I who carried the shame, not this man. I saw him once or twice after that around campus; once he even seemed to snigger at me to a male friend. Then, he disappeared. I don't imagine he ever thought much in his later life about what he did to me. I imagine I wasn't his first or last conquest. Some of the girls on the corridor had witnessed him leave in the morning and so I carried the shame of being 'loose' for the rest of that term, earning myself the nickname of 'Maneater'.

stay in the sadness

At the end of March 2009, my ex had asked me for a divorce and I hadn't given him an answer. I'm not sure why, or if it's at all connected, but the following months proved to be calamitous, men-wise. All the while, I was blogging about my writing life and could see, on my blog stats, that my ex was reading my posts not just once, but two or three times a day. He'd asked me for a psychological divorce, yet he was still tracking my life? He wanted to finally sever our connection, yet I could see he also sought to maintain one. Email, texts, the internet – I am convinced these modern forms of communication wreak havoc with affairs of the heart. I dislike and mistrust them entirely. I rail at friends who conduct their love affairs by text. Somehow it seems wrong to be negotiating the most delicate of human feelings with the pushing of buttons.

I was in a strange space. The endgame of our entire ten-year love story loomed close. Also, a lot else was happening.

Two days after the debacle on the yacht, Karsten, the masseur from the Spanish tantra festival, arrived to stay with me. While I'd cleared my diary in order to honour his visit, I was out of sorts. I was unhappy. He had a cold. And despite the fact that, when he turned up, he looked gorgeous – blue-eyed and bearded and full of a soft and mellifluous energy – I didn't want to kiss him, let alone share a bed with him. Instead, the next day, we walked the length of the canal nearby and then browsed Portobello Market. At the time my flatmate was the poet, Neil Rollinson. That night, Karsten cooked for Neil and me, fried artichokes and chicken skewers. Neil liked him and so did I. We went to bed the second night and he gave me another tender loving yoni massage which ended in body-wracking orgasm and tears of grief on my part.

'Why did you cry?' he asked.

'I've been so sad. I've tried everything to get out of it.'

'Why? You should stay in the sadness. Let it have you for

as long as it wants you. I was sad for years too, after I left my wife.'

'Stay in the sadness?'

He nodded.

'Sometimes I feel people around are impatient. I have to get on.'

'No. Stay sad. For as long as you like.'

What a good man. The following morning, with the new skills gained from Demara, I repaid the pleasure and watched, out of myself, as this tall well-built man with a large cock surrendered to my hands. It was still a new experience to say to a man, 'lie down, do nothing, this is for you'. To see this man relax enough to entirely let go. To watch his eyes roll back into his skull, to give to a man and receive nothing.

All the men, including Demara's model, I've 'given to' in this way have said the same thing: 'Women are lazy. They expect the men to do all the work.'

I knew I'd been lazy all my life, too. All my life, until I'd met Demara six months earlier and she'd shared her skills with me. Yes, I'd been a lazy bitch with men. Lazy with my ex, with all men. But also, these secrets of the flesh are well-guarded by women of the light, women like Demara. Maybe I, and many other women, lack a number of things: guidance, knowledge, sheer pluck, not to mention the imagination. And feeling we have a right to be so forward and inquisitive about a man's genital anatomy. Maybe women have been lazy because they know no better, and have been trained by society (church and state) to be demure and passive, to not lay claim to their sexual nature. While it's not *easy* to find women like Demara to teach other women sexual skills, it's not impossible.

Any women reading this interested in learning how to

pleasure a man skilfully should look in the erotic massage pages of *Time Out* or their local newspaper. There you will find all sorts of 'tantric masseuses', women who have a very woman-friendly attitude to the type of sex work they do. I'm serious. I'd advise this straight up. They are very skilled professionals and they have all the secrets. Call one of these women; say you'd like some lessons either for yourself alone or with your partner. Some teach and are happy to help.

the man with the orange underpants

Then, later that month, late April 2009, something unexpected happened. I accidentally *almost* fell for someone. I met this person on another tantra course with Jan Day. He was French, tall, with long dark hair and green eyes, eyes like iridescent lamps. Tattoos of birds and fish all over his arms. Like my ex, he was clever and funny and had a talent for drama. I can pin down the exact moment when I knew I was in trouble, the moment when all my attention collected, when my body jumped in delight, when I had that moment of *yes* – 'look who's here', the same feeling I'd had with my ex, when my arse wagged at seeing him, all those years back.

In the barn one evening, the entire group was dancing. I happened to look to my left. In that moment, I saw him, dancing wildly with another woman in the group. They were a sight, completely abandoned in their dancing. But it was his underpants that did it. They were tangerine orange. He was dancing in these tangerine underpants and then his dancing became so wild that he whipped them off. He danced even more crazily in the nude and it was then, watching him dance with such freedom with this woman that I knew I'd spotted another one.

What does it say about the likelihood of my future happiness that I fancied this man? What are the odds I'll ever be happy again? What does it say that the men I lose my heart to are showy and most irregular? They're also my type: these men make me feel less alone in the world. In all my investigations of the heart, have I come to this? I am alone in the world and I cannot find another person to pair up with because I'm also nuts.

In Plato's *Symposium*, Aristophanes makes a speech where he claims we were once all either one sex or a combination of the two. We were such powerful creatures that the gods split us up. That, he claims, is the reason why we spend our entire lives searching for the other half of our selves. Love, he said, five hundred years before Christ, is the response to another person's unique individuality. We all look for a love in another person who naturally fits our own character.

It has become clear to me that mad, mad men, men who sing and dance and show off, like my ex, men who rip off their string vests and tear off their orange underpants when they dance are the kind of men who fit my own personality. These are the type of people who will keep me company and make me less restless in the world. But, if this is the type for me, then I may be bound for singledom for a very long time, for these intelligent showy madmen are rare. Most can be found in the theatrical professions. They don't come along into my hermit-like writer's life every day or every week, or even every year. They come along now and then and when they do they make me love them.

Stuff happened between me and this mad Frenchman. After one evening workshop, we were all given mattresses as islands: we could lie on them alone or share them with another. I noticed this tall dark-haired man standing by himself, looking like he could do with some company, and so I beckoned him over. He came, happily. We spent much of the rest of the night on my mattress, kissing and fondling and gazing into each other's eyes. For hours we gazed and chatted and canoodled. No one but my ex had gazed at me so openly before. We discussed poetry and we talked about love. I stroked his armpit. He sang. He told me he had 'a history of getting intimate with women and then retreating' (I should have got up and left right then). I told him I'd been through the wringer.

'I just want to hold you,' he said, and he did.

We gazed for ages, me thinking all along, *I've had this before and I know this and can spot it, but this cannot be happening again.*

Later, I wrote in my journal:

This is what I've been mourning. For a few hours, with this man with the orange underpants, I had what I haven't had in three years. At last, I have glimpsed it again.

During the course of the week, things got a little gnarly between us. We 'said things' to each other, things which might have been a little rash. Then we were thrown together in three big tantric rituals which involved lots of nudity and intimate sexual contact. Two people chose us to be in their team of 'servers' and we made a juicy double-act. I spent most of that week writing in my journal as a way of managing my feelings around this man. I didn't slap him or call him an oaf. I maintained my distance and kept my dignity and I was proud of myself for this. I had met another person, at last, whom I considered as interesting and charming as my ex.

Later, when I talked with Jan, she said I shouldn't be so quick to give a man the keys to the kingdom. It was true – in two days, I had fallen a little in love. This was the biggest lesson of tantra, learning to be free of getting, of attachment to outcome. 'Men like to be able to win women,' Jan explained. Win? Get? So what was the difference? Was I being advised to be passive, to be more submissive? No face-slapping or tantrums? Was it men who were allowed to do all the getting? No. What she meant was that what I needed to learn, what we all need to learn, is to be open and to stay conscious and to learn how *to hold* sexual tension whenever it arises.

This was a difficult patch with men. It was as if I could no longer trust myself any more. I felt doomed. Doomed to walk forward too quickly, to be too trusting, too in need of being loved again. These tantric men, Sid of the Slap, D of the Yacht, I'd made the mistake of thinking them to be different, more conscious. But they weren't different at all; the main difference is that they were trying. And neither was I different. It all seemed to lead back to my first time. *Will you hold my leather jacket, love?* The man who got me so easily.

Was I still too easy? And if so, how could I change this? *Be your own mother*, Jan advised. By this, she meant take care of yourself, get yourself. Love your self. Self-love, the highest love of all.

dancing queen

I turned forty-four a week after this tantra course. I'd decided to throw myself a birthday party – a good sign. I was happy enough to have a party. In the three years since I'd split with my ex, I'd not been so party-spirited, had chosen not to celebrate anything for myself. This is notable because I used to throw lots of parties.

My forty-fourth birthday party turned out to be one of the best parties I've thrown to date. There was much flirting and much pot smoked and rum punch drunk and there seemed to be waves of guests. People sang me 'Happy Birthday' at one point and then my new friend Luke made my night.

I was dancing in a circle to Abba's 'Dancing Queen', when he appeared with a mischievous grin. From a bag, he brought out a fistful of something. What?

Petals! Rose petals. He threw a handful up in the air and they fluttered prettily above and around me.

Wow.

Rose petals in my hair. Pink and perfumed with rose oil. Rose petals on my shoulders, down my shirt.

I danced and twirled under the flurry of petals which seemed to rain down for ages. I danced and people sang happy birthday and rose petals caught up in my eyelashes, in my mouth.

I felt happy, like Abba's eponymous dancing queen; also exotic, like the woman in *The Song of Songs*. In the song, the man says the woman's garden is full of exotic plants: spikenard, saffron, calamus, cinnamon, myrrh. I felt equally celebrated. After so long, I was in my element that night.

'You were in your goddess, Mon,' said my friend Kate Bowes.

It was a funny evening. Curly (who complained the petals smelt like a hamster's cage) got tipsy and kept slamming the door under the stereo shut, making the CDs 'scratch' to the rhythm. A married girlfriend danced sexily with me and confessed her attraction to Luke. At midnight, a cat called Eugene arrived and hit the decks on my Lo-Fi and those who were left danced into the small hours to Kelis and Bowie and Kanye West. Lots of sexy men came. Lots of sexy women too. It was a drug- and alcohol-fuelled rampant party. No self-awareness or consciousness displayed whosoever. In the morning, the flat was trashed.

By lunch time I was back at my desk, thinking that I needed to take stock of my life. I needed to lay low. I wanted to think more about what I would do with my ex's request for a divorce. A month had passed.

So I didn't hear the stranger arrive. I was much too hungover and self-absorbed. I came out from my bunker-office around 2 p.m. for a cup of coffee and peered through the kitchen window. I saw Neil and another man sitting outside in our garden, chatting. I squinted. Neil and who? Neil and a man?

No, Mon, I castigated myself. *Lay off. Don't go there. Go back to work.* And I did just that. I was fragile from the party and bruised from the weeks of man-trouble. So I listened to my self-admonition. I turned on my heel, went back to my bunker and worked for another two hours or so. I had no wish to engage with any more men. None. Never-ever, amen. Even so, after two hours swotting, I was in need of fresh air. And so the second time I went to the kitchen widow and saw Neil and the stranger chatting in the spring sunshine I thought, *fuck it, I can't see myself getting into any more trouble.*

the northern poet

It was a perfect spring day. I ambled down the stairs to the decked area out the back of our flat, a tiny oasis of fresh mint and dill and lilies and clambering grapevines in the fox-infested backyard wastelands of Harlesden. The poets in the garden were sharing a bottle of wine and a spliff. I saw that Neil's friend was a nice-looking man with reddish hair and green eyes. He seemed open and friendly and spoke in soft Lancastrian tones. A big bloke-ish Alpha male. An Alpha-male *poet*. Rather rare. We gossiped about the poetry world and about Geoffrey Hill, a poet much admired by them both.

'Come out for a quick drink with us,' the northern poet urged. He had a feminine quality, a shy almost girlish smile. He had long eyelashes too and I swear he fluttered them.

'Uh, I can't. I'm writing tonight.'

'Oh, *go* on, just one.'

'No, I can't.'

'Oh, go on. I think you should,' said the girl-eyed northern poet, so flirtatious that it was almost camp.

And so I went with them to a local dive called the Misty Moon. There we talked of Trinidad, how it was beautiful, yes, but it wasn't some kind of paradise. He told me about he tried to row across the Irish Sea and almost made it, until, near the end, he collided with a lifeboat. We went outside and smoked while Neil watched football on TV.

We stood on the terrace of that grotty pub and flirted and I thought, *Oh God, get away, Mon.*

'I have to go now,' I said.

'Oh, *go* on, stay,' he cajoled.

'No. It was nice meeting you. I have to go, goodbye.'

I was a bit tipsy by then and I found myself weaving home along the filthy high street and doing something I'd never done before: I gave Harlesden's most infamous and relentless street beggar, One Pound Man, some money.

The next day he was up early and we chatted over coffee, again about books. He was a strapping man, Mellors-esque. He stood on our tiny kitchen balcony with a copy of *The Odyssey* and smiled at me with those girlish eyes. He was the kind of man who had never had to try with women. 'He's fearsome-looking,' Neil had said. 'Women love him.'

Yeah, yeah. He didn't have to try, only bat his eyes. I was trying to avoid men and here was one who'd just turned up on my doorstep. *No, Mon.* He seemed interested in what I was doing, or perhaps he was just northern and friendly, which to most Londoners, (especially ones like me), means too friendly. He and Neil were going to a book launch party that evening and he invited me to go along.

'I'm not sure,' I wavered.

'Oh, go on. I think you should. Why don't you come out with us for lunch and then come to the party?'

'No. I have to write. I have things to do. I'll check in with you guys later.'

I didn't go to the launch party.

In the morning, the northern poet was up early again. By

pure coincidence Curly had bumped into them at Queen's Park station on the way back from the party.

'They were both plastered,' she said. 'Funny and plastered.'

But here he was again, shockingly chipper and clear-eyed. A robust constitution for a man who'd been drinking and flirting all night. Was this a northern thing to be so 'well' first thing in the morning? In the morning I'm like a dormouse. I can barely see or speak. It takes me a while to unstick my eyes and focus properly.

Despite the difference in our morning-ness, we chatted a little more.

'We're having a summer banquet soon; you must come up for it,' he said. By 'we' he meant him and his flatmates.

'I can't, I'm going to Tibet. For research.'

'Pity you can't come. But Tibet will be more interesting than Cumbria,' he quipped. It occurred to me that I quite liked Cumbria. I'd lived in Lancaster for a year, my ex and I had visited the Lakes; I hadn't been back since. It was a part of the world sodden with nostalgia for me. Could I, should I ever go back up there again?

'Well, I *could* make one weekend,' I mumbled. I was unsure but I named the weekend – and he seemed to think this summer banquet could be arranged for then, so I could make it.

At the time I thought it a little odd that he might arrange a banquet just so I could attend. I didn't know what to think of him. He gave me a pamphlet of his poems and promised to send me his latest collection. I gave him a proof copy of my Trinidad novel, knowing it was a test. If a man is interested in me, he will read my work. When I met my ex, he'd fallen in love with me *on the page*. I guess I expected no less. I said goodbye to him and when we parted he flashed that girlish smile again and kissed me on the lips.

Later, when I quizzed Neil about him he said. 'Yes, he likes you. But leave him alone, Mon. He's too normal for you.'

A week later, his poetry collection arrived in the post with a hand-written note in a card, and an invitation for the 'summer banquet' in the Lake District at the end of May. Neil was going too. In his note, the northern poet mentioned 'rooms' for me to stay in and I imagined a room of my own, a quiet spot where I could sit in bed and write. It was a long way to go and I hardly knew this man. I *hummed* and *hah*ed and sat on the invitation for a week before I said 'yes'. If Neil was going, I'd be okay. In his note he'd mentioned otters and blue-bells and long walks. I imagined I'd spend the weekend with Neil and this big northern poet, walking in the hills, tramping through bluebells and quaffing pints of ale in the pub. So I said 'yes, I'll come up to stay'.

It was a long weekend, the last bank holiday in May 2009. He said it was fine to stay three nights; again he mentioned 'rooms' and I thought – good.

In my journal I wrote: *Give to this man, appreciate. Do not try to get anything. And, under no circumstances sleep with him.*

frieda and diego

When I got off the train at Windermere the northern poet was standing next to his car in the station forecourt. He wore blue jeans and a blazer and his hair was longer and more ragged than before. He looked at me with such a knowing and wolfish grin, that I groaned inwardly. *Shit*. I smiled and went over and kissed him on the lips.

'Hi,' I said and hoped I sounded cautious.

There'd been some kerfuffle before the trip. Neil had cancelled due to a teaching commitment days before. The banquet had been called off due to inclement weather predictions. I'd consulted all my girlfriends (and some male friends) about whether to cancel too or still go up. The jury was hung. I'd emailed the poet to let him know I'd felt a little awkward about coming alone. He'd been very encouraging. 'Your invitation is separate to Neil's. You're still most welcome.'

Soon after I arrived, we bought fish and chips and wine and he took me to my 'rooms' which were in fact his room in a large shared house. His *own room* and bed.

'I'll sleep on the sofa downstairs,' he explained. Luckily, Neil had warned me what he might have meant by 'rooms'. We ate the fish and chips and drank the wine and I began to relax. Silently, I cursed Rose and Jan Day for leading me towards being so open, towards eating fish and chips in a poet's smoky dingy room many miles north of home.

We talked. Or, rather, *he* talked. He showed me a scrapbook of his Irish Sea crossing and photographs of a trip to Kashmir. He looked a lot younger in the photos, even more ruggedly man-some. The trip up into the mountains, with gypsies, looked enviable.

'Men have all the fun,' I muttered. I meant this. Men are more active, more out there in the world and I have always envied them.

He took a glowing lava-lamp in the shape of an egg from the mantelpiece and gave it to me to play with. I lay down on his bed and he sat in a chair inches away. I listened to him tell me a lot about himself. For a man who looked like and lived like a committed bachelor, he seemed keen to share of himself with a woman. He told me about his ex-wife, his daughter; we talked about poems and poetry. It got late and I could barely keep my eyes open. I fell asleep with the glowing egg tucked up by my ear. Before I slipped into sleep I peered upwards to see him bent over me, hovering.

'Goodnight,' he said and bent to kiss me.

He brought me coffee in the morning and we went outside. A robin came to greet him. He threw it crumbs of cheese.

'Hello, little feller.'

In the same way I'd given Karsten a whole weekend, he seemed to have fully prepared himself to do the same. We spent Saturday in Morecambe. The last time I'd been to Morecambe was with my ex. We'd eaten fish and chips, trawled the many second-hand bookshops. Eric Morecambe is from Morecambe and I'd taken photos of my ex mugging next to the statue of Eric. We'd drunk tea in the Midland Hotel. It was during the first weeks of our time together, nine years earlier.

'I like this place,' I said to the northern poet.

'I can tell.'

With the poet I walked the same beach, visited the same bookshops, the same hotel, but there wasn't a whiff of romance between us.

Then, incredibly, he drove me out to Sunderland Point, possibly the most romantic spot on earth. An isthmus of land stuck out into the estuary of the River Lune, it gets cut off from the mainland twice a day. There's a small colony of people living on it, some second homers, but also many people who were born there and have lived there all their lives.

I'd visited Sunderland Point with my ex in 2000. It was sunset; we'd had to race the tide to get back. He'd shown me this romantic spot because he had felt romantic about me. I'd loved him then, truly loved him. We'd sat for some time and watched the sky change from yellow to red, watching the sun drop.

Now I was there in broad daylight with a man who cared much less, who probably had no intention of reading my soon to be published novel. We walked about. I sat on a bench and shared a cigarette with him as we gazed out into the estuary.

'I'm not ready at the moment for women,' he said at one point. His father was ill; he had family troubles. I took note.

As we walked back along the small pier, we came across an older couple, maybe in their seventies, standing outside their home, admiring the view. She had violet eyes, he had a grey-ing rockabilly haircut. They were lively and wanted to talk to us. Like my ex, the northern poet was a natural, soft-voiced, good with strangers.

We left the point, drove back to his room. There, he rolled a spliff and we chatted, me lying on his bed and him in a chair inches away. Again, I found the conversation all one way, him talking of various adventures. I was getting bored; I was maybe even a little annoyed. He wasn't asking me about what I like to read, think about, what were my dreams, had I had any adventures? I had so much to say. What on earth was I doing with this man? Did he fancy me, did he even like me or not? I was getting stoned, again.

I should have fallen asleep and started snoring.

I should have remained chatting, done nothing.

I should have remembered my pledge not to 'get' anything, to be tantric and not to sleep with him.

Instead I thought, restless, *why on earth is he ignoring me?*

In *The Song of Songs* the woman is very forward. She invites the man to: *Blow on my garden / and let its spices flow forth / Let my lover come into his garden / and eat its choice fruit.*

I felt frisky and forward too. There was that staring thing going on between us. We were stoned and staring at each other. Then I thought of something I'd seen Frieda Kahlo say to her lover Diego Rivera in the bio-pic of their lives. In the movie Frieda is too ill for sex. She has a twisted back and cannot make love to Diego any more. She says to him: *Come and lie down next to me.* It wasn't an invitation for sex. It was an invitation just to lie down.

So, that's what I asked him. 'Why don't you come and lie down next to me?'

He stared.

I thought, *oh good. That's livened him up.*

He came and sat down on the bed. Ry Cooder was playing in the background. Moments ticked past. He sat very close, our bodies touching, his body turned so he was looking down at me. He was peering at me, speculatively. Then he chose his words carefully:

'I make a better friend than a lover.'

'Wow,' I said. Through my haze, I understood. He was a womaniser; he'd assessed the situation. *Lay off her*, was his decision. 'And you seem so nice,' I said.

'I see a lot of women,' he said. 'I don't want to piss you off.'

You've already done that, I thought.

I cleared my throat. 'I haven't necessarily invited you onto the bed for sex.' I didn't want to explain about Frieda and Diego. I'd imagined some kind of clinch, yes, the clinch of Hollywood lovers – but not sex. I was too stoned for sex.

He came closer and ran his hand lightly over my arm. A light conscious touch. My skin rose up.

Fuck me, this northern poet has done some tantra, I thought.

We gazed into each other's eyes. He ran his hands up and down my arms.

I put my finger to his lips. He bit it.

Bollocks to this, I thought.

Moments passed, my finger pressed to his lips. He caressed me.

I was sure he was about to jump on my bones.

'I'm going to take a shower,' he said.

I nodded.

He disappeared.

I sprang from the bed, grabbed my mobile phone and searched for the number of a fellow tantrika, Chrissie. I was very stoned.

'Chrissie,' I gabbled.

'What?'

'It's me. I'm up here. With the poet.'

'And?'

I told her what had just happened. 'I need instructions,' I gasped.

She laughed.

'He walked away. Can you believe it? What shall I do now?'

She laughed. 'Was he inside you?'

'NO!'

'Breathe,' she advised.

'Oh, for fuckssakes.'

'Breathe!'

'Okay.' I stood there breathing and laughing and choking. 'I'm so annoyed.'

'Calm down.'

'Can you believe it?'

Peals of laughter came down the phone.

'This doesn't come in the tantra manual, does it? Man fucks off. No it doesn't.'

She laughed.

I was stoned and beside myself.

'Breathe,' she whispered coquettishly.

'Okay. I just want you to know that I'm going to kill myself when I get back.'

'Breathe,' she whispered.

'Yeah. Bye.'

I stood there, breathing.

I was beginning to see another pattern in my encounters with men – an over-active imagination. Life was dull without my ex, who'd been such a funny and dramatic man. 'Boredom: the desire for desires,' said Tolstoy in *Anna Karenina*. I was a storyteller. I wanted stories to tell, to star in myself. I loved story. Story was everything. But I liked the romantic dramatic type of story, not the real stories which lay underneath; they were far too hard to figure out. I was bored without a match. I needed to be Frieda. This need for drama, combined with drugs or alcohol, was proving to be an obstacle. I wasn't finding new ground, a new place. I was the same old, same old drama queen and I was beginning to piss myself off.

choonksy

All through my escapades I was fat. A stone heavier than my younger self. 'Healthy'-looking. 'Choonksy', as they say in Trinidad. I'd like to mention that. Not only was I in my early forties, but I was tubby, which I hope female readers will find reassuring. Not a young nubile sexpot – I was middle-aged, and no longer slim. No Botox, no injections. Yet, contrary to messages put out by the male-dominated popular press, men found me, an older, shapely woman, sexually appealing.

I was learning to live in this new older body, to grow fond of it. But even so, I began to see the extra weight as a physical manifestation of the grief, or the psychological weight I'd been carrying. So I decided I wanted to retrieve something of my younger self, something of the woman I'd been before I met my ex. And so, with the help of a personal trainer and athlete, André Williams, I began running. I could barely run two laps of the track at our local gym at first. But, slowly, slowly, often tricking me, André taught me how to run, run as far as three miles even, in the end. That summer, I ran and ran and it became a meditation, something which brought me near to a state of bliss. I ran myself into a kind of peace.

I also began dancing 5Rhythms. Invented by New York dancer Gabrielle Roth in the 1960s, it's a form of unstructured dancing with its roots in Gestalt and shamanism. It follows five musical rhythms: flowing, staccato, chaos, lyrical and stillness. These five rhythms, when danced in this sequence, form what is referred to as The Wave and can bring dancers into an ecstatic state. It's more than just a new-age disco (Rose took great pains to point this out to me); for many, this kind of dancing is a spiritual practice. At a 5Rhythms evening you dance until you are overcome, till you shed your inhibitions and your body responds in a primal and uncensored way. Some 5Rhythms dancers can feel themselves 'being danced' by their bodies, as if ancient dance movements find them in the dance.

And so, in June 2009, I went with Rose to a 5Rhythms session in Tufnell Park. I loved it immediately. It helped with the man trouble; it helped with all trouble, it *shifted* these troubles.

'This is where you can come to sweat your problems,' Sue Rickards, the facilitator, had said one night on the dance floor. She was right.

♥

By then my ex and I had started discussing our divorce. The idea of having an actual divorce ceremony had begun to materialise: it was a bizarre but practical idea. I understood what my ex meant by needing to separate, even though it was years since we'd been living together. I knew our story had to stop and I wanted this ending too.

The letter bomb had arrived from a dark place, had blown us apart. We'd never even said 'goodbye' that chilly January afternoon in 2006: I'd screamed and he'd fled, his car tyres screeching as he tore away. Our parting had been so shocking that we still felt ashamed of it. How awful to have left each other in such a hurricane of guilt and blame. We'd written books, shared a job, merged lives for years, to end it all like that?

And so, I hit on the idea of a formal ceremony, a ritual conducted by someone who knew about rituals. My ex said he'd mull over the idea. He was still reading my blog posts on a daily basis. I knew we were in the death throes of the part of our relationship which had faltered on, the remnants of our profound attachment which had never entirely died away: blog posts, Facebook, emails, they were our way of still knowing each other, of being linked.

I thought it would be a positive thing to somehow *reclaim* our split. Take it back into our own hands. Rose knew of a man, Nick Clements, who lived in Wales, not too far from my ex; a shaman who performed pagan rituals. I got in touch with him to discuss the possibility of him performing a 'hand-parting' ceremony for us; the idea being that this would be an event, a conscious act of setting each other free.

A hand-parting is the reversal of a hand-fasting ceremony. A hand-fasting is an ancient pagan ritual, the equivalent of a wedding, still performed today, where a couple will bind themselves together for a short length of time – precisely one year and a day. I'd heard about these ceremonies from John Hawken and others I'd met in my tantra workshops. I thought that having some kind of cutting of our bonds, some kind of formal separating of hands, was just what we needed.

When I mentioned the idea to my ex he grumbled. 'Can't we just go out to a field and … you know … do something alone?' he protested. 'Why does it have to be so formal?'

'You asked me for a divorce and now I'm giving you one,' I argued.

'Humph,' he said.

'It'll be good for us. I want a divorce, too. It will be a ceremony in which we can honour our time together and say goodbye.'

'Okay,' he said.

'But I don't want you to do it *for me*,' I said. 'I want you to think about this carefully. I only want you to say yes if you think it would be good for you too.'

'I'll think about it.'

And so, from the end of June 2009 onwards, we began to discuss and plan for a formal separation ceremony.

success

Also in June 2009, I visited the School of Life, a kind of modern-day school of ideas in Bloomsbury, and enrolled on a course about Love. I decided I needed to do some actual studying on Love, a subject I still didn't know enough about.

Our teacher was the philosopher and writer Robert Rowland Smith. He said many insightful things about love that weekend. The first thing he said which struck a chord was:

'There's an unspoken pressure on us all to be in love. We all have a strong urge to search for our other half, but – in the end, do we only want to be with ourselves? Is love a divine narcissism? Woody Allen once said: "I'm looking for myself, only female." Is that all we search for – our self, or the other half of our self? Not someone else.'

Robert also talked a lot about Plato's *Symposium*, about the idea of finding another person to fit our character.

'In Plato's *Symposium* Socrates also develops his theory of love,' he said. 'He says that love is not about admiring another person, but trying *to get* their qualities. We seek in others qualities we don't have in ourselves.'

That small word again, 'get': we try to get things from others. Jan Day said this, too.

'But Aristotle replies that actually, the opposite is the case. We don't try to steal the qualities from those who we love – we usually love them for who they are.

'Socrates then talks about the idea of "goodness" and the idea of "the good", about the love of good or of God. He says that we must all find our own internal goodness and develop love of the self, which is pretty much a religious state. Love of the self is the top rung of the ladder in terms of religious experience.'

Osho said something similar.

'Know thyself,' said Jesus Christ.

'Get yourself,' Jan Day once said to me over the phone when I told her about the man with the orange underpants. But self-love was boring: I wanted someone else, someone to love, to love me, to have fun with, be with. Loving myself? It didn't sound too exciting.

The Greeks had a word for spiritual bliss – *enthaos*. They were big on how to be a good lover. Giant stone phallic symbols were erected on every other street corner in downtown Athens. But the Western civilised world didn't stay sexually liberated for long.

'St Augustine was responsible for spoiling it all,' said Robert. 'He saw that sex was related to the fall of man; sexuality was the original sin. The eating of the fruit in Eden was a metaphor for sex, it was linked to sin and banishment.'

Sex, therefore, was man's first disobedience. St Augustine was one of the foremost Christian intellectuals of his time and he influenced centuries of Western thinkers to the Victorian era. Michel Foucault says in his *History of Sexuality* that we are still very much reacting against and answering to St Augustine. In the modern era, that is the last hundred years,

Robert said that human beings in the West have been in a gradual process of sexual enlightenment.

Enlightenment? I wasn't so sure. More than ever, we are in need of new structures for loving relationships, new and acceptable ways to love: shorter term arrangements, like hand-fastings for instance; a greater acknowledgement of the role of friendship in a world where families no longer live close by, a more inclusive attitude to couples and single men and women without children. Yet heterosexual monogamy and marriage, a model which has been failing for decades, is still our ideal. So much so, that now even same-sex couples have been granted legal rights to emulate this model, and are trying it.

And what about sex itself? Are we still free of taboos? Whenever I talked of my tantric experiences it had a cauter-ising effect on conversation. My friends were intrigued but, ultimately, it wasn't for them. I've had to be careful what I say and to whom about my adventures, for fear of attracting neg-ative judgement, of being labelled too active, too sexual. Tantric sex, shamanic sex, group sex, sadomasochism, liber-tine sex of the exhibitionists, anal sex, all of these are practised but still stigmatised and, in some places, totally unaccepted.

We also discussed 'what sort of person we should all try to meet'. Robert suggested that we meet people for three main reasons:

1. Because they are a good social match
2. To reproduce
3. To meet our unconscious needs

For the first of the three he asked us to calculate our own worth and social assets, to try to work out how much value others might put on our heads. When I added myself up I came to this: two novels, one PhD and nice curly hair. We use this idea of wealth, our social assets, to make ourselves attractive to the opposite sex. We weigh each other up and judge each other's worth when trying to find a mate. Had my ex judged me like this? Had I been valuable in this way? *I'm only with Mon for career reasons.* Yes, I saw then that somehow he'd seen me as an asset to him, as a way of gaining access to a world. Maybe that had been his strongest reason for being with me. I was a good social match for him, a man from the working classes; a step up.

Talking about the second idea, he showed us an online genetic DNA matching service for couples wanting partners who'd give them the right offspring – yes, an American site. This second reason is a very strong and usually unconscious motivating factor in the choosing of a mate. We choose each other to develop the race, to make strong healthy babies.

But it was the third reason I found most fascinating. 'Sexual energy is an unbound energy', Robert said. 'When we find the right love partner all this energy gets gathered, trained and bound. This is the experience of falling in love.

'The feeling of falling in love recreates the feeling of our parents' love and pride for us. When we see our love match we often have that feeling of "Daddy's here".'

I was scribbling furiously at this point.

My ex, the man with the orange underpants. I'd had that feeling with them both – 'he's here'.

'We become less special when we're older. Love is a childlike reaction. That's why so many of us have child-like names for our loved ones. Love is psychologically nostalgic. Freud said that we repeat what we don't understand.'

With my ex, had I been repeating a relationship which I didn't understand with my father? Absolutely. I didn't pick him for his social assets – he was living like a tramp in a caravan when we met. Nor did I pick him for reproduction. So, I had picked him for deeper psychological reasons – to heal the wound of neglect I had from my father. Seen this way, I had a moment of revelation: our relationship had been a *success*. Unconsciously, I picked him to love me as my father never had. And he *did* love me. It had a very healing effect – which has lasted to this day. And I will always say this about my ex – his love healed this old wound. He loved me unconditionally for a very long time and the effects have lasted.

Wow.

Robert also talked about Erich Fromm whose book, *The Art of Loving*, published in 1956, has become a Western classic.

'Fromm talks about love being economised. We shop for it. We are not trying to find love, but to *get* it. We want to be adored, prized, looked after. But we are getting things the wrong way round. There is an "art to loving" and we generally have no skills in this art. How much time do we spend making ourselves better at love?'

Again, I was nodding and scribbling. I had thought this exact thing myself. I needed to know more about how to love; I need the skill to love, both emotionally and sexually. I wanted to be good at it. But it was a lonely path; no one else around me was trying too hard. Tantra classes, this course on Love, they were rare and pricey.

'We expect to be deserving of love, and yet we are passive. We think of love as a panacea for our boring lives. We have this fantasy of this easiness, of simply "finding the right person". But few of us make ourselves better at being loved or being a good lover or being good at love.'

Being good at love. Sexual loving, as I had found out, involves some secrets and some skill, skills I hadn't taken the time to learn in forty-odd years of living. As Robert Rowland Smith made clear, emotional loving took some conscious practice too. Loving others well – this, I was sure, must start with loving oneself. But it took me some time to take this last idea on board, the least attractive idea of all. Self-love. I needed to go no further than myself, look inward, be uncomfortable for as long as it took. I needed to love myself before I could learn this art of loving anybody else.

échangisme

In early July 2009, accompanied by two glamorous and generous tantrikas, Georgie Davey and Tom Sperring, I headed for the libertine Mecca of Cap d'Agde in the south of France.

I was the one who had wanted to go, mostly in the spirit of my quest. I fancied I might be some kind of swinger. I'd loved being sexual with more than one person in my tantric workshops. I wanted to explore group sex some more, and I also wanted to meet like-minded others. I'd read *Atomised* by Michel Houellebecq years ago and thought it was very powerful: some of it is set in the famous French swingers resort of Cap d'Agde. And so, though I'd never swung, I was itching to try, and I thought the best place to start might be the biggest and baddest resort on earth, the Cap.

While naturism, nudity and swinging have been going on

at Cap d'Agde since the 1960s, 2002 saw a new wave of libertinism in France, a revival of interest twenty years on from the dawn of AIDS. Books like *The Sexual Life of Catherine M* and *Atomised* were part of this new wave. Today there are around four hundred heterosexual *échangiste* (swinging) clubs in France, forty in Paris alone: Les Chandelles, Cleopâtre and L'Abys being some of the more infamous. In France, swinging is no longer *outré* or specialist or ugly or weird. It's not something for tired middle-aged couples who've burnt out sexually; it's a leisure activity for couples in their twenties and thirties and above, for people who are sexually intrepid, often attractive and highly educated. It is for those who wish to reject and consciously live outside the basic ideas set out for them by a conservative society. Many of these couples have homes, children, pets and jobs, and choose to have sex with other couples, often complete strangers because they want to, because they find monogamy constricting. Swinging can be limited for single people: though single women are welcome, but single men are largely banned from clubs.

Besides, with writers such as de Sade, Apollinaire, Verlaine, Rimbaud, de Laclos, Anaïs Nin and more recently Michel Houellebecq, the French have a social and literary culture of outlandish and outsider sexual behaviour. Unlike the English, the French don't bat an eyelid at their politicians' mistresses. In elite circles it's considered necessary, even chic, to have a lover. We English, on the other hand, have few bona fide 'libertines'; John Wilmot, Earl of Rochester, Lord Byron, Aleister Crowley, Leigh Bowery and the late Sebastian Horsley – mostly a collection of rakes and dandies. Google 'English libertines' and you get numerous articles on Pete Doherty's old band. Oscar Wilde was Irish. The English are better known for S&M, for their interest in spanking and punishment, the dark side of being so repressed. We have Benny Hill and the sex club Torture Garden. English sexuality is famously clamped down on – hence its interest in clamps.

I wanted to know more about how and why couples swing. I'd heard that, like tantra, échangisme or libertinism is a matriarchal culture. 'No' means no. Women get to make all the rules. Was this true? And what, if anything, did sophisticated Western hedonism have in common with ancient Eastern tantra? Was there some overlap? Was there any common ground at the heart of these opposing sexual ideologies? Was it only the late and much vilified guru Osho Sri Rajneesh who'd tried to bridge the gap between Eastern and Western sexual behaviour? In short, in the basements and 'back rooms' of some of these clubs, did west and east meet?

What if there were lots of good sex clubs in the UK? What if the British were equally comfortable with a libertine ethos, if swinging was considered chic? A few good sex clubs do exist in the UK, but they are expensive, highly vetted; chic swinging is rare and pretty underground. Fever and Killing Kittens are clubs for swingers in London – but it's a world hard to, *er*, penetrate as a beginner. What if this was all very different?

I packed my bags, and, with two game-on and like-minded tantrikas, headed south.

What did I pack? Oh, the usual. Basques and see-through peek-a-boo fringed garments and stockings and g-strings and nipple tassels. Lubricant, condoms, high heels, leopard print and rabbit fur. And no bikini, for, *by day*, nudism at Cap d'Agde is compulsory – everywhere.

heliopolis

Cap d'Agde is hideously ugly. It resembles an abandoned Olympic Village, circa 1964. It's hard to imagine anywhere more spiritless or architecturally monstrous or less sexy. Swathes of sun-bleached concrete. A few parched and sand-choked palm trees. Corridors of cheap porn-star boutiques. A big libertine club, Glamour, on the beachfront. While it started out as a harmless enough naturist resort, in the 1960s buildings went up, buildings which no doubt then were the cutting edge of cool; very space age, very *Star Trek*. The entire resort is dominated by a gargantuan solid concrete donut-shaped building called Heliopolis, which is where we were staying.

Through various contacts I'd found a resident English-speaking estate agent. He picked us up at the airport and dropped us at our apartment. Apartment? The long corridor outside it was dark, the floor made of sticky gymnasium-type rubber. When he opened the door, I was so dumbstruck I almost laughed out loud. It stank of mould and contained just one large room the size of my kitchen; it was in fact a minute cell inside the donut. The furniture and décor were grim. Think eastern-block communistic tat, think plastic ducks and soft porn on the walls and broken-down and faded sofas and a sofa bed which didn't work. A scraggy unweeded garden crammed with plastic sun loungers. Sex sells. The smug agent had charged us close to £800 in rental for the week, admittedly in high season. I was too shocked to complain.

'Jesus, it's a *dump!*' I blurted the minute he was gone.

'Don't worry, Mon, we'll make it all nice,' said Georgie and Tom.

Georgie and Tom were heroic dudes from the start. For the next hour we tried our best to make our one big room less offensive to the senses. We hid all the plastic ducks and plastic hats and plastic flowers and stuffed most of the plastic furniture behind a flimsy curtain. We weeded the garden and made a dining area outside on the tiny patio.

We didn't actually know each other that well. We'd met only months before, through Jan Day, during one of her week-long intensive tantra workshops. Georgie and I had clicked and met soon after the workshop for dinner down Portobello Road. It was then that I mentioned I was looking for a suitable companion for my trip.

'I'd *love* to come,' she'd enthused. I was delighted. She was the perfect choice, an ideal companion for such a jaunt. Georgie was a natural sexual extrovert, a woman with a keen and venturesome spirit. During the workshop it was obvious that although she was younger, she was more sexually experienced than I was. Georgie was thirty and tall and blonde and had something about her of Marilyn Monroe. She was vivacious and, as I was to learn over the coming week, funny, a funny lady.

Tom was another obvious choice, a man we both liked and trusted and found amiable and attractive but whom neither of us had too big a crush on. Tom was fifty-five with a great body and long hair and a weather-beaten face. An engineer turned windsurfing instructor, Tom had retired at forty-nine to travel, do karate and work on himself with the aim of liberating himself from his past womanising ways. Tom was into everything from men's work to ayurvedic medicine. He came from Dagenham and spoke broad cockney. He was also a strict vegan.

Georgie had a good idea about how best to tackle the compulsory nudity and Heliopolis in general. As we were unpacking, she said to me: 'Here, I brought this for you.'

In her hand was a small diamanté tiara.

I smiled. 'Thank you, Georgie.'

'I'd like to go shopping tomorrow, just wearing a tiara.'

'Okay, I'll come too,' I grinned.

A tiara? As we unpacked, I noticed the significant difference between Georgie and me in terms of our sexual pallet of toys, accessories and body adornments.

Georgie: A pierced clitoris, a pierced belly button, a once-pierced tongue, a perfectly manicured Brazilian, a number of sex toys and a mountain of underwear which included a tutu, a bustle, ankle cuffs and four pairs of killer stilettos.

Mon: No piercings, a fluffy muff, which Tom said resembled an old lady's head, no sex toys, oodles of sexy clothes and underwear and one pair of Vivienne Westwood high-heeled jelly sandals.

We'd met for lunch a week beforehand, to discuss the trip. We anticipated an environment of sexual chaos and felt that having a place of calm, a 'no sex nest' at the centre of it all would be a good idea, and so we'd decide that we *wouldn't* sleep together.

Later that first day, we hit the beach. Georgie and I wore sarongs and nothing else. So did Tom, but he made a point of letting his tackle hang loose and in full view. A gentle, good-natured man, Tom is hung like a porn star. It was funny and endearing that he was so game.

We found a spot not too far from the concrete donut.

'Come on, Georgie, let's go find the libertines,' I said.

Butt naked, shoulders back, stomachs sucked in, the two of us marched along the beach. Everywhere, naked people. Orange naked people. Every man we passed stared at us, openly. Men looked us up and down, peered at our breasts, our whole bodies, with an assessing and sexually explicit gaze. *Were we fuckable?* That's what they were clearly thinking. It seemed to be okay. In fact, it seemed to be the done thing. We braced ourselves and marched on. Almost all the men wore genital jewellery. Many wore what looked like a thick silver bracelet around the neck of their flaccid cocks. Cock rings. Georgie explained that they help men to stay erect when they got hard. I thought they looked dangerous. Couldn't a man hurt himself quite seriously with one of those? Yes. But apparently some have safety release clips.

Women, too, were genitally adorned. Shaved into landing strips and letter boxes and many were utterly hairless, buffed to baby new, pierced with all manner of rings and studs. I gazed down at my spangly and unbarbered pubic hair; it was decidedly eccentric in this environment. A chic pussy is a shaved pussy, that was the obvious rule. There wasn't one other unshaved woman about on the beach. I'd never even considered this as a cosmetic option until then, that I could attend to and style my pubic hair just like the hair on my head. I felt a little ashamed and sheepish.

We marched on, taking the direct gazes of the predatory men in our stride. It was somewhere between demeaning and enraging, this open and lascivious 'looking' – and I mean looking, precisely – at my cunt. Then we came upon it.

'Ooooh,' said Georgie.

This was the part of the beach I'd read about, the seal colony, the libertine's enclave. While the long powder sand beach had been quite full, here the numbers swelled. A small patch, maybe a hundred metres wide, was heaving with orange naked bodies. It was hard not to stare, too. So we did. Oral sex. Lots of it. *Yeesh*. Couples, naked, lolling, petting, hands and fingers exploring genitals in a lazy on-the-beach sort of way. There was a curious atmosphere, an edgy huddled hush. We didn't see any wild active fucking, this wasn't a beach orgy; but the air was heavy with sexual energy, with expectation. I didn't know how I felt about it.

We pivoted in the sand and turned back, towards Tom.

Men were staring even harder at us by this point. I felt offended and annoyed. There was nothing verbal, no outright propositions, just these looks which tightened the stomach, turned me against them – and turned me off.

We sped back. We marched with such intent that we zoomed right past Tom where he sat on the beach. Georgie was equally thrown by the atmosphere. I was glad of that.

'What did you think?' I asked her.

'Ugh . . . I'm not sure if it was attractive.'

'All that staring, they seem to think it's okay.'

'Horrible.'

'Yuk.'

'I'd like to get a closer look.'

'Me too. Let's go make camp there tomorrow.'

'You were like two guided missiles,' Tom joked when we found him again.

The space-age concrete village, the hard-staring orange naked people: first impressions of Heliopolis were bad. Bad taste. I hadn't expected that. Instead, I'd projected a chic and voguish St Tropez-type environment. I'd imagined a place for people of style and culture and broad sexual experience. Not this. Everyone here had been Tangoed. Everyone had taken a pill called Hard-On. There was something ironically low-rent about everything we'd encountered in our first few hours on the Cap. Nothing, so far, had turned me on. If anything the Cap *lacked* sex appeal. I could feel my libido retracting, like a snail, into its shell.

After the beach, we went shopping. Georgie cavorted and skipped around butt naked. I waddled after her, with my arse al fresco. We headed for the café area, looking for a super-market.

The supermarket was typically French – abundant. I'd been worried about there being enough for Tom to sustain his vegan diet. But Tom would be fine. There were tons of fresh organic fruit and veg. We sat down at the café-strewn prom-enade and ordered drinks so we could people-watch. These are some of the people we saw:

A woman walking around without any clothes, her tampon string waving in the afternoon breeze.

A sixty-something woman, naked and orange, except for high heels and a broad-brimmed hat. Her breasts were so aug-mented they appeared to be made of clay, solid and mountainous, like two re-enforced fortresses.

A very fat white man who'd radiated himself in the sun. He looked like he was in great discomfort; his pubic hair, head hair and eyebrows were electric vermillion.

Naked men with cock rings.

Chihuahuas wearing hats.

Toy dogs in handbags.

An English man in a white T-shirt, a big dangly cock and white socks and sandals.

Lots of overweight people with multiple piercings.

A high proportion of amputees.

It wasn't the nudity that was offensive – it was the widespread affronts to style and dress. Did any of these people seriously consider they were going to get *laid*? At the time I lived in Harlesden where the street funk was everywhere; where not one pimp, not one street beggar, not one Afghani jeweller, not one Brazilian café owner, not one Islamic fundamentalist, not one member of the Nation of Islam, not one Christian evangelist was badly dressed. People wore hijab and Nike or wild Afro-batik, all the kids rode Chopper bikes. The whole of Harlesden got their hair done at least twice a week.

The style issue was going to be a major problem for the rest of our trip. It wasn't just our tightwad estate agent and our crappy flat; it was like dying and waking up with all the uncoolest people left over from the 1960s.

the crab shack

It was Georgie who christened it the crab shack. Georgie had the best lines all week. Indeed, it did look like a crab shack, a very low corrugated building, most unremarkable. A packing plant? A fish smoke house? From afar the bar looked anything but glamorous. In fact, it was the notorious Melrose Café, the pre-club joint that everyone who knows the Cap talks about, a place where any punter who fancies his or her chances can get up and have a pole dance.

Night One found us down the Melrose decked up in glam-hippie gear, me in leopard print flares and Georgie in a silky pink dress. This place I liked. It had wooden floors and wooden walls and a homespun down-at-heel atmosphere. There were poles everywhere, cages to dance in, the cutest waiters and fizzing fruit-stuffed cocktails. And it was busy-busy. On that first night a massive red woolly satyr stalked the crowd, laughing and 'coming' in energetic spurts of mousse. Semi-naked women were on the tables dancing; some had been hired, others had just stepped up from the throng. We sat and watched. The place rocked with high octane Euro-pop and troupes of single men stood around, waiting for something to happen.

Pretty soon two young women got up to dance on the poles. They were friends, both blondes, twenty-something. One had short-cropped hair and the other had hair to her waist.

Their dance was probably the sexiest thing I saw all week. They were obviously close friends. Their bodies were lithe and taut and they were good dancers, good at dancing generously with each other. Shaved and buffed, they were as sleek as two dolphins and were enjoying one another's sexuality. They had fun showing off their bodies, their breasts, their legs and cunts for their boyfriends, who stood beneath them, and for the crowd. They stripped from their clothes and shimmied and shook like Beyoncé; they preened and lezzed it up. These two women were impressively elastic and acrobatic, sexually strong and fit and very, very feminine. Georgie and I gazed upwards in appreciation.

'Goddesses,' we both agreed.

The other women, the ones who'd been hired, were either too slick or too hard-faced to be admired. Lots of the women at Cap d'Agde styled themselves on Victoria Beckham. They were razor-thin and hatchet-jawed and needed a good tickling.

We met all sorts of people at the Melrose over that week. There were two fifty-something French 'soft' échangistes, Martine and Rowland, he the spit of Harvey Keitel and she all Cleopatra hairdo, knee boots and slivers of leather covering her breasts and arse.

'My wife, she likes to dance. I like to watch her.' He puffed on his cigar. His wife, easily fifty-plus, was a hot vixen and loved the poles.

We met two Romanians who lived in Luton, happily married. She was a part-time escort in an exclusive club; she was very keen to sign Georgie up.

There was a Dutch couple, too. He looked like a cockatoo. She was wordless and invisible; he eyed up Tom and, realising he was with two women, said: 'You lucky bastard.'

Then, one night, a middle-aged, off-her-trolley English woman took to the poles. She wore a sack-like dress and no knickers. Everyone watched, slightly horrified, as she flashed her clit and tried to beckon anyone she could up to dance.

'Engleeesh,' people muttered. I felt ashamed. There it was again, the ugliness which went with the lunge, the grab and get. Was this lack of consciousness uniquely English? Was it only the repressed, sex-phobic Brits who got drunk and messy?

The Melrose had what the rest of the Cap lacked: a vibe. It

was noisy and chaotic and unpredictable. It reminded me of the Globe, the after-hours drinking club on Talbot Road in the 1990s. The Globe was a dive, the last of the Notting Hill she-beens, a place where celebs and street-life met and got smashed on Thunderbird or high on coke or crack and danced till 5 a.m. I spent many nights in my twenties down the Globe, many glorious hot steamy nights. I've missed it so. Yeah, the crab shack had something of the Globe about it

couples paradise

On that first night, from the crab shack we went to Glamour, the most famous sex club on the planet. Glamour is right on the beachfront. It has pink banner flags and an outdoor bar with an outdoor hot tub-cum-swimming pool and outdoor beds and two or three very serious black dudes on the door.

The rest of the club is indoors and underground.

We queued. Couples got in for thirty-five euros, single women were free. Single men, anything from fifty euros upwards.

We were as glamorous as could be: Georgie like a Hollywood star, Tom like a porn star and me in a wild flowered sundress and tangerine fake Gucci flip-flops. But when we got to the biggest and baddest dude, he shook his head.

'You,' he said, pointing at me. 'You can't come in.'

'Eh? Why?'

'Shoes. High heels only.'

'You're kidding.'

'High heels only.'

'But you don't understand. These are *expensive*,' I boasted. 'Gucci.' I flashed him one foot.

He looked unimpressed.

'They cost five hundred pounds,' I lied.

'High heels only.'

'*Shit*.'

Tom and Georgie led me away. Back at our mouldy rabbit hutch, I changed into my Vivienne Westwood jellies. When we got to the bouncer again he smiled.

'These okay?'

He nodded.

We slipped in.

Glamour was like a regular European nightclub. A spacious glass-floored nightclub with poles, a full-on chromed-up twinkling and winking black and silver emporium to Lady Gaga. Two indoor bars and an outdoor bar, plush seats. Everything was as you'd expect in an upmarket club – except for the beds.

In dark secluded corners there were beds. Four-poster king-size beds. Outside, in the courtyard-type bar area, there were two four-posters draped with muslin. And there were women of all ages everywhere dressed for sex, like the Spice Girls, in Perspex platform heels and pelmet skirts. They were the bait, we realised. The reason why the dress code was so strict, why it was 'high heels only', was to bring in the big money – the single men. And yes, there were shoals of single men, alert and looking, looking, looking.

We sat down. It was 1 a.m. A fashion show began. Lots of 'models'; women who could have been men, aggressive and bony and bold, stalking around and pouting and glaring and flashing their hard masculine sexuality at the crowd. Think Grace Jones, think Ru Paul. Heroin-thin and probably from Eastern Europe. I watched and thought of my lovely leggy tantra teacher Jan Day, wondering what she would think of this display. I wondered what *I* would have thought of this display a year ago, before I started practicing tantra. This is the red-meat heterosexual model of female sexuality; it's what we see in porn films and magazines. Its colours are black, red and silver. These women were imitation vampires; they were acting a role to please a world run by men. Any feminist worth her salt would have much to say about them. My own take was something verging more on a critique of art and taste. It lacked soul, sisters. It lacked soul.

We sat down. Tom was not only a vegan but teetotal; he nursed a glass of water. In a secluded corner there was a small neon sign which said 'Couples Paradise'. Beneath it, a winding staircase studded with red lights. It was hard not to feel a little unnerved. What was down there? Heaving knots of naked libertines humping and fucking in orgiastic clumps? My imagination cartwheeled. It had been my idea to come: Mon the Exhibitionist. But I'd imagined a different scene, something much more joyous and left-field. Jesus. Just what had I thought I was coming to? I baulked. I felt a little awestruck.

'Come on, then,' Georgie and Tom tried to coax me down. 'We'll hold your hand.'

'Give me a few minutes.'

They waited. They'd come as my escorts. Now they were baby-sitting me.

'Shit. Okay, then,' I said.

Holding hands, we approached the stairs. There was a palpable feel of descending into an dark bleak underworld.

At the end of a long corridor sat the gatekeeper, wearing a ruffed shirt. He was short and squat, smoking a cigarette, looking bored. Behind him were two signs. To the left, Trios; to the right, Couples.

We turned left, entering a dimly lit labyrinth. Immediately, we found ourselves in a flow of human traffic, all of it male. Lots of men down there, looking. And almost immediately touching and feeling Georgie and me up.

'*Ne me touché pas!*' Georgie rasped.

Stifled laughs came from the dark. We both clung to Tom. Thank God we had him with us.

There was a long chain of rooms. The first two were cavern-like, cut into the wall, with big beds in the middle. Next to the beds were piles of shoes and clothes. On the beds were naked people. On one bed, a woman was kneeling, sucking off a man. Beside her a man masturbated as he watched. Around the bed were several other single men, watching, also pulling at their cocks. In the next room, on another bed, a couple were fucking. Her legs were wide open and his testicles slapped her as he pounded. I forced myself to watch. The most striking thing was the lack of sound. No 'ooohs' and 'aahhs', no grunts or squeals or laughter. Just this slapping of testicles. No moans of female pleasure. No sex-dust in the air, no whiff of it. When couples fuck a bomb goes off; you can smell it; the air prickles with released tension. But there was none of this. Just an eerie silence. Like we'd indeed descended into another world, more a place of business. An edgy, fragile hush. Men standing and masturbating as they watched couples having mute sex.

We moved on. There were other rooms, more open, so open you could easily walk into them. Big leatherette beds in the centre of these rooms. On one bed was a knot of three people. A woman on her knees, a man entering her from behind, another man kneeling in front of her, his cock in her mouth.

'Spit-roasting,' whispered Georgie.

The woman looked like she was being tortured rather than pleasured. Again, there were no squelching sounds, no chat or banter, no sex talk, nothing seductive. They were doing it for show, presenting a kind of tableau, like a pretty unimaginative work of conceptual art. Silent cock-sucking. Again, groups of men stood around watching, some of them masturbating.

In another room, a couple were sitting on a bed, lolling, almost inert, like deflated human-shaped balloons, barely mustering the energy to touch each other.

Everyone wore the usual fetish club uniform, lots of leather and red and black. Lots of women being fucked by men and men watching these women being fucked. Hard fucked. Lots of cock being the centre of it all. Women sucking cock and men wanking. Cock, cock, cock. Room after room of it. There were no women receiving oral sex, no men being pleasured by groups of women, nothing which resembled fun or loving sex. Everything was about cunt and cock and penetration. Couples Paradise? I fought the urge to run around liberating all these women from their bonds, except they weren't bound up – there was a special room for that.

At the end of this long silent corridor there was a different room, larger, like a sitting room. On the right was a panel with 'glory holes'. Behind the panel couples were silently fucking. You could put your hands through the holes and feel them up. You could put your cock in the hole and have it sucked. There was a small oval bed in the room. A small, rather depressed-looking woman sat on it, staring at the panel.

We made our way upstairs and headed for the bar.

We bought drinks and sat on a banquette, Georgie and I huddling into Tom.

'Jesus, what was that?' I mumbled.

'Cock sex.'

'Porn sex.'

'Do you think any of those women were even close to orgasm or being turned on?'

'I didn't see one clitoris.'

'Why do these women think they like this kind of sex?'

'It's what's been shown to them, by men.'

'Ugh.'

'It's what some men want.'

'Not *my* cup of tea,' said Tom.

In front of us were the two outdoor four-poster beds. A half-clothed couple cavorted on one of them. Her legs were wide open, her feet in the air, Perspex stilettos still on. They bounced as she was pounded by her companion. Both of them had most of their clothes on. *Again*, no sound. Again, a small crowd of men gathered close to watch and wank. Just this merciless mute pounding. Her long legs flailing, her stilettos upside down. When *he* came (no sign or sound that she'd climaxed), he lay on top of her for a few moments. Then they got up and walked off. They'd been happy to fuck so casually and so without female orgasm, happy to display this lack of female sexual gratification in front of the entire club. Nothing wrong with it, nothing crass or demeaning at all. I was sad for her, even angry. But clearly, this, to them, hadn't been bad sex. They seemed self-assured and happy together. They walked off hand-in-hand.

♥

Prior to going out to Glamour, in our tiny flat, Tom had been reading excerpts from John Welwood's latest book to Georgie and me. John Welwood is a well-known American transpersonal psychotherapist, who merges Eastern and Western ideas on love and intimacy. Tom had read something about 'the mood of un-love'. The mood of un-love is a mood of lack of self-love. Tom had been keen to generate debates about love and sex. We'd all brought books. Georgie brought love poetry. Amongst others, I brought Simon Blackburn's little book, *Lust*. Tom brought John Welwood. Between the beach and going out each night we made dinner, discussed affairs of sex and love. Georgie and I would dress up, trying on stockings and bras and fussing with basques, hair, make-up. Tom loved to watch us. He'd been married for many years, but watching us he realised that he'd never seen his wife slip on a pair of stockings.

Of the three of us, I think Tom, a big red-blooded Alpha male, disliked Glamour the most. He liked to conserve his sexual energy, he said. He liked to kiss and touch for hours before releasing himself into a woman. The morning after that first night, he sat up in bed and said: 'Do you think you could be easily de-sensitised by all that sex?'

'What do you mean?' I asked.

'The more you exposed yourself to place like Glamour, the more you could get used to it.'

'And join in?'

'Yeah.'

I looked at Georgie. It was a good question.

'Yes.' I said. 'Probably.'

seals and meerkats

The day after Glamour, the three of us packed our beach bags and umbrella and headed for the seal colony. It was Saturday and the number of people had almost quadrupled from the day before. Hundred of naked bodies, including the two sexy pole-dancing chicks from the Melrose and their boyfriends. We found a spot a little apart from the main crowd and made a camp. I disrobed and tried to look natural. It was hard not to feel distracted, there was so much to see.

'*Look!*' said Georgie. 'Meerkats!'

Behind us there was the raised hump of a sand dune. On top of the dune were several lone men standing particularly upright, yes, almost like meerkats, scanning the sand, staring hard at the colony. Some of them were pulling at their dicks. They didn't seem to be part of the colony, they didn't look like they were about to join the throng of seals on the beach.

'Seals. Meerkats,' I muttered. 'It's like *Wildlife on One,*'

Some of them were naked. One or two had rucksacks with them. Some wore hats and sandals, nothing else. Thank God none had binoculars. Later, we found out that these men were not welcome at the Cap; even by libertine standards their type of voyeurism was totally uncool. They weren't libertines themselves. They were bona fide middle-aged perverts, sad fuckers. These lone men had walked in from further up the beach, they weren't paying members of the Cap. But the resort couldn't stop them. They were the reason why single men were so heavily patrolled in the clubs. They had come purely to stare at sex on the beach. No one seemed to mind them too much; they were tolerated by the people around us.

'I think lots of sex might be happening behind the dunes,' said Georgie. Yes, people were disappearing in that direction. What on earth were they doing? We found out later it was a male sex site, man on man coupling only back there.

Around us was an assortment of people, mostly couples. The men stared with open lechery at me and Georgie. I was naked. Georgie had on tiny bikini bottoms. Men stared up our cracks, at our tits. They didn't stare into our eyes much.

Within twenty minutes, we were surrounded by single men. About four stationed themselves close to Georgie; all had big cocks and cock rings and mirror shades and spiky hair. Georgie recognised one from Glamour the night before, a man called David to whom we'd got talking. He'd seemed quite nice. When he invited her to go into the sea, she agreed and they frolicked off, hand in hand.

Tom and I were left on the beach, watching.

'I don't think that was David,' said Tom.

Sure enough, half an hour later, Georgie emerged from the sea, a little breathless, with this man who was in fact someone else. We stifled a giggle.

'Well . . . he *looked* just like David,' Georgie laughed. Indeed he did. That was another thing at the Cap, this uniform of what was considered sexy: the single men, like the single women, looked alarmingly similar.

'What's his name?'

'Gregory.'

'You okay?'

'Yeah, but I did have to say "Please take your hands out of my pants".'

Georgie had kept her bikini bottoms on. We'd learnt that the nudity thing was flexible; there were sarongs and other body coverings on this part of the beach.

Gregory stood around for at least half an hour, hoping for some kind of action. Thank God for Tom. Tom, our peaceable macho man. Would he throw a punch if he had to? Yes. We were well-protected. The whole trip would have been fraught without him. Tom gave Gregory some kind of wordless *fuck off* signal men can give each other. We were his babes.

'Let's go investigate the dunes,' said Georgie.

Again, I was unnerved. But I knew I had to.

Naked, we headed for the dunes, making a wide loop to avoid the meerkats. But our plan didn't work. Once on the dunes, the meerkats appeared, keeping their distance, but nevertheless there. Middle-aged men with their cocks out, wanking at us.

'Jesus. Come on,' I urged. We tried not to run. We walked quickly along the top of the dune. One of the meerkats was running to keep up.

'Shit, there he is again,' I shrieked.

The same man we'd seen metres away popped up behind a bush. He too was wanking and looking in our direction.

'Oh God, come on, which way now?' We were a little lost. 'I'm going back down to Tom.'

'But don't you want to see what's going on behind the dunes?' asked Georgie.

'No. Not now.'

I pulled her down towards the beach. Tom was laughing when we got back, having witnessed the chase.

We sat down on our towels. Around us people were petting and stroking each other in a languid distracted manner. I felt trapped and weird. Again, this atmosphere of cool insouciance. Men feeling up their wives but looking in the opposite direction.

'Let's get an ice cream,' I said to Georgie.

Together we picked our way across the hot sand to get to the ice cream cart on the beach. Again, in the spirit of investigation, we went the long way round, passing all manner of cocks and cunts and couples and threesomes. Then, abruptly, we stopped.

'Something's going on over there,' said Georgie, pointing to a crowd. About thirty or so meerkats were standing huddled on the sand. Further up the beach, an attractive woman was sucking her partner's cock. While there was lots of this about, this was being done for display. She was half-naked, a sarong covering her thighs. She had a great body and long curly hair, maybe thirty-something. Another man was behind her, fiddling with her arse. She was sucking, sucking, sucking, her head bobbing up and down. She didn't seem to mind the crowd of perverts watching. Okay, we were watching too: it was an amazing sight up close in broad daylight: a beautiful woman being fondled while she casually sucked cock.

But it was the man she was sucking who most disturbed me. Again, mirror shades, short spiky hair, a humungous cock. He had propped himself up on his elbows. His face was set in a studiously hard glare, half-menacing, half-nothing. He was little short of an android.

'Mon,' said Georgie. The meerkats had come very close to us. One was wanking right behind us.

'I'm being touched . . .'

'Okay, let's go.'

Again we sped off, this time to get our ice cream.

We visited the seal colony three or four times in that week.

Like the clubs, it got easier, but at the same time, I never felt fully relaxed. I was constantly aware of being stared at, of being assessed. The open, sometimes aggressive, sexual inter- est was unwelcome from so many men I'd never even *consider* having sex with. Here, it was allowed. All manner of men could have a good stare and even a wank. *This is why we choose to wear clothes in general*, I decided. But while it wasn't fine for me, there were women who were happy to be on dis- play; they didn't mind the staring. *I'm a failed exhibitionist*, I realised. Or, at least, I was not quite the show-off I'd thought.

Never mind. I'd come here only to realise this was not my thing – it was a question of taste. We stuck out a bit, Tom with his long hippie hair and Georgie and I with our more natural look. Though we never started anything or got involved with others, being a trio, we attracted quite a bit of speculative attention, especially from the meerkats.

One afternoon, we were sitting on our towels, chatting. Tom began to stroke my hair.

'Mmmmm,' I said in appreciation, eyes half-closed. When I opened them, two meerkats had appeared, hoping this was the beginning of some kind of trio sex play.

Tom laughed.

I gave the men a withering look and they quickly slunk off.

It was a creepy, creepy place.

willlow, bianca and toby

Rumour got round amongst the small English contingent that we were making a porn film, that we were porn stars – or that

Tom was, at least. (Okay, I started the rumour ...) One after-noon on the beach, a naturist single male, an Englishman, sidled up to Tom.

'So, I hear ... you're in films.'

'Yup,' said Tom, casually, trying to play it down.

'I think I recognise you.'

'We're just here reccying for a project. Location, that kind of thing.'

'Oh, really.'

'Yeah.'

Tom thought it a hoot. So did we. And so from then on, we took on porn names. Georgie and I named ourselves after our first cats: Georgie became Willow and I was Bianca. Tom was Toby, after his first dog. We introduced ourselves as Willow, Bianca and Toby to everyone we met. It seemed quite apt for our new planet, Planet Sex.

On our second night in Glamour I was less on edge. We went late and spent most of our time in the underground labyrinth. Saturday night and it was like Piccadilly Circus downstairs, crowds of men down there, all sorts of people coming down to watch. Many approached me and Georgie. Again, we kept close to Tom.

The first time we visited these dark caves, it had been as virgins to this new world. This time, I braced myself; I was determined to see as much as possible.

I noticed the bins in each room for the used condoms; I noticed that some couples were not using condoms. I saw the little towels people had brought to lie on, square patches of terry-towelling for arses. It was kind of quaint, to know that French libertines are not dirty, just slutty. I saw a threesome, one big-bottomed woman and two men. One of the men wore a T-shirt and his socks; he was big and frizzy-haired, and seemed uninterested. The woman was intent on fucking the other man. She was on top of him, rasping loudly in French.

'Call me a *dog*, call me a bitch and a whore.'

Georgie and I stood close to them, against the wall and watched.

'Call me a dog,' she gasped as she fucked him.

The frizzy-haired man didn't seem to have a role. He just knelt on the bed next to them and watched.

The man she was fucking didn't call her the names she asked him to. But she fucked him and fucked him anyway, in a dry and fruitless manner. No orgasm, not much other sound. In fact, the man she was fucking looked dead, somehow flattened by her. Later, much later, we saw her on another bed, fucking the frizzy-haired man in the same barren humping manner. By then, she seemed exhausted. Had she brought both men to the club so she could fuck herself to death?

Viagra, we realised, was essential in the caves. Men had rock solid hard-ons which wouldn't be placated.

We returned to the room with the glory holes. A man stood there, completely naked, his arms bent backwards to brace himself, so he looked as though he was crucified against the panel. His body was lithe, an athlete's body, his cock was a pole.

A woman knelt in front of him sucking and sucking and grabbing at his cock. The man looked out at the crowd, watching them with intensity in his eyes, pure lust-greed, a look which said, *come and see me; this is the best damn cock, the best damn show you'll ever get*. Sweat on his brow, the sweat of concentrating to stop himself from coming? He had a Viagra hard-on which looked like it would bounce right back up even if he did.

Georgie and I wandered in and sat on the oval bed in front of the couple. We watched, as if it were a play. If this was a play, we'd become extras. The woman stood up and proffered her arse to the man with the hard-on. Then, suddenly, she placed both her hands on either side of me, her head almost in my lap as he fucked and fucked her hard from behind. *Wap, wap, wap*. Some of the energy of his thrusts made it to me, through her hands. She groaned. Then *he* reached out to grab Georgie's breasts. She backed away and then he was fucking the woman again, *wap, wap* and she was taking his thrusts and the room was then full of the hot mist of sex. Yes, here it was. This was mesmerising to watch. These two were an obvious double act; very likely they were the real things, porn stars. When he stopped fucking her from behind, she went down on her knees again to suck him off. We'd had enough, we slipped away.

'Wow, they're amazing,' I said to Georgie. Watching sex, being around the energy-bomb of what looked like real lust was exciting, a turn on.

But later, we saw them walking hand-in-hand through the crowd. He was holding his jacket and his face wore the look of man who'd in no way been satisfied. I remembered that we hadn't seen him climax. Had he, could he? Maybe he was still hard, maybe nothing, not even an ardent well-matched lover could wipe that hungry look off his face. We spent hours down in that vault that second night. Women on their backs, sometimes with the uniform Perspex stilettos, sometimes in plastic knee-high boots.

'Oui, oui, oui,' gasped one woman who was being attended to by three men.

Often the woman was at the centre of the knot. Sometimes

it was two women. And yes, I began to see how it worked for them; they were in control, no one was hurting them and they were placing *themselves* in this anti-feminist role of sexual object. They wanted to be objectified, fucked, played with. They wanted this, they liked it. They had agreed to it. And they were the real players in this adult sport. Without them, the men had no one to sport with, the crowds of voyeurs had no one to watch. These strange mute women were not at all passive, I realised. They were central to all the action; this whole underworld depended on them, on their desire to be fucked like this and watched. I now wonder if these women are sexual wolverines, the most voracious predators of the female sex. High sex drives, deep vaginas, they have restless and carnal imaginations. They're hungrier for this kind of active fucking than the average woman. They need it more. They're not faking anything.

Georgie, Tom and I returned to Glamour, again and again. To stare, to watch. Each night it got a little easier, each night we felt a little less ill-at-ease. One night, Georgie and I even went on our own. Difficult but do-able. Slowly, slowly, this hard sex, this sex that was so far away from love, which so much stirred in me a mood of un-love, began to become less distasteful. We began to move amongst the furtive wanking men and spit-roasted women with more assurance. In some rooms we'd crouch down and get real close to couples fucking on a bed. Once, Georgie and I held hands and watched a couple fucking inches away; it was fascinating and oddly private; strange little grunts which were so familiar. I said nothing, but wanted to thank the couple for letting me see them like this, bodies joined and somehow so vulnerable.

In other rooms, we placed ourselves in amongst the action, bodies heaving, arms, legs writhing; we went up close to big groups where it was hard to tell what limb belonged to what person. We stood in the dark and watched; it was like being in church; there was something similar, something old and reverent about all those bodies, like a medieval tableau. The sight triggered carnal feelings, and once or twice the urge came, a lurch of lust, up from the loins; I saw myself putting my hand out to stroke a leg. Yes, maybe I could disrobe, sink in, join the knot of lust. As Tom had predicted, it got easier to be there.

We also went to a much smaller club called Le Jules. We descended some stairs to the front door and, again, I thought to myself *down*, down rather than up – another underworld. There was an open bar and a dance floor and instead of a labyrinth of rooms underground there was one big 'back room' or play area. That night, Georgie and I had gone out dressed in tassels and stockings and basques, looking as vampy as the rest of Cap d'Agde. Think Tarts and Vicars. I'd never even consider stepping outside my home in just these undergarments. It wasn't sexy or liberating, it was most *un*cool. But we paraded down the main drag, dangling off Tom's arm. When in Rome . . .

Monday night. The club was still quiet, but we noticed something different here. Couples were practising public sex. On the banquettes, on bar stools. On the dance floor. Trying to buy a drink, I had to squeeze myself between two shagging couples.

'*Excusez-moi,*' I smiled.

'*Ah, pardon.*'

Like utter imbeciles, we sat and stared. It looked like a conga-line of sex was materialising from one particular barstool. Men and women seemed to be stuck together like dogs, groin to arse, mouth to arse. At the end of this line a man was on his knees, licking a woman's behind. He saw us looking and stopped and smiled.

'Come and join us,' he beckoned. He was rather handsome.

We shook our heads.

On the dancefloor we spotted a couple who were obviously big into 5Rhythms. They were running about the floor in a wild and uncensored manner, half-naked. It was funny. Inevitably, and in the spirit of investigation, Georgie and I headed for the back room.

It reeked of Amyl Nitrate and body odour. In corners, couples huddled. One naked woman with flat pendulous breasts just sat there, next to her fat naked husband. Were they expecting to be approached? There was a crowd of people standing up against the wall, groaning dimly. It reminded me of some kind of animal shed. It stunk. This felt like a low rent, low energy version of Glamour. We left.

An hour later, we returned to find the room had livened up quite a bit. Georgie and I became entranced with a homely looking middle-aged couple. He had greying hair and a kind face. His trousers and pants were down by his ankles and his pretty wife, with long red hair and librarian-type spectacles, was on her knees in front of him, sucking his cock. She made smiley eye contact with us, his cock in her mouth. We were standing inches from them, admiring her technique.

'Engleesh?' he asked.

We nodded.

'Ah, she's great, yes?' said the man, stroking her hair. He gestured to us as if to say, 'would either of you like to have a suck too?'

'Non, merci,' we shook our heads.

Then I saw something nice. There was a kind of cubbyhole, a group of people inside. One man was half-in and half-out. He had a taut stomach, smooth creamy loins; his cock was beautiful and erect.

'God, I feel horny all of a sudden,' I said to Georgie. 'I wouldn't mind going over there and touching that. Maybe putting my mouth on it.'

'Go on, then,' Georgie urged.

I winced. No, it didn't seem right. 'I wouldn't want to do more. It's not a petting zoo.'

She laughed. 'I get closer to doing this every day,' she said. I knew what she meant. It was a culture, wildly different, but not so terrible after all.

'Me too,' I agreed.

Finally, I'd seen something I rather fancied. Half a man, the lower half. But I left him well alone.

no philosophy

Cap d'Agde was a world. But I didn't find much philosophy. I didn't meet anyone who could tell me about the ideas behind such an environment. It was merely a place for couples who want more in their sex lives to come and play, exhibit themselves. Indulge themselves in whatever they liked or needed. And I reckon, just like the fetish scene, échangisme, the swinging scene, absorbs a lot of sexual tension and energy which would otherwise get released in bouts of frustration elsewhere. John Hawken suggests that much of the time, violence is due to unmet sexual energy. And I think he's right. BDSM, swinging, are for people who need it and enjoy the release. These 'scenes' or communities are stigmatised because the taboos in conventional society are still so strict. So, even though it wasn't entirely my thing, on balance, yes, I think places like Cap d'Agde are not only a good thing, but maybe even necessary.

Together, one afternoon, Georgie, Tom and I made a list of our likes and dislikes of the Cap. This is what we came up with:

Pros:

1. The place seemed to be fully accepting of all types of bodies. Everyone was naked, whether fat, thin, old or young, firm and saggy or even disabled. There was a lack of judgement around the body – a positive thing. It also increased our confidence in our own bodies.

2. Sex was uncomplicated, unloaded. Having sex at the Cap was easy. For the sexually hungry, it was all there.

3. There was no stigma attached to the sexually active women. No 'slut' tag. Women here could be as lascivious and voracious as they liked. If anything, here the whore was celebrated. Here women were able to exhibit their sexuality proudly and without judgement.

4. Nudity was not sexual; not outdoors, not on the beaches. We saw naked families, children and teenagers, also disabled people, a diverse range of family life during the day.

5. There was an eclectic mix of people at the Cap –

naturists, libertines, perverts. The mix seemed to work and make the place more interesting.

6. 'No' did mean no. Rejection, on sexual terms, was okay. No was okay.

Cons:

1. The resort was expensive, the architecture very dated and the Euro-pop music awful. All contributed to the 'key party' cliché of 1970s swinging. The Cap badly needed a twenty-first century update.

2. In the clubs, despite the price mark-up for single men, there were *hoards* of single men on the cruise.

3. 'This kind of sexing does away with seduction,' said Georgie. The atmosphere was hyper-sexual, so much so that mere eye contact could lead to sex.

4. The sex on display was stereotypical – much of it based on porn. There was the black and red, cheap sleazy element. No other tantrikas about, nothing other than the pierced orange naked bodies and cheap trashy nylon clothes in the boutiques.

5. Nudity at the dinner table. Cocks and cunts sailing past as you are tucking into pizza – yuck.

6. We missed modesty, both male and female. We missed what the English are best at – reserve.

east meets west

On our last night, we took a taxi to another sex super-club, L'Extasia, some fifteen minutes' drive from the resort. It was

Thursday night, a quieter night, and when we arrived, around 11.30 p.m., the crowd was thin. We bought drinks and watched the one pole dancer, a black woman in a scarlet dress, doing a wild leg-in-the-air gyration.

'Wow. She's giving it out to me,' said Tom and went to stand in front of her to watch and smile up into her charms. Georgie disappeared to explore the libertines' rooms. I chatted to a tranny at the bar. This club was a sprawling affair, mostly outdoors, a big dance floor with poles, a patio area and an acre of forest where couples could go and fuck. That night, the gate to the forest was padlocked. I felt a little jaded, a little tired, more than ready to go home.

'It's quite nice in there,' Georgie reported on her return.

'Really?'

'Yes. Go on up and have a look.'

Up? Did you go *up* in this club? Was the sex in the gods? In heaven? I was sceptical; I'd seen enough by then. But there wasn't much else to do here.

And I did go *up* this time, up some stairs, into a large space, almost like a converted barn, a wooden floor, small wooden cubicles with beds, all empty. At the back was a massive playroom. Inside this playroom were four-poster beds draped with muslin and some chaise longues round the edges, for people to sit on and watch or cavort. There was a stage with some fetish torture equipment, some stocks, what looked like a gymnasium horse. The lighting was rosy-dim. Two or three couples were fooling about. One couple stood up against the wall, another lounged on a chaise. There was a foursome on one of the beds. These people appeared to know each other; there was a relaxed whispered muffled conversation between them. It was quiet, relaxed, not one cruising single man in sight. The music was Sade or some unobtrusive background jazz. It felt like a large bedroom.

I sat down on my own and watched the couples. One couple near me were making out. He sat on the chaise longue with his pants down while she rubbed herself all over him. It was intimate, sexy. It occurred to me that I could join them.

Georgie appeared.

We sat on the chaise longue together for at least half an hour, not speaking, just watching.

'It's different here,' I said.

'Yeah.'

'I could do it here.'

'Me too,' Georgie agreed.

We watched some more.

'Tom's downstairs, shall I go and get him?'

I was still unsure about all this. 'Let's go downstairs and have a drink.'

But we didn't last long downstairs. Soon, the three of us were back upstairs in the dimly lit room, small groans around us and the faint whiff of sex. No hoards, no pushy groping perverts. I knew it was now or never. If not now, *when*?

I was wearing a dress I'd bought in one of the boutiques, filmy white lace, a slashed hemline, my jelly Vivienne Westwoods. Georgie had said before that she liked the way I'd often done things in tantra workshops that I hadn't initially wanted to do. That I'd been scared, unsure – but had gone ahead and done them anyway. This was true, I had tried many things I wasn't sure if I liked or not, it was important to try things. Could I or couldn't I do this?

Tom and Georgie must have known what was running through my head: will she or won't she? We'd agreed not to have sex in private, but this was different. This was open, others might even join in; this was new for all of us: what might happen if we began to play together? They were so up for everything, such open and loving companions. Here I was again. *Shit*.

'Would you be ... you know ... up for it?' I said to Georgie.

She smiled. God, she was beautiful, she glowed like a saintly apparition. Georgie of the Boudoir.

'If you wanted to go for it Mon, I could meet you there.'

'Er ...'

I looked at Tom.

Tom winked.

'*Fuck*, okay, then.'

And so quickly the three of us were stripping off our clothes. Tom peeled off his black shirt, Georgie stripped down to her lace leggings. I slipped off my dress and shoes and lay down naked on one of the chaise longues. Tom knelt beside me, gorgeous sexy Tom. Georgie knelt above me and rubbed energy into her hands. I shut my eyes. Carefully, and with love, they ran their hands up and down my naked body, over my breasts, thighs, loins. Tom slipped his expert fingers between my legs and began to touch me like I touch myself. *Ah*hhhh.

When I opened my eyes another woman's face was gazing down at me, she was youngish, elfin, short brown hair, her eyes wide with love. She reached forward carefully as though to ask if it was okay to touch my face. I nodded. She stroked my face and I stroked hers. She bent to kiss me on the lips. All the while, Georgie and Tom were caressing my body. Then I became aware of another man hovering – her partner? He was gazing at me and then touching Georgie. Did she like it? I wasn't sure. I could feel her tension, no, she didn't. Discreetly, Tom shooed him off.

The couple drifted away and another couple came and put their hands on me. I wasn't sure how I felt about it. But I knew I was safe with Georgie and Tom. The experience was almost out-of-body; it unfolded gently, and yet also too quickly for me to take it all in. Other couples came and touched me, joining in; it all felt soft and fluid.

The chaise longue became a little cramped for the three of us plus extras. One of the four-poster beds was empty, so we moved over.

The bed was big enough, easily, for six people, yet there were only the three of us; the other couples had melted away. No new couples tried to join us; but I was conscious that people had settled on the chaise longues opposite the bed to watch. I was also aware that we were doing things differently. At first Georgie and Tom lay next to me, gazing at me and me at them. They were my beautiful sexy friends; we all gazed lovingly at each other for a long time, drinking each other in. Slowly, they began to caress me again. I looked up at Georgie. She was in her element, somehow phosphorescent, a baby Aphrodite, a bedroom minx *par excellence*. Her skin glowed in the dark. Her hair shone. She ran her hands up and down the length of my body.

Tom kissed and caressed me too; he has hands made for touching women. For some time we writhed and squirmed and touched and kissed. I was being honoured tantra-style. Loved and adored by these two peaceable tantrikas, their hair all over me, their hands, lips, fingers. Tom stroked my yoni with his fingers, delved inside me while I wriggled on his fingertips. We laughed. It was weird; my heart surged with love for Georgie and Tom. Then, I thought to myself: *I'm going to do it.* Stroke myself, let others watch. It would be the first time I'd ever pleasured myself in front of more than one person; why the hell not? I felt like it: I was wet and loved-up, my skin felt like plum skin, cool and naked. I didn't think that having full-blown sexual intercourse with Tom, while Georgie watched, would be right, not then. We were a triple act.

I was aware that many more people were now in the room, circling our bed. I wondered what they thought of us. No cock, no penetration, no spit-roasting. Just us naked lovely people on the bed, touching and sexing. I was at the centre of it all, receiving.

I reached down to where I was wet and began to stroke myself. Yummmm. Georgie laughed, Tom watched, his long hair all over me, his cock hard against my thigh. Then, easily, I was in a place where atoms explode, where time is compacted. My body was wracked by gentle sea swells of orgasm. I could feel sweat on my brow. A rash of goose bumps rose on the back of my neck. I swooned.

I looked up at them. Tears came.

Georgie and Tom huddled close. We snuggled together and could have fallen asleep on that bed. But we didn't. Instead, I looked around. An audience of about ten people were sitting opposite on the chaise longue. How long had they been there? I didn't care. It would have been fine if they'd clapped.

After a while, we put our clothes back on. We went downstairs, sat at a table and smiled at each other.

'Thanks, guys,' I said, all dreamy and in love. 'Ten out of ten up there. You were fabulous.'

Tom grinned. He looked amused. 'And you get a twelve out of ten for wanking.'

♥

I didn't think about my ex at all in Cap d'Agde. He would've refused to step outside that grubby cell; he would've loathed the naked orange brigade. It would have disturbed him. Being there didn't make me think of our lost love or offer any answers to the tragedy of our sexual mismatch. It was a strange place. When we left the next day, neither Georgie nor Tom nor I thought we'd ever consider returning. If nothing else, at Cap d'Agde, I made two good friends.

I went back to London and then on to Shropshire to teach a course for Arvon at The Hurst. Lemn Sissay, MBE, the poet and artist-in-residence at the South Bank, was my co-tutor, a dynamic and likeable man. During that week I managed to conceal my encroaching dread of what was to come once the Arvon week was over – the ceremonial parting from my ex. In my diary I wrote:

Very worried about Saturday. Surviving without him has been a project. Getting over him has kept me busy. Will I miss it? What next after it's all officially over?

heart parting

1 August 2009 was the date we'd agreed on for our hand-parting ceremony. Prior to the day, Nick Clements, the shaman, had asked us both to write something about our relationship for him to read so he could understand our situation better, and just what kind of ceremony we needed. He encouraged

us to write about our time together, our break-up, and where we were in the present.

I wrote about the cute thug-like writer-tramp I'd met ten years ago, about Andromeda Heights, about how delighted I'd been to meet him. I wrote that our love was so hard for me to shake off that I was reduced to supernatural conclusions: had we been partners before, in another life? I wrote that I couldn't rid myself of my love for him, and had come to accept this.

I wrote that for two years when we were together, we'd both become increasingly miserable. We'd made each other very happy, but also just as unhappy. That, despite our problems, we'd been torn apart while our love was still alive. I'd been devastated by his betrayal, which had critically damaged my trust and respect for him. For years, in the aftermath, I'd lost my spirits. I'd tried everything to either enliven myself or make sense of our split. I'd come to understand the underlying cause for our flawed sexual dynamic. I'd suffered from neglect of father-love as a child, and had unconsciously chosen him to love me like my father hadn't.

What *didn't* I write?

I didn't write that sometimes I still woke up in tears.

That I was still plagued by memories, visions of our time together; like the time we once went to a country fayre and saw a 'terrier race', which was in fact a race of every kind of mutt and hound, the dogs, once unleashed, running riot across a field and into the crowd of onlookers.

That I still missed his head on the pillow next to mine, missed seeing him first thing in the morning, missed gazing into his sleeping face. I missed his voice, his walk, the shape of his hands, the shape of his head.

Mostly, I missed the conversations, our small wars. The other bigger and vivacious dynamic between us, the one which made us roar with laughter or argue like demented parrots.

I didn't write that tears still fell when I talked to friends about him.

That tears still fell when I thought of him.

I didn't write that I had always loved him for who he was, that he fitted my character, that my love for him was a response to his unique individuality.

I didn't write that I'd contemplated ending my life because I was so bored without him.

My ex sent me what he had written. It was only then I realised just how much he'd also suffered. In six hours he'd managed to write a page and a half. His writing was cramped and tight.

It is very difficult to write this ... he began. He went on to say how hard it had become for him to write anything at all; how writing, for him, had become all but impossible. For three years, since our split, he'd been crippled with uncertainty and unable to concentrate. He'd started a blog to help him write, but weeks could go by without him making an entry. He linked his chronic writer's block to the guilt of what he had written to his lover, the woman who then sent all his email correspondence to me. He felt he'd somehow manifested this writer's block with his own pen. He wanted to be forgiven so he could perhaps forgive himself and be able to write again.

I remembered that, in those final six months of our time together, after he'd ended the affair, he'd once told me he'd had suicidal thoughts. I was baffled and shocked by this, but he wouldn't tell me more. I had no idea what kind of mess he'd got himself into.

But I understand now what it is to love and lose so much that you wind up thinking it is best to end it all.

I write this by way of explanation for our hair-brained plan. To get divorced without having been married?

Our split left us both seriously injured.

Me? A voraciously broken heart.

Him? One cat disappeared, one book deal broken, two relationships severed, six teeth gone, a serious heart condition and chronic writer's block.

Even though my ex had asked for this divorce, he'd been 'yes', then 'maybe', then 'yes' and then iffy with this idea of a formal ceremony. He hadn't been able to imagine it or how it would work. He didn't believe in ley lines or earth energy. I was edgy about his iffy-ness. He'd suggested we make it official, all this was his idea. His list of injuries was longer than mine. Even so, I felt that he thought this ceremony was more for me than for him. Yet he was the one who looked like shit, he was obviously physically suffering.

'You'll like it,' I said to him. 'Remember all those things I made you do when we were together? Go on holidays, wear flip-flops. All the things you thought you wouldn't like, but did?'

'Yeah.'

'Well, this is one of them.'

Nick Clements had asked each of us to bring a close friend to act as a witness. I picked Kerry Watson, then co-director of The Hurst, and my ex picked Gilly Johnston, a friend from decades back. The six of us met at my ex's home to discuss the ceremony which Nick and Emily Fuller, the lay celebrant, had devised. We talked in rather general terms. Nick went over the whys and wheres and whats they'd planned. They tried not to be too specific and I sensed they'd already discussed some ideas they wanted to keep secret. The ceremony would take about an hour, they said. As Nick spoke my hands began to tremble and tears came into my eyes; I was flooded with dread and grief. *Can I have a rollie*, I begged my ex. I was seized, momentarily, by existential terror: it was happening, we were going to be parted. Thankfully, the cigarette calmed my nerves.

the wheat field

Emily had a breastfeeding crisis on the way to Stanlow's Tump, the burial mound we'd chosen for the ceremony. While her husband drove their three-month-old baby to meet us, my ex and I stopped at a small wooden bus shelter in Kinnerton. I was still nervous. I was also wheezy; my asthma was playing up.

'Can I have another rollie?' I asked.

He handed me his pouch of tobacco. I rolled a fag and took a hit on my inhaler before sparking up.

'I hope you don't mind if I nag you. You're smoking *and* using an inhaler?'

'I started smoking again.'

'When?'

'Recently. Anyway, *you* can talk.' His teeth were black from nicotine.

'What's that on the side of your head?' I asked.

'A wart.'

'You've grown a wart?'

'Yes.'

He didn't look good. I puffed on the fag and wheezed a little. It felt somehow appropriate to be nagging each other on the way to our divorce.

'My daughter used to come to this bus stop every day on her way to school.'

'Really?'

I'd loved his eldest daughter. Now we didn't see or speak to each other at all. I was just another ex of her father's. I sat down in the shelter. Late summer. It was getting late in the day, too. I was afraid this ceremony wasn't going to happen. My ex was ill at ease, a little embarrassed. So was I. In the end, we were awkward to be together. *I want to end this*, I thought. I wanted to stop speaking to him, nagging him in such a familiar manner; it was no longer fitting.

When the baby was fed, we all set off for Stanlow's Tump again, only to find the road was barricaded shut. I grew panicky.

'The stones!' All those who lived locally agreed this was the next best spot. 'The four stones at Kinnerton.' These were the four squat stones I'd visited in March 2009, the same stones we'd visited the day he'd asked for the divorce. They were big energy stones. Massive old fuckers. Perfect. We got in the cars and sped off.

The four stones stood in a farmer's field. Back in March, the field had been empty. Five months later, it was soft-gold with sweet-smelling wheat sheaves that stood well over waist high. The sheaves stood erect, gentle, like an army of peaceniks, or sannyasins in corn-yellow robes. The four stones huddled together in a circle, off to one side of the field. A hedge ran past them, along the road. Behind the hedge a cottage over-looked both the road and the stones.

'That's my old house,' said Gilly, her eyes a little filmy. 'I lived in that house for *years*.'

My ex and I and our two witnesses stood by the gate to the field and smoked. Emily and Nick went to prepare the stones for the ceremony. There was an element of discord between us as we stood. No one knew what to say, none of us had done anything quite like this before. I had my team, he had his. Crazy to do this. What on earth were we doing?

Then, a car pulled up and a family got out. A couple, their three children and an older woman who appeared to be the grandmother. I got nervous again. It was now nearing 5 p.m. The skies were petrol blue, beginning to glower. In fact, the sky had been most unusual all afternoon, light and then dark, a fierce sun trapped behind thick white puffs of cloud. The farmer had sown his field in such a manner as to give public access to the stones; he'd left the gate unlocked to let anyone visit. This family had come to see them, minutes before our ceremony. I wanted to say – *for Godssake, we're getting divorced. Can you come back in an hour*. But the others were more relaxed.

My ex and I glanced towards the stones. Emily and Nick had slipped into white robes, the robes of druids.

'Jesus,' he muttered.

It was a sobering moment.

They'd drawn a silvery circle in the grass around the stones. They were chanting and blessing the centre area. The family drifted past us, also a little disconcerted. The stones were being used for what they were made for. Ritual.

The wheat field calmed me. It made me think of Totleigh Barton, the time I walked home during the harvest, a silent ghost floating past. There are standing stones all over Britain and Europe, all still to be used as they once were. All of a sudden, I felt a sense of purpose. This wheat field was ripe for harvest; the following week it would be gone, and the ground naked. The seed-heads nodded their encouragement: *this will be a good thing for you. This is a fitting end for you and this man who you've loved so much.*

The family disappeared. My ex and I and our two witnesses walked sombrely along the trail to the four stones. Nick and Emily stood in their white robes, waiting to greet us.

Nick had dug a hole next to the nearest stone. The hole was deep and perfectly square. A wet sod of earth lay upturned nearby.

Nick explained that the first part of the ceremony was about severing our psychic bonds.

'Drop the rings into the ground. I want you to think of your intent. This will be the end of whatever you want.'

I thought of my loneliness. I wanted this to end. This was my intent as I dropped the ring into the hole, the ring my ex had presented to me on our first anniversary, Valentine's Day. That night, he'd approached me with a hopeful expression on his face. The ring was inexpensive, a silver band with a small violet stone, an amethyst, set into it. He took it from his pocket and held it out. I'd panicked. A ring? What was he about to say? He read my face. He smiled softly anyway: *I want you to think of me whenever you wear this,* he said. It was the closest I'd ever been to a marriage proposal; it was an engagement ring of sorts. I hadn't wanted to be married then, not to anyone. But I wore the ring a lot, both when we were together and after our split. I dropped this ring into the hole in the wet black earth.

My ex dropped the ring I'd given him, solid silver, from a hip designer on Upper Street in Islington. On it was engraved a picture of the planet Saturn, the same planet I'd had tattooed on my right hip years before we met. *Think of me when you wear it* had also been my hope.

Nick produced a gold ceremonial knife from a pouch slung round his shoulder.

'Cut the bonds between you and these rings.'

We each took hold of the knife and knelt and swiped it across the hole in the ground. I'd once done this kind of fibre-cutting ceremony with John Hawken. I could see my ex found this awkward.

'Place the sod back as it was, bury them here, forever.'

My ex put the wet sod of earth back where it had been and stamped on it, burying our rings.

I wanted my loneliness to end. Here, right at this moment. *Goodbye*.

Nick said a pledge out loud: 'I release, I let go, I give thanks. I, Monique Roffey, am no longer in a relationship with X. I want you to say this three times.'

I'd say and do anything at this point. And so I said this pledge three times, each time getting louder.

'I release, I let go, I give thanks. I, Monique Roffey, am no longer in a relationship with X.' It was good to say it out loud. It needed to be said.

The wheat field nodded. My heart sang. This was right. Yes. This was perfect.

Emily and Nick made a gateway with their bodies, arms held aloft and hands joined.

They beckoned. I went forward and fought my way through the gate. They made it hard for me to get through; I had to struggle. But I made it.

'Don't look backwards,' they advised. I didn't. I stood in the centre of the stones, feeling happier than I had in years.

Behind me, I heard my ex making the same pledge. 'I release, I let go, and I give thanks.' I heard him say it aloud three times. We were over. No longer an item. It was three and a half years since we'd been blown apart by a bombshell which arrived in the post, three and half years since I'd threatened to kill him, packed up my life with him and fled.

I heard my ex struggle to get through the gateway of their bodies; I stifled my amusement. And then he was there, next to me in the centre of the circle, looking a little befuddled and unnerved. We grinned at each other. This was good. We were ending in the same manner as we'd lived our life together. We were having one of our adventures. I smiled. He smiled. It was dawning on him that this was proper.

'I told you you'd like this.'

He nodded.

Emily brought forward a large wooden bowl full of water.

'I want you to wash each other's hands,' said Nick. Emily held the bowl between us, a small white linen towel folded over her wrist.

I looked at my ex. He was clearly thrown. His face clouded.

I held out my hands.

He took one of my hands and dipped it in the bowl. We looked straight into each other's eyes. One of us was going to cry. Who first? The air between us was stark and fluid. Beyond the stones, out in the field, Kerry and Gilly were watching us. They'd been instructed to observe the whole ceremony carefully. My ex washed my right hand in the bowl, then my left. He dried them in a hurried, self-conscious manner. I realised then, that *I'd* grown, that I'd changed since we'd split; I didn't find this kind of thing too sentimental. I'd opened.

He dried my other hand. Throughout, we didn't take our eyes off each other.

When it was my turn, I picked up both his hands and pressed them to the bottom of the bowl. I held them there for several moments, my eyes gazing directly it his. *I forgive you*, was what I was thinking.

He read the moment, how could he not?

'*Thank* you, Mon,' he said aloud.

I took my time washing his hands. I took my time with his right hand and then his left hand. I washed and soothed them in the water. I dried them carefully.

Then we stood opposite each other. The clouds above had gathered to watch. The wheat field stood on tiptoe.

Nick took two scrolls from his pouch. On them, we'd each written some words about our time together, good things and bad. He lit a match and held it under the scrolls and the paper began to collapse as the flames licked around them. Fire destroys, just like the fire which had burnt all my possessions. Fire purifies, just like the emails I'd set alight to. The fire burnt the words we'd written and they dissolved into ashes at our feet. Emily poured the bowl of water over the ashes and mixed them so they could be composted into the earth.

Then, Nick and Emily moved away.

'Now you have some time to say whatever you want,' said Nick. 'These are the last things you will ever say to each other of your time together.' He drew away and began to circle us, all the while using a singing bowl; it made a long slow melancholic toll, a sound like exotic church bells.

We stood apart. We'd almost travelled through the centre of the stones together. We were both a little wordless, a little mixed up.

I looked at this man whom I'd loved so much. Here, in this stone circle, alongside the road and in a wheat field, on the first day of August and very far from home, I was ready to be finished.

He had no words.

Instead, he came over and wrapped me in his arms.

I didn't cry. I wrapped my arms around him too. Our final embrace.

We stood like this for several moments.

Then, we separated.

We stood some feet apart. All the while Nick, dressed in white robes, walked around us, ringing the bowl.

'I want to thank you,' I said. 'For everything.'

'I want to thank you, too.'

'I want to thank you for being so good with my family.'

'Thank you for being so good with *mine*.'

We paused.

'Thank you for coming to London with me.'

He nodded.

'Totleigh was a good gig, wasn't it?' I said.

'Yes.'

'I wish I'd jumped in the bath at Bath.'

He winced. It was our most unhappy time.

He looked at me. 'I'm so sorry ... for what I did.'

I nodded.

'I can dump my guilt here. But I'll always be sorry.'

'I think you've paid enough. I had my part to play in what happened too. I forgive you.'

I meant it.

We stood there, waiting. Gazing.

Then Nick and Emily made another gateway with their arms. I struggled through it and found myself on the other side, outside the stone circle. A few metres off, Kerry was standing with a smile on her face. I beamed at her. Behind me, my ex was struggling too, through the human gate.

Directed by Nick, we made another pledge.

Three times I said: 'I am free. I step forward into my life in the beauty of all that I am. I create my own future.' I shouted the third and final pledge out into the field.

My ex said the same words three times.

It was early evening. Nick and Emily passed a lit bundle of sage, a smudging stick, between us, clearing the energy of the ceremony. Then Emily came forward and held my hand and looked into my eyes and made a formal speech. She said how much she had seen me and honoured me; how she saw my creativity, my strength and beauty. She was a small woman with big cornflower blue eyes and long silken hair. The priest's stole around her neck was embroidered with green dragonflies. She was a priestess come forward to secure my place in the word, to wish me well.

Nick made a similar speech to my ex. Nick held his hands and talked about his stepping forward into his full potential, into his creativity. I could sense my ex stiffen; this was a sore point. Would he ever write again? Nick spoke of seeing my ex in his full ability. Then, he hugged him. I knew my ex didn't like hugging men. I smiled. He'd done so many things he didn't like when we were together; this was the last time he'd do anything like this either with me or for me. I sincerely hoped this would help him.

'You're free to go now,' said Nick and Emily.

I wandered away from the stones, towards Kerry. I was so elated I almost skipped towards her. Kerry had witnessed it all; she was the keeper of what had happened.

She told me she saw a butterfly, yes, a small mauve *butterfly* fluttering about. It had settled on my sleeve just before theceremony. She described the sky, its strange heaviness, the wheat field and its attentiveness. I was glad to have her there. Kerry will always be there to talk me through it, even when I'm a very old woman; there was someone there that day, in the wheat field, on my side.

'I'm free,' I said to her. 'I'm truly single for the first time in ten years.'

I'd been so worried of being on my own, without any more association with him. 'Our story' had been so much part of my recent history, my identity: being with him, then getting over him. But I found there was nothing to worry about. I felt peaceful. We'd done a dignified thing in those ancient stones.

We left the field in separate cars. Back at my ex's house the six of us celebrated the divorce with champagne and a great mound of salty greasy chips. In turn, we each talked about the ceremony, and how we felt now. Nick gave my ex a cow's horn as a gift, Emily gave me a polished blue stone, a lump of sodalite crystal. I went outside to find Lady Violet on a wall, having a big moment with another neighbourhood alley cat.

'Hello Violet,' I said. She scowled at me, indifferent, her yellow eyes flashing.

My ex's daughters wandered past. They seemed busy and

preoccupied. They and the cat and my ex were all bound up in another life, very much without me.

My ex drove me to Leominster station to catch a train back to Paddington. Kerry came with us in the car.

At Leominster, I asked Kerry to take a photo of us, the last of us together. In the photo I'm wearing what I wore for my divorce ceremony: my favourite crumpled silver cowboy hat and an Everlast tracksuit jacket. I'm staring into the camera, grinning. My ex has his arm around me; he's looking down at me, also grinning. A pair of writers who'd once been very much in love.

He walked me to the station platform.

I smiled at him. 'That was good, wasn't it?' I said.

'Yes, Mon.'

'I'm glad I'm no longer in a relationship with you.'

He laughed but said nothing.

We parted.

I walked over the bridge to the opposite platform. I was very glad to be going home to Harlesden. Our ten-year love affair was over. This was a new era.

THE CAVE

Apollinaire said:
Come to the edge.
We might fall.

Come to the edge.
It's too high.

Come to the edge!
And they came
And he pushed them
And they flew.

Christopher Logue

♥

pilgrimage

Things didn't change instantly. Even though I was properly single again, single in the heart, head and sex for the first time in ten years, this sudden freedom didn't instantaneously catapult me into a new way of being. The shift was far more subtle. André Williams, my personal trainer, kept me running. I kept dancing 5Rhythms at Tufnell Park; life ticked along.

In the first week of September 2009, a month after my divorce, I flew to Marseilles, in the South of France. It was my second trip to France that summer, but I was returning for a very different reason. This time, I was joining a pilgrimage, led by tantric master John Hawken and his partner Gabi. The aim of the pilgrimage was to find the 'sacred feminine' in Christianity, to find out more about the elusive and enigmatic biblical figure of Mary Magdalene. If Jesus Christ ever did have a lover or a female soulmate, some would say Mary Magdalene was the most likely candidate. Much has been written about her, everything from scholarly tomes to books which claim to have been 'channelled' by Magdalene herself. Lots has been discussed, conjectured, even made up. Only one thing is sure: Mary Magdalene is the most famous prostitute on earth.

Mary Magdalene got her 'whore' reputation from a Pope. It was Pope Gregory the Great who, in an influential sermon in 594 AD, identified Mary Magdalene as a prostitute, the sinful woman who wiped Jesus' feet with her hair in chapter seven of Luke's gospel. From then on, she was known as a fallen woman, portrayed as such in countless books and paintings. In much of later Western art, she is portrayed naked with an uncovered head and luxurious flowing red hair which only just conceals her breasts and pubic hair. Despite the fact that nowhere in the Bible is Mary Magdalene ever named as a prostitute, she attracted this label – slut. Some historians say she was the victim of a patriarchal power struggle within the early church. Others say she has suffered a historical defamation of character. What is certain is that Mary Magdalene was a principal disciple – a witness to both the crucifixion and the resurrection of Christ. Yet the early Christian fathers wanted her role in Christ's (celibate) life written out. And although the Catholic Church quietly retracted Pope's Gregory's claims in 1969, it was too late. The damage had been done. Many think of Mary Magdalene only as a shady figure in the life of the pure and noble Christ.

Three guesses why I tagged along on the trip. Zoë Margolis, Brooke Magnanti (aka Belle de Jour), my friends Rosie, Demara, other women I know who *like* sex and are not ashamed to say so, I wanted to go for *us*. Yes, I include myself in this lineup; I, a woman who's had many lovers, who's taken herself on a thirsty quest for sexual self-knowledge. I wanted to know why 'slut' is such a derogatory word, why it was used to stigmatise Christ's most devoted disciple, and why it's a word used to insult, humiliate and keep sexually active women down. While I've never been called a slut or a whore or anything derogatory (to my face), born and raised a Roman Catholic, I've grown up with negative notions of Mary Magdalene.

Mary the mother of Jesus – a Virgin and a mother? She was the *right* type of Mary to be: chaste and virtuous, miraculously pregnant. But Mary Magdalene was the Virgin's dark double. Magdalene is the sexy Mary in Christ's life, the sexy Mary of the whole Christian faith in fact. However, like Eve, she is damned for being sexy. Mary Magdalene stood for female sexuality, which the Church – and also the Gnostics – believed to be the source of corruption in the world. I wanted to find out more.

no one but us hippies

There were ten of us on the pilgrimage: John and Gabi, two Czech women, Ricarda and Stefan, a German couple I'd met before in Spain, me, another English woman, a male sannyasin and yoga teacher from New Zealand and John's fourteen-year-old and resolutely *un*-hippie son Sam. Sam, a mature and handsome boy, was stoic with us throughout. We all met up with John in Aix, from where we were to make this trip in an old white Diesel minibus crammed with us, our rucksacks and tents, much other camping gear, bags of food, a primus cooker, a guitar, an inflatable boat, oars, tennis rackets, and Sam's library of forty-five fantasy fiction novels.

There are several versions of what happened to Mary Magdalene after Christ's crucifixion: she died an old woman in a siege at Magdala seventy years after Christ's death; she ended her days in Anatolia, with Mary the mother of Jesus. But the best-known version, the most popular and the most romantic, is the tale told in *The Golden Legend*, a compendium of the 'lives of the saints' compiled in 1260 by Jacobus de Voragine, an Italian Dominican and Archbishop of Genoa.

The *Legenda Aurea* tells us that, fourteen years after Christ's death, Mary Magdalene, her leper brother Lazarus, her sister Martha, the disciple Maximinus and Mary's servant Martilla were all put into a rudderless boat with no sail and sent off to sea. The authorities at the time hoped that they would perish. Instead, God intervened. Their little boat didn't sink or flounder and they didn't starve to death at sea; miraculously, the boat landed near Marseilles. There, Mary began to proselytise about Christ's life and work to the French pagans of Provence, converting them to Christianity. Later, she retired to a cave in a massive rocky mountain range not far away – the massif de la Sainte-Baume. According to the legend, she lived there for thirty years, meditating and levitating through prayer, up to the angels who fed her on spiritual sustenance. She died in Aix and her body was buried nearby by Bishop Maximinus. In 1279, her sarcophagus was excavated by the crown prince of Anjou, Charles of Salerno. Despite this amazing discovery, *other* remains which were claimed to be those of Magdalene's skeleton had long been venerated in a church in Vezelay, Burgundy.

Of course, the story is longer and more complicated, but those are the bare – ahem – bones. Mary Magdalene was ejected from the Holy Land a decade or so after Christ's crucifixion, and ended up in the South of France, where her relics are divided between two churches, one in Burgundy, and one in Provence.

♥

The skull of Mary Magdalene is in a basilica in the town of Saint Maximin la Sainte Baume. Day One of our pilgrimage was to visit the Basilica Sainte-Marie-Magdalene.

It was a balmy late summer day, a Sunday. The hills around were a reddish-brown, scrubby and bare. Pine trees, like elegant menhirs, stood everywhere, tall and still. It was a southern Mediterranean landscape, sky and air, clean sea and pine-forest scents. We rattled along in the old diesel minibus. In 1997, I'd lived in Jerusalem for nine months. For two years after that, I worked for Amnesty International, mostly on their Middle East Programme; specifically on Israel and Palestine and the surrounding countries. I was well acquainted with the Holy Land, both with its history and with its contemporary politics, post-Holocaust and post *El Naqba* (Arabic for 'the catastrophe'), when the Palestinians were driven from their farms. I'd visited the Church of the Holy Sepulchre. I'd experienced the queues of Christian pilgrims to this holy site. I had also experienced the collective iconic mystery of gazing on a Christian shrine – Calvary, the spot where Christ had supposedly been crucified. I'd been overwhelmed by the power this place possessed; I'd witnessed pilgrims prostrating themselves at the foot of the giant wooden cross. I wondered if this holy basilica would also have queues.

'Will there be many people there?' I asked John.

'No.'

'What d'you mean, *no*?'

'No one is that interested in her.'

'Really?'

'If it was the Virgin Mary, then yes, there would be queues, but not for Magdalene. There'll be no one there but us hippies.'

I took note. *No one is interested in Mary the Sinner.*

♥

And he was right. No queues. Just a smattering of visitors; we were the only group making any kind of pilgrimage. The basilica, which took two hundred years to build, is huge and gothic, an arched and vaulted doorway flanked by two subsidiary walls with stone arches. It is set in a workaday Provençal village, surrounded by narrow alleyways, with tourist shops selling soap and bags of lavender. There's a small square and a fountain out front, all quite innocent and unassuming – or so it felt, until I gazed upwards and saw several gargoyles glaring down, fangs bared.

Inside, the church is spacious and also gothic, with lots of medieval paintings in gloomy red and black (yes, just like the Cap), a dark wooden pulpit like a tower, a vaulted ceiling, stained glass windows and several smaller chapels flanking the sides. Each chapel was a shrine to Magdalene. On the left, in one chapel, very small, and below knee level, there was a wooden carving of Magdalene at the foot of an altar. She has flowing robes and hair. She is the only evidence of female sexuality on display, this small brown carving at the foot of an altar. I had to look round several times to find her.

It wasn't quiet in the church, quite the opposite. There was a baptism taking place. A small service was being held, a group of villagers blessing their baby girl. Mary's skull was not up here; it was housed in the crypt, below. I wandered down the stone stairs. In a small room, behind an ornate gilt cage, there was the skull of Mary Magdalene.

It was a small *black* skull. Most unexpected. But of course, it would be black with age; the skull was ancient, two thousand years old.

The skull was flanked by a golden headdress. It looked like

a shadowy black face with long flowing golden hair, the hair turning to two golden angels praying upwards towards her, their wings jutting out, ready to float her to heaven. The headdress stood on a gold plinth.

I went very close and stared hard at the skull.

I didn't get a buzz, or a creeping feeling up my neck. No magical puff of her essence, no shudder of awe. Not like when I'd stared at Calvary in Jerusalem.

It was a little crowded in the small room. Her sarcophagus was there too, broken but also ornate, scenes from the Bible carved into the marble.

I was oddly disappointed. I'd come for a communion, of sorts. This was my first *proper* Christian relic, this black skull. I wanted to be 'slain in the spirit', there and then, baptised by the fires of this great woman, this wronged woman. I think I had wanted an evangelical experience, a 'spirit-lash' as Trinidadians call it. I was thirty days divorced. Surely, she could say something? *Any advice, mother dearest, on lost love? I'm here. I came to see you. Some say you were the wife of Jesus. Did you miss him after he died so horribly? I bet you did.*

But there was nothing. The black skull was mute, resolute.

Reluctantly, I left. I wandered out into the sun. I took a group photo of my fellow hippies in front of the fountain.

Later, I drank a cold beer.

Magdalene, my chosen signature saint, she'd had no personal message for me.

That afternoon, we did a meditation in a nearby river. We washed each others' feet just like the sinner Magdalene had washed those of Jesus. I washed Ricarda's pretty feminine feet in the cool river water, placing tiny pebbles between her toes.

the cave

The next day, we drove out to a ridge of stone, the massif de la Sainte-Baume. Some thirteen and a half kilometres long, the massif spreads itself across several towns and two regions of France. It looked like an enormous longitudinal bone burst from the green corset of the earth. Acres of protected beech and oak trees lie beneath it, ancient trees, some hundreds of years old. Up in this great stone wall, according to legend, Mary Magdalene made her home in a cave. Looking at it, it seemed impossible such a cave could exist. The massif was solid as concrete.

We parked the minibus in a shady clearing near the road. John told us about the Gnostic belief that Mary Magdalene had been a chief disciple, perhaps even a preacher of similar ability and charisma to Christ; that maybe she was *an equal*, that Jesus Christ and Mary Magdalene were, in fact, married, a well-matched team. That they were a double act, a holy couple. These beliefs were held by the heretical early Christian Gnostics in the centuries after Christ's death; held too, by the Cathars, in medieval France who were all hounded and killed. Such ideas are also spread by present-day authors of conspiracy thrillers, of whom Dan Brown is merely the best known.

We meditated a little. It was early afternoon, late summer. The air was lit with a sylvan light. Soon the trees would shrug their leaves. We dined on baguettes and pâté and cured ham, with French beer. We left the camp at around 4p.m., and walked towards the road which led to the path up onto the rock.

I didn't feel like walking with the group. I walked alone, thinking about this idea of a *holy couple*. A couple who'd been something like our own contemporary model or ideal. Could it have been possible that Jesus Christ had known both Agape and Eros; that he'd lived with a woman of his own stature, taught with her, loved her, that they'd had children? Jesus had a notable brother, James the Just, and several other half-siblings, the children of Mary and Joseph. But the early church didn't use James's bloodline, or any of these siblings' bloodlines, to propagate his teachings. They used the *apostolic* line for their staff of missionaries and representatives of Christ on earth, from Peter, the first Pope, down. If Christ had had a lover, or offspring, well, it's easy to see why these possibilities had been suppressed by the Church.

In effect, this celebate, sexless, childless Christ was an early human projection. Today, in the West, the Church has been widely abandoned. I wondered if we needed a new model, a new Christ?

The trail was steep. It was a forty-five-minute climb, up a zigzag path cut into the rock. There were benches and one or two drinking fountains on the way up. Not many people were on this path; there were few other pilgrims. Somewhere in this sheer cliff face there was a cave, but it was invisible from the path. What *was* visible, not just from the path, but even from the road below, were some windows in the rock. A whole building had somehow been chiselled from solid stone. This was a monastery, where Dominican monks, the guardians of the cave, were housed. I learnt that there was another monastery, at the foot of the massif, nestled into the trees, which was home to about six monks. This small community took it in turns to walk up the cliff face each day, in order to keep the cave safe. Magdalene was the patron saint of the Dominican order, and they'd been guarding the cave for hundreds of years.

I wanted to make pilgrimage. I kept on alone and put one foot in front of the other, surprising myself by how sure and steady I was on the sheer path, like a little pack mule. I was well ahead of Gabi and the Czech women, who were making the pilgrimage together, bonding with each other, and, by proxy, with 'the feminine'. I walked and marvelled at the cliffs, how they seemed to shoot straight upwards from the ground, as if the massif had been formed in one great jolt, a violent thrusting upwards from the earth. The rock was bone grey and bald. Black trees rose up from the dense green verges beside the path. My head emptied. My body toiled onwards, up and up. I didn't pray or think too hard. I didn't think of my ex even though I wore the same crumpled silver cowboy hat I'd worn at the Four Stones in Kinnerton on the day of our divorce.

I liked the loneliness of the path. I realised that I'd been treading alone on a path for a very long time. It was what I'd chosen. And it suited me. I liked aloneness. I liked the melancholia and the romance and the hardiness it entailed. Yes, if not a writer, I could choose a long life of another type of solitude. I could give up sex! I could become a nun. I could choose to live in a house in a cave in a rock and guard a great woman's reputation, a woman like Magdalene. My head swirled with noble and self-righteous fantasies. I've been writing my own story, my creation myth, all my life. What did I have in common with Magdalene? Levantine looks, long wild hair. I'd always been surly and wilful and lustful. I'd had an epic love affair. Did I want to defend not just her, but my own reputation? Is that why I'd come here?

Then, there was an opening in the canopy of trees and the cliff face revealed itself. I could see a row of perfectly square windows; the small neat monastery cut into the flat face of the rock. I remembered a Daphne du Maurier short story, *Monte Verita*, about such a monastery in a cliff face high in the Swiss Alps. In the story, women of a nearby village are called to the monastery and disappear inside; there, they live forever and never grow old. Would I disappear too, into the cave? Spend a decade meditating and levitating?

I rounded a corner and found a further cluster of buildings cut into the cliff. Another corner and three wooden crosses loomed. On one was a statue of the emaciated and crucified Christ. Round yet another corner was an open square. In the square, there was a statue of Mary Magdalene kneeling. Spread across her lap was the half-naked body of the dead or half-dead Jesus Christ. What was I supposed to think? Here was a statue of a woman, a young woman, kneeling with her face turned to heaven in agony and despair. Across her was draped the body of a young dead man. Her lover?

Opposite this statue, there was a wall with stained-glass windows and a huge oak door. Behind the door was the cave. *How on earth had the monastery been built so high up?* Donkeys, pulleys, baskets on ropes? A man appeared in a flowing white monk's habit. He was young, dark-haired and studious-looking in his thick-framed glasses. I nodded at him and he nodded back, politely. I was a little unnerved.

I walked up the steps to the thick oak door. It was then that my heart began to pound. Was it the exertion of the walk up the path? I was breathless and slightly asthmatic, recovering from the climb. But my stomach was swirling, there was a churning in my gut.

I stood on the threshold, looking in. It was immense, dark; the air inside was cool and still and spiced with incense. It was a huge cavern in the rock. I was standing on solid ground, yet this cave was high up in the sky. Tears came, sudden, from nowhere. I was spooked. I crossed myself; it seemed the right thing to do. I crossed myself and bowed my head and yes, then it came, an overwhelming feeling of sadness and sweet shame, for my sins and for some kind of inexpressible love, the love I had for my ex, an old love now part of me. I was immobile, unable to take a step into the cave. Yet, standing there, I was in a state of peace. *Shit, she's here*, was what came to me. *She's really here.*

I stepped forward and sensed a great gust of power. I felt it then, the love of a great mother, a huge all-enveloping presence. My lips quivered, my breath caught in my chest. I wasn't sure my legs could carry me. I trembled as I entered the cave. Power places are well known. Earth chakras are places of sacred space on earth, portals into another time. Here was one.

I couldn't casually wander around. There was a small chapel inside the cave. I made straight for a pew in front of the altar. I sat and put my hands on my heaving chest, trying to steady myself. My breath was slow and laboured. *Breathe*, I said to myself. *Keep breathing*. Tears streamed down my face. *Breathe.*

I sat for a long time, trying to get my breath back. I sat and stared at the altar in wonder. Another cross, another statue of Mary Magdalene, long flowing hair, her face rapt with heartbreak, kneeling under the crucified Christ. Her loss, her anguish carved on her face. It was all around, a shrine to this despair of losing a partner. She'd lost her love and had come here to pray for thirty years. Here she retreated, living on food brought down by angels. I held my heart and sat and felt utterly lost and yet at home up there in the cave in the sky. Visions came, of the time my ex kicked his leg high in that shoe shop on Upper Street, so high the moccasin flew off his foot and whizzed out the door. Of waking every morning to see his head on the pillow next to me, his adult face turned slack and unlined, so that I'd seen him, every day, as a boy. I hadn't been able to extinguish this love: *stronger than death is love* says the woman in *The Song of Songs*. I'd come here to offer it up. Leave it behind. Meet with myself. Or with another me, the one which I was casting off.

twentieth-century projection

When I emerged from the cave, I spotted the young Dominican monk in the square outside. He was chatting to the woman who ran the bookshop. John Hawken was loitering on the steps.

'I'd really like to talk to him,' I said to John. 'But my French isn't great.'

'I can translate for you,' he said.

It was a bizarre conversation. Me, an author and professional sceptic, albeit one who'd try anything; a French monk; and a Cornish tantric shaman. John, be-whiskered and twinkly-eyed, was wild-looking. The monk was almost clinically shaven clean; he had the appearance of beatific calm. I wore the silver cowboy hat. I got stuck in.

'Does it bother you that not many people come up here to pay respect to Magdalene?'

'Well, recently, more people have started to come.'

'Why?'

'Because of *The Da Vinci Code*.'

'Really?'

'Yes. It has made people more interested in her.'

'And before that?'

'It was very quiet up here.'

No one wants to know about Mary, the sinner, I thought.

'And what do you think of the ideas of *The Da Vinci Code*?' I pressed. 'That Mary Magdalene was the wife or the lover of Christ?'

The young monk smiled.

'Ah, yes. That's just a twentieth-century projection. That's a romantic idea. What people would *like* to believe.'

John's eyebrows shot upwards. 'Then maybe the Bible is just a *fourth*-century projection,' he quipped.

The monk ignored this. John's face wriggled with glee.

'And,' I pressed, 'what about that Mary Magdalene has the reputation of ... you know ... a prostitute.'

'That's regrettable,' said the monk.

'It came from Pope Gregoire,' said John.

'Yes, the church itself,' I chipped in, 'said that she was sinful.'

The young monk picked up his Bible and began to leaf through. He read out the extract from Luke which says that Magdalene had seven demons which were cast out by Jesus. I think he wanted to explain Pope Gregoire, or perhaps to make the point that Magdalene had been a little ... restless.

I nodded, politely. I guess you'd expect no less from a scholarly monk. I wondered if he'd ever had sex with a woman; I had a fleeting sexual fantasy of leading him away somewhere quiet, letting my long curls fall free over his bare chest. I smiled at him with lascivious intent. We thanked him and said our goodbyes.

That night, I didn't sleep much in my thin flowery tent. My body buzzed, as though filled with new electricity. The next morning, in my diary, I wrote: *in the cave, was Mary Magdalene really there? Is that what I can still feel? Is she in me?*

gypsy

After the cave, we drove to the Carmargue, to the seaside town of Saintes Maries de la Mere. Here, according to legend, Mary Magdalene's small boat landed. There is some dispute as to who the 'servant' girl was who came with the little group. In *The Golden Legend* she is called Martilla. But others call her Sara. And some say Sara was Egyptian, had dark skin, that she was black; others that she wasn't a servant girl, but the child of Mary and Jesus.

There's another church in this town, another site of pilgrimage, mostly for Gypsies, who see this Black Sara as their patron saint and call her Sara-la Kali (Kali meaning black). In the crypt of this church, there is a strange figure of Black Sara, somehow carnivalesque. The statue is tiny, red-skinned rather than black-skinned. She wears a long tunic-type robe of many layers and colours. In late May, every year, thousands of Gypsies converge on the town and take this Black Sara from the church to the sea to be cleansed. This strange ritual is reminiscent of ceremonies in India, where pilgrims also take their gods to the river to be bathed. In India, there is also a black goddess, Kali, the consort of Lord Shiva. How could they not be related? The Gypsies, after all, can trace their origins to India.

The same day we did a meditation in the Med. John asked us to walk into the sea 'consciously', embracing its feminine qualities. He wanted us to *expand* into the warm sea. And so we lined up on the beach and walked in slowly, letting the waves lap our skin. We were to commune with the waves and the water inside us. Never before had I entered the sea so carefully. I could feel the salt nipping me, my pores singing. The waves kissed my thighs, my belly. I gave myself to the sea, to this mass of femininity. I thought of the stern and wilful Nona, my great-grandmother, of my own vivacious green-eyed mother, of my serene and elegant grandmother. My family role models of femininity were of beauty and sorrow.

I vowed to break with tradition. *I would love again*. I wasn't going to mourn for years, stay celibate. Love would come my way again, but next time I would love better. In the calm sea I floated on my back. My skin became plump and I cried and bled salt tears back into the sea.

Later, we sunbathed, did yoga and buried John's son Sam in the sand. We picnicked in the early evening next to a canal. I bought a green flouncy floor-length gypsy dress in that gypsy town. Gypsy. Black Sara. Most unlike me to wear such a garment. But I wore that dress for three days solid, till it was rumpled and camp-stained and pungent with saucisson and wine.

Yes, I think it was about then that I began to feel different about everything. Something had entirely lifted.

two other times

Soon after I returned from the Carmargue, in the autumn of 2009, I went to see Jan Day for a one-to-one session. I was happy, divorced, certain I'd little to talk to her about. I wasn't even sure why I'd asked to see her: if anything, I saw this session as a chance to sign off from seeing her, to say, 'I'm fine now, thank you for all your help'.

But, alone in a room with Jan, her steady blue-eyed gaze on me, I talked for the first time of two incidents from my childhood. Jan didn't ask me specifically to recall these events; it was over the course of more general probing that these two incidents steamed themselves out. I'm not sure why I spoke about them that day, but I left knowing that I had to include them in the story I was writing about the sexual ups and downs of my current life; they had a part in it.

Two other things happened to me before I was nineteen, before my 'first time'. My parents had moved back to the UK from Trinidad after the Black Power uprising in 1970. We were living, temporarily, in a flat in a small cul-de-sac in Weybridge, Surrey. It was close to a long slim lake ringed with dark woody trees. I think we lived there less than a year. I was five. My brothers were at boarding school, so in effect I was an only child. There was a neighbourhood gang of kids whom I knew and often played with. One grey and grizzled day, in winter, I was playing with two or three older boys from the neighbourhood. They led me for a walk. I went with them easily, naturally. I held one of the boy's hands. He was twelve or eleven. They took me to the lakeside.

When we got there, they turned on me.

'Take down your trousers,' said the oldest boy.

I was stunned: what did he mean?

'Take down your trousers and your pants.'

'Show us your bum.'

'Go, on, show us.'

There were three of them.

I cried. I was alone with them, miles from help. It was cold, dark.

I can't remember what happened next. Dim flashes of me wrestling with my pants as they tried to take them down. Not much else.

Later, aged thirteen. We'd returned to Trinidad. It was day-time, hot Caribbean sun. I'd gone to the Country Club with two girlfriends and three teenage boys. The girls I was with were hot, well-developed physically, sure of themselves; they were new friends, not friends I kept for long. My mother knew their mothers and dropped us all off. I don't think she knew we'd arranged to meet the boys. They were a bois-terous bunch. One was called Daniel Jackson, freckle-faced, an apprentice jockey. A bold, boy-man of about fifteen. My body was beginning to sprout. Small tenuous nubs for breasts. I was always skinny, lithe, as a child and adolescent. I was glad to have these new almost-woman friends.

We sunbathed and flirted with the boys. I imitated how louche these young women were.

I thought the day was going rather well, when this hap-pened:

I was swimming in the large Olympic-sized pool. A strong swimmer, I swam like a dolphin. At one point, I dove under the water and swam deep. The three boys zeroed in on me, grabbing me under the water. Daniel Jackson grabbed at my crotch. I squirmed and tried to get free. But he held me tight, and stuck his fingers inside me.

I screamed underwater and elbowed him away. I shot to the surface.

In seconds, I was out of the pool and towelling myself dry, shaking with fury.

'Penguin, penguin!' they all laughed and chanted at me.

I wasn't quite sure what they meant. Now, I know it was a reference to being frigid.

I was cold that day, with anger, with wanting to kill them. Why had they singled *me* out for this attack? Would they ever dare something like this with the other girls? I scowled at them for the rest of the day. I don't think I saw those boys again. Or those well-developed girls. Soon after, I was packed off to boarding school in the UK.

That attack, underwater, with those three teenage boys, was the first time I was touched. Penetrated. Three teenage boys.

I've never told these stories to myself or anyone else. They were so shameful I promptly forgot them. As an adult, I've heard such terrible stories of child sexual abuse that these stories don't compare.

I don't know what they are, these two early memories. I just know they aren't good. I wasn't raped, aged five, by those boys by the lake, just frightened. And the boys in the pool were ugly and hateful. Neither of these events ruined me. I recovered, just.

But these two events, combined with an Alpha-male father whose sexuality was evident all around me, made me extremely defensive with boys and men. Anything could happen. My father liked his swimming suits brief. His pubic hair often spouted out the sides. I hated to see him by the pool. While he never once touched me, he did *look* at me, as I began to develop, sexually. It was too much for me. My father drank and stank of stale sweat. I was very aware of his half-nakedness. With no emotional contact or connection with him as a younger child, with no feeling of safety around him, he became a threat. I was aloof around him, barely wanting to talk.

I became like this with most men; it was a default setting. A big aloof 'no'. A dense block, John Hawken would call it.

I was like this with the boys at sixth form college too. I was like this with all boys, until I made the mistake with the man with the leather jacket, the man cruising to fuck a Fresher on the first day of my university career.

After that, in my twenties, sex was hard to get right. How did you get as much sex as you wanted without being called a slut? Aged twenty-one, I wanted to start my sexual life, but it felt very complicated. I didn't trust, let alone love, most of the men I slept with. How did you get this balance right?

I also began to suspect that my vagina didn't work. I didn't orgasm like women did in films. I'd assumed that when a man stuck his cock inside me, and thrust and thrust, it would have the effect of working us both into a frenzied and fantastic orgasm. But it didn't have this mutual effect. It only had this effect on *men*. Men thrust and thrust until *they* came. It left me utterly baffled. Thrusting and thrusting inside a woman is just thrusting. Her nerve endings are not in the walls of the vagina.

Now, I see that much of my late life adventures have been

an attempt to reclaim these early events and experiences, put them right, neutralise their hold. I used to have so many boundaries, I was so well defended. Now, thanks to tantric workshops, most of these boundaries have been dissolved; I've tried things out. Jan Day once said that tantra is like sex education for adults: yes, that was how it felt. I was re-educating myself. These days I say 'no' to fewer sexual experiences, but when that no comes, it's a real boundary. 'No' comes softer, too.

October 2009, two months after my divorce, I was in a new era. I felt lighter, fitter. On 28 October, I ran three miles for the first time. Afterwards, I dropped round to Rose's house for a cup of tea. We gossiped and chatted and then she read my tarot cards. Tarot cards have been used for centuries to read a person's present, not their future: they provide a snapshot, a picture of what is happening in a person's life. The cards are a language, they use pictorial archetypes; they depend on the person transferring their energy to the pack. When having a reading, you are always asked to shuffle the pack slowly. I've had many tarot readings in my life, based on the cards being so uncannily accurate time and time again.

The cards I picked, the cards Rose overturned, showed a new snapshot of my life, one I recognised. The last card was the best card in the pack, the Sun card. It shows a naked child sitting on a white horse. Behind the child there is a field of sunflowers and above, an enormous and benevolent sun. This card signifies that all aspects of life are ripe; it represents accomplishment, renewal, a new innocence. *All is going well*. It's a breakthrough card, often a sign that a person has come though a long period of grief. I clapped when I saw it. Of course! The sun had arrived. I could feel it shining down. I gazed at that tiny naked child on the horse, and saw a chance to put my five-year-old self by the lake and my thirteen-year old self in the pool on that horse too. They'd journey with me into a bright future.

lesbians!

That autumn I attended another residential tantra course with Jan Day. It was Part Two of a set of five courses, my first advanced course, so to speak. It was then I *knew* the front had lifted. I felt present, active. I was no longer muddling through as I had on other courses. I was there. Over the last eighteen months, I had evolved from a reluctant to an experienced tantrika. I was comfortable with the nudity, the dynamic meditation, the effort to leave the head, to shake up and feel into the lower chakras. The ideas around being open, being conscious, had begun to settle in me. Tantra was hard work; I hated being open and I preferred to be unconscious, but changing my behaviour was beginning to pay off.

'It's lifted,' I said to Jan early one morning, dancing around the hall. 'It's gone. I'm no longer depressed!'

She smiled. It was so good to be free. And different.

I wanted to be challenged, taken to the edge. I'd jumped many times in these workshops with my eyes closed. There'd been an 'oh, shit, oh God ... what next, oh no' approach. Now, I wanted to jump – eyes *open*. Leap with a 'yes'. And sure, enough, we were encouraged to do just this.

In one morning workshop, we were encouraged to

experiment with whatever sexual encounter and experience we had wanted to try and had never tried in the past. A handsome man asked me for a prostate massage and I was only too delighted to comply; we'd be virgins at this together. Jan guided us. Latex gloves on, and then – wow. It felt glorious to explore my way up and into this part of a man, feel the tiny pea of the prostate up there, hidden deep, to make circles with my fingertips and watch him squirm, a smile spread on his face. And then I turned, proffering my behind, so he could put his fingers inside me. *Oh*, receiving an anal massage, at the same time as giving one, was sexy. Him lying on his back, me with my arse facing him, on all fours, under the skylight; a man's anus tight on my fingers, his fingers inside my anus; the unexpected intimacy of both, the pleasure of both. I was able to bend in such a way as to keep eye contact throughout; his eyes were green and pensive, his smile open. It was tender and touching to look at him. We were watched by several members of the group, which made it even sexier for me – I'd grown to like watching and being watched.

Later, another woman and I looked on as two straight men explored their boundaries with tender, loving French kisses. It was a wondrous sight, stubble on stubble, long eyelashes clashing; their sense of adventure, of being at their edge was very evident.

The next night, I found myself pleasuring a woman with my hands during a ritual ceremony which became raunchy. If you're a woman, touching a woman is easy; touch as you would touch yourself. While we all like different things, I feel I know every woman like I know myself. It was an act of solidarity, of sisterhood, to slip my fingers between her lips and caress her clitoris ever so gently, as I would myself. *Don't ever stop*, she whispered.

These workshops were a place to safely play and explore and ultimately transform. I was transforming into the adult sexual self I wanted to be. This was the right place to do it, they were the right people.

The tall dark Frenchman, the man with the orange underpants, was there, too. We were careful with each other at first. When two of my servers went down with flu, we were thrown together for the end-of-course ceremony. I wore the same white lace dress I'd worn in L'Extasia. (It is destined to be a dress which doesn't stay on long …) In the ceremony, I cried for the first twenty minutes, gripped by a random melancholia, my tears filled my ear cups. He dried my tears and smiled down at me, caressing me like a father would caress his daughter. He stared at my hands and stroked them, marvelling at them (I have nice hands). I stopped crying and then I laughed and the music changed and my mood brightened and then my dress slipped off. Slowly, he eased off my white lace knickers and parted my legs and quickly there was an explosion of mutual self-pleasure: anarchic, funny, sperm everywhere and both of us laughing like children.

Then we sat together, spent, legs and arms wrapped around each other.

'Women,' I whispered into his ear, by way of warning and explanation: *anything could happen*.

I could say a friendship blossomed in those moments. Affection? Yes. Different types of love mingle in those blurred and unpredictable moments of chemical explosion between two people. So much more can happen between men and women when they have witnesses, so much else can be expressed. My ex and I in the stone circle, me and Monsieur Pants (for that is how I know him now). Things that are too intense for two people alone can be expressed, if the atmosphere is lightened.

Later, someone drizzled honey all over my stomach.

'Lesbians!' I cried. I'd perked up considerably by then. Earlier in the week I'd expressed a desire, like Dietrich, 'to be covered in honey and thrown to the lesbians'. Sure enough, three women appeared and licked the honey from my stomach, licked me clean. Honey was poured into my mouth and I was ravished by Kara, a sexy older woman.

Yes, it's fair to say, I was no longer depressed. No longer wistful or lonely for my ex. I'd become someone else. My sex life with him had been the opposite of all this rich experience; it had been quiet and then silent. Both before and during our years together, I'd dreamt of so much more; I'd called these experiences to me, through my dreams and fantasies. This was not a phase, this was not a box I'd opened and would close again. I wouldn't go back to dating the same men, having the same inflexibly monogamous and sexually one-dimensional relationships. My relationships would be conscious, loving, sexual, and honest. I'd go forward and be with and seek out like-minded people. The sun was shining.

the edge

One thing happened during that tantra week which took me to the edge. There was a game where we were supposed to exhibit ourselves as works of art, naked or not, however we wished. The men went first. They arranged themselves in the room, all naked. Imagine a room full of various versions of Michelangelo's David. We women were allowed to look, touch, do whatever we wished, once we had asked.

I just wanted to look. I'd suffered too much from the direct gaze of men. And so I visited each of the men on display with a cushion to sit on. I placed it at the foot of each exhibit and sat down and gazed upwards for as long as I liked, drinking each man in. This is something women rarely get to do. To gaze at a man with open admiration and curiosity, to really check him out: skin tone and colour, muscle definition, unusual curves, dips, lumps and bumps, the colour, volume and texture of pubic hair.

One man in particular was astonishing to behold. An older man, a *much* older man. I found out later that he was eighty-seven. Forty-two years older than I was. I sat beneath him on my cushion and gazed for a very long time. I looked up and he looked down at me, into my eyes. His hair was thin and white. His pubic hair was snowy too. His eyes were ice blue. Clearly, he'd been a handsome man, sexually potent and attractive to women. But now his skin was slack on his bones, hanging on him, all ruched up, like one of those Japanese dogs. His skin was pale, white and pinkish.

His cock was the only piece of him which hadn't aged. It was a handsome cock, long and still vigorous-looking.

I stared up at him and his cock for a very long time, wondrous, appreciative. Here was a man at the end of his life. Still sexual, still virile in his genitals, while the rest of his body had withered.

When it came to the women's turn, I lay down on a mattress. I arranged myself as best I could like a comely courtesan, hair loose, a malachite stone pendant nestled between my breasts. It was unnerving exhibiting myself this way, as a work of art. Despite the fact that I'm a bit of a show-off, I had my reservations. Women are always on show. Here, I was naked, on display. Men came to look at me. I let two, whom I liked, caress me intimately. I enjoyed their touch. And then they left. Others came and gazed and went. Then, the much older man appeared. He stood above me for a very long time, looking down. I think he was gauging how he would be received if he lay down next to me. I looked up at him, wondering the same thing.

Then, I saw him make up his mind. Something changed in his eyes. He got down on his knees and lay down next to me. I saw one of his gnarled hands hover above my right breast. I saw his ruched skin up close. Every cell contracted. But also I wanted to make this leap, to *jump*. I didn't scream, didn't freak. I watched, outside myself, as this ancient man touched my breasts, as he kissed my neck, my arms. It was awful and powerful all at once, sickening and loving, terrifying and humanising. I wasn't the least bit aroused. But this was no sympathy fuck, no act of compassion. I wasn't being a saintly goddess, not doing this as a favour. It was beyond that. I was somewhere between panic-stricken and okay. In those moments, I saw every man in this man: my father, those teenage boys, Mr Fuck-a-Fresher, my ex. All the men who'd scared and disappointed me. I cannot quite explain the effect this ancient man had on me. I'd stopped breathing. I was watching myself from the ceiling.

These long moments were interrupted. A younger man was making his way towards us, a man I liked, even loved a little, a boyish forty-something called Bill. He had creamy smooth skin and a clear open face and he was easy in his sexuality. He came and smiled at me and began to kiss me all over. *Jump*, I told myself. *Don't freak. Stay here. Be here.* I coached myself into just being. Two men, one young and desirable, and one who made my flesh creep. Both making love to me; the younger man was tall and fair-haired, he could have been the older man's son. I stayed with it as long as I could, letting the two men merge, dissolving into a collection of experiences. Moments turned to minutes.

'Stop,' I said, at last, when I could no longer stand it. 'Please stop,' I said to the older man. He stopped but stayed and watched as the younger man began to nibble my inner thigh. I began to react to his tongue, his fingers, to utter sounds of pleasure. I was aware that several men were standing around, watching, maybe even a crowd.

I look back now and see how lucky I was to have this encounter. I think this would be called, in the language of self-development, a moment of deep healing.

the men of florida

In November 2009 I flew to Havana, Cuba to teach creative writing for Skyros Holidays. I was to tutor a small group of six students: the other twelve participants had come to dance salsa. The dancers' group was almost entirely female and they each had a male Cuban dance partner for the duration of the holiday, a partner for the classes and for trips to clubs in the evenings, if they wished. In the evenings, I tagged along. I'm a woman of the Caribbean; men and women dance together all the time in Trinidad. We are a spirited and all-dancing party-loving society, and so I figured that it would be easy to pick up salsa, easy-peasy.

How wrong I was. On our first night out, despite having no dance partner, I led the first sortie to the salsa clubs: me, an attractive woman called Jane, and Rollie, one of the Skyros dancers who spoke good English. We soon slipped away from the larger group and went to a club called Florida on Calle Obispo, a main street in the centre of old Havana. Florida, open since 1885, is a famously romantic hotel and club venue, situated on the edge of the UNESCO-restored part of old Havana. Marble floors and salmon-coloured walls and high ceilings and a wooden bar and leather chairs. A tall and handsome maître-d' sings loudly as he busies himself attending the customers. There is live music and the mojitos flow. We settled on a sofa. I wanted to watch, to soak it all up. I soon noticed there were many single Cuban men there, hanging about, on the pull, cruising women like me, single white females who couldn't dance salsa at all. They were after whatever they could get: free drinks, cigarettes, money for sex.

When I asked him outright, Rollie agreed to dance with me. I followed him on to the floor, but soon sensed he'd slowed right down and was humouring me with a soft-footed shuffle. 'Okay, Rollie,' I said.

We lasted one dance before he hurried back to his mojito.

'Come on now, out with it, how do I cut it out there?'

'You have a Caribbean rhythm,' he said politely. 'But it's not *our* rhythm.'

For a few songs I sat and watched the men of Florida in action. There were some Cuban women there, and when the

415

men danced with them, I saw arms, legs, hips, backsides
swing and connect in perfect unison. These couples were styl-
ish and ravishingly sexual and yet somehow courtly with
each other. The men, though, were the stars. They were pea-
cocks; dramatic and showy and regal. They wore skin-tight
nylon cap-sleeved tiger-print shirts, or traditional Havana-
style shirt jacks, or American bling mixed with Cuban street
style. Their shoes were either Adidas trainers or Cuban-
heeled and pointed at the toe. Mock-croc skin and sometimes
candy-coloured cowboy-esque. Some wore boots. Funk like
funk itself. I was entranced.

Soon I was being approached by one of the dance floor gig-
olos. They are bold and flamboyantly sexual in their
approach.

'Come, *come*,' beckoned a tall, coal-black man who later
introduced himself as Krema.

I was wearing Birkenstocks and in an instant he had
whipped me around so fast I'd left them behind on the floor.
He'd quite literally swept me up out of my sandals.

We danced. Okay, not quite 'danced'. I tried to keep up
with him, but it was like dancing with a hurricane. Hips and
feet moving in a blur, he held me by the wrists at one point,
thrashing me around in circles, dips, spins, double spins, smiling with great mischief at my ineptitude, my leaden feet. I
was dancing in bare feet. My soles were black and soon my
shins were covered in mauve-grey bruises. He found this so
amusing, he cast off his moccasins and danced me around in
his socks.

I wasn't deterred. I went out onto the floor with Krema several times. He tried to kiss me viciously but I managed to do
some kind of tantric peace stare on him and it worked.

I liked him a lot. But it was obvious that my experience of dancing in the Caribbean was playschool compared to this. Trinidadians have lazy feet, I realise now. We do a two-step; we chip along at carnival time. We wine our backsides. Trinidadians in full party mode are a mess, hands in the air, arses grinding, everyone holding on to their glasses of rum. We don't dance seriously, not like the Cubans.

So I went out quite a few nights. I danced with Luis, who wiped my slippery, sweaty face with his tobacco-perfumed handkerchief and treated me with care. I danced with Ramón, who was nicknamed The Electrician by the other dancers, because he never kept still. I danced with Rollie and Santiago and slowly, slowly, realised that I was getting *worse* at salsa, not better, as the nights progressed. I would wake up with hooves for feet, soles blackened, looking as though they had survived a fire. My hair would be all gummed and gooey with sweat, wildly plastered to my pillow and my face. I wouldn't know how I got to bed. I'd shower and then shampoo my feet three or four times, then rub aloe vera into them to make them re-form into shape.

I fell in love with Cuba and the men of Florida. I also felt slightly sick at the sight of their trade and ashamed of the women they were preying on, women like me. One night I felt particularly sickened to see a small group, two rich tourist couples, middle-aged, married, except they had two young black Cuban men with them. The white tourist men were fat and grey-haired and paunchy. They didn't even attempt to dance with their wives. They had hired these fit young Cuban men to do that for them. The middle-aged women were rather sprightly; all dressed up and oozing from the excitement and sexual energy these Cuban men were whipping up on the dance floor. Every time a song came on, one of the Cuban men asked one of these women to dance, as if it had only just occurred to him. He would dip his head, extend his hand. This produced a thrill of excitement in the married women and they tripped off hand-in-hand with their Cuban beaux just as though it was true, as though this was their real love match; as though they didn't look like Doris Day on MDMA.

Their husbands watched. One even filmed his wife being danced by the fit black man he'd hired. He sat on one of the leather sofas with a camcorder, tracking her around the floor. When his wife and the sexy black man finished dancing they came back to the table all flushed and talking with intimacy. The poor sexy black man sat next to the fat rich white man. No money was exchanged openly. But I noticed something very subtle in the black man's attitude and demeanour towards the white man, a mixture of pride and dislike, a quiet aloofness, a simple but unmistakeable show of resistance. This slow and quiet 'apartness' of the black man in the Caribbean is something I know well. It is self-respect in the face of utter powerlessness. It is a dark and long established human relationship which has never been entirely banished in the Caribbean – the master and the slave. Oh, it saddened my heart, to see these fit, clever young men dancing for these oafs and their wives.

And what struck me too, was the slowness of the white women on the dance floor in Florida, myself included. It was impossible to keep up with these men. They had what I'd come to recognise, through tantra, as Kundalini energy, the energy of the root chakra, the energy of the coiled serpent, shooting up though them. They were connected to the earth;

they were switched on. Their bodies glowed and writhed; their hair visibly grew from their heads; their eyes were clear and bright. They were as alive as alive can be. The white women they danced with were slow and awkward and found it alarming and difficult to dance close to these hard-bodied men. It was too much for them – for us. The difference in the energies of these men and us women was marked. Again, it made me sad, to see how we do not inhabit our bodies in the developed world. The snake within us, the shadow, the dark side has been forbidden to rise up. It has been long outlawed, living under the cloud of taboo, taboos which have only recently been lifted.

One night, at a club which was held in the open air right on the sea wall, I watched a Cuban couple standing next to me. She was tall and calmly beauteous, slant-eyed and cinnamon-skinned. He was lithe and black and wild. He wore a trilby hat and an open-necked shirt, combat trousers and pointed shoes; a Cuban spiv. A show came on, with groups of dancers, and so the pair were forced, like the rest of us, to watch *others* dancing rather than dance themselves. But the man in the trilby just couldn't keep still; the music had entered him intravenously. He fizzed, he cooked, he shook his shoulders, he whooped. The show lasted forty minutes or so, couples dancing in a rueda, some professional dancers, a foursome routine; but all the while he shivered as he watched, in agony to keep still, wanting to be set loose on the floor. His body was on fire as I stood next to him, so much so that I was set alight. *I will love differently* was what came to mind. I wouldn't allow myself to shrivel up and slow down. I'd keep the snake, the shadow flame alive inside.

sexual magick

I returned to London and made an appointment to see Gyan Nisarg, a Taoist erotic masseur. I'd met him two days before I left for Cuba at a 'sensual soirée' party hosted near Angel by the tantric goddess, sex therapist and writer Kavida Rei. At the soirée there were all kinds of tantra 'lite' massages and structures, including one where you had to 'hand dance' with various partners of the opposite sex. You sat on the floor and joined hands and danced various emotions like shyness, joy or love. The men moved round after each dance, kind of like a tantric barn dance.

Nisarg was the man I got for the hand dance of *lust*. He moved round and sat in front of me. He was wearing just his underpants: red and navy stripes. I'd seen him at Kavida's soirée the month before, the only man to have stripped to his pants. (What is it with me and men in their pants?) I hadn't been particularly attracted to him then. But when he appeared before me for the hand dance, something happened. I pretended at first to be lustful with him, and then ... well, then I got a whiff of him. Something about his chest. Musk? All I know is that I *inhaled* him and it did something uncharacteristic to me. My body responded in the manner of a cavewoman. I found myself all over him, kissing him and sitting in his lap. He beamed at me. And there it was, or rather there *he* was. Click. My mind's eye photographed him and somehow, from some other realm, I had a message, some information passed on to me. *Pay attention to this man*, the message said.

It's him. There, right in front of you. The lover you've been looking for. As though some external force was pointing him out, so that I wouldn't miss him. Because it was possible; I might have missed him.

Nisarg. Crew-cut, sweet-faced, forty-ish. I smiled and took note. I put my nose to his shoulder and breathed in. I had to stop myself from biting him.

Later, I asked Kavida about him. 'Is that one of the guys whose number you gave me a year ago?'

'Yes. He's amazing. I went to see him once a week for a year. He kept me juicy while I was single. Juicy until I met my new man.'

What she meant was that he'd kept her sexually alive, kept the flame dancing.

After the Karsten experience, I'd decided that having a tantric masseur in my life would be a good thing. But I'd stuck Nisarg's number on the wall of my office. I never called him. I was too broke; I had also somehow lost my nerve. Life, other adventures, took over. But here he was now, this shy sweet man with a thatch of a chest. I'd had his number on my wall for a *year*.

'Wow,' I said to Kavida. 'I think I'll give him a call.'

Later, during a break in the evening's activities, I spoke to Nisarg, mentioning I'd had his number on my wall for months, but was too shy to call. He fetched me his card and wrote his address on the back. 'Come and see me,' he said. I could see he was nice, that it would be all right.

'Yes. I will.'

My friend Tom Sperring, the one who'd escorted me to the Cap, was also at this party. Afterwards, we walked to the tube together hand-in-hand.

'I'm going to call that guy,' I said to him.

'You should. A woman needs to have her clitoris and G-spot massaged on a regular basis.'

I burst out laughing. '*What*?'

'Women need to have their clitoris and G-spot massaged on a regular basis. It makes them glow. Stirs up their life force. Their base energy. That's what the Taoists believe.'

'Fuck's sake,' I chortled. 'That's brilliant. Never thought I'd hear *that* from a man.'

He smiled. Tom's like a big old lion. Three women had thrown themselves at him at the party; women are always throwing themselves at Tom. But Tom was waiting for the right woman to come along, a woman who fit with him. We'd become good friends; we had avoided the 'becoming lovers' issue. He kissed me and ran for his train.

And so, after Cuba, I called Nisarg and went to see him, worrying a little, thinking that while I *was* interested in having a massage, I was more curious about him as a potential lover, that I was arranging to meet him for the wrong reason. His Camden flat was tiny and his massage table was set up in the front room. It all felt easy. We chatted while he smudged the room with sage and tree resin, wafting it about. He lit candles. He asked me some questions. Had I ever had an erotic massage before, did I have any medical problems, did I mind him working nude? I said I was asthmatic and slightly deaf, had nerve damage on the soles of my feet. I have a lump under my left shoulder blade, and have very sensitive skin. I was happy for him to be nude.

He left the room. I took off my clothes and lay face down on the table. Here I was again. *The sun is shining*, I thought.

The room was dimly lit. As he moved around me, I caught glimpses of him, the reddish-bronze skin on the flanks of his stomach, his forearms, his hands, his rounded arse, his perfect neat genitals. My hair was loose and once or twice he moved it from my neck; another time he got up and knelt on the table, his knees either side of me. My legs, he said later, were tense from all the running; my shoulders, arms and hands were also tense, from all the typing. We chatted and laughed a little throughout. I was conscious that, just like Karsten, he was keeping his professional boundaries. When I turned over, he massaged my stomach, my ribs, my breasts. We gazed at each other.

'Is that nice?' he said.

I nodded.

Eventually his hands moved down to my pubic bone and he pressed around it. And then he was stroking and massaging my clitoris and our eyes were locked for several minutes before he asked, very gently, if he could put his fingers inside me.

'Yes,' I whispered.

Earlier, in the questionnaire, I'd told him I hadn't come for healing, that there was no trauma locked inside me. Funny how I lied, even with such an expert who could help. No, there's nothing wrong with me. That's the official story. Nothing. No boys by the lake, no boys in the pool. I'd buried them until I started to write this book. I thought of what Tom had said to me at the soirée: *what women need*. It was there and then, on the massage table, a man's hands all over me, that I came up with some answers.

What do women need?

They need to have their sexuality safeguarded by their

families until such time that they are ready to venture forward, sexually, into the world.

They need to feel safe around their fathers and brothers.

They need to be educated about how to be sexual in the world. They need this information prior to puberty.

· They need to know how they work, on all levels: head, heart and sex.

They need gentle loving touch, a lot, especially in the place where they are most powerful, their sex. This makes them glow. Without this they get restless. They grow sad.

Soon Nisarg was probing inside me, gently, lovingly. I put one hand to the flank of his stomach. He pressed his free arm across my chest, proffering me his other hand and I clasped it. We gazed at each other and he stroked me again until the sexual energy in me was raised so high I sat upright. It wasn't quite orgasm, more like a row of lights inside me switching on. I was alight.

'Breathe,' he whispered, stroking my back, stroking the energy back down and it was hard, then, not to kiss him.

Afterwards, he left me covered on the table. When he reappeared in a sarong and T-shirt minutes later I got dressed. It was then that I kissed him, a light peck on the lips. We sat on his sofa and drank English Breakfast tea and rolled cigarettes and smoked. I was keen to ask him about Quodoushka, a type of Native American Indian neo-shamanic teaching around magick and sexuality.

Nisarg explained he'd done lots of this Quodoushka, or 'Q-training'; he was then in the Deer Tribe First Gateway training. He'd spent most of the Q workshops either writing copious notes or working one to one with a partner. I was intrigued.

Quodoushka echoed the ideas and themes of Western sexual magick. This involves harnessing and using sexual ecstasy to do the Great Work; to achieve knowledge and wisdom of one's Divine Immortal Self.

Sex magick puts sex on a high idealistic plane. It involves rituals which encourage non-climactic sex for the purpose of transcending the self. Sexual magicians see sexual energy as a powerful force which can be directed with intent to achieve various aspirations, be it oneness-with-self or more material- istic goals. The rituals of sex magick aim to clear the sex act of emotion and personality so that the imagination can be fully harnessed. The magickal imagination is 75 per cent of all willed magick.

'If the imagination is energised and intense enough, it can produce a vital subjective reality', says Louis T. Culling in his 1971 manual, *Sex Magick*.

I was attracted to the idea of sex magick. I can see the con- nection between sex magick and the alchemical process of writing. Poets and writers, artists, too, are magicians of sorts. I'm something of a 'magickal realist' as an author. Talking cheeses, trees, hills. I've always seen what Cuban writer Alejo Carpentier called 'the marvellous real' in landscapes and inanimate objects. Since childhood I've possessed a vivid, sometimes hallucinatory imagination which has been reflected in my fiction. I'd harnessed my imagination with intent to produce novels. Could I do the same with the sexual act? Was this the next obvious step? Did I want to venture into dabbling with the potent forces of sexual energy, creating more, much, much more from the coupling of two people?

I stared at Nisarg's perfectly formed feet as he talked. Of course he would have nice feet, just like he had nice hands. I thought of the photograph of him my mind had snapped weeks before: *it's him, pay attention.* I was being shown this man, somehow. I was a little spooked. I wasn't sure why or for what reason but I didn't stay too long. We kissed on the lips and hugged goodbye. 'I'll be back,' I told him.

♥

The next night, I went to Kavida Rei's house to talk about sex. It was a Meet Up group affair; three men turned up, another woman and me. Kavida gave us a wooden dildo to use as a talking stick to keep the conversation guided. There was a lot of sexual grief in the room; two of the men were in their fifties or early sixties. One man said he missed being touched, that his partner didn't touch him at all. The other, living alone in a big house, had no sexual activity in his life, had been living like this for years after his wife had died. The woman, newly divorced, like me, wanted to venture forth and experiment. One man had been living in a tantric community. I had also been journeying consciously with my sexuality. Kavida, who'd quite recently started a serious relationship, was the only one to talk about her current sex life. She and her partner Roland, also there, were the only ones who were happy, who were exploring the depths of an alive and compatible sexual partnership. Kavida, who'd been teaching and counselling in tantric and non-tantric sexual affairs for fifteen years, had, at forty-six, only just found this exquisitely well-matched sexual partner.

I was beginning to realise a couple of things.

It's *possible* that a uniquely compatible sexual partner might fall out of the sky into your lap either early or later on in one's life. Yes, it's possible that you might luck out big time.

But, more often, this is what happens: we believe in the white princess/white knight myth, that we will meet the 'right person' with whom we will fall in love and make a castle, raise children, live a small good life. We believe we deserve this, that it's our birthright. Of course, there will be hardships and compromises to make, but, in general, we still think of ourselves falling into some kind of agreeable and satisfying long-term monogamous relationship – despite all the massive social changes in the world around us.

And so, most of us wait. We might experiment a little, even take drugs, be promiscuous. But most of us wait – for this 'right person' to show up. Often a pretty good or a good enough person does show up, and so we fall in love with them for a period of time, until things mess up. Then we split. We recover. Then, we wait again. People wait, sometimes, for years. We wait, celibate, lonely, restless. But we *wait*. I know many people who have waited for, three, six, even ten years – doing absolutely no work on themselves, making no investigations whatsoever into any aspect of love or loving or how to love better, emotionally or sexually.

As we get older this waiting period becomes longer and longer. In the process of waiting, we age physically; we die, spiritually. Yet, incredibly, we still believe, somehow, in the quintessential goodness of ourselves and the good luck we deserve. We *do* very little. We don't work out, flex our love muscles, and yet we expect to be rewarded with the grand prize, the Cup, our very own romantic Grail, The Right Person. Given that a woman like Kavida, who's loved many times, committed much of her life to exploring her sexuality, has only just met her sexual match at forty-six; given all my adventures, it took three years before I met a man like Nisarg,

I now see that waiting around is a ridiculous option for anyone wanting to be loved.

♥

In the course of our conversation, one person mentioned a method of finding the right mate which I hadn't tried. Magick. Meditating, putting the request out to the universe with intent. I was coming across this idea again and again. It's a current meme, seemingly everywhere, even spelled out in a best-selling book *The Secret*. A simple secret: thought influences chance.

If you consciously ask and believe with intent – you *will* receive. Rubbish, I thought. It sounded to me like more waiting around. The man from the tantric community suggested that finding the lover would happen if I simply asked for him. But I had to *really* want this, really want it in my heart. I had to harness my intent.

And so, ever ready to try something new, I set about this task. Returning home, I sat in the dark in my sitting room, wrapped in a blanket, meditating long and hard in front of a candle's flame. I thought of Nisarg. What I wanted was for him to call me up or email me, ask me out for a drink. That would be nice. I gazed into the flame. Visions of birds came. Sparrows, robins, bigger birds, too. Lots of birds fluttered in the flame. I sat there for quite some time.

In the morning, sleepy and hazy, more birds appeared to me. I thought I'd give it a week. For a week, I'd energise and direct my imagination; I'd send my request, send it out to the universe, see if the magic worked. Would he call? Drop me a line? It sounded like a challenge.

By midday, I cracked.

Have you been pestered by any birds today? I emailed him. *I've been trying to use magick to get you to ask me out.*

Sounds like fun, he replied. *You free next week?*

Simple as that. No waiting or messing about with magick or asking the universe for anything. Action is always a good idea.

However, later that night, something odd happened. Despite the fact that we'd arranged a drink, that I'd already got what I wanted from the universe, I decided to practice magick again. *I'll keep sending you birds, see if they arrive . . .* I'd said to him in another email.

I was tired. I'd drunk a couple of glasses of wine. I sat in bed wrapped in a blanket and gazed into the lit candle on my bedside table. It was dark. Nothing. Then, I put one hand on my yoni, one finger inside me. I pulsed my PC muscles on my fingers. I could feel myself, hot and wet and juicy. I gazed into the flame. I started to feel quite sexy. Wow. I began to feel the force of sexual energy inside me, an energy all of its own, newly awakened. I began to pleasure myself slowly and then . . . well . . . the energy ran upwards very quickly, running upwards and out of me.

I ended up on my back, twisted up in the blankets, knickers flung from the bed, panting and breathless, ecstatic with orgasm. And when the orgasm cleared, I had a vision. Yes, a vision of a brown bird of prey. A hawk. A fearsome creature, black-eyed and yellow-beaked, yellow rings around its eyes. I couldn't believe it.

Andrew Miller, a brilliant contemporary writer, once said to me, *image forward* when writing. By this he meant, go forward with the images from dreams. I frequently take his advice while writing. I close my eyes, dream things up – and

then write them down. I find this all very easy. Simple magickal alchemy. Had I image-forwarded a hawk? For fuckssake.
Yes. This bird had blossomed from the depths of me. Cool.
But I didn't know what to do with it; I hadn't magicked it forward with either aspiration or intent. And so, I lay there all
naked and post-orgasmic and decided there and then to send
the hawk on its way, towards Nisarg, towards Camden.

FOX

'You have even taught me a woman's way to weep'

Aleister Crowley, *Divine Synthesis*

♥

a new type of man

I guess it was inevitable that during the course of this quest I might 'meet someone' I liked a lot, and I did. For the first few months of 2010, I got involved again. While there'd been other lovers who'd lasted a few months here and there, they were mostly sexual affairs. By 2010, I'd had enough of them. This man was different: I *liked* him, and I cared about him a lot; and, after a while, I even began to recognise the first stirrings of love.

And what a man my heart had chosen! 'The heart is small and fussy and knows exactly what it wants', I'd written in my novel, *The White Woman on the Green Bicycle*. My ex; the man in the orange underpants, my heart chooses the showy men, the outlaws and sometimes the shy outsiders.

Nisarg was an entirely new type of man; I'd never met a man like him before – or since. He was a male version of Demara, a body worker and sex worker who believed he had 'erotic gifts' to give or sell – and indeed he did. Like Demara, he worked in the rather esoteric and outré fringes of the sex industry. Not only was he a skilled and well-trained erotic masseur, he'd also trained and advertised himself online as a sexual surrogate, which he saw as his true calling. He'd been interested in sex from an early age, educating himself in the practices of tantra, BDSM, sexual magick and all manner of out-there sexual practices.

Nisarg was quiet and shy, yet his sexual experience was

broad and his attitude to sex was grounded. He only had sex or sold sex if it was a spiritually connected experience, or so he claimed. Sometimes I thought he was handsome and sometimes I thought he wasn't; he had blue eyes and dirty blond hair, a wide-open face and a disarming gaze. His body was compact and curvaceous; he reminded me of a small bear.

Nisarg was further advanced on the path of sexual self-knowledge, that was clear. He was where I was going and maybe even, like so many men I've been with, including my ex, he was a model of what I wanted to be. I've so little respect for men of actual authority, ever happy to trash prime ministers and policemen in fiction. I now see that I fancied this man because he had some kind of 'spiritual otherness', maybe even a spiritual authority, something I do respect. And so, briefly, unconsciously, I gave him some authority over me. He looked beatific, spoke softly, was only ever courteous and polite; he was some kind of angel-man, a 'man of the light'.

Nisarg talked of having a number of 'sexual hungers' and ideals which included staying open to sexual relations with men and wanting to live in some kind of polyamorous community. He wasn't monogamous, not even during his marriage which had ended years back. His current thing was Quodoushka and the neo-shamanic teachings of the Deer Tribe started by the maverick Harley SwiftDeer Reagan. SwiftDeer claimed that he had once been a student of a man called Tom 'Two Bears' Wilson, a man some think is none other than Don Genaro, one of the shamans who taught American anthropologist Carlos Castaneda.

Wooky shit. I sort of loved it. Nisarg was a new type of man and for the time being I didn't question the shamanic models he described. He told me about himself and about his other lovers, the other women in his life, and at first I didn't particularly care or mind. This man was far too interesting to pin down or pass up.

I'd been bold and asked him out myself. That was before Christmas 2009. In early 2010, we met again in a pub in Hampstead. We chatted for a couple of hours before he looked at me and blinked and said: 'Wanna come home and play?'

After that, we saw each other quite a lot. It was the beginning of a fairly standard and exciting love affair. During these early weeks it was easy to forget all about the other women, his exotic sexual nature. We walked down the street hand in hand, we stared at each other over dinners in restaurants; he'd watch my curls as I talked. We had sex at his flat, sex at my flat. He was intelligent, a polymath and well-read. He met some of my friends; he came to a party I had and we milled about, hugging and chatting, and stayed in bed till noon the next day.

Sex? It was different, all right. One night we were canoodling on the sofa at his tiny Camden pad.

'Let's smudge each other,' he said. From the shelf he brought a pearly shell. In it was a nub of resin. When he lit it, violet curls of smoke lifted up from the bowl. With a large striped feather, we wafted the smoke and cleansed every part of each other's body, chasing away the day's dead energy. In his bedroom, we made love for an hour or so. He'd been 'de-armoured', a lengthy process, a hybrid combination of Reichian bioenergetics and Native American shamanic techniques. As a result, his body was hyper-orgasmic. It was like making love to an electric eel. His whole body would convulse with orgasm, even at the slightest touch. His thrusts sent currents of sexual energy through me, right up to my ears. Making love with Nisarg was a totally original experience.

We made love and fell asleep in each other's arms, his body still shuddering in post-orgasmic shocks. The next day we drank coffee and ate porridge in bed, then gave each other full-body erotic massages, at which I was still very much a beginner. The massage session lasted hours and ended with sex on the massage table. We had lunch, chilli con carne and champagne, and then, in the shower, soaped and washed each other clean.

He didn't just have other lovers, but clients, too. He even visited prostitutes in the right circumstances, like when he went with one male client to Amsterdam. In the Netherlands, prostitution is legal and the entire concept of selling sex is much less taboo. 'Not all, but some of the girls there can be open-hearted and friendly,' he said.

I didn't mind the clients and the call girls, the money changing hands. He brought me handmade chocolates back from Amsterdam. Things were getting confusing: gifts from a man who didn't want to be exclusive? He bought me books; I gave him books, too. Once, he even suggested I meet his mother. I declined.

I didn't know I was falling for him until one night in late March when we went to see an author give a talk in Soho. We sat through the talk holding hands, his body electric at our touch. Later, in the bar, we were discussing the points the author had made. Rose had come with us. I was moving house two days later, and Nisarg said he might be able to help. He checked his diary, and then, in front of Rose, said, quite casually: 'I can't come and help because Susan is coming to stay that night.'

Susan was his lover of the last four years; she lived in Brighton. My stomach surged. My heart smacked my ribs. He came with me to the bar to buy the next round. The distress must have been evident on my face. I'd heard about Susan, but she had sounded like an old love, someone he no longer cared about.

'I'm afraid I can't go on with this any more,' I said.

He nodded. 'I'm sorry. I saw how sad you were when I said that.'

'Yes.'

Rose left tactfully after we finished our drinks. In a burger joint next door to the theatre we talked.

'This can be simple or complicated,' I said. 'You can't change and neither can I. You don't want to be monogamous, and I do.'

He looked in pain.

'You're asking me to change a lifetime's way of thinking in one night.'

'No, I'm not. I don't want to change you. But I just can't go on.' I felt sure of myself and business-like. This love affair was doomed. It had to stop.

Tears welled in his eyes. 'I feel overwhelmed with sadness,' he said.

'So do I. I'm going to go home and cry.'

We smoked a cigarette outside on the pavement. My stomach was in knots. I kissed him and said, 'Goodbye,' and stumbled away down Frith Street and then on to the tube. Tears streamed down my cheeks. Of all the men to choose again, after all these years, of all the men to *like*, get close to – a frigging sacred prostitute.

I called Curly. She said, 'What on *earth* are these men all playing at?' I laughed and then went home and drank two beers and smoked more fags and sobbed loudly. My flatmate Kina heard and came downstairs and said nice things. I held my heart. I was amazed, dumbfounded. How hadn't I seen this, it, him, all coming? My heart actually hurt inside my chest.

It wasn't the end. This was the first of three rather dramatic endings. I moved house. Emails shot back and forth. Two days later, he came over for dinner. We talked in my kitchen as I stir-fried vegetables. I quizzed him extensively on his ideas and practices of being polyamorous. He said he'd only been monogamous once in his life, seven years back. He said that monogamy restricted him, his true nature; it was some kind of domestic trap. He talked of books he'd read, ideas; primary relationships, secondary relationships, communities where it worked.

'It sounds like horseshit to me,' I said. 'A set of half-baked Utopian ideals. It sounds like refried sexism, like a type of authorised infidelity, like old-fashioned sexist desires dressed up in New Age rhetoric.'

I soundly believed these ideas were unworkable, or only workable for the few, for those who write manuals like *The Ethical Slut* (ironically, written by women). Even so, I was weak. I wanted him, wanted to stay connected. And so I said:

'Maybe I could meet you as an equal in this non-monogamy thing. Maybe I could do this, or at least try it for a short time. Maybe three months.'

His face lit up and he came forward with open arms.

'Not so fast,' I said, forcing him backwards with a spatula.

We talked some more, went to bed, made love. We drank prosecco and talked of our new future as lovers with other lovers.

A week later, I got fully sexually tested for the first time. If we were to be regular lovers and not use condoms, Nisarg insisted this was a must. (Condoms were for our other lovers.) He got himself tested every six months. Until then, I'd always taken my sexual health for granted. I'd enjoyed rude health and good luck in this respect; no herpes, no thrush, no crabs, no itching or burning, no outbreaks of anything, no reason to worry. I'd been careful. Even so, it was nerve-wracking getting the results – which were negative. I was clean.

I saw him again a week later. As lovers we were only just getting to know each other. He liked things slow and tantric; I liked things slow too, sometimes, I also liked it hot and fast. We had lots to explore with each other, how we each liked to be touched and where. He loved to have his testicles licked; for me, it's gentle nibbles on the neck. He liked eye contact throughout sex, I found it hard not to swoon and close my eyes. Our journey as lovers was nascent. Natural compatibility is something of a gift; most couples need an early period of patient and loving exploration. What kept me on board was this new enquiry, our potential.

I really thought I might be able to handle it all, even though I'd already tried and failed with my experiment in not being monogamous, with the man with the bongos and split-toed socks; even though I thought the women who'd written *The Ethical Slut* had neatly avoided the whole notion of romantic love. Mad, I know.

Our non-monogamous relationship lasted all of ten days. He was busy with his own plans to move house; he went to Devon to do a 'massage swap' with another woman. We spoke on the phone; he was with this other woman, another erotic masseur. He sounded awkward, as though he didn't really want to talk. I sent him an email saying that I was only human, that we needed a better way to communicate between seeing each other. He said he understood.

He moved house. Susan helped him move. We spoke on the phone again and he told me that she'd stayed the night.

'This isn't working for me,' I said.

'Me neither.' Already he felt I was making demands he couldn't meet. He was seeing three women, including me; he was also attending to the sexual needs of his – mostly male – clients. How was he managing it? I didn't know. Years of practice? Probably. Or had it become a habit to spread himself so thinly? He saw it as his calling to be so sexually active, so generous with his skills. But to me it felt wrong, impossible. I suddenly wanted out of it. I felt cramped. I'd started to love this man but it was a stifled, crippled love. This non-monogamous type of loving only works, if at all, with those rare creatures who also want to love more than one person at a time. These people are usually men.

I'd been foolish to try this, foolish even to date him, to get involved at all. But I'd been intrigued, even captivated by the entire notion of this unusual man, his 'erotic gifts'. The universe had conspired to point him out: he'd been the Lover I'd been seeking; only there was one big catch. I needed to save myself, pull out. Do it with some kind of honour. He was coming over to talk, to say goodbye again. I felt relieved that I didn't have to try any more to be someone I wasn't.

on that bench

April 2010 was an eventful month. I went 5Rhythms dancing a lot. One Saturday evening, on the dance floor in Tufnell Park, I met Sid of the Slap again. I'd never seen him there before. He spotted me too and we spent a good hour dancing around each other. Then I found myself near him and we made eye contact and we both laughed out loud in memory of the slap. We danced closer to each other and then spontaneously hugged, almost happy to see each other again.

'We did a couple of intense meditations together,' he said, once we'd disentangled from our embrace. Around us people were dancing madly to the rhythm of chaos.

'Uh-huh,' I said, remembering him saying I had a homely heart.

And then a strange look passed across his face, and he became serious. He came closer and looked at me carefully. What on earth was he going to say?

'I'm sorry I hurt you.'

I was caught off guard. I nodded slowly. 'You didn't just hurt me, there was another woman too.'

'No,' he said. 'I'm sorry I hurt you.'

'That's okay.' And it was. Everything was okay in the dance. I smiled and we hugged again and drifted apart.

Exactly three days later, I encountered another man on the same dance floor. His name was Adam. We'd met out in Spain, at the festival. He liked me and we'd kissed and then he got too keen and I was mean to him. I was sorry; I'd been a pig. I danced around Adam for an hour or so. He was tall and had curly strawberry blond hair and was dancing to the beat of his own drum. He was very handsome, but still I didn't fancy him. *Damn.* As with Sid, we came closer together and made eye contact and smiled at each other. He put his hand on his heart and gave me a warm, understanding grin. I melted and knew, then, exactly what to say. It seemed perfect, right there in the dance. I knew I should pass on the right words. I went towards him and put my arms around him and whispered into his ear. 'I'm sorry I hurt you.'

The next night, Nisarg came round again; this time to call it all off – *again*. In a moment of inspiration, I'd decided to prepare a magick circle for us to talk in. I used Margot Anand's *The Art of Sexual Magic* and followed her instructions: for the ritual I needed seven stones and seven pieces of different-coloured cloth. Symbols of the lingam and the yoni were also required. I found the stones in Curly's collection in the bathroom (I'd moved in with her a month earlier, a temporary arrangement) and the strips of cloth were tied to a wire fence down the road.

To make a magick circle you have to address the spirits of the north, south, east and west; you proclaim incantations and call on these spirits for their powers. Before doing this you have to drive other energies out. You have to burn sage and use sound (I used a tambourine) both of which will clear the air. You need to state your intentions, so I did: I wanted my affair with Nisarg to end with love and dignity.

I hid the stones and the cloth under the kelim rug, so he couldn't see them. I put the yoni and lingam symbols on the mantelpiece. By this time, I'd come to like the use of ritual. I'd been divorced in some ancient standing stones, I'd had numerous tantric rituals, one in which I'd even celebrated the onset of irregular periods, the coming of menopause.

When Nisarg arrived, he hugged me tightly and growled a small lustful sound into my ear. I felt awkward. It was too late for him to fancy me still. I hadn't seen him for almost two weeks. I was friendly and polite; I'd even prepared a meal of cold salads and we took them into the front room to eat and listen to Billie Holiday while we chatted. The pieces of cloth were under the rug, the stones in the corner of the room. I knew the spirits were with me. *This is cool*, I thought. *I have new ways of ending things.*

After a while, our chit-chat dried up. 'Let's talk about us,' he said.

'Okay.'

'I like you, I like you a lot,' he began. But it didn't really matter what he had to say. It was over. Soon we were horizontal on the sofa, honest and intimate. We spent a few hours like this, entwined, saying goodbye. He didn't want to be monogamous with me. If anything, he said, one day he might be monogamous with another person like him! Another shamanic tantric sex worker? Yes. It was rather a cruel thing to say: *you're not quite what I want.* His shadow revealed itself. But it was then that I understood, knew in my heart, that he'd met that person in Devon during the massage swap, that he had actually found this other woman, had known her some time.

So we said our goodbyes. Well ... sort of.

Sorry, dear reader, I know, I know – I should have known better. I should have said 'no' to any other dates we had left in the diary. But we'd had these plans for some time, and they were too exciting to pass up. And so we agreed to meet again twice, once to go to a sex party in London, the second time to do a workshop together, one I was very keen to attend: Chuluaqui Quodoushka, in Herefordshire at the end of May.

Nisarg left and I didn't feel bereft. The circle had made everything feel soft and contained.

♥

A few days later, I headed to Sheepwash, Devon, once more, to act as temporary centre director for Arvon. And it was there, on a bench outside the kitchen at Totleigh Barton that I heard my ex was planning to get married. It was my lovely friend Julia Wheadon, the centre's administrator, who told me.

We were having a catch-up, and inevitably my ex's name was mentioned. 'Oh, someone said he was getting married,' Julia said, almost in passing.

Nothing. Not a flutter of pain, not a twinge, not a murmur in my heart.

'That's not surprising,' I replied. 'He likes to be married. He's the marrying type.'

It was the perfect place to hear this news, there on that bench at Totleigh Barton, a bench we'd bought together for that great house we'd both loved so much. Now, as I write, I think of what he'd said: *the cure for me isn't me*. And he was right. I don't want a man with bad lungs, a ticky heart, shot teeth and a wart on his head. I have a new type of man in my sights, someone perhaps closer to my age who is fit and active and who has maybe even taken some time to explore his sexuality. And so when, two months later, pictures of his 'secret' registry wedding appeared on Facebook, it was okay. I even sent him a message saying I was happy for him – and I was. He did look very happy on his wedding day.

The next day, Tuesday, 21 April, the shortlist for the Orange Prize for Fiction 2010 was announced and my novel was on it. This is an amazing thing to happen to any writer. I was in a remote part of Devon, out of mobile signal, out of touch with close friends and family. Even so, it was, again, the right place to be when the news was announced, at Totleigh Barton. I'd spent ten years as an apprentice to the pen and I owed much of this to having been a student, mentee, and centre director for the Arvon Foundation.

At lunch time, I climbed the hill with my mobile and found it clogged with calls from friends and well-wishers. I spent an hour squawking with delight while around me cows looked on with a total lack of interest. Oh, how I love Arvon for this, for its level-playing-field attitude when it comes to anyone who writes; the well known and the student writer are treated alike.

Four days later, I turned forty-five. I spent it in Cornwall with Demara; we went for lunch and a long walk on the beach. The next day she treated me to an erotic massage – hours of pleasure in her temple. *Ahhhh*. It was so nourishing to be loved and tended to by a woman of the light.

shipwrecked

When I returned to London I received an invitation via Facebook to read in front of an audience of six hundred; some big writer had pulled out of an event, would I cover? *No, sorry*, was my reply. *I'm going to a sex party tonight.*

The party in question was Night of the Senses, organised by long-time sex activist Tuppy Owens. I'd agreed to go with Nisarg. The evening would be Fellini-esque, a celebration, a carnival of sex, a party for every type of sexual animal in town: gay people, straight people, those into BDSM, into exhibitionism, swinging, into anything. Also, notably, this event is disability-friendly. Tuppy Owens is a great champion of raising awareness around the sexuality of disabled people. She has launched a charity called Outsiders and runs a website on behalf of the TLC Trust, both of which actively promote and support disabled people and their carers in the realm of sexuality.

I wore a flouncy gauzy dress with orange wedge heels and a silky, tasselly boa. Nisarg wore leather chaps and not much else, letting his perfectly formed cock hang free. A fretted whip swung from his belt. He had a crew cut and army boots. It was wonderful to see this other side of him: darker, more butch. Julie, a friend of Nisarg's, came with us, a cool chick with long black hair, silver false eyelashes and satin camiknickers. My mate Georgie was on the door of the venue, a cavernous place called the Cable Club near London Bridge.

The place was packed. On the stage a beautiful woman was doing a striptease, her arms shortened by Thalidomide. She stripped using her mouth, peeled stockings off with her toes. She was very sexy, laughing all the way through it, stripping down to heart-shaped nipple tassels and a tiny g-string.

Nisarg, Julie and I cruised about in a threesome. There were stalls and tents all over the club where you could have a tantric massage, have your breasts fondled by women, a cup of tea, a hug; there was a dungeon where you could be strung up.

One tent, the Couples Tent, looked rather intriguing; it had holes that you could peek through. Inside, couples could make love and be watched. A woman stood there in top hat, corset and stockings, playing the violin. The room was otherwise still empty.

There was a café too, a shebeen run by a man with a fez and a long white nightshirt. It had carpets and sofas and cushions. Erotically half-dressed able-bodied and disabled people lay around canoodling or having all manner of sexual intercourse.

'Doesn't it look pretty?' Nisarg said, as we passed.

And it did. Lines of couples were making out or fucking and chatting and laughing amidst low lights and a Bedouin-type feel. It was a long way from what I'd witnessed in Cap d'Agde.

We bumped into Kavida and Roland and some other friends of Nisarg's, got some beers and sat down. A woman next to us was getting frisky with her partner and rolled about to such an extent that she fell into our hands. She was in her fifties, sexily chubby with long bleached hair and a suntan, half-naked in a spangly skin-tight dress.

Her partner rolled his eyes in mock despair and so Julie and I ran our hands all over her and she laughed.

Later, we visited the tent with the breast fondling. We found a women-only makeshift boudoir full of babes, all chatting and lying about caressing each other's breasts. A pretty woman in a bowler hat said 'hello' and soon I was half-naked sipping wine and allowing her hands to roam all over me. *Ahhhh*.

Eventually, Julie and I scampered out and found Nisarg

being seduced by an older woman. I didn't intend to interrupt, but I was suddenly horny. The woman seemed to understand and melted away. Holding hands, we peered into the Couples Tent. It was like looking into a shipwreck of sex. The space had filled and there were couples all over the place, their party gear half-shed; they were naked and groaning and writhing, smiling languorously with lust. The woman with the violin stood in the middle, serenading them.

'I'd like to go in there,' I whispered to Nisarg.

He led me in by the hand.

We found a sofa and got comfy. Another couple, more friends of Nisarg's, were making out at the other end; a pretty young woman with a shaved head who was sucking her partner's cock. He sat on the arm of the sofa, legs parted, his chest bare, his long silk dressing gown open, a look of bliss on his face as her head bobbed back and forth. Nisarg sat down and I straddled him. We began to kiss. It was weeks since we'd been together and it was all over between us. Even so, we kissed hungrily, his firm probing kisses sending me into rapture. When the other couple left, we lay down. And then he was inside me and kissing me and around us other couples were also fucking and the woman playing the violin was above us. We writhed and groaned and locked eyes. Nisarg whispered, 'I'm close to coming.'

'Come inside me,' I whispered.

He looked perplexed. I didn't care how foolish this sounded right then; it was a unique request under the circumstances. Momentarily, I'd lost myself. But, wisely, he didn't comply. We kissed and ravished each other until we both fell into swoons of bliss. I loved him then. I still feel love for Nisarg as I write this.

quodoushka

Chuluaqui Quodoushka, or Q-training, is a type of neo-shamanistic teaching on sexuality taught by a man known as Harley SwiftDeer Reagan. Reagan, who claims to be half-Cherokee, set up the Deer Tribe Metis Medicine Society in 1986. Chuluaqui means life force, supposedly, in the ancient star language of the Cherokee. Quodoushka is what happens when two energies come together through lovemaking, creating more.

'Quodosh', according to sex magician Louis T. Culling, is also the name of the Third Degree ritual in Western sex magick, where bodily emissions during intercourse are mixed and used as powerful elixirs.

The Deer Tribe claim that their brand of teaching comes from the Twisted Hairs Council of Elders, one that it takes knowledge from many different places and tribes and weaves (or twists) it together. This council of elders is most mysterious. Apparently, it's a council of the 250 tribes in North, South and Central America. These elders are intertribal medicine people who can transcend traditional earthly limitations to collect and share knowledge; they are known in their tribes, but don't necessarily represent them. In some tribes these elders might even be hated. All of them, however, are 'high vibration' operators, that is people with great luminosity, who exhibit the highest points of light. SwiftDeer is one of these elders. He was among those chosen by the council to share some of the teachings of the Twisted Hairs with people of all races in preparation for 2012, the dawn of the New Age.

Googling SwiftDeer is somewhat disconcerting. Serious academic historians call him a clown. The Cherokee Nation call him a 'plastic shaman' and many others deride and denounce his claims of heroism in Vietnam and that he has various martial arts medals and awards. He is also known as 'Gunnie' Reagan because of his fondness for guns, and he is the president of an organisation called Keep and Bear Arms.

I'll stop there.

Needless to say, despite all of this, in the spirit of my quest I signed up for round one of quodoushka, known as Q-training.

Nisarg and I had agreed to share a room and do all the structures together. He'd attended Q-1 twice before and felt there were always new things to learn. The main reason I'd agreed to do the course with him was that I was expecting it to be the most challenging and intimate of all the workshops I'd done so far. I didn't want to be thrown into an advanced course with a complete stranger; an ex-lover was preferable by far.

A couple called Batty Gold and Rose Fink were our teachers. Batty, in his early sixties, was tall, with white curls tied up in a ponytail, clear blue eyes and striking Hawaiian shirts. Rose was in her late forties, thin as a broom and sexy. She wore a skin-tight scarlet dress throughout and red high heels, and talked in a quick, funky Austrian staccato. They both smoked in the breaks, as did most of the class participants – in tantra workshops, smoking is unheard of. They'd been together for twenty-seven years and, they explained, their relationship veered from open to closed. They taught Quod-oushka all over the world.

They were an immediately impressive and likeable

couple, attractive to be around. I forgot my reservations about SwiftDeer: he had two very cool cats representing him.

Nisarg was right, this was a very different kind of workshop. Much less experiential. Batty and Rose talked a great deal, sometimes together, sometimes in turns. They had a lot of information to pass on – and we sat taking notes.

First, they showed us the general principals of the medicine wheel and how it relates to sex. The medicine wheel is something you either accept or don't – a metaphor for the cyclic nature of the natural world. But the language of the medicine wheel is still used by shamanistic communities on every continent.

In Quodoushka, each point on the wheel relates to an elemental force and so to a type of sexual energy. For example, the north is associated with air and the head and this is a receiving energy; the west is the element of earth, a holding energy. The medicine wheel can also be used to depict various types of relationship: in the north, open, or shared; in the east, celibate; in the south, a triadic relationship and monogamy in the west. Even types of sexuality can be mapped on to the wheel: bi-sexuality in the north, homosexuality in the east, ambi-sexuality in the south and heterosexuality in the west.

Rose and Batty also described the various and invisible human shields which are all around us. We use these to protect and defend ourselves at any given time; they switch and revolve as needed. I found I didn't want to ask too many questions; they were unpacking a whole system of knowledge so alien to my Western secular rationale that it would have been pointless, even disrespectful. I found it fascinating.

They discussed the different levels of orgasm, first level

orgasm being the most common – the 'untrained male' takes 2.5 minutes to achieve this type. The 'untrained female' takes maybe twenty minutes. This is pleasure which spreads to the base chakras only in men; in women it can balance the first three chakras. A quick fuck or wank ensures a level one orgasm. The second level orgasm can be achieved by conscientious students of tantra and yoga. These are orgasms which reach the heart. Some people, however, don't need this training. Having a heart orgasm can be a matter of simply being more attentive and conscious of one's body, being more sensitive. Third and fourth level orgasms unite the body and soul with the rest of the universe.

My head was bulging from all the information. That night we practised the Fire Breath, something I'd already tried with both John Hawken and Sarita, a heart meditation ritual that involves raising the sexual energy up the chakras. This meditation can be done alone and is all about healing the self; by using your imagination you can learn to 'run the energy' up and down your body. If you do this meditation three times a week you can learn a lot about how your body functions. We all stripped off and did this naked in the group room. It takes about an hour and leaves the body fizzing and energised.

The next day, more note-taking, this time about the elemental expressions of orgasm. Batty and Rose talked of the four types of male and female orgasm, relating them to various birds, animals and elemental extremes. In the west of the wheel, for example, there's the earthquake orgasm for women, associated with the raven or crow. It is a very physical experience and shakes the body. The build up is slow, but gets faster and a woman usually makes loud staccato noises.

'This is the kind of orgasm which you see women making in Hollywood films,' said Rose. *Ha*. Indeed.

foxy lady

That second afternoon we were to find out about our own genital types. This was demonstrated first on the wheel, then on a flipchart and then via photographs of anonymous genitals. The teachings passed down to the Deer Tribe claim that there are nine different genital types, eight of which are associated with a specific animal. The ninth type are either Dancing Men or Dancing Women.

According to the Deer Tribe, around fifty per cent of all women are in the centre of the wheel: these, they call Dancing Women. These women, the teachings say, have their clitoris placed quite high above the entrance to the vagina and their G-spot is also deep and hidden by a fold of tissue; therefore just 'in and out' thrusting doesn't give them pleasure. They need a patient and skilful lover to bring them to orgasm, one who'll deliver a lot of manual and oral stimulation as well. All too often these women do not have the luck of finding such a lover; especially post-childbirth, they give up on themselves or their partners; they physically and spiritually dry up. They turn to other options: settling into celibate relationships, that, or they self-pleasure, or turn to their own sex, other women.

This made me sad and thoughtful. It seemed an eerily plausible explanation for so much female dissatisfaction, why so many women claim they don't orgasm, don't even like sex. They need careful loving attention; they don't want to be hard fucked by a man with a big cock. Very few women do, is my guess.

The Deer Tribe say these teachings have existed for thousands of years. The modern day teachers use photographs to show Q students, but these in turn have been verified by the elders.

What amazed me was the detail they went into: what a particular type of woman's outer and inner lips looked like, where her G-spot was located, where her clitoris was, high or low, what a woman's secretions smelt like, sweet or bitter, if she was hot or cool inside, if she ejaculated, if she had a tilted cervix, if she liked to have intercourse while menstruating, if she was noisy or quiet during orgasm, the depth of her vagina. It was also fascinating to discover what kind of women were the deepest and made the best porn stars (deer), which women were the natural hunters (wolves, foxes and cats), which women were always wet (sheep), which women were shallow (buffalo). We learnt that genital types and personality types are also linked. Nisarg said he thought I was probably a wolf; this is the great hunter of the female pack, the big extrovert. *Qui, moi*?

The Indian *Kama Sutra* has similar types of animal names for genitals, but these are much less sophisticated, relating to size only, three types for each sex. In Quodoushka, there are eight animal names for male and female genitalia. For women, you can be a wolf, antelope, deer, fox, sheep, cat, buffalo or bear. For men, a horse, elk, deer, ram, coyote, dog, bear, or pony.

What type was I? There was only one way to find out.

Rose drew the curtains. She arranged a chair in the centre of the room. The women formed a circle around the chair, the men formed a circle around the women. Rose went first. She wasn't wearing underwear; she simply hitched up her skirt, sat on the chair and opened her legs.

'I am an antelope,' she said.

We all leant forward.

One by one every woman slipped off her knickers and sat on the chair. One by one Batty and Rose, who sat on the floor on either side of the chair, judged our genital types. There was one bear woman. The rest were either wolves or antelopes (who are full of energy and like to jump about). I went near the end; I can't remember if I was nervous. As with all my adventures, curiosity pushed me forward. I peeled off my knickers and took a deep breath. I sat on the chair and parted my legs.

'I think I'm a wolf, too,' I said.

Batty and Rose leant forward. Rose frowned. 'No, I don't think so,' she said.

'Really?' I murmured. I spread myself wide open, both pairs of lips now visible.

'Ah,' said Batty. 'See? Those little ears?'

I certainly couldn't see any ears, couldn't see myself at all from my vantage point. But he seemed so sure, even affectionate in his judgement. Rose nodded.

'You're fox,' said Batty.

I felt a flush of pride. Me? A fox? It was the nicest thing anyone had said to me in a long time. *You're a fox.* Of course I was.

I beamed and closed my legs. 'Thank you,' I murmured. I was a hunter, yes, but a smaller creature than the wolf; cuter, too.

Fox women are on the southeast of the medicine wheel, in

between sheep and deer. We have a hood over our clitoris, and this is clearly visible. The inner lips, when open, curve a little and are serrated. We are quite deep. The G-spot isn't spongy, but smooth, three centimetres inside the vagina. Fox women are quick and fast movers (along with antelope, deer and cats); we can do long and short build-ups to orgasm, have fast or long rolling climaxes. We hunt at night and are private, family-orientated people. We can be loners – and we like to give our lovers breakfast. These were the facts Rose had given us earlier. I dislike being easily typified; yet these facts are not only complex, but also accurate.

Knowing what genital type you are is helpful, according to Rose. You can explain yourself to lovers, who you are and what you're like inside and out. I was grateful for the infor-mation. I looked forward to telling the next man I met that I'm a fox woman.

submission

Later that night, Nisarg and I did a structure together. There was a final medicine wheel to look at, one for the different 'Lovers' Masks'. By this, Batty and Rose meant different types of sexuality, the choices of sexuality out there: the shy curious child, the explorer, the wanton lustful lover, the socially con-ditioned lover, the master/slave scenario, the tantric couple, the exotic and shamanic 'firewoman', the goal-orientated lover, and so on. We were asked to choose one of these types, the one we felt *least* comfortable with – and invite our partner to try it out in private.

I chose the master/slave scenario. I knew Nisarg was very experienced, even professional at these BDSM games, that he was the perfect person to experiment with. I'd seen glimpses of his butch side at the sex party a month earlier, but of the two of us I was definitely the dominant personality. And so I didn't want to be the dominatrix in the game. I wanted to be submissive. I wanted him to be dominant, tie me up. I'd never really seen this in him, and I rarely got to be submissive myself. I borrowed what I needed from the course organiser: a couple of whips, some strips of cloth for him to tie me up with, a jar of honey, a blindfold.

When he entered the room I was in a green silk spotted dressing gown, open to reveal fine black lace underwear. He sat down on the bed next to me.

'I want you to tie me up,' I said. He looked surprised. His blue eyes shone like an angel's.

'I don't particularly want you to hurt me. Use the whip lightly. But I don't want to know what's coming. Be creative, do what you want.' I chose a safe word: *frog*.

He nodded. 'Go and stand in the corner,' he commanded. 'Raise your arms.'

In moments, he was lashing my hands together, pulling the strip of cloth into an expert knot. Then he led me to the bed.

'Lie down,' he said and pushed me so I fell backwards, my hands tightly secured above my head. He pulled off my knickers.

Over the next forty-five minutes, the length of time we were given, he kissed me, licked me, whipped and fucked me; he tied me up in knots, and performed the most excellent cunnilingus. I was on my back and then my stomach, all the while bound and blindfolded. My love for him, in those minutes, doubled. At one point, he gently put his fist to my pubic bone and pressed down. The pain was hard and soft. I loved him then. I loved him drizzling honey into my pussy and licking so long and lovingly he complained that his jaw ached the next day.

It was a sad, sweet, bitter game, because I fell for him all over again.

When it was his turn, the game he chose was wantonness. He wasn't a confident dancer. My heart burst as he danced around the room naked, trying to be sexy, a game that I knew how to play well. He was exposing his vulnerability to me. I danced with him, naked too. He didn't want to kiss, just tease me. I loved his compact body, the body of some kind of wood spirit, perfectly formed. He was neither big nor small, a half-god. A sweet face and a hard body, great legs and feet. *Pay attention to him*. The universe had shown him to me. I could have missed him.

Then he asked for a massage. It was my turn to be surprised.

'I can sometimes find it hard to ask for what I want,' he said.

The next day was our last. There would be a sweat lodge in the morning: twenty of us in a small hut which looked rather like an igloo made from wattle boughs and blankets. There was a pre-breakfast ceremony of making the lodge and laying the stones in the fire to heat. The ritual itself was also explained. Once the spirits were called in, there would be three rounds of incantations, almost like prayers. The third round would be called the 'give away' round, a chance to give away something we no longer wanted. In preparation for the sweat, we were all asked to do a tree meditation, to go and sit by a tree and consult its wisdom, ask what it was we needed to give away: the tree would have the answers. This is, in effect, tree hugging. I found a slim white-trunked sapling and sat under it: what did I need to give away?

After lunch, we lined up naked. One by one we filed in. I made sure I was near the door; this was my first lodge. Inside it was so dark I could barely see inches from my face. It was sauna hot. When we were all in, Batty closed the blanket door. Utter night. Batty began to address the elders of the spirit world. He was a man approaching his winter years; his hair white, his voice soft. There was something deeply dig-nified about the way he called out to these spirits. Yes, it did cross my mind to ask what we were doing in a hut in Herefordshire, calling to the spirits of Native American Indians. What about our own spirits, those of the soil beneath us, what of the Celtic and Saxon gods? What on earth were we all thinking?

I didn't care. I was near the end of my journey, I could feel it. I poured with sweat. Water seeped out of my body; rivulets of water. I lay on my back. I prayed and sweated and prayed and cried and found myself floating in some unknown melan-choly. Were there really spirits with us? It felt holy in there. *Quodosh* – Hebrew for holy. That's what it felt like. And when the 'give away' round came I surprised myself again. There were two things I found I wanted to give away: my fear of reading in front of nine hundred people at the Queen Elizabeth Hall the following month, and what was left of my heart, my love for my ex. I wanted to give both these things away. My ex had given me so much; so much that was there for me to keep. So much of him had become part of me. But I no longer needed any part of his heart; that was for the woman who was soon to be wife.

And, dear reader, this part of my story ends, like so many, with a mixture of elation and sorrow. I didn't get back with my ex, and I didn't get together with the next man who came along either.

We drove back to London later that day. In the evening, in *Os Amigos*, a Brazilian restaurant in Harlesden, Nisarg and I ate our last meal together and said our goodbyes once more. He didn't want to be with me. I wasn't the woman he wanted for himself. He'd fallen for someone else, a woman who was more like him. I thought of what Robert Rowland Smith had said about love being some kind of 'divine narcissism'; and Woody Allen's 'I'm looking for myself, only female'. Nisarg had chosen a fellow masseur; my ex had also chosen to marry a woman who was a quizzer, like him.

I was okay then. Nisarg came to see that reading ten days later, the night before the Orange Prize awards; he showed up like my mother did, from Trinidad, and so many of my friends and students. He wanted to be there. We saw each other again, but eventually, I said no, that I didn't want to be his friend just yet. We needed some time apart, some months, the whole summer at least. I cancelled the date we'd made in the diary to see the musical *Hair* together. I was heartbroken – again. It was totally shit – and yet it was a sign that I was better. I was back in action. Properly working once more.

We met again in September and Nisarg was suntanned and sad. The love affair with the other woman had never got off the ground. I didn't get him; he didn't get her – but we will always be friends.

sexual fantasy store

Foxes appeared on walls all over my neighbourhood. They appeared on corrugated shop fronts, on pub walls in Salusbury Road, Queen's Park, on the corner of Harvest Road, trotting past shops on Chamberlayne Road in Kensal Green: all of them in black stencils Banksy style. A lone artist? Curly and I did a trawl on Google and found that other local residents were curious about the foxes too; it had started some kind of blog. Who was the Black Fox of Brent?

Soon after Q-1, I signed up to an eighteen-month intensive tantra training with Jan Day. I realised I was no longer a complete beginner in the art of love. Jan's training offers weekend seminars, longer residential workshops, and one-to-one coaching sessions. I still needed to unlearn old tricks and bad habits, to try a whole new approach to loving and sexing. My days of ad-hoc exploration were over. After two years of these crazy workshops, I realised I couldn't confine them to a neat chapter in my life, and move on. I wanted this learning to continue. I'd learnt a lot on my own, but now I needed continual and steady guidance. Transformation was underway.

Two years on, I know a few things about myself. I'm not a swinger; I'll never share a man, be polyamorous. In fact, I'll run a mile from the next man who brings this word up. I am not a 'top' or dominatrix in BDSM games. I don't have a wildly voracious sex drive either. I've had twelve lovers since these adventures began – not that many, really.

The biggest change has been in my attitude to my body. Breath work, tantric meditations, a full realisation of the chakras; all this has made an enormous difference. Being penetrated by a man used to be so disappointing. Many women keep this disappointment a secret. I liked and wanted the energy of cock – but cock didn't deliver me to heaven as promised by Hollywood. I was somehow expecting to be jump-started by a man's sexual energy; that the cock was the key, and my yoni was some kind of curious lock. I just had to find the right key to unlock me. But I'd got it all the wrong way round. Now I see that my body is a far subtler vehicle than I'd ever understood, that I'd been driving myself about in the wrong gear. I had my body in passive, in Neutral, waiting for a man to start me up. Now I'm in Drive all the time, always on, always humming. These days, a touch or a lick in the right place can make my body shake.

Today, if I walked into the sexual fantasy store, I know more about my broad sexual tastes, so I'd know where to browse. What I am is a tantrika, and also an ethical slut. I'm lightly bi-sexual, or ambi-sexual, open to threesomes here and there, with the right men and women. I'm an exhibitionist, sure, and love having sex in public, and at parties, with an atmosphere of consciousness. I'm also a writer-magician, one who enjoys using magick in my work and is keen to test this in sex. I seek like-minded people to befriend and play with sexually, because I've outgrown my former self, the confines of the everyday world.

Also, I am this fox woman. Monogamous at heart, a lone hunter, private, smaller than the wolf, bushy-tailed. Wily and adventure-prone. I'm an omnivore, both sexually and actually – I'll eat anything. I was able to negotiate Craig's List so easily because of my lone hunter instinct; I see this now. But I also know I must pay attention to this hunting instinct, learn to lay low, hunt differently. Be more playful. Let men hunt me. I've learnt that good sex doesn't equal love. And I have vowed to learn to trust once more. I'll keep opening to the good in men, notice what I *like* about them. This feels important, to trust men again.

the song of songs

I have an old photograph of my mother and two brothers, taken in 1967. My father took the photograph; he is behind the camera. It was taken in Hong Kong: there is water in the background, they are on a boat of some kind. My brother Nigel, blond, toothy, handsome, sits on my mother's lap; he is six. He is wearing a blue Hawaiian shirt. My brother Ian is on the right, next to my mother, a tubby freckly boy of nine; he wears a red Hawaiian shirt. Between them is my mother, thirtysomething, honey-skinned, blonde and glamorous in her tortoiseshell Jackie-O sunglasses.

I am not in the photograph. I was two years old. My whole family, my parents and two brothers, had gone on a three-month holiday, a sightseeing trip, and left me behind, in Trinidad. My parents were taking my brother Ian to boarding school and the trip was some kind of treat to compensate. They were depositing one child, their oldest son, in the care of a dour English school, while leaving their youngest child behind, in the care of a rather aloof woman, my grandmother. My elegant grandmother, Maman, had had servants to care for her own children; she had no maternal qualities at all.

I don't remember much of those three months in her care.

But I do remember the day my mother and father arrived home. I was dressed up to greet them. When my mother came to hug me, saying *Monique, Monique, hello, hello, we're back, look at all the lovely presents we've brought you*, I tore away from her in a wild rage, screaming with fury and resentment.

This begs the question: did I really have a broken heart when I split from my ex or do I have the mother of all abandonment issues? I would say both. Perhaps that first loss, aged two, of my entire family, has underpinned all later losses in my life, including the loss of my ex. My ex was a man whom I chose on some deep and unknowable psychological level to heal the wound of being unseen by my father. And this unconscious need was fulfilled. His powerful and unconditional love had healed me. Our catastrophic parting broke me again – but, with time, eventually I recovered. My subsequent sexual adventures have been the making of a new me.

I think again of *The Song of Songs*.

On one level, this magnificent poem may be about a mystical love so holy, so beyond us, that we today cannot comprehend its actual meaning and quality. On the other hand, it can be read as a clear celebration of authentic human love, which shows men and women as equals; which is a positive representation of male/female sexuality and male/female friendship. The lovers in the poem are everything to each other: friend, sexual partner, family. In which case, we need to ask, is this a model which can only bring heartbreak and dissatisfaction as we try to live up to its ideal in modern times?

All I know is *The Song of Songs*, to a large degree, echoes my own experience of love. I have tasted something of the epic nature of the love portrayed in the poem: *he is the one my soul loves*. I would call this love holy – in Hebrew, *kadosh*. And this love has never died or gone away: love, as far as I know, is as strong and arbitrary as death. Once upon a time, in my adult life, I found my companion on earth, the person I wanted to live with and be with all the hours of my waking life. I stared at his face every morning and this made me feel rich and peaceful.

The poem has a strong erotic charge: the man and the woman are desperate for each other, to copulate, to fuck, and to eat in the garden of delights. *The Song of Songs* is ornate and declaratory, Middle Eastern and grand, flamboyant sacred erotica, a celebration of a love between two people who lust for each other's flesh. And in this respect, my love affair with my ex did not match up. Our love did not live up to the ideal it represents, this *everylove*.

I now see that finding a truly compatible sexual partner is very, very difficult. The sexual adventures in this book are those of a sexually forward and lustful woman, just like the woman in the Song. But also, to begin with, a woman on the rebound; they are reactive, and they are the adventures of an amateur. While I'm not planning to write a sequel to this book, I *am* planning to continue my journey, to take my investigations to another level and to keep sexually active. I won't be returning to my old self, the one who knew little of the art of love, the skills of sex. I'm 'out' now. I've crossed over, stepped into the same room, joined the small community of like-minded people who are conscious sexual seekers. It is a small group, but who knows; I am advised by others of us that we are part of 'a rising movement' out there in the world, who want to be more physical, more conscious in our sexual affairs.

465

Love, I know now, is something we can seek out, accomplish, celebrate and learn from. We can grow love; we can grow from it, too. We can create children from love, great works of art. And so, it seems to me, it is worth taking love seriously enough to study it, to train for it, to somehow make sure that when it comes around, we are ready for it and good at it. This, for me, is my future homework: to be better at love, emotionally, sexually, in every aspect; to recognise it as one of the great human arts and to honour it as such. I'm still an apprentice at the art of love. I try, I fail – and will keep trying to love better. Being good at love seems both sensible and worthwhile.

As I write, it is late October 2010. It's been well over a year since my psychological divorce in a stone circle in a wheat field in Wales. The planet Earth is turning on its axis, beckoning a new season, the northern hemisphere is leaning away from the sun. And so, in a few weeks I shall be following that sunshine, heading south, to an island I call home, where the sun shines all year round and where fine poets also write about love. And I'll be dancing up the flame inside me when I'm there and celebrating the wantonness of the woman in the song: *come kiss me on the mouth*, I like the way you taste, like wine. Yeah, yeah. Just like wine.

♥

Postscript

Love after Love

The time will come
when, with elation,
you will greet yourself arriving
at your own door, in your own mirror,
and each will smile at the other's welcome,

and say, sit here. Eat.
You will love again the stranger who was yourself.
Give wine. Give bread. Give back your heart
to itself, to the stranger who has loved you

all your life, whom you ignored
for another, who knows you by heart.
Take down the love letters from the bookshelf,

the photographs, the desperate notes,
peel your own image from the mirror.
Sit. Feast on your life.

Derek Walcott

ACKNOWLEDGEMENTS

Between October 2008 and May 2010 I met once a month at the Welcome Collection café, Euston, with fellow writer Emily Pedder in order to exchange chapters of this book and hers. In those months we formed a structured and mutually supportive 'writer buddy' relationship in order to get our deeply personal memoirs finished. I can honesty say that without this relationship, this book would never have been written. Emily Pedder is the midwife, first reader, first editor, and ever-encouraging mentor who kept me writing all that time. I owe her a huge debt of gratitude for her keen instincts around the subject matter of this memoir. This working relationship was exciting and dynamic and very much a story within which I was able to write this story. Thank you, Emily.

The poet Neil Rollinson was my second reader. My flatmate at the time, he also read every word of the first draft and his encouragement also kept me writing. Thanks, Neil.

Thank you Deborah Dooley and Sarah McCloughry, for standing me upright in the beginning. Thank you Nick Clements and Emily Fuller for the work you did for me at the end of things.

I'm blessed with the friendship of a number of brilliant women, all of whom I want to thank for their tireless support during my years of recovery and enquiry into all matters of love and sex. Thank you Emma Wallace, Amanda Berry, Kitty

Stirling, Hydrox Holroyd and Rose Rouse: I love you all. Thank you Rose, for the tarot readings, for numerous adventures; you are part of this story: Thank you for introducing me to Jan Day.

Which brings me to the teachers and mages who've helped shape my recent life. The Buddhists say: *when the student is ready, the master appears.* Thank you Jan Day for all your loving guidance; you appeared just in time and saved my life. Thank you, also, John Hawken for all you have taught me about energy and consciousness and for carrying me, fireman-style, across a puddle of mud. Thank you for the stones, for showing me what they are. Thank you Michele Bosc, I sleep well knowing you are always nearby. Thank you Dina Glouberman for your wisdom and our new friendship, you have been an influence too. Thank you Darby Costello for showing me what is written in the stars. Demara, as ever, thanks for the tips.

My friends Georgie Davey and Tom Sperring also deserve praise and thanks for accompanying me to the swinger's resort of Cap d'Agde in July 2009. Thanks for the breakfasts, the 'potato salad', for your courage, good humour and enthusiasm. Without you both, I may never have explored the caves of Glamour.

This book, amazingly, was generously supported by the Arts Council of England. Thank you Charles Beckett, book man, nice guy, for helping me write this memoir. Thank you Eileen Gunn at the Royal Literary Fund for bailing me out. Thank you to the Society of Authors, again for much appreciated financial support.

Francesca Main, my editor at Simon and Schuster UK, has also been something of a guiding star, her feedback always accurate, always making this book stronger, better. Isobel Dixon, my agent at Blake Friedmann has gone beyond and above the call of duty to ensure I not only kept writing but breathing while writing this book. Isobel, you know what I mean. I feel lucky to have you on my side.

Finally, a number of peers and friends came forward to read my penultimate draft. This support and feedback, at the last hurdle, made a difference. Thank you Louisa Young, Daisy Goodwin, Amanda Smyth, Clare Sims, Robert Rowland Smith, Saara Marchadour, Gyan Nisarg and Jan Day. Your sound feedback gave me the confidence to make up my mind and go ahead and publish this book. I'd like to thank my ex, too, for giving me the nod.